Regional Maintenance of Peace and Security under International Law

This book explores the scope and limits of what is appropriate for regional action in the maintenance of peace and security. It offers a comparative study of legal regulation of the use of force in the maintenance of peace and security of different security regions in the context of the UN system and general international law. The book examines the post-Cold War legal documents and practice of the regional organisations of six security regions of the world (Africa, Asia, the Americas, the Middle East, the Russian sphere of influence and the Euro-Atlantic region), and in doing so offers a unique international and comparative perspective towards regional characteristics that may influence the possibility for coherent action in a UN context.

Dace Winther explores the controversial topics of regional humanitarian intervention and robust regional peacekeeping without a UN mandate, what is regarded as appropriate for regional action in different security regions of the world, and if the approaches of the regions differ, what factors could have an influence. The book is highly relevant in a global climate where regional mechanisms take an ever more active part in the maintenance of international peace and security, including the use of force. The book will be of great interest to students and academics of international law, international relations and security studies.

Dace Winther has worked as a legal advisor for the Ministry of Defence of the Republic of Latvia. She has received a PhD in Law from Aarhus University, Denmark. Her research interests are general international law, the use of force and international organisations.

Routledge research in international law

Available:

International Law and the Third World
Reshaping justice
Richard Falk, Balakrishnan Rajagopal and Jacqueline Stevens (eds)

International Legal Theory
Essays and engagements, 1966–2006
Nicholas Onuf

The Problem of Enforcement in International Law
Countermeasures, the non-injured state and the idea of international community
Elena Katselli Proukaki

International Economic Actors and Human Rights
Adam McBeth

The Law of Consular Access
A documentary guide
John Quigley, William J. Aceves and Adele Shank

State Accountability under International Law
Holding states accountable for a breach of jus cogens norms
Lisa Yarwood

International Organisations and the Idea of Autonomy
Institutional independence in the international legal order
Richard Collins and Nigel D. White (eds)

Self-Determination in the Post-9/11 Era
Elizabeth Chadwick

Participants in the International Legal System
Multiple perspectives on non-state actors in international law
Jean d'Aspremont

Sovereignty and Jurisdiction in the Airspace and Outer Space
Legal criteria for spatial delimitation
Gbenga Oduntan

International Law in a Multipolar World
Matthew Happold (ed.)

The Law on the Use of Force
A feminist analysis
Gina Heathcote

The ICJ and the Development of International Law
The lasting impact of the Corfu Channel case
Karine Bannelier, Théodore Christakis and Sarah Heathcote (eds)

UNHCR and International Refugee Law
From treaties to innovation
Corinne Lewis

Asian Approaches to International Law and the Legacy of Colonialism
The law of the sea, territorial disputes and international dispute settlement
Jin-Hyun Paik, Seok-Woo Lee, Kevin Y. L. Tan (eds)

The Right to Self-determination Under International Law
"Selfistans," secession, and the rule of the great powers
Milena Sterio

Reforming the UN Security Council Membership
The illusion of representativeness
Sabine Hassler

Threats of Force
International law and strategy
Francis Grimal

The Changing Role of Nationality in International Law
Alessandra Annoni and Serena Forlati

Criminal Responsibility for the Crime of Aggression
Patrycja Grzebyk

Regional Maintenance of Peace and Security under International Law
The distorted mirrors
Dace Winther

Forthcoming titles in this series include:

International Law, Regulation and Resistance
Critical spaces
Zoe Pearson

The Cuban Embargo under International Law
El bloqueo
Nigel D. White

International Law-Making
Essays in honour of Jan Klabbers
Rain Liivoja and Jarna Petman

The Changing Nature of Customary International Law
Methods of interpreting the concept of custom in international criminal tribunals
Noora Arajärvi

Technology and the Law on the Use of Force
New security challenges in the twenty first century
Jackson Maogoto

Criminal Diversity in International Law
The effectiveness of the UNESCO convention on the protection and promotion of the diversity of cultural expressions
Lilian Hanania

The United Nations and Collective Security
Gary Wilson

Regional Maintenance of Peace and Security under International Law
The distorted mirrors

Dace Winther

LONDON AND NEW YORK

First published 2014
by Routledge
2 Park Square, Milton Park, Abingdon, Oxfordshire OX14 4RN

and by Routledge
711 Third Avenue, New York, NY 10017

First issued in paperback 2015

Routledge is an imprint of the Taylor & Francis Group, an informa business

© 2014 Dace Winther

The right of Dace Winther to be identified as author of this work has been asserted by her in accordance with sections 77 and 78 of the Copyright, Designs and Patents Act 1988.

All rights reserved. No part of this book may be reprinted or reproduced or utilised in any form or by any electronic, mechanical, or other means, now known or hereafter invented, including photocopying and recording, or in any information storage or retrieval system, without permission in writing from the publishers.

Trademark notice: Product or corporate names may be trademarks or registered trademarks, and are used only for identification and explanation without intent to infringe.

British Library Cataloguing in Publication Data
A catalogue record for this book is available from the British Library

Library of Congress Cataloging-in-Publication Data
Winther, Dace.
  Regional maintenance of peace and security under international law : the distorted mirrors / Dace Winther.
    pages cm. – (Routledge research in international law)
  Based on the author's thesis (Ph.D.)–Aarhus University, 2011, under title: The distorted mirrors of regional maintenance of peace and security.
  Includes bibliographical references and index.
  ISBN 978-0-415-85499-3 (hbk) – ISBN 978-0-203-79735-8 (ebk) 1. Security, International. 2. International law. I. Winther, Dace. Distorted mirrors of regional maintenance of peace and security. II. Title.
  KZ5588.W56 2013
  341.7'3–dc23   2013018374

ISBN13: 978-1-138-93748-2 (pbk)
ISBN13: 978-0-415-85499-3 (hbk)

Typeset in Garamond
by Cenveo Publisher Services

To my Mark

Contents

Abbreviations xiii
Acknowledgements xvi
Introduction xvii

1 **The historical development of regionalism in the maintenance of peace and security: regionalism through universalism** 1

   General overview 1
   Early regionalism 2
   The beginnings of modern regionalism 5
   Regionalism during the Cold War 9
   Post-Cold War regionalisation 11

2 **The universal perspective on the maintenance of peace and security: law and practice** 14

   The law 14
   The practice of the United Nations 27
   Post-Cold War doctrinal developments 38

3 **Africa: African solutions for African problems** 49

   General description of the region 49
   Economic Community of West African States 53
     General description 53
     The practice 54
     The legal basis 58
     Decision-making 59
     Co-operation with the United Nations 59
   Southern African Development Community 60
     General description 60
     The legal basis 61

x   *Regional maintenance of peace and security under international law*

        Decision-making   62
        The practice   63
        Co-operation with the United Nations   65
   African Union   66
        General description   66
        The legal basis   66
        Decision-making   72
        The practice   74
        Co-operation with the United Nations   76
   Summary   78

4   Asia: the ASEAN way   80

   General description of the region   80
   Association of Southeast Asian Nations   85
        General description   85
        The legal basis   87
        Decision-making   90
        The practice   91
        Co-operation with the United Nations   92
   Shanghai Cooperation Organisation   93
        General description   93
        The legal basis   95
        Decision-making   96
        The practice   97
        Co-operation with the United Nations   98
   Summary   99

5   The Americas: intervention without intervening   101

   General description of the region   101
   Organization of American States   106
        General description   106
        The legal basis   108
        Decision-making   111
        The practice   113
        Co-operation with the United Nations   115
   South American Union of Nations   116
        General description   116
        The legal basis   117
        Decision-making   120
        The practice   121
        Co-operation with the United Nations   123
   Summary   124

		Contents xi

6	The Middle East: in the absence of regional unity	126

General description of the region   126
League of Arab States   127
   General description   127
   The legal basis   128
   Decision-making   133
   The practice   135
   Co-operation with the United Nations   137
Organization of Islamic Conference   140
Summary   142

7	The Russian sphere of influence: the matryoshka of military peacekeeping	144

General description of the region   144
Commonwealth of Independent States   146
   General description   146
   The legal basis   146
   Decision-making   151
   The practice   152
   Co-operation with the United Nations   156
Common Security Treaty Organization   158
   General description   158
   The legal basis   159
   Decision-making   160
   The practice   161
   Co-operation with the United Nations   163
Summary   163

8	The Euro-Atlantic region: going global	165

General description of the region   165
European Union   166
   General description   166
   The legal basis   166
   Decision-making   171
   The practice   173
   Co-operation with the United Nations   183
North Atlantic Treaty Organization   185
   General description   185
   The legal basis   187
   Decision-making   194
   The practice   196
   Co-operation with the United Nations   202
Summary   203

9 **Comparison of the regions: the house of mirrors**   206

Factors influencing different regional approaches   206
Appropriate for regional action   211
A Chapter VIII organisation   213
Security and defence   214
Humanitarian intervention   217
    Support for unilateral regional humanitarian intervention   217
    The role of the UN Security Council   219
    Counter-reaction in other regions   220
    Possible justifications of intervention   221
Qualifying factors for the legitimacy of action   222
Summary   225

10 **Suggestions: where there's a (political) will, there's a (legal) way**   227

Measures taken by the United Nations   227
Measures taken at the regional level   235

Bibliography   241
Index   246

Abbreviations

ACS	Association of Caribbean States
ACTO	Amazon Cooperation Treaty Organization
AEC	ASEAN Economic Community
ALADI	Latin American Integration Association
AMIS	African Union Mission in Sudan
AMISOM	African Union Mission in Somalia
APEC	Asia-Pacific Economic Cooperation
APSC	ASEAN Political-Security Community
ARF	ASEAN Regional Forum
ASCC	ASEAN Socio-Cultural Community
ASEAN	Association of South-East Asian States
AU	African Union
AUPSC	African Union Peace and Security Council
CAR	Central African Republic
CARICOM	The Caribbean Community
CEMAC	Central African Economic and Monetary Community
CENTO	Central Treaty Organization
CFSP	Common Foreign and Security Policy (EU)
CIS	Commonwealth of Independent States
CSCE	Conference on Security and Cooperation in Europe
CSDP	Common Security and Defence Policy (EU)
CST	Collective Security Treaty
CSTO	Collective Security Treaty Organization
DPKO	Department of Peacekeeping Operations (UN)
DRC	Democratic Republic of Congo
EC	European Community
ECCAS	Economic Community of Central African States
ECJ	European Court of Justice
ECOMOG	Economic Community of West African States Monitoring Group
ECOWAS	Economic Community of West African States
ESDP	European Security and Defence Policy (EU)
EU	European Union

EU BG	European Union Battlegroups
EUFOR	European Union Force
EUNAVFOR	European Union Naval Force
EUTM	European Union Training Mission
FARC	Revolutionary Armed Forces of Colombia
FYROM	Former Yugoslav Republic of Macedonia
ICJ	International Court of Justice
IFOR	NATO Implementation Force
IGAD	Intergovernmental Authority on Development
ILC	International Law Commission
ISAF	International Security Assistance Force
ISDSC	Inter-State Defence and Security Committee
ISPDC	Inter-State Politics and Diplomacy Committee
KFOR	Kosovo Force
MERCOSUR	Southern Common Market
MICIVIH	International Civilian Mission in Haiti
MINURCAT	United Nations Mission in the Central African Republic and Chad
MINUSTAH	United Nations Stabilization Mission in Haiti
MONUC	United Nations Observer Mission in the Democratic Republic of Congo
NAC	North Atlantic Council
NATO	North Atlantic Treaty Organization
NEACD	Northeast Asia Cooperation Dialogue
NGO	Non-governmental organisation
NRF	NATO Response Force
OAS	Organization of American States
OAU	Organization of African Unity
OECS	Organization of Eastern Caribbean States
OIC	Organization of Islamic Conference
OSCE	Organization for Security and Cooperation in Europe
SADC	South African Development Community
SADCC	Southern African Development Coordination Conference
SCO	Shanghai Cooperation Organisation
SEATO	Southeast Asian Treaty Organization
SFOR	NATO Stabilization Force
SHIRBRIG	United Nations Stand-by Forces High Readiness Brigade
SICA	Central American Economic System
UN	United Nations
UNAMI	United Nations Assistance Mission
UNAMID	AU/UN Hybrid Operation in Darfur
UNAMIR	United Nations Assistance Mission in Rwanda
UNASUR	Union of South American Nations
UNEF	United Nations Peacekeeping Force
UNMIT	United Nations Integrated Mission in Timor-Leste

UNMOGIP	United Nations Military Observer Group in India and Pakistan
UNOMIG	United Nations Military Observer Mission in Georgia
UNOMIL	United Nations Observer Mission in Liberia
UNSAS	United Nations Standby Arrangement System
UNSC	United Nations Security Council
UNSF/UNTEA	United Nations Security Force/United Nations Temporary Executive Authority
UNTAC	United Nations Transitional Authority in Cambodia
UNTAES	United Nations Transitional Administration for Eastern Slavonia
UNTSO	United Nations Truce Supervision Organization
WEU	Western European Union
WMD	Weapons of Mass Destruction

Acknowledgements

An in-depth study of the various regional mechanisms of maintenance of peace and security has resulted in this book. It has been a long trip both mentally and geographically. I am grateful to all the people who have contributed to my work through their professionalism, personal qualities and skills, either through action – or abstention.

First of all, I would like to thank my supervisors at Aarhus University, Jens Hartig Danielsen and Sten Shaumburg-Müller, who guided me through my PhD project which serves as the basis for this book. Thanks also to my colleagues at the Department of Law at Aarhus University School of Business and Social Sciences, who helped me with all issues possible: professional, practical and personal. I would also like to thank all those who helped me during my research stay at the Faculty of Law at Copenhagen University, especially Professors Jens Elo Rytter, Michael Rask Madsen and Henrik Palmer Olsen, and the administrative staff.

I am grateful to my fellow PhD students both at Aarhus University and Copenhagen University for their important moral support and for creating for me a sense of belonging to a group of people who share the same common challenges and aspirations as I do.

Gratitude goes to my colleagues at the Ministry of Defence of the Republic of Latvia – the place where I got the inspiration for the topic of this book. A special thanks to my supervisors, Anita Rimsa and Svetlana Araslanova, I highly value all the practical and moral support for my professional and personal growth and my aspirations as an academic.

I am grateful to my parents, Zigismunds and Iveta, to my wider family and to my friends for their support and their taking pride in what I am doing, and for their continuous 'cheering' for me in this mental marathon of mine. I am greatly thankful to my children, Eliza and Lukas, for all their love and patience. And lastly, a special thanks to my dearest husband, Mark, for being my steady rock, a friend, an advisor and a true fighter for peace and security in this world. Therefore, this book is dedicated to him.

Introduction

Since the end of the Cold War, regional organisations have become a tool widely used by the United Nations (UN) for both peacekeeping and in peace enforcement. The UN has not been able to cope with the large number of threats to peace and security requiring a resolution by military means and has thus been increasingly calling for the involvement of regional organisations. Nearly all regions of the world have updated their mechanisms for the maintenance of peace and security over the past 20 years (especially in the past decade), and even created new ones. As with any new developments in practice, new legal issues have consequently arisen.

A row of operations have taken place upon the initiative of the regional organisations, including many operations based on controversial grounds. According to international law, regional military operations are legal if they are authorised by the UN Security Council or take place based on an invitation. Nevertheless, the authenticity and legitimacy of such invitations, and the actual amount of force used in these operations have been questionable in a long row of regional military peacekeeping operations, especially some undertaken by the Commonwealth of Independent States (CIS) and the Economic Community of West African States (ECOWAS). In addition, the invocation of humanitarian intervention in Kosovo has sparked further regional developments, most importantly the inclusion of a right to regional humanitarian intervention in the African Union Constitutive Act. At the same time, and in contrast to the practice of the aforementioned organisations, the Asian regional organisations fully maintain the principle of non-interference, prioritising it even above the responsibility to protect. The American organisations, though active in regional maintenance of peace and security, draw the line at diplomatic measures. The regions and their mechanisms for the maintenance of peace and security are thus very different, even though, in theory, they apply the same set of basic rules contained in the UN Charter. This diversity of the regional mechanisms for the maintenance of peace and security and their differing ways of interpreting and applying the UN Charter rules resemble a set of distorted mirrors.

This book intends to study the complex mass of provisions relevant to regional maintenance of peace and security in order to clarify the details of the diverging regional approaches and their compatibility with general international law. This is done both from a UN perspective and from the perspective of a wide range of regional organisations, in order to establish what the content of the rules is, how they are interpreted and applied by regional organisations, and why. The regions selected for this analysis are the *de facto* security regions developed politically, with a coherent approach towards the maintenance of peace and security. The regions are: Africa, Asia, the Americas, the Middle East, the Russian sphere of influence and the Euro-Atlantic region.

Some of the issues studied in this book from the general law perspective are, for example, what is a regional arrangement, what is appropriate for regional action and what are the exceptions to the prohibition of the use of force. Each regional organisation is studied in detail, analysing the issues of the internal mandate in the legal acts of the organisation, the decision-making procedure and whether the practice of the organisation complies with international law. The background of each region is studied in order to determine what factors have influenced the development of this particular region's unique approach to maintenance of peace and security. The book also studies a wide range of comparable criteria, for example, the formal Chapter VIII status of each regional organisation, what the regional organisation considers appropriate for regional action, whether the organisation has a defence function, whether the use of force is allowed, and what is the regional approach to humanitarian intervention.

The structure of the book

The book sets out with the historical background of regionalism, and the relationship between universalism and regionalism. Then the universal mechanism for the maintenance of peace and security is presented as the yardstick against which to evaluate the legality of the practice of each regional organisation. The book uses UN law and practice as the benchmark for what is the existing consensus of the international community on the permissibility of regional use of force. Even if the UN is not an infallible mechanism, it still serves as the common denominator for diverging interests of different states and regions of the world. Thus, the individual regional position on the permissibility of the use of force will be held up against the general international law, which has been established as consensus by the international community in the UN framework. Further on in the book each individual regional organisation is analysed, describing the activity of the organisation in the maintenance of peace and security. In analysing the regional organisations, the book uses the following template: a general description, the legal basis, the decision-making procedure, the practice and the co-operation with the UN.

The general description of what characterises each individual security region as a whole is given as an introduction to each of the regional chapters, and a summary of the common characteristics of the region is made at the end.

Following the regional chapters, a comparative analysis is made in order to establish the similarities, the differences and the influencing factors when applying the rules of general international law in the individual regions.

The overall structure of the book is as follows: Chapter 1 describes the development of regionalism from the ancient world until today. Chapter 2 depicts the universal approach towards regional maintenance of peace and security, and regional use of force in particular. Chapters 3 to 8 are dedicated to the analysis of the individual regions, and their regional organisations. Chapter 3 is thus a study of Africa (ECOWAS, SADC, AU), Chapter 4 – Asia (ASEAN, SCO), Chapter 5 – the Americas (OAS, UNASUR), Chapter 6 – the Middle East (Arab League, OIC), Chapter 7 – the Russian sphere of influence (CIS, CSTO) and Chapter 8 – the Euro-Atlantic region (EU, NATO). Chapter 9 is a comparison of the regions which contextualises the findings of the previous chapters.

Chapter 10 concludes the book by making suggestions, mainly of a procedural nature, on how to improve the compliance of organisations dealing with the maintenance of peace and security, to the rules of international law, in order to ensure legality and legitimacy in regional military action, and in order to limit unilateralism in regional use of force.

Literature and other sources

The sources used in the book are legally binding documents and documents containing general political commitments and doctrine of the organisations analysed, as well as literature and factual information on the practice of organisations. The documents analysed include the UN Charter, UN Security Council resolutions, the basic documents of the regional organisations, UN General Assembly resolutions and many other documents of both the UN and regional organisations. Press materials are also widely used in the book, as this is often the only possibility to acquire the necessary information about the newest practice of the organisations.

Two of the regions studied in this book have been analysed more widely in literature, namely, Africa and, especially, the Euro-Atlantic region. As to other regions, there is a shortage of legal analysis of the regional use of force (and permissibility of action in the maintenance of peace and security in general). Many of the developments, such as a new mechanism for the maintenance of a peace and security in the League of Arab States (2006), the newly established South American Union of Nations (UNASUR, established 2008), or the new Charter of the Association of Southeast Asian Nations (ASEAN, entered into force in 2008) have so far not been analysed in depth for the objective reasons that they have only been created within the last few years. Due to the very limited amount of post-Cold War literature on the regions of Asia, the Russian sphere of influence, the Americas and – most of all – the Middle East, the author has, in addition to the analysis of the primary sources, used news releases and information of the activities of the organisations on the websites of the organisations.

The implications of the diversity of accessible material relating to the content of the different chapters influence both the depth of the factual background and the extent of the legal debate in the actual chapter. In regions that are more broadly analysed in literature, it is more apparent what the problems of the practical application of the law are, and what contradictions have been discovered. In general, the author has made an effort to facilitate the comparability of the regional mechanisms as much as possible.

1 The historical development of regionalism in the maintenance of peace and security
Regionalism through universalism

General overview

Maintenance of peace and security is one of the basic tasks any society has had to perform since the beginning of time. With the emergence of States it became one of their core tasks. Collective maintenance of peace and security, however, has had a less systematic character in the course of history. Alliances, unions and coalitions of collective maintenance of peace and security have come and gone, shifting war after war. An undefined regionalism in the maintenance of peace and security precedes universalism.[1] It has, in fact, been a step between an individual State-based maintenance of peace and security to an all-encompassing universal collective maintenance of peace and security. Universalism in the maintenance of peace and security cannot truly be traced further back than to the establishment of the League of Nations, followed by the present universal mechanism of the United Nations (UN). Nevertheless, it was not until the past decade that regional organisations started taking up space in law books as significant actors of maintenance of peace and security. With the gradual developments of regionalisation in the maintenance of peace and security, such as the creation of autonomous regional co-operation of the Americas in the nineteenth century, and a few brief provisions in the UN Charter, the modern regionalism in the maintenance of peace and security has truly taken up speed in the twenty-first century, supplementing and sometimes contradicting the post-UN Charter universal order. The aftermath of 9/11 has dramatically catalysed regional activity. Most of the regional mechanisms in place at the moment have undergone a significant make-over in the few years of the twenty-first century to increase their efficiency. On the other hand, the regionalisation of the maintenance of peace and security is, in a way, the return to the roots of the international order that date back to the ancient world. The matter of making political alliances and coalitions has

---

1 W. Hummer and M. Schweitzer, 'Chapter VIII. Regional Arrangements', in B. Simma (ed.), *The Charter of the United Nations. A Commentary*, 2nd edn, Vol. 1, Oxford: Oxford University Press, 2002, pp. 811–12.

traditionally been connected to a coherent area – a region.² Before the creation of the universal order, however, regionalism in the maintenance of peace and security was not about regional coherence and speaking in one voice, as today, but rather about constraining the settlement of matters of peace and security within the borders of a limited region. Nevertheless, regionalism was also about distinguishing 'us' – the members of the 'club' – and 'them' – the outside world – even if the restraints on the use of force as such were minimal. The examples of such regional forums for the maintenance of peace and security over the course of history include the amphictyonic leagues in ancient Greece, the *Dar al-Islam* collective security of medieval Islam and the medieval Christian Europe.

Early regionalism

Since the ancient times regions of security and defence formed on the basis of religion. In the ancient world religious amphictyonic (neighbour) leagues were created by neighbouring Greek cities sharing temples. The most significant of such was the Amphictyonic League of Delphi. The ancient beginnings of the regional religious leagues, however, were not about establishing peace among the States participants, but rather establishing the rules of warfare somewhat restraining the use of force against fellow members of the league,³ amounting to what could be regarded as humanitarian law in modern terms. For wars outside the framework of the league, such limitations were not set; there was a constant natural state of war between Greek and barbarian worlds.⁴ Ancient Rome, on the contrary, had a practice of concluding bilateral, and not multilateral, alliances. In the early period of expansion, any State that did not have a treaty of friendship or alliance with Rome was considered to be permanently at war with Rome.⁵

In ancient China an approach was influenced by Confucianism. China was regarded as the only civilization and the outside enemies surrounding the 'Middle Kingdom' of China were not regarded as enemies, but as 'imperfectly integrated into the great global order'.⁶ The use of force against the 'uncivilized' outsiders was not regarded as waging war but rather as law enforcement.⁷ The Roman approach of putting Rome into the centre of the world security structure was thus similar to the Chinese rather than the Greek model. In antiquity the powers did not interact globally, thus the areas

---

2 Hummer and Schweitzer, ibid.
3 S. C. Neff, *War and the Law of Nations. A General History*, Cambridge: Cambridge University Press, 2005, pp. 23–4.
4 Neff, ibid, p. 41.
5 Neff, ibid, p. 31.
6 Neff, ibid, p. 32.
7 Neff, ibid, p. 20.

of influence of China and Rome did not overlap and they could perceive themselves as the global rulers. This type of ancient regionalism can, therefore, in today's perception, be argued to be the universalism of the ancient world. In contrast, the equal-member Greek regions of collective security system were created as a unity against the outside world and thus, dominated by a self-perception as of a distinct region in a wider world. From the ancient world lines can be drawn to the modern world. Today one can also distinguish the maintenance of peace and security in regions with more-or-less equal State participants from that of regions with one hegemon in the centre.

In the Middle Ages, the Islamic States and Christian Europe provide examples of regional maintenance of peace and security. The Qur'an prescribes *jihad*, translated as struggle or fight, according to Islamic principles. Based on that, Islamic scholars created a security and defence community of the Islamic States – *Dar al-Islam* (the house of Islam) – outside which was the *Dar al-Harb* (the house of war). No specific wrong-doing was necessary to start a war against the outsiders.[8]

The European medieval regionalism was determined by Christianity, thus, once again, on a common religious ground. Here the just war doctrine became the central concept of war-fighting. There had to be a just cause to start a war. However, just as in Islam, war against the infidels was a just cause in itself.[9] The prototype of a just war in medieval Europe would thus be a war carried out under the authority of the pope for the defence of the Christian world as a whole against a common outside enemy who threatened the faith or the faithful.[10] Thus, the examples of ancient Greek leagues, *Dar al-Islam* and medieval Europe all evidence a set of rules concerning internal conduct for the members of the regional 'club', whilst hardly any limitations have been set up for starting wars against outsiders.

In seventeenth-century Europe, the order of maintenance of peace and security found its expression in the Westphalian State sovereignty-based power-balance system. This system replaced the Europe religiously united under the pope. The Westphalian system with the balance of power in the centre,[11] however, was not able to ensure a long-lasting peace, with wars frequently raging in Europe.

After the Napoleonic wars, in 1815 the Concert of Europe was created to re-establish public law and the principle of balance of power in Europe.[12] The Concert of Europe depended on the agreement of the great powers.[13]

---

8 Neff, ibid, p. 41.
9 I. Brownlie, *International Law and the Use of Force by States*, Oxford: Clarendon Press, 1963 (reprinted 2002), p. 7.
10 Neff, op. cit., n. 3, p. 53.
11 Brownlie, op. cit., n. 9, p. 16.
12 Ibid, p. 19.
13 Ibid, p. 20.

The right to go to war was now generally unlimited.[14] In fact, until as late as the signing of Kellogg-Briand Pact in 1928, there were no restraints on using war in international relations as a means of settlement of disputes. While today the right to go to war is strictly limited, the agreement of the great powers is still a leading principle of the maintenance of peace and security, reflected even in the balance-of-power provisions in the UN Charter regarding the role of the Permanent Members of the UN Security Council (UNSC).

The nineteenth century marked the establishment of Eurocentrism in international law, which was still based on the European balance of power.[15] The civilized, Christian European States were at the centre of the world order, having a global influence over their colonies around the world. The European States were members of the club, or league – just as in ancient Greek leagues – fighting against and colonising territories outside the region. Over the centuries, starting from the age of discovery (sixteenth century), major parts of the rest of the world were colonised and split between the colonial powers. Especially the African continent was split up and divided along oftentimes straight, rather than ethnically determined lines. This division is still one of the causes for African conflicts, making it the most conflict-burdened region of the world. Also most of the Far East and the Pacific was in the realm of various Western colonisers.

The nineteenth century was also the time when the formerly colonial Latin America gained independence from Europe, establishing the first modern regional system in the world. This regional system for maintenance of peace and security was created to counterbalance the outside superpower influence – that of Europe. The beginnings of the Latin-American system date back to 1826, when Simón Bolivar summoned the Congress of Panama,[16] with a formal co-operation framework being established many years later, in 1889.[17] The US Monroe doctrine furthermore illustrates the American position of keeping the European influence out of the region.[18]

In Europe, large-scale and devastating conflicts had usually taken place between the powers within the region, though, occasionally, affecting other parts of the world due to conquests and the colonial influence. Both the Peace of Westphalia and the Concert of Europe, and their balance of power principle had failed to secure not only peace, but also a sense of a regional unity. In the pre-League of Nations world, Europe was a region, but not one of many regions of the world. Europe was, instead, the region that was the centre of

---

14 Brownlie, op. cit., n. 9, p. 20.
15 M. N. Shaw, *International Law*, 6th edn, Cambridge: Cambridge University Press, 2008, p. 27.
16 H. McCoubrey and J. Morris, *Regional Peacekeeping in the Post-Cold War Era*, The Hague: Kluwer Law International, 2000, p. 93.
17 *Organization of American States. Our history*, OAS official website. Available at <http://www.oas.org/en/about/our_history.asp> (accessed 3 March 2013).
18 On Monroe doctrine see, for example, McCoubrey and Morris, op. cit., n. 16, p. 101.

power, radiating its influence globally, hence, Eurocentrism. Perhaps the new Eurocentrism was not that far from the ancient perceptions of world order. Just like the Greek amphictyonic leagues, the European core of the world was a group of States with their individual, different, competing interests; despite internal wars – a club of the civilized. The characteristic of the post-Concert of Europe, pre-League of Nations regionalism was the absence of a universal system of maintenance of peace and security, other than the European influence over most of the rest of the world. It is this world-governing European order that the American States broke off from, by establishing a separate region of maintenance of peace and security, and thus setting the example for the modern day regionalism in the maintenance of peace and security.

The beginnings of modern regionalism

It was with the creation of the universal organisations – the League of Nations and subsequently the UN, that closer regional co-operation became distinguished as a separate category. The universalist approach assumed that regional systems would create rivalries, being a cause to future conflicts in themselves, thus a universal system would be needed to avoid the development of conflicts.[19] The new regionalists, on the other hand, claimed that regional sub-systems represented indispensable intermediary structures of co-operation over which a universal structure of supervisory nature could span.[20] The universalist system was proposed and seen by many as the ideal mode for ensuring peace and security around the world.

The first universalist attempt in the maintenance of peace and security was the establishment of the League of Nations. Universalism was a new alternative for ensuring peace and security, by making every international conflict anywhere in the world a matter of the whole international community. The Covenant of the League of Nations contained a provision on regional co-operation in Article 21. This Article reads: 'Nothing in this Covenant shall be deemed to affect the validity of international engagements, such as treaties of arbitration or regional understandings like the Monroe doctrine, for securing the maintenance of peace'.[21] This provision secured the priority of regional security regimes over that of the League of Nations provisions.[22]

The Covenant referred to regional understandings – alliances, rather than institutions. The only regional organisation dealing with peace and security

---

19 Hummer and Schweitzer, op. cit., n. 1, p. 813.
20 Ibid.
21 The Covenant of the League of Nations. Available at the Avalon Project – Documents in Law, History and Diplomacy, Yale Law School, Lillian Goldman Law Library. Available at <http://avalon.law.yale.edu/20th_century/leagcov.asp#art21> (accessed 1 March 2013).
22 Hummer and Schweitzer, op. cit., n. 1, p. 813.

existing at that time was the International Union of American Republics.[23] Other examples of regional co-operation of the inter-war period included the 'Small Entante' (Czechoslovakia, Yugoslavia, Romania), the Balkan Pact (Greece, Yugoslavia, Romania, Turkey), the Baltic Union (Estonia, Latvia, Lithuania), the Oriental Pact (Afghanistan, Iraq, Iran, Turkey) and the Locarno Treaty (Germany, Belgium, France, Great Britain, Italy), none of which were formalised institutions resembling international organisations. The inclusion of the reference to regional alliances was not in line with the idealism of creating a new – universal – system. Yet the reference was included in Article 21, to receive the approval of the US Senate.[24] The attempt was in vain; the USA never became a member of the League of Nations.

The *Agenda for Peace*[25] of 1992 refers to Article 21 of the League of Nations as the beginnings of regional involvement in the maintenance of peace and security. Through this Article the creation of a universal mechanism of maintenance of peace and security gave shape to the regional mechanisms as well. The historically chaotic regional systems were, for the first time in history, regarded from a common perspective.

The universalist model of maintenance of peace and security failed to bring a *panacea* to the world that was plagued by conflicts between different groups of allies within different regions. The conflicts, however, did not take place region against region, but within regions, still influenced by Eurocentrism. In mere 20 years the League of Nations universal mechanism failed to guarantee the commitment of the great powers of the time and prevent the Second World War, which can hardly be seen as an improvement from the Westphalian system statistical record of wars.

At the time of the establishment of the UN there was no mention of a category of regional organisations in international law. The sole example was the regional co-operation in the Americas with over a hundred years of history of development, of which 50 years as institutionalised co-operation. The predecessor of the Organization of American States (OAS) – the International Union of American Republics for the Prompt Collection and Distribution of Commercial Information, had been established by 18 American States as early as 1890 (renamed Pan-American Union in 1910). The second institutionalised regional system – the League of Arab States – was established on 22 March 1945 – at the time between the Dumbarton Oaks Conference and the San Francisco Conference as a result of which the UN was created. Apparently this development had some influence on the political balance in the UN negotiations, as during the Dumbarton Oaks Conference the proposals were dominantly universalist, whereas in San

---

23 *Organization of American States. Our history*, op. cit., n. 17.
24 Ibid.
25 *An Agenda for Peace, Preventive Diplomacy, Peacemaking and Peace-keeping*, Report of the Secretary-General, A/47/277–S/24111, 17 June 1992 (*Agenda for Peace*).

Francisco the debate was to find a compromise between universalist and regionalist tendencies.[26]

Traditionally, in Europe the concept of regionalism had been power-balance based, rather than based on institutionalised co-operation. The history of the eternal rivalry of the European powers and the two world wars were not a promoting background for regionalism in Europe at the time of the creation of the UN. Neither was the earlier European domination of the world a factor for limiting European participation in the maintenance of peace and security to the geographic region of Europe, since the European influence had traditionally been global. The only regional interest of the European States at the time was the right to conclude bilateral treaties for their mutual protection against Germany.[27] Interestingly enough, of the 51 founding members of the UN, 20 were members of the Pan American Union (to become the OAS in 1948) and five were members of the newly established Arab League. Relatively few – eight – Western European States were represented.[28] However, the power-balance eventually established as the basis for the UN did not correspond to the number of representatives promoting regionalism. Two out of five Permanent Members of the UN were European,[29] and despite the regionalist pressure from Latin America, the UN gained the primary status in the enforcement of peace and security. This result had reasons dating back to 1941 described below, mainly connected to establishing a power-balance among the Second World War allies.

The balance between regionalism and universalism in the maintenance of peace and security, as we know it today, was established during the drafting negotiations of the UN Charter. The *Agenda for Peace*[30] notes that in the past, regional arrangements were often created because of the absence of a universal system for collective security; thus their activities could on occasion work at cross-purposes with the sense of solidarity required for the effectiveness of a world organisation. But in this new era of opportunity regional arrangements or agencies could render great service if their activities were undertaken in a manner consistent with the Purposes and Principles of the UN Charter, and if their relationship with the UN, and particularly the

---

26 C. Schreuer, 'Regionalism v. Universalism', *European Journal of International Law*, Vol. 6, 1, 1995, p. 478.
27 M. Akehurst, 'Enforcement Action by Regional Agencies, with Special Reference to the Organization of American States', *British Year Book of International Law*, Vol. 42, 1967, p. 175.
28 Belgium, Denmark, France, Greece, Luxembourg, Netherlands, Norway, the United Kingdom.
29 Or even three, if Russia is included as one of the Concert of Europe great-powers, though the political coherence of the region was already lost with the establishment of the USSR in 1917. The USA, in addition, is also a Western State and part of the Euro-Atlantic region.
30 *Agenda for Peace*, op. cit., n. 25.

UNSC, were governed by Chapter VIII of the UN Charter.[31] Regionalism was to become a tool for universalism.

During the drafting years of the UN Charter (from 1941 on), the rival proposals for the common system for the maintenance of peace and security were either purely universalist or supervisory universalist with a strong regional element. The whole long-term drafting over the years of the Second World War, before the Dumbarton Oaks Conference, was a matter of co-operation between the sponsors of the UN Charter. The drafting initiative and specific proposals came from Great Britain and the USA, with the USA being the principal drafter.[32] The process then included involving the other allied powers – the Soviet Union and China – in the negotiations. It was necessary to achieve co-operation among the great powers through the composition of the UNSC with its five Permanent Members and their right to veto decisions.

Where Roosevelt suggested a concept of four great powers leading a world of nation-States in their peaceful behaviour as a common group, Churchill envisaged entrusting the function of maintaining peace to regional organisations – a Council of Europe and a Council of Asia under the common roof of the world organisation.[33] The regionalist position was supported also by Latin America and the Arab States, as well as those of the Commonwealth of Nations (i.e. the former British colonies).[34] The general consensus that was reached, however, was that regional institutions should be made subordinate to a universal organisation, and should only be used for the purposes of the pacific settlement of disputes.[35] The regional agency model for the preservation of peace is said to have failed due to the strong position of the USA that there ought to be a universal peace-enforcing mechanism which would accommodate regional agencies only under the roof of general authority, namely, the UNSC.[36] A central concern was that smaller States might become involved in regional matters and lose interest in the UN, at the same time forming power blocs or military alliances regionally under the hegemony of the great powers.[37] In addition, a reason for failure is the fact that even though 36 out of 50 States were supporting the regionalist approach, the views on what shape this *regionalism* should take were too split to create a common position.

The negotiations on the basis of a universalist draft Charter combined with a great number of proponents of regionalism ended up in a universalist Charter that contains a compromise regionalist Chapter VIII. Peace and

---

31 *Agenda for Peace*, op. cit., n. 25.
32 B. Simma, 'Drafting History', in B. Simma (ed.), *The Charter of the United Nations. A Commentary*, 2nd edn, Vol. 1, Oxford: Oxford University Press, 2002, pp. 2–8.
33 Simma, ibid, p. 6.
34 Hummer and Schweitzer, op. cit., n. 1, p. 814.
35 Ibid.
36 Simma, op. cit., n. 32, p. 9.
37 Akehurst, op. cit., n. 27, p. 175.

security matters are the only sphere in which regionalism as such is mentioned in the UN Charter. In Chapter VIII of the Charter the UN recognises the role of regionalism in the peaceful settlement of disputes, yet maintains the primary responsibility over the maintenance of peace and security in the universal mechanism through the UNSC. This is a significant change from the League of Nations system, where the regional understandings were to have priority in the maintenance of peace and security. In contrast, according to Chapter VIII of the Charter, no enforcement action could be taken without UNSC authorisation, and collective regional action in self-defence would have to be reported to the UN immediately.

In the drafting negotiations of the UN Charter the Latin American States had strongly demanded a general regional right to settle disputes by all means without UN supervision. However, the specific right was demanded as applicable exclusively to the region of Americas. The Latin Americans claimed that the requirement for enforcement action to be authorised by the UNSC would enable the extra-regional great powers to veto regional action in the Americas and to interfere in their regional affairs.[38] These efforts ended up in the compromise provision of a right to collective self-defence in Article 51. This right, however, was included in the UN Charter as a common right of all Member States – not limited to a specific region – and in the final version of the Charter this turned out to be the only possibility for legal use of force that regional organisations could employ without a specific authorisation from the UNSC. Chapter VIII, moreover, is said to have been included in the UN Charter to show that regionalism as such plays a subordinate role to the UN and to re-emphasise that securing peace is one indivisible aim which is to be achieved on all levels and by all means.[39]

Regionalism during the Cold War

The role of the UN in the maintenance of global peace and security has been a great improvement compared to that of the League of Nations. Yet, the UN was neither able to prevent the Cold War with its constant threat, nor the occasional unilateral use of force, especially, by the Permanent Members of the UNSC and their allies. During the years of the Cold War the UN military action in order to maintain peace and security remained limited to peacekeeping, with 15 peacekeeping operations throughout the years of the Cold War. In comparison, in 2013 there were 14 UN peacekeeping operations ongoing simultaneously.[40]

---

38 Akehurst, op. cit., n. 27, p. 176.
39 Hummer and Schweitzer, op. cit., n. 1, p. 815.
40 *UN Peacekeeping Factsheet*, United Nations Peacekeeping official website. Available at <http://www.un.org/en/peacekeeping/resources/statistics/factsheet.shtml> (accessed 1 March 2013).

During the second half of the twentieth century, and in contrast to the UN standing still, other – regional – developments took place. Greatly influenced by the establishment of the UN and the provisions of Chapter VIII of the UN Charter, institutionalised frameworks of regional organisations started developing. Regionalism was, in addition, promoted by the general growth and expansion of interdependence of the States at the time.[41] In the years after the establishment of the UN, regional organisations, including those dealing with security and defence, mushroomed. These regional arrangements, however, were not put to use by the UN in the maintenance of the global peace and security until the end of the Cold War. Only a couple of regional organisations were regarded as Chapter VIII organisations during the Cold War. The OAS and the Conference on Security and Cooperation in Europe (CSCE; later the Organization for Security and Cooperation in Europe (OSCE)) claimed themselves explicitly to be Chapter VIII organisations.[42] In addition, the UN General Assembly recognised Chapter VIII status not only of the OAS and the CSCE (OSCE) but also of the League of Arab States and the Organization of African Unity (OAU).[43]

The level of activity of the regional organisations was also low, compared to the post-Cold War period. There were a few controversial cases of unauthorised regional action. Examples of regional operations launched during the Cold War years include action by OAS and the League of Arab States. The OAS undertook a couple of controversial military operations on its own: Cuba (1962) and the Dominican Republic (1965). In addition, an example of a controversial regional intervention is the intervention in Grenada in 1983 by the Organization of Eastern Caribbean States (OECS). The three Latin American operations involve examples of what is generally accepted to be *de facto* US interventions formalised as regional operations. The Arab League also took up a couple of peacekeeping operations: Kuwait 1962 and Lebanon in 1976. The North Atlantic Treaty Organization (NATO) and the Warsaw Pact were not intended to be Chapter VIII organisations subject to the control of the UN by definition. The Warsaw Pact launched controversial interventions into Hungary in 1956 and Czechoslovakia in 1968. NATO's intents remained on paper during the Cold War.

---

41 L. Fawcett, 'Exploring regional domains: a comparative history of regionalism', *International Affairs*, Vol. 80, 3, 2004, p. 430.
42 Schreuer, op. cit., n. 26, p. 482. References to Art. 1 of the Charter of the Organization of American States of 1948, 119 UNTS 4 and Declaration and Decisions from Helsinki Summit 10 July 1992, 31 ILM (1992) 1385 at 1403.
43 Schreuer, op. cit., n. 26, p. 477. With references to UN General Assembly Resolutions 47/11, 47/10, 48/19, 48/21, 48/25; Shaw, op. cit., n. 15, p. 1274, note 343: organisations self-identifying themselves as being Chapter VIII organisations: OAS (see Art. 1 of the Charter of OAS 1948), OSCE (para. 25 of the Helsinki Summit Declaration, 1992 and the Charter for European Security 2000, 39 ILM, 2000, p. 255 and UN General Assembly Resolution 47/10, and the CIS (see 35 ILM, 1996, p. 783).

Post-Cold War regionalisation

In contrast there has been a high level of regional activity since the end of the Cold War. The Commonwealth of Independent States (CIS) has launched five long-term peacekeeping operations in 20 years and the European Union (EU) has launched 23 operations in eight years. The Economic Community of West African States (ECOWAS), the African Union (AU) and NATO have also launched numerous operations in the past two decades making up for the stand-still during the Cold War. Moreover, activity not involving military assets has been high both in the organisations mentioned above, and others described in this book. Regional maintenance of peace and security without the use of military force has, for example, intensified significantly in Asia and South America over the past few years.

Since the end of the Cold War regional organisations have gained a more significant role than the UN Charter had foreseen. The reason for this development is said to be the partial failure of the UN to come to terms with many of the tasks entrusted to it, in combination with a strong resurgence of group solidarity among Member States, their unwillingness to be subject to outside influence, and their preference to deal with certain problems in a smaller arena, seemingly better adapted to co-operation for these specific purposes.[44]

The political map of the world has changed beyond recognition since the early days of the UN. At the time of creation of the UN the international community consisted of 51 States – a number relatively easily co-ordinated in comparison with the 194 States of today. Of the initial 51 members, five States (10 per cent) were the Permanent Members of the UNSC, and 11 States (roughly 20 per cent) were represented in the UNSC. In comparison, the International Union of American Republics had 18 members and the League of Arab States had seven members. All the members of the International Union of American Republics were the original founders of the UN, and so were five out of seven original members of the Arab League. If we compare it to today's regional map, we can see that, for example, the OSCE has 56 members, the EU – 27 members, NATO – 28 members, the AU – 53 members, the Association of South-East Asian States (ASEAN) – 10 members, the OAS – 35 members and the ECOWAS – 15 members. There is a limit to the abilities of a single organisation. Co-ordinating 194 countries and their security issues has proved to be a challenging task for the universal organisation. In this situation regional organisations may be able to respond better to the threats located within a limited geographic area.

The regionalisation of the maintenance of peace and security has been intentionally catalysed by the universal organisation itself. It may not have been in the interest of the UN to promote regional security activities during the Cold War, but today the UN is increasingly willing to utilise all the

---

44 Schreuer, op. cit., n. 26, p. 479.

available security and defence organisations. Following the end of the Cold War, the criteria for determining the status of a Chapter VIII organisation appear to have been nearly abandoned by the UN, which is now adopting a much broader interpretation of a Chapter VIII regional arrangement. From the side of the UN this has been done with regard to efficiency – to be able to utilise the widest range of regional organisations possible for the maintenance of peace and security. It was stated in the *Agenda for Peace* that the UN Charter deliberately provides no precise definition of regional arrangements and agencies. This would allow for a useful flexibility for undertakings by a group of States to deal with a matter appropriate for regional action, which also could contribute to the maintenance of international peace and security. Such associations or entities could include treaty-based organisations, whether created before or after the founding of the UN, regional organisations for mutual security and defence, organisations for general regional development or for co-operation on a particular economic topic or function, and groups created to deal with a specific political, economic or social issue of current concern.[45] Thus, the *Agenda for Peace* is the turning point of the involvement of regional organisations in the global maintenance of peace and security, ensuring the widest contribution to the maintenance of peace and security possible, irrespective of how these organisations may have been classified earlier.

The intensification in regional maintenance of peace and security brings with it a danger of regional action which is not subordinated to the UN and not in conformity with the UN Charter. Though generally displaying loyalty to the UN and respecting its primary responsibility in the maintenance of global peace and security, regional organisations have taken up actions that are controversial under international law.

A landmark case for this trend is the NATO intervention in Kosovo in 1999. This case may have been qualified as an illegal but legitimate[46] exception to the prohibition of the use of force. Yet, the subsequent regional developments in the maintenance of peace and security appear to prove that Kosovo has had a greater influence on spreading the idea of autonomous action by regional organisations than initially presumed. Following the development of practice over several years following the Kosovo intervention, Aidan Hehir concludes that the discourse to humanitarian intervention 'has come to be seen as a necessary rhetorical component in any intervention'.[47]

---

45 *Agenda for Peace*, op. cit., n. 25.
46 See the analysis of the legality-legitimacy paradigm in the Report of the International Commission on State Sovereignty, *Responsibility to Protect*, Ottawa: International Development Research Centre, 2001, and Danish Institute of International Affairs, *Humanitarian Intervention. Legal and Political Aspects*, Copenhagen: DUPI, 1999.
47 A. Hehir, *Humanitarian Intervention after Kosovo. Iraq, Darfur and the Record of Global Civil Society*, New York, NY: Palgrave Macmillan, 2008, p. 95.

Where in 1999 the International Court of Justice (ICJ) did not express its authoritative opinion on the claims brought on by the Former Republic of Yugoslavia (Serbia and Montenegro in other cases) against the NATO Member States that participated in the Kosovo intervention in the cases concerning 'Legality of Use of Force'[48] stating that it lacked jurisdiction, regional and national authorities have since expressed strong and diverging views on the regional right to intervene. The controversial cases of the regions of Africa, the Russian sphere of influence and the Euro-Atlantic are analysed in detail in the respective chapters and contrasted to the non-interventionist approach of the Americas and Asia, with the passive Middle East on the side-line.

Even though the developments in regional maintenance of peace and security are extensive and diverging, their legality needs to be measured against the general international law. The most relevant international law provisions are stapled in the UN Charter. Describing these provisions may not be an easy task in itself, as the UN Charter rules are brief and not without controversy. Chapter 2, nevertheless, clarifies the main concepts and rules regulating regional maintenance of peace and security included in the UN Charter and deriving from subsequent practice.

---

48 The full list of cases can be found under advisory opinions from the year 1999. Available at <http://www.icj-cij.org/docket/index.php?p1=3&p2=2> (accessed 1 March 2013).

2 The universal perspective on the maintenance of peace and security

Law and practice

> ... *their obligations under the present Charter shall prevail* ...
> Article 103 of the UN Charter

The present day regionalism can be officially said to have been demarcated with the inclusion of Chapter VIII in the UN Charter. Also the process of practical use of regional mechanisms in the maintenance of peace and security has been initiated by the UN. The UN law and practice are thus the main sources of provisions regarding regional use of force.

The aim of this chapter is to clarify what is expected from the regional organisations viewed from the universal perspective. In the first part of the chapter the general rules of international law, relevant for regional use of force, are described to depict the background against which the legality of regional action is to be evaluated. The second part is dedicated to the developments in UN military peace operations within the universal system. This part describes the UN practice which has lead towards the practical utilisation of the regional organisations, provided for in Chapter VIII of the UN Charter. The third part of the chapter is dedicated to the post-Cold War doctrinal developments on the utilisation of the regional organisations, in order to depict how the UN envisages and intends to utilise the regional mechanisms for the maintenance of peace and security. The UN law and practice described in this chapter give a background that allows placing the legality of individual regional practice into a universal context.

The law

The provisions embedded in the UN Charter are the ultimate background against which to evaluate the legality of regional action. The provisions of the Charter that apply to the activity and, in particular, the use of force by the regional organisations, are both those referring to the responsibilities of UN Member States in general, as well as those regarding regional organisations specifically. The most relevant provisions are found in Articles 2(4), 24, 25 and 103, as well as in Chapters VII and VIII, with provisions of Articles 39,

42 and 53, in particular. Regarding the possible exceptions to the prohibition of the use of force, subsequent developments in doctrine are also of relevance.

The UN was established with the aim to save succeeding generations from the scourge of war, to reaffirm faith in fundamental human rights, to establish conditions under which justice and respect for the obligations arising from treaties and other sources of international law can be maintained, and to promote social progress and better standards of life in larger freedom.[1] The core reason for establishing the universal organisation for the maintenance of peace and security was the prevention of large-scale inter-State conflicts, like those of the First and Second World Wars. The underlying principle of the UN Charter therefore is the prohibition of the threat or use of force, which is widely accepted as *jus cogens*,[2] and is considered by many to be the most important rule contained in the UN Charter.[3] Article 2(4) of the UN Charter reads:

> All Members shall refrain in their international relations from the threat or use of force against the territorial integrity or political independence of any state, or in any other manner inconsistent with the Purposes of the United Nations.

The rule traditionally prohibits using military force for solving disputes between States. The term 'use of force' is not defined in the UN Charter. The content of Article 2(4) is very comprehensive and subject to many controversies. Even though a nuanced approach to what types of action may be considered use of force, including the debate on political and economic pressure, can be found in literature,[4] in this book the term 'use of force' is limited to coercive military action.

Even the use of force through military action has itself turned out not to be an obvious concept. One of the most contested interpretations of Article 2(4) is that the prohibition of the use of force applies only to force that is directed against the territorial integrity and political independence of a State, however, the dominant view, supported by the UN Charter text and the *travaux*

---

1 The Charter of the United Nations, 1 UNTS XVI.
2 I. Brownlie, *Principles of International Law*, 6th edn, Oxford and New York, NY: Oxford University Press, 2003, p. 489; M. Shaw, *International Law*, 6th edn, Cambridge: Cambridge University Press, 2008, p. 126; C. Gray, *International Law and the Use of Force*, 3rd edn, Oxford: Oxford University Press, 2008, p. 30; O. Espersen, F. Harhoff and O. Spiermann, *Folkeret*, København: Christian Ejlers' Forlag, 2003, p. 225; Case Concerning Military and Paramilitary Activities in and against Nicaragua (Merits), *ICJ Reports* 1986, pp. 100–1, para. 190.
3 A. Randelzhofer, 'Chapter I. Purposes and Principles', in B. Simma (ed.), *The Charter of the United Nations. A Commentary*, 2nd edn, Vol. 1, Oxford: Oxford University Press, 2002, p. 66.
4 I. Brownlie, *International Law and the Use of Force by States*, Oxford: Oxford at the Clarendon Press, 1963 (reprinted 2002), pp. 361–64.

preparatoires, is that the phrase 'against territorial integrity and political independence' was used to qualify and emphasise the prohibition of the use of force, and not to specify separate cases when the use of force would be prohibited.[5] Nevertheless, the invocation of the abovementioned interpretation gives an example of how creatively the UN Charter rules may be interpreted, if a politically motivated action requires legal justification.

The UN Charter itself provides very limited exceptions to the prohibition of the use of force. There are only three. First, under Chapter VII, Articles 39 and 42, the UNSC authorises the use of force to maintain or restore international peace and security, if military force is deemed necessary to counter a threat to peace, a breach of peace or an act of aggression. Second, individual or collective self-defence and, third, measures against enemy States.

Even though it was originally intended that the UN itself takes the enforcement measures envisaged in Article 42 of the UN Charter with the help of the forces provided for in Article 43, it is now accepted that the UN may authorise Member States to use force. This has been invoked in practice with an increasing frequency since the end of the Cold War.[6] The wording of Article 53 and the practice of the UN in the past two decades clearly show that not only Member States, but also regional organisations may be authorised by the UNSC to use force.

Along with individual self-defence, Article 51 also allows for collective self-defence. Even though organisations like NATO and the Warsaw Pact have argued that they are Article 51 organisations and not Chapter VIII organisations, the provision on the right to collective self-defence, among others, applies also to Chapter VIII organisations that have a defence function. In fact, as described above, the self-defence provision was included in the UN Charter upon request from the predecessor of the OAS – the first formally recognised Chapter VIII organisation.

The clause permitting action against enemy States without a UNSC authorisation was included in the UN Charter to satisfy the concerns of some European States relating to their perceived need for protection against Germany.[7] The provisions on enemy States were embedded in Articles 53

---

5 S. D. Murphy, *Humanitarian Intervention. The United Nations in an Evolving World Order*, Vol. 21, Procedural Aspects of International Law Series, Philadelphia, PA: University of Pennsylvania Press, 1996, p. 72; Randelzhofer, op. cit., n. 3, p. 123. See also the description by M. Byers and S. Chesterman, 'Changing Rules about Rules? Unilateral Humanitarian Intervention and the Future of International Law', in J. L. Holzgrefe and R. O. Keohane, (eds), *Humanitarian Intervention. Ethical, Legal and Political Dilemmas*, Cambridge: Cambridge University Press, 2003, ref. 82.
6 J. Frowein and N. Kirsch, 'Chapter VII. Action with respect to Threats to the Peace, Breaches of the Peace, and Acts of Aggression', in B. Simma (ed.), *The Charter of the United Nations. A Commentary*, 2nd edn, Vol. 1, Oxford: Oxford University Press, 2002, pp. 756–58.
7 M. Akehurst, 'Enforcement Action by Regional Agencies, with Special Reference to the Organization of American States', *British Year Book of International Law*, Vol. 42, 1967, p. 175.

and 107, thus being directly relevant also for regional organisations. The clause is intended to apply only to the former enemy States of the newly created UN in 1945,[8] and not to any 'rogue' States gaining such status later in time. Action against enemy States, however, is nowadays commonly regarded as obsolete and inapplicable, as all the former enemy States are now members of the UN.[9] The UN Charter text itself, disregarding *travaux preparatoires* and the doctrine, would not clearly prohibit a modern interpretation. Nevertheless, a modern application of the clause is not to be supported, as it would allow too wide a leeway for using force unilaterally.

In addition to the exceptions to the prohibition of the use of force provided for in the UN Charter text, Charter-related exceptions and extra-Charter exceptions to the use of force have developed through subsequent practice. The Charter-related exceptions refer to the 'Uniting for Peace' procedure, where the UN General Assembly can, in theory, act in case of the non-functioning of the UNSC. The right of National Liberation Movements to employ 'all means necessary', and to seek international assistance for the use of force in their legitimate struggle against colonialism, racist regimes or alien occupation is mentioned as another. The extra-Charter exceptions include the rescue of nationals in a life-threatening emergency situation abroad, if necessary, by military coercion and humanitarian intervention.[10] Humanitarian intervention thus is also named as a ground, though controversial, for the use of force.[11]

It has been argued that action in common interest is not subject to the general prohibition.[12] This is also linked to the presumption that acting consistently with the purposes and principles of the UN Charter (as stated, e.g. in the Treaty on European Union[13]) may sometimes differ from the Charter text and UNSC decisions. In the initial blueprint document of the UN Charter – the Atlantic Charter of 1941 – and later repeated in the Dumbarton Oaks Proposals, contained a commitment 'to unite our strength to maintain peace and security' and that 'armed force shall not be used, save in the common interest'.[14] The interpretation of 'common interest' has in the past couple of

---

8 G. Reiss and J. Bröhmer, 'Chapter VIII. Regional Arrangements', in B. Simma (ed.), *The Charter of the United Nations. A Commentary*, 2nd edn, Vol. 1, Oxford: Oxford University Press, 2002, pp. 876–77.
9 Ibid., p. 884.
10 Ibid.
11 For example, Brownlie, op. cit., n. 4, p. 338; M. Wood, 'Towards New Circumstances in Which the Use of Force May be Authorized?', in N. Blokker and N. Schrijver (eds), *The Security Council and the Use of Force. Theory and Reality – A Need for Change?*, Leiden and Boston, MA: Martinus Nijhoff Publishers, 2005, p. 79.
12 D. Kuwali, 'Protect Responsibly: The African Union's Implementation of Article 4(H) Intervention', *Yearbook of International Humanitarian Law*, Vol. 11, 2008, p. 68.
13 [2010] OJ C83, 30 March 2010.
14 R. Wolfrum, 'Chapter I. Purposes and Principles', in B. Simma (ed.), *The Charter of the United Nations. A Commentary*, 2nd edn, Vol. 1, Oxford: Oxford University Press, 2002, pp. 36–37.

decades become the focal point of discussion of the use of armed force on humanitarian grounds, even without a UNSC mandate in the cases of humanitarian catastrophes. The common interest has been connected to the notion of '(in)consistent with the Purposes of the United Nations', where the need to protect the fundamental principles included in the UN Charter is countered against the compliance with provisions of Articles 24 and 53 of the UN Charter on the primary role of the UNSC in the maintenance of peace and security.

The Preamble of the UN Charter contains a significant reference to fundamental human rights – the dignity and worth of human persons and equal rights of men and women – which were neglected throughout the years of the Cold War. Only in the past decade has the provision gained the attention of scholars and practitioners and had a significant influence on the matters of the use of force, eventually leading to the consensus on the principle of 'responsibility to protect' at the 2005 World Summit.

In general, the right to humanitarian intervention is supported as an existing customary right by legal realists[15] and denied by classicists.[16] The argument used against the right to humanitarian intervention is that there is not enough evidence of a pre-Charter right to humanitarian intervention, and that such a right would in any case have been abolished by the UN Charter prohibition of the use of force. Moreover, there is consistent evidence that States that launch humanitarian interventions justify them with other legal grounds: 'If there is presently a right to unauthorized humanitarian intervention, it is a right that dares not speak its name'.[17] An argument used to support a right to humanitarian intervention is the list of actual post-Charter unauthorised interventions: USA in the Dominican Republic (1965), India in East Pakistan (1971), Vietnam in Kampuchea (1978–93), Tanzania in Uganda (1979), ECOWAS in Liberia (1990–95), Britain, France and the USA in Iraq (since 1991), ECOWAS in Sierra Leone (since 1998), and NATO in Kosovo (since 1999); that evidence the continued existence of a practice.[18] Though it appears to be generally accepted that there is no right to unilateral humanitarian intervention, including unilateral regional intervention,[19] the debate spurred after the NATO intervention in Kosovo has led to the creation of the 'responsibility to protect' principle and different levels of acceptance of

---

15 J. L. Holzgrefe, 'The Context for Humanitarian Intervention', in J. L. Holzgrefe and R. O. Keohane, (eds), *Humanitarian Intervention. Ethical, Legal and Political Dilemmas*, Cambridge: Cambridge University Press, 2003, p. 44. For example, Richard B. Lillich, Jean-Pierre Fonteyne, Michael J. Bazyler.
16 Holzgrefe, ibid., p. 45
17 Holzgrefe, ibid., p. 49.
18 Holzgrefe, ibid., p. 46.
19 All action without a UNSC authorisation, even that taken by regional organisations, is classified as unilateral action, even if the level of legitimacy may be higher in regional interventions than interventions launched by one State.

the right to humanitarian intervention in regional organisations. The right to humanitarian intervention without a UN mandate is now suggested to be at least an 'emergency exit' solution.[20]

The classical view on enforcement action is that all action not taken by the UN is unilateral action, and there is no legal difference in enforcement action taken by an individual State or a regional organisation;[21] moreover, the humanitarian aspect is not decisive. The absence of theoretical distinction between a State and an organisation has, however, been challenged in the aftermath of the NATO intervention in Kosovo.[22]

Though not formally an exception to the prohibition of the use of force,[23] intervention by invitation needs to be mentioned. It is often used as the legal basis for operations launched by regional organisations. Intervention by invitation is deemed to be consensual, without coercion, and thus it is not essentially a use of force. This legal ground for intervention is, however, subject to potential misuse and, in fact, has been contested as a legitimate ground for action by regional organisations in the past two decades. The justification problems when invoking intervention by invitation include those of *pro forma* invitations, invitations by governments of dubious authority, as well as action exceeding the limits of non-coercive peacekeeping.

For an operation to be classified as a peacekeeping operation (non-coercive), State consent is required.[24] In practice this is usually settled in a Memorandum of Understanding and Status of Forces Agreement, or Status of Mission Agreement between the host State (its government) and the forces present (organisation or each participating State individually). In practice, however, there is usually no written agreement at the time when an operation is being launched. When consent of a State is alleged, it may be difficult to determine whether it has been voluntary and, if pressure has been exerted, to what degree of pressure may be regarded as vitiating the consent.[25] The scope of internal conflicts for which intervention may be invited is not clear either. The majority of scholars appear to agree that in civil wars intervention by another State would be considered illegal, even with an invitation of the government in control.[26] It is considered to be customary law that prohibits

---

20 Danish Institute of International Affairs, *Humanitarian Intervention. Legal and Political Aspects*, Copenhagen: DUPI, 1999, p. 127.
21 D. Sarooshi, *The United Nations and the Development of Collective Security. The Delegation by the UN Security Council of its Chapter VII Powers*, Oxford: Clarendon Press, 1999, p. 248.
22 Danish Institute of International Affairs, op. cit., n. 20.
23 Wood, op. cit., n. 11, p. 28.
24 A. Randelzhofer, 'United Nations Peacekeeping System' ('Host Country Consent'), in R. Bernhardt (ed.), *Encyclopedia of Public International Law*, Vol. 4, Amsterdam: North-Holland Publishing Company, 1982, p. 261.
25 Brownlie, op. cit., n. 4, p. 317.
26 A. Arend and R. Beck, *International Law and the Use of Force*, London and New York, NY: Routledge, 1993 (republished 2003), pp. 84, 85, 92.

intervention in civil wars.[27] Further, the discussion extends to whether intervention by invitation is valid in order to quell an insurrection. The reasons for this controversy are the inability of a shaky regime to represent the State as its government, the conflict of such intervention with principle of self-determination and a violation of the duty of non-intervention in the internal matters of another State.[28] This is true to an even larger extent in failed States, where the government has lost control over the territory and institutions fail to carry out public functions.[29]

The purpose of the invitation is an important element in ensuring the legality of the intervention. The consent of the territorial State to the presence and operation of foreign troops on its territory normally acts as a circumstance precluding wrongfulness of the otherwise unlawful presence of foreign troops, deriving from the law of State responsibility.[30] As the International Law Commission's (ILC) Article 20 on State Responsibility suggests, consent precludes the wrongfulness of the act to the extent of the consent that is given.[31] Thus any action that exceeds the limits of the consent is *ultra vires* and *de facto* becomes coercive, breaching the prohibition of the use of force. The analysis of regional organisation practice in the following chapters reveals numerous cases where the theoretical concerns mentioned above find expression in real life.

The UN Charter further provides for the responsibilities of the UNSC and the Member States. Article 24(1) of the UN Charter reads:

> In order to ensure prompt and effective action by the United Nations, its Members confer on the Security Council primary responsibility for the maintenance of international peace and security, and agree that in carrying out its duties under this responsibility the Security Council acts on their behalf.

Article 24(2) nevertheless, does not put the UNSC above the law: the UNSC has a responsibility to abide by the law provided for in the document giving

---

27 L. Doswald-Beck, 'The Legal Validity of Military Intervention by Invitation of the Government', *British Year Book of International Law*, Vol. 56, 1985, p. 189. Also the comment to this in M. Dixon and R. McCorquodale, *Cases and Materials on International Law*, 4th edn, Oxford: Oxford University Press, 1991, p. 557.
28 Doswald-Beck, ibid.
29 For a nuanced analysis of what is a failed State, see D. Thürer, 'The "failed state" and international law', *International Review of Red Cross*, No. 836, 1999.
30 A. Orakhelashvili, 'Legal Stability and Claims of Change: The International Court's Treatment of *Jus ad Bellum* and *Jus in Bello*', *Nordic Journal of International Law*, Vol. 75, 2006, p. 380.
31 Report of the International Law Commission on the work of its fifty-third session, *Draft Articles on the Responsibility of States for Internationally Wrongful Acts, with Commentaries*, A/56/10, 2001. Available at <http://untreaty.un.org/ilc/texts/instruments/english/commentaries/9_6_2001.pdf> (accessed 25 March 2013).

it the powers, namely – the UN Charter: 'In discharging these duties the Security Council shall act in accordance with the Purposes and Principles of the United Nations'. No commonly accepted provisions, however, exist in either the UN Charter or customary international law on what to do if the UNSC fails to discharge its duties in accordance with the purposes and principles of the UN. The 'Uniting for Peace' procedure where the UN General Assembly would take charge of the maintenance of peace and security has not become the common practice. The humanitarian intervention launched by a regional organisation – NATO – in the absence of a UNSC consensus on intervention, has not been accepted by the international community as a legal precedent that would make regional action as a substitute for the UNSC action. There exists no formal judicial review of the decisions of the UNSC. Neither the UN General Assembly nor the ICJ has a balance-of-power control over the UNSC, analogous to that of a democratic State system.

As a corollary to the Article 24(1) provision, Article 25 requires the members of the UN to 'agree to accept and carry out the decisions of the Security Council in accordance with the present Charter'. But as with the Article 24 provision, the law is silent about the abidance by the decisions of the UNSC if these decisions are in breach of international law. There is no legal right of regional organisations to act contrary to the UNSC decisions, even if the decisions are contestable under international law.

The UN Charter provides for 'equal rights of nations and peoples and sovereign equality of all its members'. These principles embedded in the UN Charter, however, are conditioned by the privileges of the Permanent Members of the UNSC.[32] The 'some are more equal than others'[33] principle of the UNSC composition has given a ground for discontent revealed in the UNSC reform proposals.[34] On the other hand, the importance of the balance of power in international relations and the need to ensure the commitment of the great powers was thought through by the drafters of the UN Charter after the failure of the League of Nations, which did not contain such preconditions for ensuring the interest of the powers. Nevertheless, the UNSC is the only authority that in accordance with the Article 39 of the UN Charter has the right to determine the existence of any threat to peace, breach of peace, or act of aggression and to make recommendations, or decide what measures shall be taken in accordance with Articles 41 and 42, to maintain or restore international peace and security. The records of both the Dumbarton Oaks and the San Francisco Conferences plainly show that the drafters of the UN Charter wanted the UNSC to have wide discretion in determining the

---

32 Wolfrum, op. cit., n. 14, p. 35.
33 G. Orwell, *Animal Farm. A Fairy Story*, Harmondsworth: Penguin Books in Association with Martin Secker and Warburg, 1945 (reprinted 1977), p. 114.
34 See *In Larger Freedom: towards development, security and human rights for all*, Report of the Secretary-General, A/59/2005, 21 March 2005.

existence of any threat to the peace.[35] In the cases of Kosovo (1999) and Iraq (2003), there was such a general prior acknowledgement by the UNSC. In other cases of controversial use of force such a requirement has been disregarded and other legal grounds for launching operations have been used. The examples of legal grounds include peacekeeping by ECOWAS in Liberia and Guinea Bissau, or self-defence by Russia in Georgia in 2008, where a UN mandate would thus theoretically not be required.

Both the geography and the content of threats have changed beyond recognition since the establishment of the UN. The concept of a 'threat to peace' has been expanding, until at the beginning of the nineties[36] the concept of the 'responsibility to protect'[37] developed, and humanitarian catastrophes came to be regarded as a threat to peace. In addition, most conflicts on the agenda of the international community today are internal, not international, whereas the UN initially intended to be involved only in international conflicts.

Article 103 of the UN Charter is of high relevance to regional agreements. The Article states that in the event of a conflict between the obligations of the members of the UN under the present Charter and their obligations under any other international agreement, their obligations under the Charter shall prevail. Thus this Article restricts a creation of regional rules for the maintenance of the peace of security, in the way that they must comply with the UN Charter. No regional customs, laws or treaties may be created that contradict the general international law contained in the UN Charter.

Chapter VIII of the UN Charter contains the core of provisions regarding the participation of regional organisations in the maintenance of peace and security. Article 52 contains the general provisions on regional arrangements and deals with the peaceful settlement of disputes in particular, while Article 53 contains the core provisions on the use of force by regional organisations. Article 54 provides for a duty to report regional action to the UNSC.

The maintenance of international peace and security – both peaceful settlement of disputes and enforcement measures – is the only topic on which regional arrangements have received specific regulation in the UN Charter.

---

35 J. L. Holzgrefe, 'Chapter I. Purposes and Principles', in B. Simma (ed.), *The Charter of the United Nations. A Commentary*, 2nd edn, Vol. 1, Oxford: Oxford University Press, 2002, p. 42.
36 K. Månsson, 'Reviving the "Spirit of San Francisco": the Lost proposals on Human Rights, Justice and International Law to the UN Charter', *Nordic Journal of International Law*, Vol. 76, 2007, p. 222: 'When in 1992 Boutros Boutros-Ghali made the statement that the "time of absolute and exclusive sovereignty [had] passed"', it was perceived as the turning point in the work and activities of the UN'. See also *An Agenda for Peace, Preventive Diplomacy, Peacemaking and Peace-keeping*, Report of the Secretary-General, A/47/277–S/24111, 17 June 1992, para. 17 (*Agenda for Peace*).
37 International Commission on Intervention and State Sovereignty, *Responsibility to Protect*, Report of the International Commission on Intervention and State Sovereignty, Ottawa: International Development Research Centre, 2001.

The UN Charter provides for the hierarchical relationship between the UN and the regional organisations. Whereas Article 52 gives the primary responsibility for peaceful settlement of disputes to the regional arrangements and agencies, Article 53 reinforces the provision of the primary authority of the UNSC regarding the use of force. Otherwise, the only requirement specified in Article 52 is that regional organisations and their activities have to be consistent with the purposes and principles of the UN Charter.

Article 53 provides that the UNSC shall, where appropriate, utilise regional arrangements or agencies for enforcement action under its authority. Enforcement action may not be taken under regional arrangements or by regional agencies without the authorisation of the UNSC. Paragraph 1 of Article 53 provides only one type of exception to that: the use of force against an enemy State (as in Article 107).

Even though included in a different chapter of the UN Charter, collective self-defence in Article 51 should also be taken into consideration in this context, as regional organisations may also have the purpose of collective self-defence and, in the case of self-defence, a UNSC authorisation for enforcement action would not be required.

Regional organisations have obligations towards the UN not only before taking action. Article 54 provides for the duty of the regional arrangements and agencies to keep the UN informed of their activities in the maintenance of international peace and security, both those already undertaken and also those contemplated.

Chapter VIII of the UN Charter is very concise with the central terms not clarified, thus leaving room for confusion and controversial interpretations. Two significant clauses that were left open by the drafters of the UN Charter were the term 'regional arrangements and agencies' (relevant today in how it relates to 'regional organisations'), and the content of what is 'appropriate for regional action'.

Chapter VIII of the UN Charter is entitled 'Regional Arrangements', and the content of the chapter refers to 'regional arrangements and agencies'. Thus, the Charter text distinguishes between regional 'arrangements' and 'agencies', but does not contain the commonly used term 'regional organisations'. No definition of the term 'regional arrangements' was ever accepted, and thus there is no consensus on the meaning of the term in doctrine.[38] All the proposals for defining a regional agency in the UN Charter were also subsequently rejected.[39] In addition, it is notable that for two decades following

---

38 M. Zwanenburg, 'Regional Organizations and the Maintenance of International Peace and Security: Three Recent Regional African Peace Operations', *Journal of Conflict and Security Law*. Vol. 11, 3, 2006, p. 488.
39 W. Hummer and M. Schweitzer, 'Chapter VII. Regional Arrangements', in B. Simma (ed.), *The Charter of the United Nations. A Commentary*, 2nd edn, Vol. 1, Oxford: Oxford University Press, 2002, p. 817.

the creation of the Charter, the UN refrained from naming any arrangement as a Chapter VIII arrangement or creating a definition. It came to be argued at the beginning of the nineties that the definition of 'regional agencies and arrangements' was left deliberately open, in order to provide flexibility, enabling the term to cover a wide range of regional organisations going beyond those strictly established for security and defence co-operation.[40]

The UN Charter thus confusingly distinguishes between 'arrangements' and 'agencies', and in addition these terms are further blurred with the term commonly used today, 'regional organisations'. The difference between an agency and an arrangement is that an agency possesses an institutional structure, whereas an arrangement does not.[41] According to Hummer and Schweitzer, the distinction of these terms is to provide for application to a wide range of regional co-operation forums: from a treaty to a regional organisation.[42] In this interpretation 'arrangement' would refer to a treaty under international law, whereas an 'agency' would be exercising its functions with organs of its own, though not necessarily having to be an international organisation proper. The distinction, however, is theoretical, and has no practical application. It can briefly be said that all the agencies are also agreements, as an agreement is necessary to establish an agency. More relevant is the connection between the wording of the Charter and the commonly used terminology nowadays.

The term 'regional organisations' is nowadays commonly used in doctrine, as well as by the UN in the official language regarding the maintenance of peace and security. It appears to be interchangeably usable shorthand for 'regional arrangements and agencies'.[43] Examples can be found in a long list of UN documents, for example, UNSC Resolution 1197 (1998) uses the terms 'regional and subregional organisations' and 'regional and subregional arrangements' interchangeably, also using the term 'mechanisms' as a synonym. UNSC Resolution 1809 (2008) uses only the term 'regional organisations', also in the context of the Chapter VIII of the UN Charter. UNSC Resolution 1769 (2007) regarding the establishment of the AU/UN Hybrid Operation in Darfur (UNAMID) uses both terms, with an apparent distinction, where 'regional arrangements' refers specifically to the AU, while also noting the efforts of other regional 'organisations' that have assisted in the deployment of UNAMID. Nevertheless, UNSC Resolution 1631 (2005), which is the first resolution adopted by the UNSC on regional organisations in general, uses only the phrase 'regional and sub-regional organisations' clearly in the understanding of Chapter VIII of the UN Charter. Furthermore, the Statement by the President of the UNSC of 13 January 2010 refers to 'Cooperation between the United Nations and regional and sub-regional organizations in

---

40 *Agenda for Peace*, op. cit., n. 36; Shaw, op. cit., n. 2, p. 1274.
41 Akehurst, op. cit., n. 7, p. 177.
42 Hummer and Schweitzer, op. cit., n. 39, p. 822.
43 Zwanenburg, op. cit., n. 38, pp. 491–92.

maintaining international peace and security'.[44] It appears that the use of the word 'organisation' today is as flexible, if not more, than that of the word 'arrangement' in 1945, and that the former appears to have replaced the latter in application in documents referring to Chapter VIII. 'Arrangement' is generally used only to refer to the Charter text or quoting a title of an earlier document, but otherwise the word 'organisation' is used in the same sense. The word 'agency' is generally omitted. The phraseology has instead been supplemented by 'subregional' organisations, which are as much of interest to the UN as 'regional' organisations.

There is a concern expressed in the literature regarding the imprecision in abbreviating the term 'regional arrangements and agencies' to 'regional organisations', as not all regional organisations are regional arrangements and agencies in the understanding of Chapter VIII of the UN Charter.[45] Article 52 of the UN Charter requires that a regional arrangement must have been created for dealing with matters relating to the maintenance of international peace and security and that doctrine requires that a procedure for the settlement of disputes between the members is established, in order to qualify as a regional arrangement or agency.[46] Hummer and Schweitzer list the following requirements for a regional arrangement: constituted by States, has a constitutive treaty that must be valid under general public international law, and is created to last. In addition, no States may be incorporated into the organisation by coercion.[47] A group of States can be a regional organisation, without qualifying to be a Chapter VIII agency or arrangement, and vice versa. A regional organisation requires legal personality, and this is not necessarily the case of regional arrangements and agencies. From an institutional theory perspective one can argue about many details of the terminology used and the regional mechanisms referred to. The interchangeability of the terms is a new development started after the end of the Cold War, and reflects the (re)discovery of the utilisation of Chapter VIII by the UN. The approach of the UN towards the Chapter VIII classification of regional organisations is not conditioned by legal-theoretical nuances but aimed at achieving broader participation of regional organisations by disregarding such nuances.[48]

The debate on what is appropriate for regional action (Article 52 of the UN Charter) is wide, yet unresolved. In the Commentary to the UN Charter, Hummer and Schweitzer limit the question of appropriateness of regional action only to peaceful measures of Article 52 and conclude that it is the regional organisations determining themselves what is appropriate for

---

44 S/PRST/2010/1.
45 Zwanenburg, op. cit., n. 38, pp. 491–92.
46 Ibid.
47 Hummer and Schweitzer, op. cit., n. 39, p. 823.
48 *A regional-global security partnership: challenges and opportunities*, Report of the Secretary-General, A/61/204–S/2006/590, 28 July 2006.

regional action.[49] As a general rule, Article 53 provides the limit for regional action, stating that no enforcement action shall be taken by the regional organisations without a UNSC mandate. The UNSC can, nevertheless, authorise a regional organisation to carry out enforcement action by virtue of Article 39. The division of labour between the UN and regional organisations was not even debated at the time of the drafting of the UN Charter.[50] This was most likely due to the unsystematic incorporation of a regionalist Chapter in the otherwise universalist Charter. A view expressed in literature is that a provision was included in Chapter VIII that the UNSC would control all enforcement (Chapter VII) action.[51] At the time of the creation of the UN this provision meant all military action, since the alternative use of military capabilities, such as peacekeeping, was not invented. In 1962, however, the ICJ in 'Certain Expenses Advisory Opinion'[52] confirmed that UNSC authorisation was necessary for enforcement action[53] and counter-positioned it to the peacekeeping operations of the time – operations that had been established to cease hostilities and had the consent of the States involved. Peacekeeping as such was thus not regarded as enforcement action and the UN General Assembly was exercising the authority it had alongside the UNSC to authorise peaceful settlement of disputes. Later, peacekeeping became an even more loosely applicable means of dispute settlement, without any UN authorisation. It is commonly accepted that peacekeeping may nowadays be carried out autonomously by regional organisations. The limits of autonomous peacekeeping and the borderline between peacekeeping and illegal enforcement action, as well as action outside the region, are the core problematic issues in drawing the line on what is appropriate for regional action today.

Action outside the region is a problematic issue that applies generally to the Euro-Atlantic regional organisations. Is regional action outside the region legal at all, and is there a difference between peacekeeping and enforcement outside the region? Generally, out-of-area enforcement action authorised by the UN and carried out by a regional organisation is regarded as covered by Article 53 of the UN Charter. Consequently, therefore, UN-authorised peacekeeping outside the region is also legal: the UNSC has the right to authorise a regional organisation to act outside the region. There does, however, exist an opposing opinion, that Article 53 by its nature prohibits action outside the region: any action outside the region is not appropriate for regional

---

49 Hummer and Schweitzer, op. cit., n. 39, p. 824.
50 Z. Deen-Racsmány, 'A Redistribution of Authority Between the UN and Regional Organizations in the Field of the Maintenance of Peace and Security?', *Leiden Journal of International Law*, Vol. 13, 2000, p. 308.
51 Deen-Racsmány, ibid, p. 309; Akehurst, op. cit., n. 7, p. 186.
52 Certain Expenses of the United Nations. Advisory Opinion, 20 July 1962, *ICJ Reports* 1962, p. 151.
53 Certain Expenses of the United Nations, ibid., p. 17.

action, not even with a UNSC authorisation.[54] A supportive argument to this view is the debate in the San Francisco Conference that the regional organisations would deal with the settlement of local disputes only.[55] The world has moved on since San Francisco. Just as with many other developments in the law on use of force, the needs of the international community have changed since the signing of the UN Charter, and what was meant by the drafters may not be relevant today. The practice of the UN itself, actively involving regional organisations in the global maintenance of peace and security, and specifically requesting and authorising EU and NATO operations outside their region, appears to be a strong enough argument that, in general, action outside the region is permissible.

The legality of regional action outside the region without a UN mandate remains an open question. If coercive action within the region is not permissible, it would, by no means, be any more legally permissible outside the region. This would also apply to humanitarian intervention as enforcement action outside the region. The question of permissibility of unauthorised regional peacekeeping outside the region is also complicated. There is potential controversy surrounding the legality of the invitation, as well as crossing the border between peacekeeping and enforcement in the action taken by the military forces.

The practice of the United Nations

The context of the universal perspective towards regionalism is not completely illustrated by only listing the UN Charter provisions of 1945. As noted, at the time of the creation of the UN there was no clear vision on how regionalism would work within the universal UN system. It was not even clear which criteria the various forums should meet in order to classify as regional arrangements and agencies under Chapter VIII of the UN Charter, and it was even less clear how the UN would utilise these arrangements. The practice that developed subsequently was not foreseen by the drafters of the Charter and has developed according to an innovative path.

The need for innovation came from the very outset of the UN system of maintenance of peace and security, as the mechanism for military action that was intended by the UN Charter was never set into place. Article 43(1) of the UN Charter provided all Member States were to make forces available to the UNSC. No agreement, however, was reached in practice, and no obligations were made for the Member States to contribute troops.[56] For the following 45 years the UN relied almost solely on *ad hoc* contributions from Member States for every single one of the 15 peacekeeping operations.

---

54 Deen-Racsmány, op. cit., n. 50, p. 309.
55 Ibid.
56 Frowein and Kirsch, op. cit., n. 6, pp. 762–63.

Peacekeeping became the phenomenon developed outside the provisional scope of the UN Charter, as no solution was feasible in line with the Charter provisions. It is considered to be the most important development in the history of the maintenance of peace and security.

The term 'peacekeeping' is not found in the UN Charter, and neither are any provisions directly relating to this 'trademark' of the UN. Rather, peacekeeping has been created independently and accepted as not being in contradiction with the Charter. Some answers to what the rules for peacekeeping are can be found in the practice of the UN developed over 60 years.

Chapter VI of the UN Charter provides for peaceful settlement of disputes, while Chapter VII, 'Action with Respect to Threats to the Peace, Breaches of the Peace and Acts of Aggression', provides for enforcement measures: economic and political in Article 41, and military in Article 42. The non-violent use of force that UN peacekeeping stands for has developed as something in-between peaceful measures, such as negotiations and mediation under Chapter VI, and enforcement action under Chapter VII, and is unofficially called 'Chapter Six and a Half', a term introduced by Dag Hammarskjöld, the second UN Secretary-General.[57]

Peacekeeping had no direct basis in the UN Charter and did not operate under Chapter VII of the Charter.[58] The rules on peacekeeping were derived from practice, and apart from the very basic principles, they have shaped and developed according to the needs of the time and the specific operation in question.

There are various suggestions as to what could theoretically be the legal basis for peacekeeping in the UN Charter. Gray observes that the legal basis for peacekeeping may be found in the right of the UN General Assembly to establish subsidiary organs, or under Chapter VI regarding peaceful settlement, or under Article 40 regarding provisional measures. However, in practice there has been no express reference to any of these in the resolutions establishing peacekeeping operations and the debate appears to be without practical significance.[59] In its comprehensive document, *United Nations Peacekeeping Operations. Principles and Guidelines* (Capstone doctrine),[60] the Department of Peacekeeping Operations (DPKO) includes a very brief explanation of the legal basis of UN peacekeeping, and links it to the purpose of the UN. It notes that UN peacekeeping has traditionally been linked to Chapter VI of the UN Charter, but adds that the UNSC does not need to

---

57 United Nations Peacekeeping website. Available at <http://www.un.org/en/peacekeeping> (accessed 18 March 2013).
58 Gray, op. cit., n. 2, p. 282.
59 Ibid, 261–62.
60 Department of Peacekeeping Operations, Department of Field Support, *United Nations Peacekeeping Operations. Principles and Guidelines*, New York, NY: United Nations, 2008, p. 12.

specify the Chapter of the Charter when authorizing peacekeeping.[61] The generally agreed principles that evolved through State practice required that peacekeeping forces should: be impartial, not take sides, be lightly armed, not use force except in self-defence, operate with the consent of the host State and not usually include forces from the Permanent Members of the UNSC or States with political interest in the host State.

The first peacekeeping operation was an observer operation, the United Nations Truce Supervision Organization (UNTSO). These were unarmed military observers, set up by the UNSC in the Middle East in 1948.[62] The second UN peacekeeping operation was an observer mission as well – United Nations Military Observer Group in India and Pakistan (UNMOGIP).[63] The third operation brought about a new development – the authorisation of a peacekeeping force by the UN General Assembly under the 'Uniting for Peace' resolution in 1956 in the Suez Crisis. The 'Uniting for Peace' procedure itself deserves special attention.

The 'Uniting for Peace' resolution,[64] adopted by the UN General Assembly, challenged the provisions of the UN Charter by the General Assembly taking action in the maintenance of peace and security in a situation where the UNSC failed to act. The resolution was adopted by the UN General Assembly in connection with the paralysis of the UNSC in the Korean Crisis. The most important part of Resolution 377 A (V) is section A, which states that where the UNSC, because of lack of unanimity of the Permanent Members, fails to exercise its primary responsibility for the maintenance of international peace and security, the UN General Assembly shall seize itself of the matter.[65] Resolution 498 (V) (1951) remains the only example of a situation where the UN General Assembly, at that time under domination of Western influence, recommended taking enforcement action, notwithstanding the firm resistance of a Permanent Member of the UNSC.[66]

To date, ten emergency special sessions, as provided for in the resolution have been convened by the UN General Assembly, mainly discussing topics of threats to international peace and security, but not taking action. In a couple of cases, however, peacekeeping forces have been established by the UN General Assembly. The first session took place on the occasion of the

---

61 Department of Peacekeeping Operations, ibid., pp. 12–13.
62 United Nations, *The Blue Helmets. A review of United Nations Peace-keeping*, 3rd edn, New York, NY: United Nations Department of Public Information, 1996, pp. 4 and 13. The operation is still continuing.
63 The operation is still continuing.
64 UN General Assembly Resolution 377 A (V).
65 C. Tomuschat, 'Uniting for Peace General Assembly Resolution 377 (V) New York 3 November 1950', UN Audiovisual Library of International Law, Codification Division, Office of Legal Affairs, 2008. Available at <http://untreaty.un.org/cod/avl/ha/ufp/ufp.html> (accessed 21 April 2013).
66 Tomuschat, ibid.

1956 war between Israel and Egypt and the British-French attack on the Suez Canal zone. This lead to the establishment of the first UN peacekeeping force. The tenth emergency special session, dealing with the Israeli occupation of Palestinian territory, started in 1997 and has not yet come to an end.[67] The 'Uniting for Peace' procedure presumes that the veto of the Permanent Members of the UNSC does not operate, since referral to the UN General Assembly is considered to constitute a procedural determination and hence not subject to such blocking power.[68] Although the shifting of responsibilities to the UN General Assembly may not be consistent with the original intentions of the drafters of the UN Charter, it is today fully accepted that emergency special sessions have become an integral part of the legal order of the UN. On the other hand, the significance of these meetings is very low and does not impact the work of the UNSC.

The legality of the 'Uniting for Peace' resolution has been challenged on the grounds that the primary responsibility for the maintenance of international peace and security lies with the UNSC (Articles 5, 24, 39, 50, 53, 99 and 106). On the other hand, those who uphold the validity of the resolution argue that even if the UNSC has the primary responsibility, the UN General Assembly has a residuary or secondary responsibility based on the wide terms of Articles 10 and 11(4).[69] The UN General Assembly passed the resolution stating that where the UNSC, because of lack of unanimity of the Permanent Members, fails to exercise its primary responsibility for the maintenance of international peace and security, the UN General Assembly would seize itself of the matter, also calling emergency meetings, if necessary.[70] In its Advisory Opinion on the 'Legal Consequences of the Construction of a Wall in the Occupied Palestinian Territory', the ICJ has formally confirmed that the prohibition of simultaneous action has been superseded by practice.[71] Article 11(2) says that the UN General Assembly may discuss questions relating to the maintenance of peace and security and make recommendations (except as provided in Article 12); but any such question on which action is necessary shall be referred to the UNSC. Article 12 is designed to prevent clashes between the two bodies; it provides that while the UNSC is exercising its functions with regard to a particular dispute or situation, the UN General Assembly shall not make any recommendation unless the UNSC so requests. These two provisions have been flexibly interpreted in such a way that there is no strict division of functions.[72] Brownlie admits,

---

67 Tomuschat, ibid. (The emergency special session was adjourned by resolution RES-10/16 of 17 November 2006, para. 13, and can at any time be resumed upon request by Member States.)
68 Ibid.
69 Brownlie, op. cit., n. 4, p. 334.
70 UN General Assembly Resolution 377 A (V).
71 *ICJ Reports* 2004, p. 136, paras 27–28.
72 Gray, op. cit., n. 2, p. 259.

though, that the controversy is academic to a considerable degree, since the opponents of the resolution in the UN have since approved the use of its machinery in practice in several crises and are presumably estopped from reopening the question of interpretation.[73]

Despite the discretion on matters of peace and security the 'Uniting for Peace' procedure would give to the UN General Assembly, it has not been efficiently utilised. Even in a case like the Kosovo crisis this option for bypassing a UNSC paralysis was not utilised, thus leading to unilateral regional action. Perhaps the reason was that the majority support would not have been likely to have been achieved in the UN General Assembly. Nevertheless, the achievement of the 'Uniting for Peace' resolution is that it secured that in 1956 the UN General Assembly was able to establish the first UN peacekeeping force that provided the model for classical peacekeeping, which requires the consent of the protagonists, impartiality on the part of the UN forces, and the resort to arms only in self-defence. The immediate objective of this classical form of peacekeeping is to facilitate conditions for a more comprehensive peace agreement. It offers the combatants an opportunity to stop fighting, to explore fresh avenues towards peace and allows time for the UN Secretary-General or other negotiators to do their work.[74]

The impact of the 'Uniting for Peace' resolution on UN peacekeeping practice is broad and accepted as legal, despite having no legal basis in the UN Charter and, perhaps, even despite its possible contradiction with the Charter. The First United Nations Peacekeeping Force (UNEF I) was created based on UN General Assembly Resolution 999[75] (ES-I) of 4 November 1956 (which was recommendatory). All in all, peacekeeping units have been created by the UN General Assembly in a couple of exceptional cases – the aforementioned UNEF I, as well as United Nations Security Force/United Nations Temporary Executive Authority (UNSF/UNTEA). The peacekeeping practice with the use of military force with a strictly limited mandate, and the 'Uniting for Peace' procedure are strong examples of how something not provided for in the UN Charter, and formally full of controversy, has become the accepted in international law. It proves that if there is a political will, there is a possibility to find a solution acceptable to the majority. The 'Uniting for Peace' procedure, in addition, shows that the paralysis of the UNSC does not support the direct necessity to seek alternatives outside the UN. If the UN is willing to work on retaining the central role in the maintenance of peace and security, there are measures that can be taken by the organisation itself to ensure control over the regional mechanisms, not only relying on the voluntary compliance of the latter.

---

73 Brownlie, op. cit., n. 4, p. 334.
74 *The Blue Helmets*, op. cit., n. 62, p. 4.
75 Ibid, p. 37.

UN peacekeeping has come a long way since the first peacekeeping operation in 1948. Since then there have been a total of 64 UN peacekeeping operations around the world.[76] Compared to the UN peacekeeping activity in the Cold War years the number of peace operations after the end of the Cold War has sky-rocketed. Over 50 new operations have been launched in the decade following the end of the Cold War, and several of the Cold War operations are still ongoing. Over the years, peacekeeping has undergone continuous transformation. Some of the more significant developments include a widening of tasks for the UN, the introduction of the use of force beyond self-defence in peacekeeping, and the introduction of the long-forgotten provision of utilisation of regional arrangements under Chapter VIII of the UN Charter. The developments in peacekeeping are classified either in the four generations of peacekeeping[77] or by distinguishing between traditional and modern peacekeeping.[78]

The first peacekeeping operations consisted of military observers and lightly armed troops having roles of monitoring, reporting and confidence-building in order to support ceasefires and limited peace agreements. Whereas the first generation of peacekeeping covers operations launched over 40 years, the last two decades have seen a tripled number of operations, and also three more generations of peacekeeping. The world, the balance of power and the types of conflicts changed dramatically after the end of the Cold War. So did the strategic context of UN peacekeeping. The nineties saw a shift and expansion of field operations from traditional operations involving strictly military tasks, to complex multidimensional enterprises designed to ensure the implementation of comprehensive peace agreements and assist in laying the foundations for sustainable peace.[79] Today, the operations contain a wide range of tasks, such as helping to build sustainable institutions of governance, human rights monitoring, security sector reform, disarmament, demobilisation and reintegration of former combatants and others. The military presence today is complemented by a wide range of civilian specialists. Moreover, whereas

---

76 United Nations Peacekeeping website, above, n. 57.
77 Gray, op. cit., n. 2, pp. 261–74; *The Blue Helmets*, op. cit., n. 62, pp. 4–5; M. Malan, 'Peacekeeping in the New Millennium: Towards Fourth Generation Peace Operations?', *African Security Review*, Vol. 7, 3, 1998. Available at <http://www.iss.co.za/pubs/asr/7no3/Malan.html> (accessed 25 March 2013).
78 N. Blokker, 'Security Council and the Use of Force: on Recent Practice', in N. Blokker and N. Schrijver (eds), *The Security Council and the Use of Force. Theory and Reality – A Need for Change?*, Leiden and Boston, MA: Martinus Nijhoff Publishers, 2005, p. 18, and E. Fanta, 'The Capacity of African Regional Organisations in Peace and Security'. Paper presented at the ERD (European Report on Development) Workshop: 'Transforming Political Structures: Security, Institutions, and Regional Integration Mechanisms', Florence 16–17 April 2009. European University Institute website. Available at <http://erd.eui.eu/media/fanta.pdf> (accessed 18 March 2013).
79 United Nations Peacekeeping website, above, n. 57.

initially peacekeeping was to be used in international conflicts, it has now became increasingly used in internal conflicts and civil wars.[80]

First generation peacekeeping has mainly been used to assist in resolving conflicts between States. The basic characteristics of first generation peacekeeping are the use of force only in self-defence, the impartiality of the peacekeepers, the consent of all parties involved and an inter-State conflict. Impartiality implies that the States participating ought not to have a special interest of the State in the conflict, i.e. States with a particular interest in the territory of conflict, like former colonial States, should abstain from sending their troops. The first generation peacekeeping pattern was rather unchanged until the end of the Cold War, though the list of the operations stretching over nearly 40 years was not excessive – 15 peacekeeping operations, including observer missions.

After the Cold War, peacekeeping mainly became a tool for addressing conflicts within States, sometimes in situations where the government would no longer be functioning.[81] UN forces were now facing irregular forces, rather than the regular armies.[82] The statement of the UN Secretary-General, that the nature of peacekeeping precludes the employment of peacekeeping forces in situations of an essentially internal nature, and that force should be used only in self-defence,[83] lost its relevance and applicability. Another core characteristic of peacekeeping – impartiality – showed its dark reverse side. In the case of, for example, Cambodia and Rwanda, the lack of individual State interest meant an inability for the UN to stop the mass killings and genocide. An earlier example of the lack of interest of the international community is the genocide in Cambodia: Vietnam intervened in Cambodia in 1978 illegally – unilaterally. Along the same lines, the UN was reluctant to stop the Rwanda genocide, leaving France and Belgium – the States directly interested – to take the only action, and thus the effort being too little and too controversial.[84] Rwanda was another landmark in the transformation of peacekeeping: individual State interest in participating in a certain peacekeeping operation that had been prohibited before was now legitimised. Belgium, participating in the ill-fated United Nations Assistance Mission in Rwanda (UNAMIR) in 1993, was the first country with an alleged interest to participate in a peacekeeping operation.[85] The interest was the fact that

---

80 United Nations Peacekeeping website, above, n. 57.
81 *The Blue Helmets*, op. cit., n. 62, p. 3.
82 Gray, op. cit., n. 2, p. 272.
83 Ibid, p. 263.
84 The first UN peacekeeping operation in Rwanda, UNAMIR, was too small-scale and with a very restrictive mandate for the extent of the crisis. Belgium withdrew its UN peacekeeping troops after the killing of ten Belgian peacekeepers. After that France intervened, launching Operation Turquoise. Even though the operation had UNSC authorisation under Chapter VII of the UN Charter, it was accused of not being impartial.
85 Gray, op. cit., n. 2, p. 293.

Rwanda had been under Belgian Trusteeship from 1918 to 1962.[86] Since 1992, peacekeeping operations have also included personnel contributions from all five Permanent Members of the UNSC and some neighbouring or near-neighbouring States, such as Thailand and China in Cambodia in the United Nations Transitional Authority in Cambodia (UNTAC) 1992–93.[87] Also, the concept of self-defence has become conditional. The violence faced by the UN peacekeepers has given the UNSC reason to often add Chapter VII use of force elements to peacekeeping, where the use of force is allowed not only for the peacekeepers in self-defence, but also to accomplish the mission. The requirement for impartiality on the ground, however, remains unaltered. Within the context of the abovementioned principal post-Cold War changes in the basic rules of peacekeeping, i.e. modern peacekeeping, the next three generations are distinguished.

The second generation peacekeeping operations mark the beginning of multi-functionality in peacekeeping. The new situations are conflicts, in which the UN or other multinational organisations have guided the adversaries to political settlements based on compromise (Namibia, Cambodia, El Salvador, Mozambique and Angola).[88] In these cases, the peace process has started with a ceasefire determined by comprehensive peace agreements, after which peacekeepers have been deployed in the affected areas with the consent of the involved parties reflected in these agreements. The so-called 'multidimensional' processes include separation of combatants, the disarmament of irregular forces, the demobilisation and transformation of regular and irregular forces into a unified army, assistance with reintegration into civil society, the establishment of new policing systems and the monitoring of elections for new governments.[89]

Peacekeeping forces created in 1999 in Kosovo and Timor Leste marked a further development establishing what is referred to as the third generation of peacekeeping. The UN tasks here turned from complex to comprehensive, all-inclusive, resembling the functions of a State. Fiscal management, judicial affairs, municipal services and civilian experts became an integral part of peacekeeping as much as the deployment of military personnel.[90]

Fourth generation peacekeeping has been linked to the developments in regionalisation. In Darfur, Chad, the Central African Republic (CAR) and other places, peacekeeping operations have been launched in co-operation between the UN and regional organisations. For example, UNAMID and the United Nations Mission in the Central African Republic and Chad (MINURCAT) are hybrid operations involving co-operation between the

---

86 *The Blue Helmets*, op. cit., n. 62, p. 341.
87 Malan, op. cit., n. 77.
88 Ibid.
89 Ibid.
90 UN Press Release, DSG/SM/91, 3 April 2000.

UN, the AU and the EU.[91] In addition, greater emphasis is put on peace-building, conflict prevention and the establishment of preventive peacekeeping forces.[92]

Thus, simultaneously with the extension of the scope of the general peacekeeping mandate and the complexity of UN peacekeeping operations, a significant new characteristic of peacekeeping is also the involvement of regional organisations. It must be noted that, as the following chapters on regional organisations reveal, peacekeeping by regional organisations alone is as robust as post-Cold War UN peacekeeping proper, but does not contain the same complex set of tasks. The wide scope of functions and tasks of the second, third and fourth generation UN peacekeeping operations sets in only when regional peacekeeping operations are conducted in co-operation with the UN itself. The autonomous regional peacekeeping operations, in most cases, contradicting the scholarly defined frames, combine the simplicity of tasks of the first generation of peacekeeping and the robustness of the post-Cold War modern peacekeeping. The scope of robust peacekeeping action and the border between peacekeeping and peace enforcement in both universal and regional practice are of relevance in discovering what is appropriate for regional action.

Since the end of the Cold War, the global maintenance of peace and security has witnessed a significant increase in the use of military enforcement elements. First, the majority of peacekeeping operations are authorised by the UN by referring to Chapter VII of the UN Charter, thus providing a mandate for the use of force exceeding traditional UN peacekeeping (i.e. robust peacekeeping). Second, also since the end of the Cold War the UNSC has been authorising enforcement operations, both by coalitions of the willing and by regional organisations. The UN does not carry out enforcement action itself but outsources peace enforcement operations as well as peacekeeping operations with enforcement elements to subcontractors, namely coalitions of the willing and regional organisations.[93]

One of the fundamental problems of what is permissible for regional action is subsequently the blurring of the concepts of peacekeeping and peace enforcement in the past two decades. In the ICJ Advisory Opinion in the 'Expenses' case, it was stated that the UNSC exclusive powers are confined to coercive or enforcement action.[94] This statement leaves space not only for UN General Assembly recommendations (as was the matter of the 'Expenses' case), but also for the autonomy of action of regional organisations in peacekeeping. As Chapter VIII of the UN Charter provides that the regional organisations may

---

91 Gray, op. cit., n. 2, p. 273.
92 Ibid.
93 *A More Secure World: Our Shared Responsibility*, Report of the High Level Panel on Threats, Challenge and Change, A/59/565, 2 December 2004, para. 210.
94 Advisory Opinion of 20 July 1962, *ICJ Reports* 1962, pp. 163–64.

settle local disputes by peaceful means, peacekeeping has developed as an inherent part of this practice.

The problem of distinction between peacekeeping and peace enforcement in the post-Cold War era has two main causes:

(a) The peacekeeping forces are allowed to use force beyond self-defence, even getting engaged in combat action. This way the action carried out by peacekeeping forces goes beyond what is traditionally accepted as peacekeeping, and as a peaceful means of settlement of disputes in general. By extensive use of force, military peacekeeping comes closer to enforcement action than to means of peaceful settlement of disputes.
(b) Traditionally, peacekeeping operations are to be launched once peace has been established and in order to keep this peace. The post-Cold War peacekeeping operations have been launched in situations where there was a deep ongoing crisis, in situations of civil war. Thus, in addition to using force beyond self-defence, there have been problems with acquiring the consent of all the warring parties, and ensuring that the operations were not coercive.

The modern robust peacekeeping was first used in Somalia in 1992. The significant legal element in the case of this operation was that Chapter VII of the UN Charter was used for the first time not to authorise force against a wrongdoing State, but with a humanitarian aim during a civil war.[95] It was the first time in UN history that a force was established with the primary purpose of making possible the delivery of emergency assistance to civilian population. UNSC Resolution 794 contained the phrase characteristic to enforcement operations: 'use all necessary means', but with the specification 'to establish a secure environment'.[96] The traditional understanding of peacekeeping implies that there is already a situation that can sufficiently be characterised as 'peace', the purpose of such an operation being to 'keep' the peace. Today, however, the tasks of peacekeeping operations start in situations where there is no peace to keep, but where peace is first to be created. Thus, while the aim of the operations is peacekeeping by content, the execution is enforcement by form. Hence the problem of blurring between the concepts of peacekeeping and peace enforcement.

The blurred distinction between peacekeeping and peace enforcement refers, among others, to the example of the United Nations Transitional Administration for Eastern Slavonia (UNTAES) force in Croatia when the UNSC issued Resolution 1037 (1996) mandating the operation under Chapter VII of the UN Charter, even though there was a host State consent.[97] A Chapter VII

---

95 Gray, op. cit., n. 2, p. 287.
96 S/Res/794.
97 Gray, op. cit., n. 2, p. 285.

reference was also included in UNSC Resolution 918 (1994) on peacekeeping in Rwanda.[98] Other early examples of blurring the distinction between peacekeeping and peace enforcement on the ground include the ECOWAS operations in Liberia (the 1990 operation) and Sierra Leone and CIS operations in Georgia, Azerbaijan and Tajikistan. All these are cases where combat action has taken place and the existence of a legitimate invitation has been dubious. None of these operations, however, has been formally authorised with a reference to Chapter VII,[99] but classified as autonomous regional peacekeeping operations instead, without the UN debating their actual content.

Whereas peacekeeping functions may either be performed by UN-led forces or other formations of States, such as regional organisations or coalitions of the willing, peace enforcement operations are always outsourced. As an illustration, the *Report of the Panel on United Nations Peacekeeping Operations* reads: 'The Panel recognises that the UN does not wage war. Where enforcement action is required, it has consistently been entrusted to coalitions of willing States, with the authorization of the Security Council, acting under Chapter VII of the Charter'.[100] The need for an efficient response to conflicts is reflected also in the sudden decrease in UN peacekeeping operations in the past few years,[101] while in the same period the activity of regional organisations has intensified significantly in both robust regional peacekeeping and UN-authorised peace enforcement.

During the Cold War the UNSC authorised (though in a form of a recommendation) the use of force only once – in 1950, regarding Korea.[102] After that, the next UNSC resolution, involving military enforcement authorised by the UN, came only after the end of the Cold War. It was UNSC Resolution 678 (1990) on the Iraqi invasion in Kuwait, in which the UNSC authorised all Member States to use all necessary means and called for Iraq to withdraw its forces from Kuwait.[103] Operation Desert Storm was thus the first enforcement operation outsourced by the UN to a coalition of the willing.

In 1993, the UN requested NATO to enforce the arms embargo against all States of the former Yugoslavia and to implement sanctions against the Federal Republic of Yugoslavia.[104] In fact, most of the UN-authorised enforcement operations have been and are being carried out by NATO (or alternatively by coalitions of the willing, yet also mainly with USA in the leading role). Such were the cases of enforcement operations in the Balkans in

---

98 S/Res/918.
99 Gray, op. cit., n. 2, p. 295.
100 Blokker, op. cit., n. 78, pp. 15–16; Report of the Panel on United Nations Peacekeeping Operations, A/55/305–S/2000/809, 21 August 2000, p. 10, para. 53 (Brahimi Report).
101 Malan, op. cit., n. 77.
102 83 (1950).
103 S/Res/678.
104 A row of resolutions, among them S/RES/816, S/RES/820 and S/RES/836.

the beginning of the nineties (NATO), and the operation in Afghanistan (NATO). Unfortunately, some of the largest enforcement operations have been authorised by the UN *ex post facto*. These operations are the 2003 operation in Iraq carried out by a US-led coalition, and the NATO operation in Kosovo in 1999. Both sparked a concern that the UN may become marginalised when enforcement action is taken unilaterally by a group of States. In the light of *ex post facto* authorisations, Mark Malan's concern that 'the UN now seems willing to hand over responsibility for peace and security to any form of "coalition of the willing", without necessarily having any clear notion of legality, higher direction, or the concerned support of the international community',[105] appears to be founded. Even though in the first few years after the end of the Cold War the number of UN peacekeeping operations skyrocketed, the proportion of UN-led operations has decreased in comparison to the operations led by regional organisations. The action taken by the regional organisations (both peacekeeping and peace enforcement), as a rule, tends to be more robust than that of peacekeeping forces led by the UN. An example is the NATO-led IFOR/SFOR in the mid-1990s. There has been little critique and counter-action from the side of the UN towards certain cases of regional action, despite the controversy, or even clear-cut illegality of such operations. Examples of UN silence towards controversial regional action are found in several of the following six chapters. The problem of the UN in this context is that it lacks the tools for response to illegal regional action, especially if it involves a member of the UNSC. Those who have the capabilities to take action are not willing to fully subordinate themselves to the UN either. Thus a problem of the consistency of a global network of maintenance of peace and security arises. A solution needs to be found on how to consolidate the military enforcement capabilities of individual regional organisations and the control of the UN over a coherent network of regional mechanisms for the maintenance of peace and security.

Post-Cold War doctrinal developments

In the beginning of the 1990s the UN saw an overstretching of its capacities, financially, along with the unwillingness of States to put troops under UN command. The task of maintaining global peace and security had become too complex for one institution to handle.

After 50 years of turning a blind-eye to the Chapter VIII provisions on utilising regional organisations for the maintenance of peace and security (for the objective reasons of the Cold War), the UN changed its policy drastically. The developments in the UN doctrine on the involvement of regional organisations are now depicted in various UN documents, most widely in the UN

---

105 Malan, op. cit., n. 77.

Secretary-General's reports. The UN Secretary-General's reports and the reports prepared by experts for the UN Secretary-General are not the annual reports on the work of the organisation to the UN General Assembly pursuant to Article 98 of the UN Charter. The reports themselves are an innovation brought about by UN Secretary-General Boutros Boutros-Ghali, starting with his *Agenda for Peace*.[106] These documents are analysis with recommendations on matters relevant to peace and security, prepared for an internal debate and reflection in the UN organs. Formally, Boutros Boutros-Ghali is said to have invoked Article 100 guaranteeing the independence of the post of the UN Secretary-General for elaborating these reports.[107]

The 1992 *Agenda for Peace*[108] was a significant turning point for the involvement of regional organisations in the global maintenance of peace and security. A special chapter in this report by UN Secretary-General Boutros Boutros-Ghali was dedicated to the co-operation between the UN and regional arrangements and organisations.[109] The UN envisaged the utilisation of the regional organisations on a case-by-case basis, without creating a specific system, as the regions are very different.[110] The *Agenda for Peace* otherwise repeats, emphasises and elaborates on the basic Chapter VIII provisions. It points out that the efforts of the regional organisations should be complimentary, that the regional organisations should act as prescribed in Chapter VIII and that the UNSC maintains the primary responsibility for the maintenance of peace and security. The regional organisations are encouraged to contribute, so that the efforts in the maintenance of peace and security can be decentralised, delegated and in co-operation with the UN could lighten the burden of the Council and contribute to a deeper sense of participation, consensus and democratisation in international affairs.[111] Thus, the first attempt was made to utilise the Chapter VIII rules in a systematic way.

In 1995, the UN Secretary-General prepared a follow-up report, *Supplement to an Agenda for Peace: Position Paper of the Secretary-General on the Occasion of the Fiftieth Anniversary of the United Nations*.[112] This document contains more detail regarding the maintenance of international peace and security, including the involvement of regional organisations. Section III of this document specifies the instruments for peace and security, and their use. The most significant instruments mentioned are: preventive diplomacy and peacemaking;

---

106 S. Bailey, and S. Daws, *The Procedure of the UN Security Council*, 3rd edn, Oxford: Clarendon Press, 1998, p. 123.
107 Bailey and Daws, ibid.
108 *Agenda for Peace*, op. cit., n. 36.
109 Note: both terms 'regional arrangements' and 'regional organisations' are used here simultaneously, whereas the later practice has developed to regard them as synonyms.
110 *Agenda for Peace*, op. cit., n. 36.
111 Ibid.
112 *Supplement to an Agenda for Peace: Position Paper of the Secretary-General on the Occasion of the Fiftieth Anniversary of the United Nations*, A/50/60–S/1995/1, 3 January 1995.

peacekeeping; peace-building; disarmament; sanctions; and peace enforcement. Of these, preventive diplomacy, peacekeeping and peace-building need the consent of the host State. Sanctions and peace enforcement need a legal basis under Chapter VII, and disarmament can be undertaken with either one of the two aforementioned legal bases. The section further states that the UN does not have or claim a monopoly in the use of any of these instruments, and that these can be employed by regional organisations, by *ad hoc* groups of States or by individual States. The paragraph does not distinguish between actions taken by regional organisations, *ad hoc* groups of States and individual States, but rather puts them into a 'non-UN' category.[113] The report emphasises that the UN system is better equipped than regional organisations or individual Member States to develop and apply the comprehensive, long-term approach needed to ensure the lasting resolution of conflicts. The shortcomings in the performance of the UN are described as 'perceived', but that, nevertheless, they appear to have inclined Member States to look for other means, especially, but not exclusively, where the rapid deployment of large forces is required. The report concludes that it is thus necessary to find ways of enabling the UN to perform better the roles envisaged for it in the UN Charter.

With the fading of the post-Cold War optimism about the functioning of the UN, in 1997 the new UN Secretary-General Kofi Annan recognised that:

> The United Nations does not have, at this point in its history, the institutional capacity to conduct military enforcement measures under Chapter VII [of the UN Charter]. Under present conditions, *ad hoc* Member States coalitions of the willing offer the most effective deterrent to aggression or to the escalation or spread of an ongoing conflict. The Organization still lacks the capacity to implement rapidly and effectively decisions of the Security Council calling for the dispatch of peacekeeping operations in crisis situations. Troops for peacekeeping missions are in some cases not made available by Member States or made available under conditions which constrain effective response. Peacemaking and human rights operations, as well as peacekeeping operations, also lack a secure financial footing, which has a serious impact on the viability of such operations.[114]

Nevertheless, the continued requirement for a UNSC mandate to ensure international support and legitimacy of enforcement action was also noted.[115]

---

113 *Supplement to an Agenda for Peace*, ibid.
114 *Renewing the United Nations: A Programme for Reform*, Report of the Secretary-General, A/51/950, 14 July 1997, para. 107.
115 *Renewing the United Nations*, ibid, paras 107 and 109.

Thus, at this stage the UN recognises the need for a regional input to cope with the international maintenance of peace and security, due to the inability to achieve sufficient State-level input. From this point, regional organisations have the potential of becoming important actors in the maintenance of peace and security, and the regionalisation of the maintenance of peace and security can start. The *Agenda for Peace* is the hopeful call for the activation of regional capabilities, as no practice – either positive, or negative – in the new, post-Cold War world has taken place. The following reports, including the follow-up to the Agenda, and other documents, however, contain ever more reservation about the freedom of action by regional organisations, to prevent regional maintenance of peace and security from becoming a Frankenstein monster of UN's own creation.

A very significant landmark in the peacekeeping doctrine is the Brahimi Report of 2000.[116] The report repeatedly encourages co-operation in the field of maintenance of peace and security between the UN and regional and subregional organisations. The list of possible activities specifically includes conflict prevention, peacemaking, elections and electoral assistance, human rights monitoring, humanitarian work and other peace-building activities. The report emphasises a need for caution with peacekeeping operations:

> [...] because military resources and capability are unevenly distributed around the world, and troops in the most crisis-prone areas are often less prepared for the demands of modern peacekeeping than is the case elsewhere. Providing training, equipment, logistical support and other resources to regional and sub-regional organizations could enable peacekeepers from all regions to participate in a United Nations peacekeeping operation or to set up regional peacekeeping operations on the basis of a Security Council resolution.[117]

This provision has become one of the core points of co-operation between the Euro-Atlantic and African regional organisations, while such practice is hardly found elsewhere. There is an important point in helping weaker regions in giving them a 'fishing rod, instead of a fish', as local regional participation is likely to attribute more legitimacy to military action, than military involvement from another regional organisation. In addition, assisting the weaker regions in building regional capacities would also help those who truly have an interest in conflict-resolution in a positive sense. The problem with this suggestion, however, is the actual extent of the possibility to boost up regional capabilities of a region that does not have them itself.

The Brahimi Report is not disregarding the new regional activity, however, in the report it is referred to as a negative development. This is very likely

---

116 Brahimi Report, op. cit., n. 100.
117 Ibid.

due to the fact that the report was prepared soon after the Kosovo intervention by NATO. References to regions are most commonly made for two reasons: to encourage common regional training and to emphasise that regional powers can misuse force against weaker States in the region. European States are reproached for strengthening regional efforts and not contributing to UN peacekeeping efforts.[118] On the other hand, the Brahimi report is realistic about the reasons why the UN peacekeeping is having difficulty attracting volunteers. The report mentions the peacekeepers murdered in Mogadishu and Kigali and those taken hostage in Sierra Leone. However, it also puts the blame on the strategic interests of developed States, which do not include participating in peacekeeping in Africa. The report is rather negative about the European regional peacekeeping initiatives prioritised above participation in UN operations.[119] The Euro-Atlantic reasons for reservations towards UN operations are understandable: the relatively well-structured and efficient Euro-Atlantic regional capabilities would lose these advantages when being put under a less coherent UN lead. In addition, there is a limit of how many human and financial sacrifices a region is willing to make, if it has no other interest than altruism and higher values. Nevertheless, at least the EU appears to have been putting a lot of effort into implementing the recommendations of the Brahimi Report, including the establishment of rapid reaction forces that can be used to assist the UN.

The next in a line of reports depicting a growing tendency of regionalisation in the maintenance of peace and security is the UN Secretary-General's High Level Panel on Threats, Challenge and Change report, *A More Secure World: Our Shared Responsibility* of 2004.[120] It is once again repeated in the report that the UNSC ought to enhance the co-operation with regional and subregional organisations even more. The report is critical of the failure of the UNSC to act in the face of humanitarian catastrophes.[121] The report does not propose to find ways around the inefficient UN mechanisms, but rather to reform the UNSC[122] – a proposal that in itself is not new, but has never been carried out. This report introduces the criteria for legitimacy in decision-making (decisions being made legally, on solid evidentiary grounds, and for the right reasons[123]). These criteria should be used by the UNSC when deciding whether to authorise or endorse the use of force. The criteria listed are: proper purpose, last resort, balance of consequences and proportional means. The UNSC has, however, in practice failed to react in cases of unilateral action that do not meet the given criteria (e.g. Iraq in 2003), and the UN

---

118 Brahimi Report, op. cit., n. 100.
119 Ibid.
120 *A More Secure World*, op. cit., n. 93.
121 Ibid, paras 12, 87, 201 and others.
122 Ibid, paras 197, 198.
123 Ibid, paras 204–9.

lacks tools for responding to such cases in general. The report, on the other hand, recommends the same requirements for the authorisation of both peacekeeping and peace enforcement, thus implicitly not supporting the right for regional peacekeeping without a UN mandate.[124] This is due to the blurring of peacekeeping and peace enforcement, and the frequent reference to Chapter VII of the UN Charter even in formal peacekeeping operations. At the same time regional capacity-building is encouraged, especially the creation and strengthening of rapid reaction capabilities, both peacekeeping and peace enforcement, in support of the UN. This expert panel report is thus not concentrating on criticising the weakness of the UN mechanism for the maintenance of peace and security and its consequences. Instead, it is focusing on what causes the weaknesses in the UN system, and how more control over the regional developments can be gained through measures within the UN system.

The next UN Secretary-General's report, *In Larger Freedom: towards development, security and human rights for all*, followed *A More Secure World*, one year later in 2005. The document is briefer on the matters of use of force, but in general repeats the content of *A More Secure World* and is in line with numerous other UN reports preceding it. The report emphasises the need for Member State contribution to strengthen UN peacekeeping, and especially, building a rapid response capability. The request is specified: '[…] the time is ripe for the establishment of an interlocking system of peacekeeping capabilities that will enable the United Nations to work with relevant regional organizations in predictable and reliable partnerships'.[125] Special attention in the UN reports is paid to the involvement of the AU in maintaining peace and security regionally, and especially in the *In Larger Freedom* report. This is not surprising, as since decolonisation Africa has been plagued by the greatest share of conflicts in need of international peacekeeping assistance. The report calls for global assistance to the regional African efforts.[126] The temptation to use force unilaterally is recognised, but the suggested solutions to the problem include only a part of those included in *A More Secure World*. The UN Secretary-General's report, *In Larger Freedom*, reinforces the more detailed expert report, *A More Secure World*, by recommending that the UNSC adopts a resolution setting out the principles for when deciding whether to authorise or mandate the use of force. Once again the paragraph refers to the UNSC not only 'authorising', but also 'endorsing' the use of force.[127] The use of the term 'endorsement' as a subsequent approval of unilateral action is not coincidental, it has become frequently used regarding regional peace operations. The recommendation of the high-level panel to set the same requirements of

---

124 *A More Secure World*, op. cit., n. 93, para. 213.
125 *In Larger Freedom*, op. cit., n. 34.
126 Ibid, para. 111.
127 Ibid, para. 126.

authorisation for regional peacekeeping as for regional enforcement action, however, is not picked up by the UN Secretary-General, who is silent on the matter.

The World Summit Outcome of 2005 must be noted as an important UN General Assembly document reflecting the existing consensus of the international community on a wide range of matters, including the maintenance of peace and security. In great part, the World Summit Outcome contains the confirmation by the UN General Assembly of some of the recommendations contained in the UN Secretary-General's reports. One of its most significant contributions is the acknowledgement of the 'responsibility to protect' principle, the concept of which was first included in the *Responsibility to Protect* report.[128] The World Summit Outcome document concludes that each individual State has the responsibility to protect its populations from genocide, war crimes, ethnic cleansing and crimes against humanity. The international community is encouraged to assist the UN through, among others, establishing an early warning capability, utilising peaceful means as provided in Chapters VI and VIII of the UN Charter.[129] The international community is prepared to 'take collective action, in a timely and decisive manner, through the UNSC, in accordance with the Charter, including Chapter VII, on a case-by-case basis and in cooperation with relevant regional organizations as appropriate, should peaceful means be inadequate'.[130] As distinguished by Bellamy, the World Summit Outcome marks the divide where the 'responsibility to protect' develops into a principle, as opposed to having been a concept (an abstract idea) since the *Responsibility to Protect* report.[131] According to him, the acquired status of a principle means that there is a shared understanding and a significant consensus on the responsibility to protect, to allow it to function as a foundation for action.[132] The extent of the application of the principle in different regions, in balance with the principle of the prohibition of the use of force, however, is not unequivocal.

A special focus in the document, repeated throughout the text, is on the rapid response capabilities, such as the peacekeeping capabilities established by regional organisations (the EU is specifically mentioned, as a regional 'entity', implicitly falling under Chapter VIII) and in particular, to assist the African region.[133]

The World Summit Outcome document also makes a significant acknowledgment that 'many of today's threats recognize no national boundaries, are interlinked and must be tackled at the global, regional and national levels',

---

128 *Responsibility to Protect*, op. cit., n. 37.
129 World Summit Outcome, A/RES/60/1, 24 October 2005, paras 138–139.
130 World Summit Outcome, Ibid, para. 139.
131 A. Bellamy, *Responsibility to Protect. The Global Effort to End Mass Atrocities*, Cambridge: Polity Press, 2009, pp. 5–7.
132 Bellamy, ibid, p. 6.
133 World Summit Outcome, op. cit., n. 129, paras 92–93.

though, it is added, 'in accordance with the Charter and international law and pursuant to purposes and principles of the UN Charter'.[134]

The provisions specifically dedicated to co-operation between the UN and regional organisations state that in order to achieve a stronger relationship between the UN and regional and subregional organisations, the signing of co-operation agreements between the secretariats of the UN and regional organisations, and the placing of peacekeeping capacity under the United Nations Standby Arrangement System (UNSAS) by regional organisations are necessary.[135] Both of these intentions have been followed up in practice by regional organisations.

In all the innovations regarding the interconnection of threats, the responsibility to protect, and the involvement of regional organisations (especially strengthening African peacekeeping capacities), it is strongly emphasised that the primary responsibility in the maintenance of peace and security lies unchangeably with the UNSC that has the authority to mandate coercive action.[136] Nevertheless, the flaws of the UNSC are faced in the World Summit Outcome document by recognising that the UNSC needs to be reformed to increase its transparency, effectiveness and the legitimacy of its decisions.[137] The latter contention has not been followed by practical steps.

In Larger Freedom is, to date, the last of the major reports on the developments of the maintenance of peace and security in the period from 1993 to 2005. This series of reports appears to have been sealed and concluded with the World Summit Outcome. Today, the UN Secretary-General and expert panel reports have been replaced by UNSC meetings on the issue, UNSC co-operation meetings with individual regional organisations, the signing of declaratory co-operation documents between the UN Secretary-General and the regional organisations, smaller scale UN Secretary-General reports made upon the request of other organs, and other documents.

Judging from the unilateral and bilateral documents of the UN, relating to regional organisations, the UN is persistently increasing co-operation with regional organisations, putting an extra emphasis on the strengthening of the capabilities of the AU. The enhancement of co-operation with regional organisations was started in the realm of the UN Secretary-General in 1992, and in 2005 the UNSC issued its first resolution specifically on co-operation with regional organisations – UNSC Resolution 1631 (2005). The resolution refers to Chapter VIII and numerous preceding UN documents, UNSC meetings and debates. The main points in the resolution are: the call for placing the regional military capacity under the framework of UNSAS, emphasising the strengthening of the capacities of African regional and subregional

---

134 World Summit Outcome, op. cit., n. 129, paras 71–72.
135 Ibid, para. 170.
136 Ibid, paras 79–80.
137 Ibid, paras 152–154.

organisations, improving and structuring the co-operation between the UN and regional organisations, and inviting the UN Secretary-General to strengthen the accountability of regional organisations to the UN.[138]

Following UNSC Resolution 1631 (2006) the UN Secretary-General issued a special report on the co-operation of the UN with regional organisations, *A regional-global security partnership: challenges and opportunities*.[139] The report in major part repeats the content of the general reports mentioned above and makes a number of practical suggestions on how to enhance the co-operation between the UN and the regional organisations, and how to ensure the subordination of the regional organisations to the UN. The measures include high-level meetings with the UN Secretary-General, thematic meetings of the UNSC, operational co-operation, and others. Throughout the document the concern about the respect of the supremacy of the UN Charter and the primary responsibility of the UNSC is expressed along with the need for the clarification of the roles of the UN and the regional organisations.

The UNSC had expressed in Resolution 1631 (2005) the intention to hold regular meetings with regional and subregional organisations to strengthen co-operation in the field of peace and security. This initiative received strong support from the UN Secretary-General in his follow-up report, above. One of the more recent activities to the point was a UN Secretary-General's Retreat with Heads of Regional and other Organisations on 11–12 January 2010, followed by a UNSC meeting of 13 January 2010 with the participation of the representatives of a wide range of regional and subregional organisations dealing with the matters of peace and security.[140] The representatives of the UN and the representatives of regional organisations exchanged views on the co-operation between the UN and regional and subregional organisations in maintaining international peace and security. The general political language of this document does not contribute significantly to the understanding of the legal nature of regional maintenance of peace and security. Nevertheless, the relevant message of the UNSC in the document is that the aim of the UN co-operation with regional organisations in the maintenance of peace and security is to utilise their contributions for the peacekeeping efforts of the UN.

A tool for improving international maintenance of peace and security that has been particularly highlighted is the development of rapid reaction capabilities – a call that appears in nearly every UN document mentioned. The main cause for the failures of the UN has been its slowness in reacting to global crises due to the lack of readily available troops. The first call for rapid deployment capabilities was therefore included in the 1995 *Supplement to an*

---

138 S/RES/1631.
139 *A regional-global security partnership*, op. cit., n. 48.
140 S/PV.6257.

Agenda for Peace,[141] where the UN Secretary-General recommended that the UN should consider the idea of a rapid deployment force. The call for rapid response capabilities was reinforced in the 2000 Brahimi Report.[142]

In the mid-nineties, the ground was set for creating an enhanced UNSAS, along with Civilian Police Capabilities.[143] Attempts are still being made to establish the standby system, but it is not yet in place. The main, at least on paper, achievement of the standby system initiative was the establishment of the UN Stand-by Forces High Readiness Brigade (SHIRBRIG). It was founded in 1996 by a minor group of contributing States on a Danish initiative.[144] The brigade was praised for its impartiality, as it did not belong to a regional organisation but was created to be under the direct command of the UN. In practice, SHIRBRIG was employed for a couple of peacekeeping organisations in its years of activity from 2000 to 2009, but without ever gaining a significant role in promoting the aims of the UN in the field. It was closed down by 2008/09. Thus, the only seriously intended universal rapid reaction initiative after the end of the Cold War had failed, just like the intent to bring to life the Article 43 provisions after the end of the Second World War. The failure of the brigade was not due to lack of resources, but rather the political will to utilise it. Perhaps SHIRBRIG is a good example, among many others, of how the best intentions for the maintenance of global peace and security are destined to fail if they do not have the commitment of the Permanent Members of the UNSC.

Meanwhile, the regional organisations also started developing their rapid reaction forces, based on the recommendations by the UN. Thus, NATO established NRF (NATO Response Force) and the EU established its Battlegroups. The AU is currently in the process of developing its rapid reaction units,[145] and so is the Collective Security Treaty Organization (CSTO).[146]

The accusations of the Brahimi Report of the developed States denying troop contributions for UN peacekeeping operations[147] coincide with the growth in autonomous activity of regional organisations. Nevertheless, the events of the few years following the Brahimi Report evidence an increasing

---

141 *Supplement to an Agenda for Peace*, op. cit., n. 112.
142 'Introduction to SHIRBRIG', SHIRBRIG website. Available at <http://www.shirbrig.dk/html/sb_intro.htm> (accessed 18 March 2013).
143 'UN Standby Agreements System Description', United Nations website. Available at <http://www.un.org/chinese/work/peace/rapid/sys.htm> (accessed 18 March 2013).
144 Argentina, Austria, Canada, Denmark, Finland, Italy, Ireland, Lithuania, the Netherlands, Norway, Poland, Portugal, Romania, Slovenia, Spain and Sweden.
145 'Profile: African Union', *BBC News*, last updated 1 February 2012. Available at <http://news.bbc.co.uk/2/hi/country_profiles/3870303.stm> (accessed 25 March 2013).
146 'CSTO Rapid Reaction Force to Equal NATO's – Medvedev', *RIA Novosti*, 4 February 2009. Available at <http://en.rian.ru/russia/20090204/119984654.html> (accessed 25 March 2013).
147 *A More Secure World*, op. cit., n. 93, para. 103.

support for regional aspirations by the UN itself, especially in Europe and in Africa, and in recent years also in Asia.

Already in 2001 the Brahimi Report was counterbalanced with the Report of the International Commission on Intervention and State Sovereignty, *Responsibility to Protect*.[148] In addition to generally praising and supporting regional action (note is made also about the danger of such action), the report goes as far as to regard as legitimate possible *ex post facto* authorisation of regional enforcement operations:

> The UN Charter recognizes legitimate roles for regional organizations and regional arrangements in Chapter VIII. In strict terms, as we have already noted, the letter of the Charter requires action by regional organizations always to be subject to prior authorization from the Security Council. But as we have also noted, there are recent cases when approval has been sought *ex post facto*, or after the event (Liberia and Sierra Leone), and there may be certain leeway for future action in this regard.[149]

The last phrase by the Independent Commission on State Sovereignty appears to have been picked-up by some regional organisations, and strictly opposed by others. The right to unauthorised regional humanitarian intervention has subsequently become a highly relevant legal and political topic of the twenty-first century.

Today, the UN calls both for input into more rapid response capabilities and for more subordination from the regional organisations. How the individual organisations interpret and tackle these requests is left up to the goodwill of each one of them. Chapters 3 to 8 depict how the aspirations of the UN on regional input to the maintenance of peace and security are reflected through the perspectives of different regions.

---

148 *Responsibility to Protect*, op. cit., n. 37.
149 Ibid, para. 6.35.

3 Africa
African solutions for African problems

General description of the region

In the field of maintenance of peace and security, Africa has been the most troubled region in the world since its decolonisation. Ever since the calls from the UN for the regional organisations to take action, at the beginning of the 1990s, the focus on Africa has increased – both for the reason that most conflicts occur in Africa, and also because of the difficulty of the African countries and regional organisations to cope with the conflicts on their own.[1] The efforts of the UN to deal with African issues are reflected in an overwhelming amount of documents – from the UN Secretary-General's reports, to High Level meetings of the UNSC, UN Secretary-General and the representatives of regional organisations,[2] and a wide number of UNSC reports, presidential statements and resolutions. The World Summit Outcome,[3] for example, emphasises the need for the international community to assist Africa, including the sphere of peace and security.

The efforts of the UN to strengthen the African capabilities are apparently connected to an overload of African issues at the UN. While up to 1990 the number of UNSC resolutions ranged from a mere one in 1959 to a peak of 22 in 1980, their number sky-rocketed after the end of the Cold War, with an average of approximately 60 resolutions per year. Nevertheless, ever since the first resolutions on the admission of African States to the UN throughout the sixties, the lion's share of UNSC resolutions have been dedicated to Africa, mainly concerning intrastate conflicts.[4] For example, in 1963

---

1 United Nations, Office of the Special Adviser on Africa, *The Emerging Role of the AU and ECOWAS in conflict prevention and peacebuilding*. Background paper prepared for the expert group meeting, pp. 27–32. Available at <http://www.un.org/africa/osaa/reports/Emerging%20Role%20of%20AU%20and%20Ecowas%202007.pdf> (accessed 18 March 2013).
2 Such is, for example, the 13 January 2010 UN Security Council 6257th meeting, S/PV.6257.
3 World Summit Outcome, A/RES/60/1, 24 October 2005.
4 See the complete listing of UNSC resolutions at the UNSC website. Available at <http://www.un.org/documents/scres.htm> (accessed 18 March 2013).

seven out of eight resolutions were on Africa; in 1972 – 13 out of 17; in 1995 – 32 out of 76; in 2002 – 25 out of 67; in 2006 – 46 out of 86; and in 2009 – 21 out of 47. Only in 1991 the number of the resolutions regarding Africa was at a low of three out of 41.

In 2009 to 2011 the list of resolutions contained ongoing conflict situations in the Democratic Republic of Congo (DRC), Côte d'Ivoire, Somalia, Guinea-Bissau, Sudan, Sierra Leone, Liberia, Libya, Chad and the Central African Republic (CAR), Djibouti and Eritrea. The latter two are at the centre of resolutions broadly entitled as 'Resolutions on Peace and Security in Africa', UNSC Resolutions 1809 (2008), 1862 (2009) and 1907 (2009). Thus, at least 20 per cent of the States in Africa are currently struggling with an internal or international conflict – this number depicts only the conflicts that are handled under the supervision of the UN. In all the conflicts listed above, except for Guinea-Bissau, the UNSC acted under Chapter VII of the UN Charter, while none of them, apart from Libya, is a formal enforcement operation. This fact illustrates the problem of the application of the concept of peacekeeping in today's violent reality. The conflicts of the twenty-first century, at least in the case of Africa, are hardly ever on such a low scale, that the use of force beyond self-defence would not be necessary. Thus, almost every operation in reality contains enforcement elements, even if it is entitled and formally launched as a peacekeeping operation.

Several of the UNSC resolutions on Africa contain another common feature: a reference to the region or subregion in which the State concerned is located. While UNSC Resolution 1951 (2010) is concerned with Chad, it refers also directly to peace and stability in the subregion. Similarly, the above-mentioned resolutions on the conflict between Djibouti and Eritrea, entitled 'Peace and Security in Africa' – indicate a concern of the region as a whole. Resolutions 1923 (2010), 1922 (2010) and 1913 (2010) are entitled 'The situation in Chad, the Central African Republic and the subregion'. The mention of the region as the area impacted by an intra- or interstate conflict depicts the growing importance of the concept 'region', as opposed to the traditional counter-positioning of the concepts of a 'State' and 'the international community'. The mention of regions in the UNSC resolutions reflects the recognition that the conflicts in one or between two States can cause instability and a threat to peace and security in a whole region. If a conflict arises in Chad, or in Djibouti and Eritrea, the spill-over effects of refugee flows, warring parties roaming and other factors will greatly influence also the social and security situation in the neighbouring countries, and create a threat to peace for a wider region without a specified border limitation; a threat to peace and security in the African region.

Several of the resolutions also mention or provide for the involvement of regional organisations in reaching the aims set out in the resolutions, such as Resolution 1950 (2010) on Somalia, Resolution 1923 (2010) on Chad and the Central African Republic and Resolution 1938 (2010) on Liberia. In Resolution 1950 (2010) regional organisations, alongside States are called upon to assist the UN in combating piracy. In Resolution 1938 (2010) the concern about subregional stability (especially in the form of drug trafficking, organised crime, and illicit arms) is expressed, and a note is made on the contribution of ECOWAS and the AU in dealing with the instability in Liberia. In Resolution 1923 (2010) the situation in Chad is regarded as a region-wide threat, and regional organisations (without specifying) are also called upon to propose solutions for the conflict. The UN does not tend to specify a single African regional organisation, but requests the organisations to work in concert.

As any other region, Africa has experienced considerable regionalisation and fragmentation since the end of the Cold War. The number of regional organisations has mushroomed, fulfilling economic, social, security and other functions. The African region has been showing a post-Cold War initiative of taking matters into its own hands through increased regional activity. Africa is very much concerned with economic growth, and at the moment there are at least 14 regional economic communities alone.[5] The AU, however, is trying to limit the number of subregional organisations, by formally having recognised only eight of them.[6] Of these, there are four organisations in Africa with experience in peace and security: the AU, the Southern African Development Community (SADC), ECOWAS and the Intergovernmental Authority on Development (IGAD).[7] There is a general tendency to include peace and security on the agenda of the economic co-operation forums in Africa. The mechanisms for the maintenance of peace and security in ECOWAS and the AU, created at the turn of the last century, have been joined by other mechanisms on their way, such as those of the Central African Economic and Monetary Community (CEMAC) and the Economic Community of Central African States (ECCAS).[8] This illustrates the general African approach to peace as the necessary pre-requisite for any economic or social development.

In this book only SADC, ECOWAS and the AU are analysed in detail. IGAD is, in comparison, a small organisation (six Member States[9]) with few resources, and subsequently little action taken. It is a regional organisation that consists of some of the world's most conflict-plagued countries (in particular, Sudan and Somalia). The situations in them have been a long-time concern of the whole international community and have primarily involved the efforts of other organisations, such as the UN, the AU, the EU

---

5 *The Emerging Role of the AU and ECOWAS in conflict prevention and peacebuilding*, op. cit., n. 1.
6 'General Information', African Court of Human and Peoples Rights website. Available at <http://www.african-court.org/en/court/mandate/general-information/> (accessed 20 February 2013).
7 *The Emerging Role of the AU and ECOWAS in conflict prevention and peacebuilding*, op. cit., n. 1, p. 3.
8 Ibid.
9 Djibouti, Ethiopia, Kenya, Somalia, Sudan and Uganda.

and even NATO. The three other organisations have the only three mechanisms in Africa for dealing with matters of peace and security through military intervention. These are: ECOWAS Mechanism on Conflict Prevention, Management, and Resolution, Peace-keeping and Security, SADC Organ on Politics, Defence and Security Cooperation and the African Union Peace and Security Council (AUPSC).[10] The AU is a regional organisation, and ECOWAS and SADC are subregional organisations. The system of organisations is co-ordinated and subordinated. The SADC Treaty refers to the Constitutive Act of the AU in its Preamble. The ECOWAS Treaty merely refers to the OAU[11] and the UN as organisations they co-operate with. Otherwise, reference to the UN in both treaties is made with regard to depositing documents.[12] However, the fact that both organisations deposit their documents both with the UN (which is the general practice), and the AU in addition, is an evidence of the authority of the AU with respect to SADC and ECOWAS. The Constitutive Act of the AU also provides for a multi-level co-ordination of peace and security matters – both with the UN and the subregional organisations (Articles 16 and 17).[13] Article 16 stipulates the primary responsibility of the AU for the maintenance of peace and security in Africa (with regard to the subregional mechanisms),[14] while Article 17 stipulates the primary responsibility of the UNSC in line with the UN Charter. The relations between the organisations with regard to unmandated operations, however, are more complicated than general 'primacy of the United Nations Security Council'. A dual approach to the authority of the UNSC derives from the 'non-indifference' doctrine[15] or pro-interventionism, that is said to have developed as a norm in the African continent, replacing the

---

10 J. I. Levitt, 'The Peace and Security Council of the African Union and the United Nations Security Council: the Case of Darfur, Sudan', in N. Blokker and N. Schrijver (eds), *The Security Council and the Use of Force. Theory and Reality – A Need for Change?*, Leiden and Boston, MA: Martinus Nijhoff Publishers, 2005, pp. 213–14.
11 Amendments in connection with the replacement of the OAU by the AU as its legal successor in the text have not been made. Treaty of ECOWAS, 24 July 1993, (1996) 8 *AJICL* 187; (1996) 35 *ILM* 660, Art. 83. Available at <http://www.comm.ecowas.int/sec/index.php?id=treaty> (accessed 25 March 2013).
12 Treaty of ECOWAS, Arts 83 and 93; Treaty of the SADC, of 17 August 1992, Art. 43. Available at <http://www.sadc.int/files/9113/5292/9434/SADC_Treaty.pdf> (accessed 18 March 2013).
13 The Constitutive Act of the AU, 11 July 2000, OAU Doc. NO. CAB/LEG/23.15, Preamble and Art. 3. Available at <http://www.africa-union.org/root/au/Aboutau/Constitutive_Act_en.htm> (accessed 18 March 2013).
14 Constitutive Act of the AU, Art. 16, para. 1 reads: 'The Regional Mechanisms are part of the overall security architecture of the Union, which has the primary responsibility for promoting peace, security and stability in Africa'.
15 The 'non-indifference' doctrine can be found in numerous writings on the African regional organisations, for example, Levitt, op. cit., n. 10 and B. Kioko, 'The right of intervention under the African Union's Constitutive Act: From non-interference to non-intervention', *International Review of Red Cross*, Vol. 85, 852 (December) 2003, p. 819.

traditional 'non-intervention' doctrine that corresponds to the generally accepted law on the use of force.

The roots of the doctrine of non-indifference are said to date back to the lack of international response in Uganda in the 1970s.[16] However, the considerable number of autonomous regional peace operations, that set ground for the existing legal regulation, took place throughout the 1990s. The main reason for this development was the failure of the international community to respond timely and efficiently to the genocide in Rwanda, as well as the long-term political and humanitarian catastrophes in Sudan and Somalia.[17]

The developments in regionalisation of the use of force in Africa can be derived from the combined practice of ECOWAS and SADC in the nineties and the subsequent creation of the AU in 2000, enhancing the African post-Cold War practice into a legal-doctrinal framework. The African unilateral regional interventions throughout the nineties have served as the basis for the development of the subsequent 'non-indifference' (pro-interventionist) clause stapled in the basic documents of the African regional organisations. Thus, they form a two layer practice and doctrine mass of evidence for the regional right to use force without a UNSC mandate in specified cases. The relevant law and practice is analysed below in this chapter.

Economic Community of West African States

General description

ECOWAS was founded in 1975 and comprises 15 Member States.[18] The aims of the organisation, as stated in Article 3 of the ECOWAS Treaty are:

> […] to promote co-operation and integration, leading to the establishment of an economic union in West Africa in order to raise the living standards of its peoples, and to maintain and enhance economic stability, foster relations among Member States and contribute to the progress and development of the African Continent.[19]

Nothing in this paragraph refers to the organisation having a function of the maintenance of peace and security. The provisions on co-operation in regional security were added with the amendments of the Treaty in 1993, in Article 58.[20]

---

16 Kioko, ibid, p. 812.
17 Ibid.
18 Benin, Burkina Faso, Cape Verde, Côte d'Ivoire, Gambia, Guinea, Guinea-Bissau, Liberia, Mali, Niger, Nigeria, Senegal, Sierra Leone, Togo.
19 Treaty of ECOWAS, Art. 3.
20 'Profile: Economic Community of West African States', African Union website, p. 2. Available at <http://www.africa-union.org/Recs/ECOWAS Profile.pdf> (accessed 24 March 2013).

The Member States are to work to safeguard and consolidate relations conducive to the maintenance of peace, stability and security within the region, and in pursuit of these objectives 'Member States undertake to co-operate with the Community in establishing and strengthening appropriate mechanisms for the timely prevention and resolution of intra-State and inter-State conflicts'. Furthermore, paragraph 3 of Article 58 states that the detailed provisions governing regional peace and stability shall be defined in the relevant Protocols. The core document provided for in the aforementioned article of the Treaty is the Protocol Relating to the Mechanism for Conflict Prevention, Management, Resolution, Peace-keeping and Security, dated 10 December 1999 (ECOWAS Protocol).[21] This Protocol depicts the increasing focus on security by a co-operation forum of a generally economic nature. Both the Treaty and the Protocol provide a reference to the overarching regional organisation, the OAU, which has now been succeeded by the AU.[22] The ECOWAS Protocol replaces the ECOWAS Protocol relating to Mutual Assistance in Defence signed on 29 May 1981.[23] It appears to be a globally widespread post-Cold War trend that where there has formerly been a regional document on mutual defence, it is now replaced by a more general, wider in scope regional security agreement.[24] While the general structure of this book follows the pattern of analysing the legal basis of each organisation first, the subchapter dedicated to ECOWAS starts out with the analysis of its practice. This is due to the fact that early post-Cold War ECOWAS experience from regional operations in Liberia and Sierra Leone set the precedent for the development of the African pro-interventionist doctrine, which was subsequently included in the regional legal documents currently in force.

The practice

The ECOWAS intervention in Liberia is a case that still, after 20 years, influences the debate on issues, such as, what is appropriate for regional action without a UN mandate, the authenticity of invitation, the distinction between peacekeeping and peace enforcement, and UNSC endorsement. The intervention by ECOWAS in Liberia in 1990 was regarded as dubious for several reasons: it was questioned whether or not the invitation to intervene in the failed State was received from the right authority.[25] The use of enforcement

---

21 Protocol Relating to the Mechanism for Conflict Prevention, Management, Resolution, Peace-keeping and Security, 10 December 1999. Available at <http://www.comm.ecowas.int/sec/index.php?id=ap101299&lang=en> (accessed 25 March 2013) (ECOWAS Protocol).
22 ECOWAS Protocol, Arts 2, 26, 27, 36, 41, 52.
23 ECOWAS Protocol, Art. 53.
24 The same is valid for UNASUR, NATO, CSTO and other organisations described below.
25 C. Gray, *International Law and the Use of Force*, 3rd edn, Oxford: Oxford University Press, 2008, pp. 401–3.

measures[26] in what was defined as regional peacekeeping and not a peace enforcement operation was also questioned. Also there was suspicion of the lack of impartiality on the part of the regional hegemon – Nigeria.[27]

None of these issues received an official clarification, when the UNSC endorsed the operation launched on 27 August 1990 through UNSC Resolution 788 of November 1992. The UN commended ECOWAS for its efforts in restoring peace, security and stability in Liberia. The legality of the ECOWAS operation was not discussed in UNSC meetings and the enforcement measures taken by ECOWAS were neither mentioned, nor authorised by the UN.[28] The UNSC authorised, or rather, endorsed the operation as a peacekeeping operation by a Chapter VIII organisation, for which a UN authorisation would not be a mandatory requirement. Subsequently, in 1993 the UN Observer Mission in Liberia (UNOMIL)[29] became the first UN operation to be undertaken in co-operation with a peacekeeping operation established by another organisation (ECOWAS) – a trend to be followed in a number of other crises, not least in Africa.

By endorsing the ECOWAS operation as peacekeeping, the UNSC avoided confronting the legally complicated issues that might have arisen from the circumstances of the case. It cannot be judged from the text of the resolution whether the UN would have approved of enforcement action by a regional organisation based on humanitarian grounds, if it had concluded that such action did take place. Being treated as a peacekeeping operation by the UN, the ECOWAS intervention in Liberia did not establish a precedent for a legal endorsement of enforcement action. There are, however, authors who claim that the intervention in Liberia, and subsequent ECOWAS interventions are examples of retroactive authorisations of otherwise illegal operations.[30] Nevertheless, the case of Liberia, among others, was never elaborated on by an authoritative organ, such as the UNSC. The legal considerations of the UN authorisation remain blurred and, apparently, the response by the UN was based on political rather than legal reasons. The UNSC may have a general concern that if all legal controversies were to be analysed, no real action would be taken. If the UNSC had endorsed the ECOWAS operation as a peace enforcement operation, having analysed it in detail, the Council may

---

26 Z. Deen-Racsmány, 'A Redistribution of Authority Between the UN and Regional Organisations in the Field of the Maintenance of Peace and Security?', *Leiden Journal of International Law*, Vol. 13, 2000, p. 314. Gray, ibid, p. 400.
27 Deen-Racsmány, op. cit., n. 26, p. 314; Gray, op. cit., n. 25, pp. 400 and 402.
28 Deen-Racsmány, op. cit., n. 26, p. 315–16; Gray, op. cit., n. 25, p. 400. However, in Resolution 788 (1992) the UNSC implemented an embargo under Chapter VII itself.
29 UNOMIL website. Available at <http://www.un.org/en/peacekeeping/missions/past/unomil.htm> (accessed 24 March 2013).
30 Levitt, op. cit., n. 10, p. 233. D. Kuwali, 'Protect Responsibly: The African Union's Implementation of Article 4(H) Intervention', *Yearbook of International Humanitarian Law*, Vol. 11, 2008, p. 56.

have acted illegally itself. Even though there is no true remedy against illegal action by the UNSC, no State, not even the Permanent Members of the UNSC wish to set a precedent of unjustified illegal action. If the UNSC endorses the operation as a peacekeeping operation, the authorisation has symbolic value and does not set a precedent of a new legality, nor does it create a political tumult. By not interfering in the legality and legitimacy issues concerning controversial, short of clear-cut-illegal regional operations, the UN gives discretion to the regional organisations in deciding on the specific regional limits of what is appropriate for regional action. From a development of law perspective, however, this undecided precedent has become one of the first building-blocks in a trend towards regionalisation in the maintenance of peace and security in Africa, including regional autonomy in the use of force, depicted in the basic legal documents of the region.

In 1997, ECOWAS once again launched an operation without a UN mandate. ECOWAS intervened upon the request of the president of Sierra Leone, after a coup had taken place, and when the president had already been exiled and lost control over the territory of Sierra Leone.[31] In this case the troops consisted, once again, mainly of a Nigerian contribution, and the troops of the Economic Community of West African States Monitoring Group (ECOMOG) were engaged in full-scale enforcement action.[32] Nevertheless, just like in the case of Liberia, the UN did not debate the legality and legitimacy of the intervention.[33] The UN merely mandated the operation two months later as a peacekeeping operation.[34] UNSC Resolution 1132 (1997) invokes Chapter VII of the UN Charter, however its contents mandate a peacekeeping operation, not an enforcement one, which is usually characterised by the presence of the phrase 'all means necessary'. Levitt and Deen-Racsmány argue that this authorisation provides for a retroactive authorisation of the use of force, at least tacitly.[35] Gray opposes this position stating that it is not only dangerous to claim a right for enforcement action without a UNSC authorisation, but also that neither ECOWAS, nor the UNSC made statements approving of this position.[36] Nevertheless, no statements were made of the opposite, and the aforementioned right to enforcement action has been consequently cemented in the ECOWAS and AU basic documents. By not restricting the use of force by ECOWAS without a UN mandate, the UNSC is very likely to have contributed to the perception of permissibility of an inclusion of an African regional pro-interventionist clause in the region's legal documents.

---

31 Deen-Racsmány, op. cit., n. 26, pp. 316–17.
32 Ibid, p. 318. ECOMOG was fighting the Revolutionary United Front that had taken over the country in full-scale battles. See also Gray, op. cit., n. 25, p. 414.
33 Ibid, pp. 318–19.
34 Ibid.
35 Levitt, op. cit., n. 10, pp. 233 and 235; Deen-Racsmány, op. cit., n. 26, p. 330.
36 Gray, op. cit., n. 25, p. 418.

Another example, representing an ECOWAS military involvement following an election crisis, is the Côte d'Ivoire (2003). The operation was launched to assist the government after an attempted coup.[37] The issues of the legality of enforcement action to restore democratic government without UNSC authority did not arise on the facts.[38] This is concluded from the facts that the ECOWAS operation, in co-operation with France, was a peacekeeping operation that had been commended by the UN. The reason for France to deploy its troops, however, was the protection of its own citizens in Côte d'Ivoire,[39] which is in theory a controversial legal ground for launching an intervention,[40] prior to any mandate. Nevertheless, France merely provided transportation and security to the ECOWAS mediation team.[41] In addition, the difference between the Côte d'Ivoire case and those in Liberia and Sierra Leone is that in Côte d'Ivoire there was a peace agreement between the parties to the conflict reached,[42] so there was a 'peace to keep'. Furthermore, the forces were not involved in violent fights. With UNSC Resolution 1464 (2003), the UN endorsed the deployment of ECOWAS and the French peacekeeping troops, acting under Chapter VII. With UNSC Resolution 1479 (2003), the UN created its own peacekeeping force to work parallel to and co-operate with the former two. Further on, with UNSC Resolution 1528 (2004) the UNSC merged the former UN operation and the ECOWAS operation into one, also acting under Chapter VII of the UN Charter.

The operation in Côte d'Ivoire is not controversial from the legality perspective, but it is an example of the shortage of resources to carry out an operation successfully. In this case – both regionally, and under the UN lead.[43] On 7 December 2010 the Côte d'Ivoire membership of ECOWAS was suspended, along with UN sanctions imposed due to the unwillingness of the losing party to acknowledge the election results and give up power.[44] The reason why the intervention in Côte d'Ivoire is mentioned here is that, as classified by Levitt,[45] it is an example of the so-called 'pro-democratic' interventions, i.e. the purpose of the intervention falling short of mass atrocities on a scale of genocide to legitimise it, instead, the operation is launched

---

37 Gray, op. cit., n. 25, p. 419.
38 Ibid, pp. 421–22.
39 J. Levitt, 'Pro-Democratic intervention in Africa', *Wisconsin International Law Journal*, Vol. 24, 3, 2006, p. 809.
40 I. Brownlie, *International Law and the Use of Force by States*, Oxford: Oxford at the Clarendon Press, 1963 (reprinted 2002), pp. 298–301.
41 Levitt, op. cit., n. 39, p. 809.
42 UN Press Release SC/7758.
43 Gray, op. cit., n. 25, p. 420.
44 Final Communiqué on the Extraordinary Session of the Authority of Heads of State and Government on Cote d'Ivoire, N°: 188/2010, 7 December 2010, Abuja, Nigeria. Available at <http://news.ecowas.int/presseshow.php?nb=188&lang=en&annee=2010> (accessed 25 March 2013).
45 Levitt, op. cit., n. 39, p. 787.

to restore the legal democratic order. In Africa, elections cause the greatest internal conflicts, as even initially democratically elected leaders may become dictators and stay in power until death, with military juntas ruling the countries. Such rulers include Gnassingbé Eyadéma, and his son Faure Gnassingbé of Togo, Lansana Conté and Moussa Dadis Camara of Guinea, and numerous others. The attempts to overthrow the regimes by violence, or to impose the results of new democratic elections often cause bloody civil wars. Not only the operations in Liberia, Sierra Leone, and Côte d'Ivoire, but also Guinea Bissau, Guinea and Togo are among the examples of pro-democratic interventions by ECOWAS mentioned in literature.[46]

The legal basis

The legal documents of ECOWAS depict the stipulation of a right to regional intervention – both humanitarian and pro-democratic. The ECOWAS Protocol (signed in 1999, and in force from 2001) is the document that describes the principles and procedures for launching regional operations among other security measures.[47] According to Article 25 of the ECOWAS Protocol, the Mechanism is to be applied not only in the case of humanitarian catastrophes and collective self-defence, but also in cases where rule of law or democratic order is threatened. The measures taken do not necessarily have to be enforcement measures; however, nothing in the document excludes or limits the authority of the Mediation and Security Council to take any measures necessary.

Article 26 of the ECOWAS Protocol lists the authorities that can initiate the mechanism. The Authority of Heads of States and Governments, which is the supreme institution of ECOWAS, and the Mediation and Security Council have a right to initiate the mechanism. In addition also a Member State, the executive secretary of ECOWAS, the OAU (now the AU) and the UN can request the initiation of the mechanism. In Article 52 it is stated that 'in accordance with Chapters VII and VIII of the United Nations Charter, ECOWAS shall inform the United Nations of any military intervention undertaken in pursuit of the objectives of this Mechanism'. The Article, thus, does not express a requirement to act upon a request or with an authorisation of the UN, but only a requirement to inform the UN of regional action subsequently. The necessary compliance with the UN Charter requirement not to take enforcement action without UN authorisation does not derive from the text of the Protocol. The ECOWAS Protocol article on co-operation requires full compliance and co-ordination with the OAU (the predecessor of the AU) Mechanism for Conflict Prevention, Management and Resolution. The current AU and ECOWAS Mechanisms are alike and equally contradictory

---

46 Levitt, op. cit., n. 39, p. 787.
47 ECOWAS Protocol, in particular Chapter V.

with regard to the UN Charter provisions on unilateral regional use of force. Nevertheless, they maintain a coherent African approach with the doctrine of non-indifference in the centre.

Decision-making

The ECOWAS Treaty provides that the Authority of the Heads of States and Governments acts by decisions that are taken by unanimity, consensus or by a two-thirds majority of the Member States, unless provided otherwise in the relevant Protocol. In the case of matters of peace and security, such a Protocol exists.[48] According to the ECOWAS Protocol the Authority in turn mandates the Mediation and Security Council to take, on its behalf, appropriate decisions for the implementation of the Mechanism. The Mediation and Security Council, among others, is specifically mandated to 'authorise all forms of intervention and decide particularly on the deployment of political and military missions'.[49] ECOWAS has both the legal basis and the procedure for launching regional interventions, without a requirement for a UNSC authorisation stipulated in them.

The Mediation and Security Council comprises nine members, of which seven are elected by the Authority, along with the former and present chairman of the Authority. The quorum is two-thirds of the members. The vote necessary for making decisions is two-thirds of the members present. Thus, the number of votes necessary can be as low as four. This is a surprisingly low quorum requirement for a decision, potentially, on launching a coercive operation. The legitimacy of such a small group to decide on behalf of all its members on taking action that is not only highly controversial in the light of international law, but can potentially have dire consequences, is highly debatable. Such a decision-making procedure does not guarantee a procedural restraint for dominating States to use the subregional organisation for furthering their national interests.

Co-operation with the United Nations

In the ECOWAS Protocol, ECOWAS makes a reference to Chapter VIII of the UN Charter, thus recognising itself as a Chapter VIII organisation. It is a subregional organisation. ECOWAS and the UN have a long history of co-operation and co-ordination regarding specific military operations that the UN has either authorised (or endorsed) or led. The first such case is the ECOWAS operation in Liberia and the subsequent establishment of UNOMIL in 1993.

As to the formal co-operation beyond *ad hoc* cases, the co-operation with ECOWAS is enhanced in the ten-year co-operation framework with the AU,

---

48 ECOWAS Protocol, Art. 7.
49 Ibid.

which is to co-ordinate the efforts with the subregional organisations.[50] The interaction of the AU and ECOWAS with the UN is not fully co-ordinated,[51] and in addition to the UN co-operation with the African region through the AU, there is also some direct co-operation between the UN and ECOWAS. ECOWAS has had an observer status with the UN General Assembly since 2004.[52] The background paper for the expert group meeting on the emerging role of the AU and ECOWAS in conflict prevention and peacebuilding, prepared by the UN Office of the Special Adviser on Africa, highlights the significance of something as simple as the location of the offices of the UN and ECOWAS in different countries, and lack of flights between these countries, as a serious impairment for the co-operation between the two organisations.[53] Thus even purely practical issues, not only high-level political considerations, contribute to strengthening the autonomy in African regional maintenance of peace and security.

Despite the practical and political difficulties of the UN-ECOWAS co-operation, it has a significant place in the post-Cold War development of law on the use of force. ECOWAS was one of the first regional organisations that caught the specific attention and recognition of the UN after the end of the Cold War, even before the UN Secretary-General's hopeful *Agenda for Peace* report was published. In the beginning the UN lacked experience, including negative, with the subordination of regional organisations to the UN. Perhaps this explains the lack of hesitation by the UN to endorse operations, the legal basis of which was contradictory by way of challenging the limits of what is appropriate for regional action, including the use of military force.

Southern African Development Community

General description

The Southern African Development Coordination Conference (SADCC) was created in 1980 and transformed into an organisation, SADC, in 1992.[54] SADC comprises 15 Member States.[55] The SADC Treaty provides mainly for

---

50 T. Ajayi, 'The UN, the AU and ECOWAS – A Triangle of Peace and Security in West Africa?', Friedrich Ebert Stiftung: New York, Briefing Paper 11, November 2008, p. 4. Available at <http://library.fes.de/pdf-files/bueros/usa/05878.pdf> (accessed 25 March 2013).
51 Ajayi, ibid, p. 7.
52 A/RES/59/51.
53 *The Emerging Role of the AU and ECOWAS in conflict prevention and peacebuilding*, op. cit., n. 1, p. 37.
54 'SADC Facts and Figures', SADC website. Available at <http://www.sadc.int/about-sadc/overview/sadc-facts-figures/> (accessed 24 March 2013).
55 Angola, Botswana, DRC, Lesotho, Madagascar, Malawi, Mauritius, Mozambique, Namibia, Seychelles, South Africa, Swaziland, United Republic of Tanzania, Zambia and Zimbabwe.

socio-economic co-operation between the Member States, however, an organ on politics, security and defence co-operation subsequently has been added to the treaty with Article 10A (amendment of 28 June 1996).[56] A Protocol on Politics, Security and Defence Cooperation[57] to implement Article 10A was signed by SADC Member States on 14 August 2001 – a development common in the twenty-first century, when security and defence issues rose high on the agendas of both States and international organisations. The SADC subregion had also its individual reasons that allowed it to bring the security and defence co-operation further, starting from mid-nineties, namely, the end of the apartheid regime in South Africa.[58] The SADC practice regarding action without a UN mandate has not been frequently analysed in literature. The SADC documents, in contrast to those of ECOWAS and the AU, do not contain controversies regarding the UN Charter law on the use of force. There is, however, relevant SADC practice that raises the question on what is appropriate for regional action.

The legal basis

The Protocol on Politics, Security and Defence Cooperation starts out by declaring in its preamble that SADC is a regional arrangement under Chapter VIII of the UN Charter and reaffirms the primary responsibility of the UNSC in the maintenance of peace and security.[59] The Preamble further states that a prerequisite for development is peace, which can be achieved through close co-operation in security and defence matters. The Protocol puts an emphasis on the peaceful settlement of disputes and also contains provisions on self-defence (also the Mutual Defence Pact (2003) which eventually came to be signed only in 2011[60]). Paragraph 1(a) of Article 11 in essence combines and repeats Articles 2(4) and 51 of the UN Charter.

Article 15(2) of the Protocol again emphasises that 'this Protocol in no way detracts from the responsibility of the United Nations Security Council to maintain international peace and security'. On the other hand, Article 15(1) states that 'this Protocol in no way detracts from the rights and obligations

---

56 Agreement Amending the Treaty of the South African Development Community, 14 August 2001. Available at <http://www.sadc.int/files/3413/5410/3897/Agreement_Amending_the_Treaty_-_2001.pdf> (accessed 25 March 2013).
57 South African Development Community, Protocol on Politics, Security and Defence Cooperation, of 14 August 2001. Available at <http://www.sadc.int/files/3613/5292/8367/Protocol_on_Politics_Defence_and_Security20001.pdf> (accessed 25 March 2013).
58 H. McCoubrey and J. Morris, *Regional Peacekeeping in the Post-Cold War Era*, The Hague: Kluwer Law International, 2000, pp. 145–46.
59 The Preamble reads: 'Bearing in mind that Chapter VIII of the UN Charter recognises the role of regional arrangements in dealing with such matters relating to the maintenance of international peace and security as are appropriate for regional action'.
60 SADC Mutual Defence Pact (2003), 1 August 2011. Available at <http://www.sadc.int/documents-publications/show/1038> (accessed 24 March 2013).

of State Parties under the Charters of the United Nations and the Organization of African Unity'. As is revealed further in this chapter (the AU being the legal successor of the OAU[61]), the rights and obligations under the UN Charter and those under the Constitutive Act of the AU might not always coincide. Thus, acting in compliance with the Constitutive Act of the AU might in reality mean breaching the UN Charter prohibition of the use of force. Nevertheless the SADC documents are generally non-interventionist. The Article 7 of the Mutual Defence Pact, entitled 'Non-interference', in paragraph 3 reconfirms that action will be taken against a Member State only with its request or consent, unless the Summit decides that action needs to be taken. This is to be interpreted in the way that self-defence measures can be taken against a Member State. Yet, the article's wording appears to be addressed to finding a compromise position for SADC in pro-interventionist Africa.

Decision-making

Even though SADC is not formally among the pro-interventionist organisations of Africa, it does have a practice of launching unauthorised regional interventions. Therefore it is necessary to look into the way decisions on such interventions can be made. SADC does not have a detailed decision-making system like ECOWAS. Article 10 of the Treaty provides that the Summit takes decisions by consensus and they are binding. It may also delegate authority as it deems necessary. The institution of SADC responsible for the defence and security co-operation is 'the organ'.

The decision-making principle in the organ, provided for in Article 10A(7) of the SADC Treaty, is also consensus. Article 10A(5), in addition, reads: 'The structure, functions, powers and procedures of the organ and other related matters shall be prescribed in a Protocol'. Yet, there are no additional provisions on the decision-making procedure for conflict prevention, management and resolution. In general, the organ is responsible for promoting peace and security in the region.

The organ reports to the SADC summit and consists of:

(a) the chairperson of the organ;
(b) the Troika;
(c) a Ministerial Committee;
(d) an Inter-State Politics and Diplomacy Committee (ISPDC);
(e) an Inter-State Defence and Security Committee (ISDSC); and
(f) such other sub-structures as may be established by any of the ministerial committees.

---

61 Constitutive Act of the AU, Art. 33, para. 1, reads: 'This Act shall replace the Charter of the Organization of African Unity'.

In general, the decision-making procedure in SADC is consultations and consensus, without detailed procedural rules. The cases of Lesotho and the DRC, described below, evidence that, just like the UNSC, the intransparent SADC decision-making mechanism may become impaired due to the interests of an individual Member State.

The practice

The practical record of SADC operations is limited to the operation 'Boleas' in Lesotho[62] and operation 'Sovereign Legitimacy' in the DRC, both in 1998. Neither has been widely analysed in major legal-scholarly writings. However, the details of the operations to a great extent resemble the above-described ECOWAS operations.

The relevant legal concerns in the Lesotho case, formally a peacekeeping operation, were the questionable legality of the invitation, as well as suspicion of lack of impartiality on the side of the sole contributor to the force – South Africa. In addition, the intervention by SADC caused an increase in violence and civil unrest which again brought about full-scale use of military force from the side of SADC, with casualties on all sides.[63]

The SADC operation in Lesotho took place within the region of the organisation – in one of its Member States. The operation was launched upon the invitation by the democratically elected prime minister of Lesotho, and based on an SADC mandate after growing unrest following elections.[64] The SADC mandate itself was questioned, as it endorsed an operation launched in reality by South Africa alone,[65] thus, there was no multilateralism in the intervention. The South African forces were only supplemented by a symbolic contribution from Botswana. In addition South Africa was reproached for not being impartial – having interests in Lesotho (Katse Dam water scheme[66] and, rather obviously, the fact that Lesotho is an enclave fully surrounded by South Africa from all sides). The prime minister was not the proper authority to invite the intervention as the constitution reserved this right for the king, and in addition the authority and actual control of the formal government at the time of the unrest was dubious.[67] Further on, a considerable contradiction

---

62 T. Neethling, 'Conditions for Successful Entry and Exit: An Assessment of SADC Allied Operations in Lesotho', in M. Malan (ed.), *Boundaries of Peace Support Operations: The African Dimension*, Pretoria: Institute for Security Studies, 2000. Available at <http://www.operationspaix.net/IMG/pdf/Conditions_for_Successful_Entry_and_Exit_An_Assessment_of_SADC_Allied_Opera.pdf> (accessed 24 March 2013).
63 K. P. Coleman, *International Organizations and Peace Enforcement. The Politics of International Legitimacy*, Cambridge: Cambridge University Press, 2007, p. 163.
64 Coleman, ibid., p. 161.
65 Coleman, ibid., p. 160.
66 Neethling, op. cit., n. 62, p. 1.
67 Coleman, op. cit., n. 63, p. 167.

was that the operation, by its form, was an enforcement operation. This case can, thus, be compared to the ECOWAS intervention in Liberia. In Liberia there was also an invitation from a questionable authority, the action without a UN mandate had enforcement character, and suspicions were raised about the abuse of power by the regional hegemon. On the other hand, in line with the later-developed non-indifference doctrine, the proponents of the operation in Lesotho claimed the need to intervene in order to prevent a tragedy. Thus, for example, the 'Boleas' commander, Colonel Robbie Hartslief, suggested that '[...] this kind of intervention [in Lesotho should] be accepted as a new kind of peace operation in Africa, because such operations may prevent a massive loss of lives and enormous economic damage'.[68] The intervention received neither condemnation, nor endorsement by the UNSC.

Even more controversy surrounds the 1998 intervention (operation 'Sovereign Legitimacy') of a few SADC Member States (Angola, Zimbabwe and Namibia) in the DRC. The intervention was formally based on invitation by the president of the DRC, Laurent Kabila, whose authority in the situation of the conflict was questionable.[69] Though unilateral, the action by the three Member States subsequently received endorsement from SADC. The endorsement is said to have come as a political trade-off between Zimbabwe (operation 'Sovereign Legitimacy' in the DRC) and South Africa (operation 'Boleas' in Lesotho).[70] Operation 'Sovereign Legitimacy' was thus *de facto* not a SADC operation. The status of a SADC operation was apparently sought by Zimbabwe, Angola and Namibia as one giving greater legitimacy than a unilateral intervention by individual States. In UNSC Resolution 1234 (April 1999) on the situation in the DRC no mention of the SADC operation was made. There was only a call for the involvement of the OAS. In August 1999, in UNSC Resolution 1258, the UNSC commended the efforts of both SADC and OAU to find a peaceful settlement to the conflict. In November of the same year the UNSC established the UN Observer Mission in the Democratic Republic of Congo (MONUC) with UNSC Resolution 1279. Thus, even in the case of operation 'Sovereign Legitimacy', which was a *de facto* unilateral individual State intervention, the UN abstained from debating the issues of legality. Instead, not analysing the preceding events, the UN chose a practical solution, entrusting the operation to the African regional organisations. And once again, just as in the ECOWAS cases, the regional effort was not sufficient, and a UN peacekeeping operation was launched alongside.

---

68 M. Hough, 'Collective security and its variants: A conceptual analysis with specific reference to SADC and ECOWAS', *Strategic Review for Southern Africa*, Vol. 20, 2 (November) 1998, pp. 37–38.
69 Neethling, op. cit., n. 62, p. 3.
70 Coleman, op. cit., n. 63, pp. 155–57.

Newer developments in SADC include the Memorandum of Understanding on the creation of a SADC stand-by force in 2007.[71] The SADC Summit decided to deploy the standby force to the DRC in December 2012.[72] No deployment, however, has taken place at the time of writing.

Co-operation with the United Nations

SADC has until recently acted unnoticed by the UN. In the cases of the operations in Lesotho and the DRC, there were no reactions from the side of the UN. In the case of the intervention in Lesotho the UN General Assembly and UNSC did not comment on the issue, while the UN Secretary-General commended the operation.[73] In the case of intervention in the DRC that SADC endorsed, no direct action was taken by the UN, until a UN resolution calling upon the OAU to deal with the conflict, without a reference to any previous SADC involvement.[74] The efforts of the UN were generally directed at co-operating with the AU as the overarching security organisation in Africa.

SADC has, nevertheless, declared itself to be a Chapter VIII organisation, and has observer status at the UN General Assembly since 2004.[75] Moreover, on 21 September 2010, the UN signed a Framework for Cooperation in the matters of peace and security.[76] As the only information the present author could find on this document is one single article, it is difficult to suggest what the legal nature of the agreement is. It does appear from the UN News Centre material, that, though politically the agreement strengthens co-operation between the UN and SADC, it also limits approved SADC action to conflict prevention, mediation and elections. The Framework for Cooperation aims to strengthen and draw upon the capacities of both organisations, including SADC's knowledge and understanding of the region and the mediation, peacemaking and peacebuilding experience of the Department of Political Affairs (UN).[77] The emphasis on elections in this co-operation document is

---

71 Memorandum of Understanding on Establishment of SADC Standby Brigade, 16 August 2007. Available at <http://www.sadc.int/documents-publications/show/1022> (accessed 25 March 2013).
72 Extraordinary Summit of SADC Heads of State and Government, 8 December 2012, Dar Es Salaam, United Republic of Tanzania, 'Communique'. Available at http://www.sadc.int/files/4213/5523/4282/SADC_EXtraordinary_Summit_COMMUNIQUE_8_DECEMBER_2012_English.pdf (accessed 25 March 2013).
73 Coleman, op. cit., n. 63, p. 186.
74 S/RES/1234(1999).
75 A/RES/59/49.
76 *Southern African bloc and UN agree to boost cooperation on peace and security issues*, UN News Centre, Available at <http://www.un.org/apps/news/story.asp?NewsID=36037&Cr=peace&Cr1=security> (accessed 25 March 2013).
77 *Southern African bloc and UN*, ibid.

not surprising, as it echoes the general African problem, also faced with by ECOWAS.

African Union

General description

The AU was created in 2002 to replace the OAU, established in 1963. The OAU had proved to be an unsuitable mechanism for dealing with the African regional threats to peace and security,[78] therefore a new regional mechanism was established to replace it.[79] While the main aim of the OAU was to eliminate external interference in the African continent (decolonisation),[80] the aims of the AU are unity and peace among African nations, democracy and sustainable growth.[81] The Constitutive Act of the AU is a document that depicts the realities of the twenty-first century: the link between socio-economic and military threats in Africa. The AU takes a view from the reverse perspective compared to, for example, the EU[82] and the Shanghai Cooperation Organisation (SCO). The Preamble of the Constitutive Act recognises '[…] that the scourge of conflicts in Africa constitutes a major impediment to the socio-economic development of the continent and of the need to promote peace, security and stability as a prerequisite for the implementation of our development and integration agenda'.[83] Thus, in order to achieve economic development, the organisation gives itself a mandate to deal with threats to peace and security. In comparison, the EU approach is that economic and social well being is a pre-requisite for peace and stability, and in the SCO security is the primary aim of co-operation, with economic issues supplementing and extending the former.

The legal basis

The legal basis of the AU has developed on the background of the African practice of the 1990s, most significantly the ECOWAS practice. An additional

---

78 Ajayi, op. cit., n. 50, pp. 2–3. Kioko, op. cit., n. 15, pp. 813–14.
79 Abbas also notes the strengthening of ECOWAS and the SADC as the reason for the redundancy of the OAU. In A. Abass, *Regional Organizations and the Development of Collective Security: Beyond Chapter VIII of the UN Charter*, Oxford and Portland, OR: Hart Publishing, 2004, p. 33.
80 McCoubrey and Morris, op. cit., n. 58, p. 15.
81 Constitutive Act of the AU, Preamble and Art. 3.
82 The EU Security Strategy emphasises that military threats are caused by socio-economic burdens: 'In much of the developing world, poverty and disease cause untold suffering and give rise to pressing security concerns'. European Security Strategy, 'A Secure Europe in a Better World', Brussels, 12 December 2003, p. 2. In the case of the SCO, the primary aim of co-operation is security, and social and economic co-operation are new additions to the scope of the co-operation.
83 Constitutive Act of the AU, Preamble.

factor for the development of the existing legal basis is the historical inaction of the UN in African crises, such as Uganda, Rwanda, Sudan and Somalia.[84] The core provisions on the maintenance of peace and security can be found in Article 4 of the Constitutive Act of the AU, as well as the Protocol establishing the AUPSC.[85]

According to the principles of the Constitutive Act of the AU, the responsible thing to do is not to await international response from outside the continent, but to deal with threats to peace and security, if necessary, with a solely regional mandate. Thus Article 4(h) provides for 'the right of the Union to intervene in a Member State pursuant to a decision of the Assembly in respect of grave circumstances, namely: war crimes, genocide and crimes against humanity'. The intent of the African politicians to be able to act regionally, without a UN mandate is deliberate. It was the absence of international assistance rather than its presence that influenced how the new AU was to be shaped. The politicians of the African continent joined the criticism saying that the UN and the rest of the world in general lack interest in resolving crises on the troubled African continent.[86] The cases that highlight this reasoning are the currently ongoing Sudan and Somalia crises and, especially, the lack of response by the international community to the genocide in Rwanda. The tragedy of the Rwandan genocide is the case specifically mentioned when permitting the option of legalising a regionally authorised operation in the absence of an efficient UN response.[87] Some other listed cases of UN failure to act are Liberia (1990, 2003), Sierra Leone (1997), the CAR (1997), Guinea Bissau (1998), Lesotho (1998), Congo (1998), Guinea (1999) and Côte d'Ivoire (2003) – a number of cases greater than the total number of threats to peace and security in any other region over the same time-span. African leaders seem to believe that new solutions are necessary to curb the devastating effects of civil conflict on African people, and that sovereignty is no longer a shield from intervention when human suffering exists on a great scale.[88] They have consciously and willingly contracted away sovereignty for greater aspirations of peace, security, stability and development.[89] Today's reality is that the inviolability of the principle of non-intervention in Africa has become strongly contested in favour of the principle of the responsibility to protect.

Article 4(j) of the Constitutive Act of the AU also notes the right of Member States to request intervention from the AU in order to restore peace

---

84 Kioko, op. cit., n. 15, pp. 812–16.
85 Protocol relating to the establishment of Peace and Security Council of the African Union, 9 July 2002. Available at <http://www.africa-union.org/root/au/organs/psc/Protocol_peace%20and%20security.pdf> (accessed 25 March 2013) (AUPSC Protocol).
86 See Kioko, op. cit., n. 15, pp. 810–17 for a more detailed account of reasons.
87 Kuwali, op. cit., n. 30, p. 43; Kioko, op. cit., n. 15, p. 815; Levitt, op. cit., n. 10, p. 229.
88 Levitt, op. cit., n. 10, p. 226.
89 Ibid.

and security, however, an invitation is not mandatory for launching a regional intervention. Along with the principle of non-indifference, Article 4 reaffirms traditional principles: the sovereign equality and interdependence among the Member States of the Union (a), peaceful resolution of conflicts among the Member States (e), prohibition of the use of force (f), and non-intervention in the internal matters of another Member State (g).

The provision of the Constitutive Act of the AU on the right to regional intervention in a case of a humanitarian catastrophe is repeated in the Protocol relating to the establishment of the AUPSC of 2004. The AUPSC is established pursuant to Article 5(2) of the Constitutive Act of the AU, which empowers the AU General Assembly to establish other organs.[90] The AUPSC is a standing decision-making organ for the prevention, management and resolution of conflicts and to serve as a collective security and early-warning arrangement to facilitate timely and efficient response to conflict and crisis situations in Africa.[91]

The Constitutive Act of the AU and the AUPSC Protocol reveal that while the AU acknowledges the 'primary' role of the UN in maintaining international peace and security, it reserves the right to authorise interventions in Africa – seeking UN involvement 'where necessary'.[92] Ademola Abass, however, draws a more radical conclusion from his interview with the director of the AUPSC, who has expressed the view that the AU needs to act on its own without waiting for and relying on the UNSC and the politics behind its decision making.[93] In addition, the director of the AUPSC has stated, in an interview, that there is a tacit agreement with the UN on such an approach.[94] Indeed, no debates in the UN have been raised over the past decade on the legality of African regionalism. The mention of the issue in a positive light can even be found in UN documents described below.

An authentic interpretation of Article 4(h) can be found in the Common African Position on the Proposed Reform of the United Nations: the Ezulwini Consensus.[95] This document reveals that the AU does agree that a UNSC-authorised intervention should be the norm, but that in certain situations approval could be granted subsequently. Interestingly, this position also includes an approach that if the UN mandates the operation, it also pays for it:

> Since the General Assembly and the Security Council are often far from the scenes of conflicts and may not be in a position to undertake effectively

---

90 Levitt, op. cit., n. 10, p. 215.
91 AUPSC Protocol.
92 Levitt, op. cit., n. 10, p. 230.
93 Abass, op. cit., n. 79, p. 166.
94 Ibid.
95 The Common African Position on the Proposed Reform of the United Nations, the Ezulwini Consensus, AU doc. Ext/EX.CL/2 (VII), 7–8 March 2005. Available at <www.africa-union.org/.../Ext%20EXCL2%20VII%20Report.doc> (accessed 25 March 2013).

a proper appreciation of the nature and development of conflict situations, it is imperative that Regional Organisations, in areas of proximity to conflicts, are empowered to take actions in this regard. The African Union agrees with the Panel [High Level Panel on Threats, Challenge and Change] that the intervention of Regional Organisations should be with the approval of the Security Council; although in certain situations, such approval could be granted 'after the fact' in circumstances requiring urgent action. In such cases, the UN should assume responsibility for financing such operations.[96]

Moreover, the Ezulwini Consensus lists the Article 4(h) norm as an exception to the UN Charter prohibition of the use of force, on the same level as that of Article 51 of the UN Charter:

With regard to the use of force, it is important to comply scrupulously with the provisions of Article 51 of the UN Charter, which authorise the use of force only in cases of legitimate self-defence. In addition, the Constitutive Act of the African Union, in its Article 4(h), authorises intervention in grave circumstances such as genocide, war crimes and crimes against humanity. Consequently, any recourse to force outside the framework of Article 51 of the UN Charter and Article 4(h) of the AU Constitutive Act, should be prohibited.[97]

Such a statement raises the question, whether the African classification of Article 4(h) right to intervention ought to apply globally or be a specific regional exception to the prohibition of the use of force in Africa. On one hand, the exception is listed here as equal to that of Article 51, but on the other hand, there does not exist a global consensus on such a norm. According to the UN Charter itself (Articles 2(4) and 103) such a norm is actually illegal under international law.

To defend the African regional norm, it must be noted that the developments in African regional legislation have not been condemned by the UN. On the contrary, in 2008 the UN Secretary-General submitted a report of the AU-UN panel on modalities for support to AU peacekeeping operations to the UN General Assembly and the UNSC, in which it is stated:

The United Nations Security Council has primary responsibility for the maintenance of peace and security. While regional and sub-regional organizations act on its behalf in resolving conflict, it is necessary to ensure that they are able to exercise their comparative advantage in initiating an operation before a situation becomes protracted. A timely and effective

---

96 Ezulwini Consensus, ibid., Part B, p. 6.
97 Ezulwini Consensus, ibid.

response to crises is needed, especially in cases of war crimes, genocide, crimes against humanity and major humanitarian situations.[98]

This statement gives ground to consider that there is a political flexibility for endorsement from the side of the UN (at least the UN Secretary-General) for unilateral regional action (at least regarding Africa) in cases of a humanitarian catastrophe. While the need for a more rapid regional action in the report is illustrated by humanitarian catastrophes, it is not specified as the only possible exception either (as opposed to, e.g. pro-democratic interventions). Thus, the position of the UN Secretary-General can be understood to be that unilateral regional action may be permissible: at least as a humanitarian intervention and at least with regard to the AU. Jeremy Levitt writes that:

> African states and their organizations have sought to fashion African solutions to African problems by creating innovative rules and mechanisms for pro-democracy and human rights-based intervention. These rules and structures are, in turn, evolving the law of intervention and, in [his] view, have been the most credible examples and the single most important force in the development of pro-democratic intervention and humanitarian intervention norms.[99]

Even if the legality of the pro-interventionist African norms in theory is very questionable, the fact remains that a pro-intervention or non-indifference clause has been included in the Constitutive Act of the AU. Jeremy Levitt's submission that pro-democratic intervention is a part of the package is a further debatable issue. The amendment of the Constitutive Act of the AU of 1 July 2003, among others, provides for the amendment of Article 4(h) to have the following wording:

> (h) the right of the Union to intervene in a Member State pursuant to a decision of the Assembly in respect of grave circumstances, namely: war crimes, genocide and crimes against humanity as well as a serious threat to legitimate order to restore peace and stability to the Member State of the Union upon the recommendation of the Peace and Security Council;[100]

---

98 Report of the African Union-United Nations panel on modalities for support to African Union peacekeeping operations, A/63/666–S/2008/813, 31 December 2008, p. 13, paras 36 and 37.
99 Levitt, op. cit., n. 39, p. 786.
100 Protocol on Amendments to the Constitutive Act of the African Union, 3 February and 11 July 2003. Available at <http://www.africa-union.org/root/au/Documents/Treaties/Text/Protocol%20on%20Amendments%20to%20the%20Constitutive%20Act.pdf> (accessed 24 March 2013).

Thus, the amendment would provide also for a right to pro-democratic intervention (intervention to restore the legitimate order), the legality and legitimacy of which has considerably less general support than humanitarian intervention.[101] The amendment has not, however, come into force, even though it was adopted in the Assembly of the AU already in 2003. Jeremy Levitt argues that pro-democratic intervention has become customary law in Africa.[102] The fact that the relevant amendment to the Constitutive Act of the AU has not come into force does not talk in support of such a claim. On the other hand, a corresponding norm is in force in the ECOWAS legal acts. In addition, what speaks in the defence of a need for accepting that a right to pro-democratic regional intervention ought to exist is the endless row of interstate conflicts arising following elections, with one of the most recent examples being the aftermath of the elections at the end of 2010 in the already long-troubled Côte d'Ivoire.

A legal-theoretical issue arises on the compatibility of a regional right to intervention (humanitarian, pro-democratic) with the prohibition of the use of force as *jus cogens*. In theory, there may not exist a custom or a treaty provision which is in contradiction with a *jus cogens* norm. Nevertheless, ten years of existence is a long enough time-span to conclude that the norm exists in African regional documents and has not been condemned or contested by any organ of the UN or any other State. During this period the norm has only been the topic of the scholarly debate.

There are numerous bids for how to justify African regional interventions. Yoram Dienstein, for example, points out that the use of force is abolished in Article 2(4) only in the 'international relations' of the Member States, and that intrastate clashes are therefore out of reach of the UN Charter provisions.[103] Levitt concludes that the possible justification for a regional humanitarian intervention is that general and regional customary international law and treaty law developments permit it. Such conflicts arguably fall outside of the jurisdictional mandate of the UN, and the UN law does not forbid it.[104] He admits that it is debatable whether intrastate conflict falls outside the jurisdictional mandate of the UNSC, given the way in which the UNSC has interpreted its discretionary powers and the language of Article 39 of the UN Charter since the end of the Cold War.[105] The UNSC has not delegated internal conflicts, and in particular, African conflicts to full African discretion of action, thus the above-mentioned arguments cannot justify the regional right to unilateral humanitarian intervention. At the present moment the

---

101 Gray, op. cit., n. 25, p. 56.
102 Levitt, op. cit., n. 39.
103 Y. Dienstein, *War, Aggression and Self-Defence*, Cambridge: Cambridge University Press, 2001, p. 80.
104 Levitt, op. cit., n. 10, p. 234.
105 Ibid.

actual exercise of the African right is acquiesced to by the UN only as an exceptional – emergency – solution, and cannot be considered to have become a general right.

Dan Kuwali comes with some interesting suggestions for the interpretation of a regional right to humanitarian intervention. He goes further into a debate whether a treaty-based acquiescence can give legitimacy to regional humanitarian interventions. He concludes that the consent of regional States to a pro-intervention norm relates rather to the *pacta sunt servanda* principle, than to a violation of a norm of non-intervention.[106] Nevertheless, it can be argued contrary to his claim, that *pacta sunt servanda* is not a *jus cogens* principle, and thus, could not override a *jus cogens* principle of prohibition of the use of force. However, looking at the issue from the *pacta sunt servanda* perspective does give more legitimacy to an intervention, if a State of the region has accepted the obligations to observe human rights, and signed for it, acknowledging the possible sanctions if the responsibility to protect principle is breached. There is a higher legitimacy to action within the region – a mutual principle agreed by the Member States of one organisation, than a unilateral intervention by any State or organisation trans-regionally. Such an agreement does provide a kind of a *carte blanche* invitation, the validity of which is more verifiable than in the case of many real-life operations on the ground. The general acquiescence, however, does not make humanitarian intervention a peacekeeping operation, because it does imply enforcement action against the State authority that has previously acquiesced to the pro-interventionist norm.

Moreover, Dan Kuwali argues that as mass atrocities are a breach of *jus cogens* themselves, the humanitarian intervention constitutes a universal *erga omnes* obligation, with the sole purpose of the intervention being apprehending the perpetrators and deterring armed attacks against civilians.[107] Today the principle of prohibition of the use of force is counterbalanced with the principle of responsibility to protect. Where even the UNSC's right to intervene forcefully in the case of humanitarian catastrophes was debated before the universal consensus on the principle of the responsibility to protect was reached, today the very existence of the principle diminishes the clear-cut illegality of humanitarian intervention.

Decision-making

A correct and transparent decision-making procedure is an important factor for the legitimacy of interventions carried out by regional organisations. The decision-making mechanism of the AU has been thought through in order to make it transparent and efficient. In the case of ECOWAS, as well as the AU,

---

106 Kuwali, op. cit., n. 30, p. 76.
107 Ibid.

the mechanisms have been created according to the model of the EU and the UN.[108] Levitt writes that from a structural standpoint, the AU's collective security framework should have a greater longevity and legitimacy than prior OAU conflict mechanisms because of its robust mandate to enforce peace – authority lacking in those organisations that preceded it.[109] However, while the ECOWAS peace and security mechanism developed gradually, the AU mechanism started out with a detailed conflict management mechanism. The strong structure is the key to the capability of the AU to undertake peace operations and engage in conflict prevention activities.[110]

The decision-making procedure in the supreme organ of the AU – the Assembly, described in Article 7 of the Constitutive Act of the AU – is consensus or, failing it, a two-thirds majority vote of the members of the AU. The quorum is also two-thirds majority. The necessary votes, however, are counted from the number of Member States, not from the number present.

In the AU it is generally the AUPSC that makes decisions on the matters of resolution of conflicts.[111] According to the Protocol, the AUPSC has a wide scope of functions in the maintenance of peace and security, with one exception. As to humanitarian interventions provided for in Article 4(h) of the Constitutive Act of the AU, the AUPSC recommends humanitarian intervention to the Assembly, which then makes the decision.[112] This can be explained by the highly sensitive character of humanitarian intervention both from a legal and a political perspective, requiring the decisions to be made at the top level, with the greatest possible participation. The AUPSC is, nevertheless, responsible for the implementation and follow-up of the decisions on intervention.

The AUPSC resembles the UNSC, not only by name, but also by composition. It consists of 15 members, of which ten are elected for two years, and five for three years. In addition to the principle of equitable regional representation and rotation, candidate Member States are evaluated according to listed criteria on compliance with and promotion of the requirements and aims of the AU.[113] More importantly, even though the AUPSC is established after the example of the UNSC, there is no veto right for any Member State. Parties to a conflict are excluded from the debate, which is another difference from the UNSC. The required quorum is two-thirds. The decisions are generally to be taken by consensus. However, more flexibility is provided: In cases where consensus cannot be reached, the decisions on procedural matters

---

108 *The Emerging Role of the AU and ECOWAS in conflict prevention and peacebuilding*, op. cit., n. 1, pp. 23–24.
109 Levitt, op. cit., n. 10, p. 226.
110 *The Emerging Role of the AU and ECOWAS in conflict prevention and peacebuilding*, op. cit., n. 1, pp. 23–24.
111 Ibid, p. 12.
112 AUPSC Protocol, Art. 7(e).
113 AUPSC Protocol, Art. 8, para. 5.

are adopted by a simple majority, while decisions on all other matters – by a two-thirds majority vote of its members voting. On the one hand, this mechanism helps avoid a paralysis (which has been a significant problem in the UNSC), but on the other hand, decisions having serious implications can be taken by down to seven members of the AUPSC.[114] Seven States are not even a half of the members of the Council, therefore the legitimate representation of all AU Member States in taking a decision by seven votes can be questionable. However, the rules are clear, and it is apparent that if a Member State has an opinion, boycotting the relevant AUPSC meeting is not to its benefit.

A region-specific feature of the AU is the Panel of the Wise which corresponds to the cultural peculiarities of the region. It is an advisory body to the AUPSC, consisting of five African personalities from various segments of society who have made outstanding contribution to the cause of peace, security and development on the continent. They are selected by the Chairperson of the Commission of the AU after consultations with the Member States concerned, on the basis of regional representation and appointed by the Assembly to serve for a period of three years.[115] The Panel of the Wise corresponds to the tribal model and the authority of the elders, familiar in many African societies. This may add more legitimacy to the action taken by the organisation in the eyes of the public, being a more natural component than the structures directly copied from the EU model.

The EU model, though created to ensure greater representation and transparency is also known to be a very complex and cost-ineffective system. In the African region, where financial and human resources are short, trying to take over such an effort-consuming system can in itself turn out to be a major capabilities issue. As the report on ECOWAS and the AU suggests, the manning of the posts in the supporting staff in itself is one of the greatest challenges.[116] Having these practical difficulties, it can be assumed also that the AU does not have an overflow of resources for launching interventions, and thus would not be likely to launch interventions, unless in a true case of necessity (if even then). Not only the legal considerations, but also the financial issues are a significant factor that may limit unilateral regional action.

The practice

Since its creation, the AUPSC has considered situations in Burundi, the CAR, Chad, Comoros, Côte d'Ivoire, the DRC, Guinea-Bissau, Liberia,

---

114 Presuming the minimum number of States necessary for a quorum – ten. Two-thirds of ten are seven States.
115 AUPSC Protocol, Art. 11.
116 *The Emerging Role of the AU and ECOWAS in conflict prevention and peacebuilding*, op. cit., n. 1, pp. 27–30.

Mauritania, Rwanda, Somalia, Sudan (the Darfur region and South Sudan), Togo,[117] Libya and others. The cases of intervention have not been frequent despite the permissive legal basis of the Constitutive Act of the AU. An AU peacekeeping force was deployed in Burundi in 2003 before the UN force arrived.[118] The AU has been involved in co-operation with the UN in Chad, Côte d'Ivoire, Somalia and Darfur.[119] An AU regional intervention, along with other enforcement measures, took place in Comoros in 2007[120] to oust a separatist leader; there was government consent. The operation was labelled as being election monitoring. It was successful and attracted little international attention.[121]

The attempts of the AU to deal with Somalia since 2007 (the African Union Mission in Somalia (AMISOM)) have seen little progress. The force contributions do not exceed 5,000 troops, though at least 8,000 were called for,[122] and the AU, with its limited resources cannot offer a stronger response. The UN remains reluctant to re-enter Somalia.

The largest of the AU's operations in the past decade is the operation in Darfur, which is by essence a humanitarian intervention. The humanitarian catastrophe in Darfur (Sudan) in 2003 was slow in receiving international response. The UN could not launch a peacekeeping operation without the consent of Sudan due to the non-interventionist position of China and Russia.[123] In this situation the UN left it up to the AU to deal with the situation.[124] The AU, on the other hand, was also not willing to intervene without the consent of the government of Sudan.[125] As a result, the AU sent a small monitoring force of 150 troops. Even though the monitoring force was transformed into a considerably larger peacekeeping force (6,171 personnel),

---

117 *The Emerging Role of the AU and ECOWAS in conflict prevention and peacebuilding*, op. cit., n. 1, p. 12.
118 E. Svensson, *The African Mission in Burundi. Lessons Learned from the African Union's First Peace Operation*, Stockholm: Swedish Defence Research Agency, 2008, p. 11.
119 Security Council Report, *Update Report No. 3 The UN and Regional Organisations*, 23 March 2007. Available at <http://www.securitycouncilreport.org/site/c.glKWLe MTIsG/b.2616247/k.893B/Update_Report_No_3BR_The_UN_and_Regional_ OrganisationsBR_23_March_2007.htm> (accessed 24 March 2013).
120 Communiqué of the 95th Peace and Security Council Meeting, PSC/PR/Comm(XCV). Available at <www.africa-union.org/root/.../Communiqué%2095%20(Eng.).doc> (accessed 25 March 2013).
121 S. Hanson, *The African Union*, Council of Foreign Relations, 1 September 2009. Available at <http://www.cfr.org/publication/11616/african_union.html#p5> (accessed 25 March 2013).
122 AMISOM Bulletin, Issue 1, February 2010, p. 2. Available at <http://www.africa-union. org/root/au/auc/departments/psc/amisom/Bulletin/2010/AMISOM%20Bulletin%20 No.%201.pdf> (accessed 24 March 2013).
123 Gray, op. cit., n. 25, p. 53.
124 Ibid, p. 380.
125 Ibid, p. 55.

it was unable to stop the violence.[126] The government of Sudan resisted the efforts of the UN, until in 2007 it finally accepted the creation of the hybrid AU/UN force, UNAMID.[127] UNAMID was established on 31 July 2007 with the adoption of UNSC Resolution 1769.[128]

It must be noted that the AU is among the few regional organisations to have a rapid reaction force – the African Standby Force, with readiness reached at the end of 2010. Actual activity of the force, however, does not appear to have taken place from the materials available, apart from the military exercise 'Carana' in October 2010.[129]

It appears that even if the creation of the non-indifference clause in Africa has not brought more order, it has not created more chaos in regional interventions either. The problem of the AU is not that it has the legal mandate to intervene unilaterally in regional conflicts, but rather that it is not able to deal with the great number of crises that are constantly present in Africa. The inability of the international community to respond to all African crises can be justified with the vast number of African intrastate conflicts. Thus with the claimed post-colonial disinterest of the international community in African issues, the subsequent introduction of the non-indifference clause, though not according to the UN Charter, might be the better solution for Africa. However, with the shortage of resources in Africa, the situation remains principally the same as before the introduction of the non-indifference clause. The Darfur case also shows that without at least a *pro forma* invitation from the government, even a regional organisation with a non-indifference clause in its basic legal document may be reluctant to react to a humanitarian catastrophe.

Co-operation with the United Nations

Just as the OAU was, the AU is presumed to be a Chapter VIII organisation. This derives from the fact that the AU is the legal successor of the OAU and is regarded as such by the UN. However, no such statement is made either in the Constitutive Act of the AU, nor the Protocol establishing the AUPSC. Nevertheless, the co-operation of the UN with the AU has been more enhanced than with any other organisation. In addition to a general call for strengthening the African region through the AU, the World Summit Outcome calls for the development and implementation of a ten-year plan

---

126 Gray, op. cit., n. 25, pp. 54 and 380.
127 Ibid, p. 54.
128 UNAMID African Union/United Nations hybrid operation in Darfur website. Available at <http://www.un.org/en/peacekeeping/missions/unamid/> (accessed 24 March 2013).
129 P. Heinlein, 'New African Standby Force Faces First Test', *Voice of America*, 22 October 2010. Available at <http://www.voanews.com/english/news/africa/New-African-Standby-Force-Faces-First-Test-105518428.html> (accessed 25 March 2013).

for capacity-building with the AU. These calls have been followed up in documents ranging from political reports to practical co-operation working papers, and to actual practical co-operation in the field. Some of the examples of such documents are the reports of the UN Secretary-General, for example, report A/61/256 of 2006 on co-operation between the UN and regional and other organisations, and UNSC resolutions, such as UNSC Resolution 1809 (2008) welcoming the proposal to establish an AU-UN panel to consider the modalities of how to support AU peacekeeping operations established under a UN mandate. Further, these documents have been followed by practical steps to develop a plan proposed by the UN Secretary-General[130] and, lastly, by the creation of the framework plan itself.[131]

On 16 November 2006, the UN Secretary-General and the Chairperson of the Commission of the AU signed a declaration 'Enhancing UN-AU Cooperation: Framework for the Ten-Year Capacity Building Programme for the African Union'.[132] This declaration differs from other regional co-operation declarations, such as the ones signed between the UN and the EU,[133] the UN and the CIS,[134] the UN and NATO[135] in that it provides for a supervisory ten-year development plan for the development of the AU Peacekeeping Capacity Building. Thus, the UN intends to participate closely in the development of the AU maintenance of peace and security. The response of the UN and its great efforts to promote peace and security in Africa are perhaps a result of the great number of problems in Africa. At second glance, the African practice and doctrine on action without a UN mandate has, perhaps, been a catalysing factor for a UN to become more interested in African regional matters.

---

130 For example, A/63/666–S/2008/813, op. cit., n. 98.
131 Declaration. Enhancing UN-AU Cooperation: Framework for the Ten-year Capacity Building Programme for the African Union, Addis Ababa, 16 November 2006, annex to A/61/630.
132 Declaration, ibid.
133 European Union @ United Nations, Partnership in Action, 'Joint Declaration on UN-EU Co-operation in Crisis Management', New York, 24 September 2003. Available at <http://www.eu-un.europa.eu/articles/en/article_2768_en.htm> (accessed 25 March 2013).
134 'Joint Declaration on UN/CSTO Secretariat Cooperation', Moscow, 18 March 2010, CSTO website. Available at <http://www.dkb.gov.ru/start/index_aengl.htm> (link under the icon – Documents) (accessed 27 July 2011).
135 *Breaking News. Secret UN-NATO Cooperation Declaration*, The Transnational Foundation for Peace and Future Research, 3 December 2008. Available at <http://www.oldsite.transnational.org/Resources_Treasures/2008/TFFBoard_UN-NATO.html> (accessed 25 March 2013). (This source is used because information on the declaration cannot be found on either the NATO or the UN websites, or any other official source.)

Summary

A characteristic of the African region is the pro-intervention or non-indifference clause. This is set against a historical background of the failure of the international community to respond to several conflicts in Africa with dire consequences, most significantly the Rwanda genocide.

The main threat that the African region is faced with, is internal conflicts, especially the rivalry over power following elections, and the humanitarian catastrophes caused by these conflicts escalating. Though not fully excluded, interstate conflicts in Africa are rare, compared to intrastate conflicts. The threats to a great extent are related to the low economic development. The connection between economic issues and security is reflected in the basic documents of the African regional organisations.

The African regional organisations are commonly regarded as Chapter VIII organisations and have a blended security and defence function. The threats may come from outside, but the main focus is on the threats within: within the individual countries and within the region. The use of military force in the region is allowed in its full range: it includes both peacekeeping and peace enforcement. The practice and law of the AU and ECOWAS even support the existence of a regional right to launch unilateral regional interventions without a UN mandate in extreme cases. The right to humanitarian intervention however, is more clearly established than a right to pro-democratic intervention.

As the use of military force is regarded as permissible for regional action in Africa, this brings along the problem of drawing the line between the extent of permissibility of military peacekeeping and peace enforcement. The practice of the African regional organisations to launch military interventions, sometimes involving enforcement elements and being based on dubious invitation, has neither received condemnation, nor created debate at the UNSC. The African practice is limited to operations within the region, with no intentions or capacity to act outside it, even with a UN authorisation. Just as the conflicts are oftentimes related to economic underdevelopment, also African unilateral action is in reality more limited by its financial resources than by law. The practice of African regional organisations does not show an increase in unmandated regional operations with enforcement elements since the stipulation of the pro-interventionist norms in the regional documents. This may be the reason why the UN has not shown more political caution in endorsing African regional operations.

Another legal issue that the African regional example raises is how to justify regional humanitarian intervention without a UN mandate under international law: Articles 2(4), 53 and 103 of the UN Charter. The pro-intervention norm exists *de facto*, and has not been objected to by the international community – neither a UN organ nor an individual State. The less supportable justifications of the pro-intervention norms include referring to the principle of *pacta sunt servanda* instead of the prohibition of the use of force as the applicable provision, and the argument that intrastate conflicts are outside the scope of issues dealt with by the UNSC. The UNSC has competence regarding internal conflicts in its modern practice. The contractual agreement argument, though not fully justifying the contradictory norm, is a factor adding to the legitimacy of regional humanitarian intervention. An explicit consent of Member States to the applicability of the regional right to humanitarian intervention gives more legitimacy to such action compared to regions where the concept of regional humanitarian intervention is rejected. The argument that makes the most sense is that the right to regional humanitarian intervention can be justified as the balance between prohibition of the use of force, which is a *jus cogens* principle, and the protection of population against humanitarian atrocities, which is an obligation *erga omnes*. Human rights may need to be protected at cost of the prohibition of the use of force. The principle of responsibility to protect, invoked in such cases, however, does not alter the UNSC primary responsibility in the maintenance of peace and security, and the obligation of regional organisations not to launch enforcement action without a UN mandate. It must be noted that the African regional example does not create a norm of international law, for permitting regional intervention: either in any region or in any case. The acceptance of the African regional norms is political, not legally conditioned. The UN has tacitly weighed the problems the African region faces and the need to respond to them, and subsequently acquiesced to a certain African *carte blanche* right to regional intervention without a UN mandate in emergency cases, based on regional agreement. The lack of sufficient response to regional conflicts, and not the existence of a pro-intervention norm, still remains the core problem of Africa.

4 Asia

The ASEAN way

General description of the region

Asia is geographically a continent ranging from the Ural Mountains in the West, to the Pacific Ocean in the East. As a security region, however, its core is the Far East, bordering and overlapping with the Middle East and the Russian sphere of influence. Asian regional co-operation has not traditionally been shaped after the Western models. It is a region having a very distinct non-interventionist culture. Multilateralism in the maintenance of peace and security in Asia, as such, is a new phenomenon, starting out gradually only after the end of the Cold War.[1]

Asia has classically been the strongest proponent for non-interventionism in international relations. In 1954, two of the largest and most influential countries in Asia, China and India, elaborated the Five Principles of Peaceful Co-existence. The principles are: mutual respect for each other's territorial integrity and sovereignty, mutual non-aggression, non-interference in each other's affairs, the principle of equality,[2] and peaceful co-existence. While the international community in general has reached a consensus that sovereignty and non-interference are not unconditional and unlimited, in Asia these principles are still strongly defended. For example, they appear in the official position of China.[3] Further on, China's new common security concept for Asia, published in 2002, provides for, among others, non-alliance,

---

1 X. Wang, 'Regional Peace Architecture and Multilateralism in Asia', in *Regional Security Architecture and Multilateralism. Proceedings of the Second Workshop on Global Governance. June 21–23, 2004*, Shanghai: Friedrich-Ebert Stiftung, March 2005, pp. 23 and 30.
2 M. N. Shaw, *International Law*, 6th edn, Cambridge: Cambridge University Press, 2008, p. 214.
3 China's Position Paper on the New Security Concept, 31 July 2002, Ministry of Foreign Affairs of the People's Republic of China. Available at <http://www.mfa.gov.cn/eng/wjb/zzjg/gjs/gjzzyhy/2612/2614/t15319.htm> (accessed 25 March 2013).

non-confrontation and that building security on the basis of force and the threat of force is rejected.[4]

In a similar way the co-operation in the Association of Southeast Asian Nations (ASEAN) is based on the principles of non-interference, sovereignty and non-use of force, as stapled in the Treaty of Amity and Cooperation in Southeast Asia of 1976. Regarding the right to unilateral regional intervention in specific, many ASEAN members saw the Kosovo case as a matter of power politics rather than a moral question.[5] Not only were most Asian countries opposed to Kosovo in particular, but reject the concept of humanitarian intervention as an imposition of Western values, or an attempt of more Western dominance in general.[6] China holds the position that humanitarian intervention is inconsistent with and violates the UN Charter, it has no legitimate basis, and is conducted in the interests of the intervening, not target State.[7] The position of South Korea is that intervention is illegal without the authorisation of the UNSC, unless justified as self-defence.[8] India's perception of humanitarian intervention is that the needs of humanitarian assistance are to be met with assistance aimed at building the nation-State, rather than military intervention. Intervention is said to be carried out by the strong States against the weak, and by the developed countries in the West against the developing countries in the south.[9] Article 9 of the 1947 constitution of Japan stipulates that Japan renounces the use of force and that intervention in the domestic affairs of other States would be a sensitive issue.[10] The position of Japan has become more open to the use of force since 9/11.[11] In recent years, Japan has become more willing to participate in multilateral operations – either UN or other regional forums.[12] Thus, Japan took part in the coalition of the willing in Iraq 2003.

The approach of ASEAN is very different from the Western countries and, in particular, the Euro-Atlantic regional organisations like the EU and

---

4 T. Zang, 'Peaceful Coexistence, Common Security, Good Neighbourly Relations – A Brief Analysis of China's Asian Security Policy', in *Regional Security Architecture and Multilateralism. Proceedings of the Second Workshop on Global Governance. June 21–23, 2004*, Shanghai: Friedrich-Ebert Stiftung, March 2005, p. 47.
5 K. Watanabe, 'The Debate on Humanitarian Intervention', in K. Watanabe (ed.), *Humanitarian Intervention. The Evolving Asian Debate*, Tokyo: Japan Centre for International Exchange, 2003, p. 17.
6 C. Tremewan, 'Asia-Pacific Regional Integration and Human Rights', in R. F. Watters and T. G. McGee (eds), *New Geographies on the Pacific Rim: Asia Pacific*, Vancouver: University of British Columbia Press, 1997, p. 65; Watanabe, ibid, p. 12.
7 Watanabe, op. cit., n. 5, pp. 13 and 20.
8 Ibid, p. 15.
9 Ibid, p. 16.
10 Ibid, p. 14.
11 J. Gilson, 'Japan and East Asian Regional Security', in S. Hoadley and J. Rüland, (eds), *Asian Security Reassessed*, Singapore: Institute of South Asian Studies, 2006, p. 75.
12 Gilson, ibid., pp. 81–82.

NATO. ASEAN claims that it is not a security, nor a defence organisation.[13] In general, Asia, being a more pacifistic region, does not go further than engaging in conflict prevention. There are exceptions though, as evidenced by the participation of South Korea and Japan in the peace enforcement operation in Iraq. The non-interventionist position, nevertheless, remains dominant in the region. Thus, the responsibility to protect principle, along with the development of human rights and limitation of State sovereignty with regard to its own citizens, and the *erga omnes* obligation to protect human rights, have not had the same impact on the Asian non-interventionist approach, as in other regions. For this reason, it is highly unlikely that a regional norm for unilateral regional humanitarian intervention could develop in Asia. Nevertheless, the traditional non-interventionist position of Asian States has not prevented developments in the Asian regional maintenance of peace and security, impacted by the global developments. Changes in regional security co-operation are underway, especially with regard to ASEAN. Every region has its particularities: just like in the case of Africa there are calls for regional solutions to regional problems, there are also Asian solutions to Asian problems, in particular, the 'ASEAN' way.

The fact that the region is not pro-interventionist is not synonymous with concluding that the region is not undergoing regionalisation in the maintenance of peace and security. The persistence of the principle of non-intervention in Asia, while at the same time the principle of responsibility to protect has become accepted by the UN, can also be of evidence to increased regionalisation of peace and security in Asia – in its own way.

Historically regional mechanisms for the maintenance of peace and security have not been common in Asia. During the Cold War, the security co-operation in Asia took place mainly through bilateral agreements.[14] One of the few regional co-operation forums in Asia during the Cold War – ASEAN specifically avoided military co-operation, in order not to be manipulated by the Cold War situation.[15] After the end of the Cold War the security needs of individual States in Asia led to an arms race.[16] To stop this development, a multilateralism trend in Asia started, thus, the Asia-Pacific Economic Cooperation (APEC), ASEAN, ASEAN Regional Forum (ARF), ASEAN 10+3, Northeast Asia Cooperation Dialogue (NEACD) and the SCO were developed as forums enhancing security co-operation in Asia.[17] All of these organisations are small in size, comprising an average of ten Member

---

13 A. Acharya, 'Conclusion: Asian norms and practices in UN peace operations', *International Peacekeeping*. Vol. 12, 1 (Spring) 2005, p. 147.
14 Wang, op. cit., n. 1, p. 25.
15 A. Acharya, *Constructing a Security Community in Southeast Asia. ASEAN and the problem of regional order*, 2nd edn, New York: Routledge, 2009, p. 55.
16 Wang, op. cit., n. 1, p. 26.
17 Wang, op. cit., n. 1, p. 26.

States, and there is no wider overarching Asian regional organisation. The most dynamic of these organisations are ASEAN and the SCO.

At present, the major security issues facing Asia are: relationships with and between powers, disputes over territory, boundary and maritime rights, hotspots such as the Korean peninsula, the proliferation of weapons of mass destruction (WMD), economic security and non-traditional security, regional security and co-operation mechanisms.[18] The non-traditional security challenges include terrorism, piracy, environmental pollution, international crime, illegal immigration, drug trafficking, sandstorms, AIDS/HIV and others.[19]

A characteristic of Asian multilateralism in the twenty-first century is said to be multilateralism replacing bilateral treaties – to ensure democracy, the protection of the interests of smaller States and institutionalisation in order to facilitate co-operation and the rule of law in international relations.[20] Thus also security co-operation in a formalised framework is new in Asia. The concept of democracy, from the perspective of Asian co-operation, relates to the equality of States, and not necessarily to that of individuals. The treatment of individuals remains an internal matter of each individual State, where other States do not interfere.

The problems of multilateralism in Asia are the same as in most other regions: the problem of restraining the major powers in a multilateral framework, and the problem of efficiency and time-consumption in decision-making.[21] Yet, the Asian forums are not as institutionalised and formalised as elsewhere in the world. In Asia, the peace and security matters are dealt with through informal institutions and forms of co-operation.[22] The flexibility of the co-operation forums has the flip-side of institutional mechanisms not being developed enough for effective crisis management.[23] Multilateral alliances, power co-ordination and collective security in Asia, based on a common collective security model, are still impossible. Therefore co-operative security is the only way to reduce the negative effect of the Cold War alliances, balance power, enhance power co-ordination, and eventually to establish an institutionalised security mechanism. From there on there can be talk of collective security in the future.[24] However, as described below, a movement towards a more enhanced co-operation in the maintenance of

---

18 Zang, op. cit., n. 4, p. 47.
19 X. Liping, in *Regional Peace Architecture and Multilateralism in Asia in Regional Security Architecture and Multilateralism. Proceedings of the Second Workshop on Global Governance. June 21–23, 2004*, Shanghai: Friedrich-Ebert Stiftung, March 2005, pp. 149–50.
20 Wang, op. cit., n. 1, p. 23.
21 Ibid, p. 24.
22 Ibid, p. 27.
23 Ibid.
24 Ibid, pp. 28–29.

peace and security can now be sensed through the developments in ASEAN and the SCO.

The co-operation of the UN with Asia as a region has been conditioned by the absence of an overarching Asian regional peace and security organisation. The main organisation in Asia with which the UN has an increasing co-operation is ASEAN, with constant enhancement of the co-operation since the First ASEAN-UN Summit in 2000.[25] In addition, the UN has been encouraging more initiative and co-operation with and within the SCO. The low level of regional co-operation has led UN Secretary-General Ban Ki-moon to extensively lobby regional co-operation in peace and security matters in individual Asian States.[26]

During the twenty-first century, the UNSC has issued resolutions only on situations in Timor Leste and North Korea, regarding the region of Asia. In addition to that the international community, of course, continues to be seized with the matters of Afghanistan, which, due to the nature of the situation on the ground, cannot be regarded as a pure Asian concern. UNSC Resolutions 1912 (2010), 1867 (2009), 1802 (2008), 1745 (2007) (among others) on Timor Leste are resolutions extending a peace building mandate, staying strictly within the limits of Chapter VI of the UN Charter. UNSC Resolution 1928 (2010) on North Korea addresses the issue of non-proliferation specifically with regard to the Democratic Republic of Korea (North Korea). This resolution is issued under Chapter VII, in line with UNSC Resolutions 825 (1993), 1540 (2004), 1695 (2006), 1718 (2006), 1874 (2009) and 1887 (2009), as well as the statements of the President of the UNSC of 6 October 2006 (S/PRST/2006/41) and 13 April 2009 (S/PRST/2009/7), which recognise that proliferation of nuclear, chemical and biological weapons, as well as their means of delivery, continue to constitute a threat to international peace and security.

In the India-Pakistan conflict, UNMOGIP is a UN peacekeeping operation that has lasted for decades. It is a ceasefire observation mission since 1949.[27] The contributions to the operation come from Chile, Croatia, Finland, Italy, the Philippines, the Republic of Korea, Sweden and Uruguay. The operation comprises only 42 military personnel and around 60 civilian personnel, most of whom are local.[28] The current UN operation in Timor-Leste – United Nations Integrated Mission in Timor-Leste (UNMIT), active

---

25 UN Press Release, SG/2167, 1 November 2010.
26 For example, on his visits to Vietnam, Tajikistan and Mongolia: 'Development, co-operation and security the focus of Ban's talks with Asian leaders', UN News Centre, 21 September 2010. Available at <http://www.un.org/apps/news/story.asp?NewsID=36028&Cr=mdgs&Cr1=> (accessed 25 March 2013).
27 'Observing the Ceasefire in Jammu and Kashmir', UNMOGIP website. Available at <http://www.un.org/en/peacekeeping/missions/unmogip/> (accessed 25 March 2013).
28 'UNMOGIP Facts and Figures', UNMOGIP website. Available at <http://www.un.org/en/peacekeeping/missions/unmogip/facts.shtml> (accessed 25 March 2013).

since 2006 – is the latest in a series of UN operations since 1999.[29] The operation consists mainly of police personnel (approximately 1,500) with contributions from countries from all regions of the world.[30]

The operation in Afghanistan is also classified as falling geographically within the Asia-Pacific region by the Department of Peacekeeping Operations (DPKO).[31] The UN Assistance Mission in Afghanistan works parallel to that of NATO. The mission is political, not military, and 80 per cent of the personnel are Afghan.[32] Thus, one can observe, that the international operations in Asia are not established in co-operation between regional organisations and the UN, but only under direct supervision of the UN, involving State-participation from all over the world. This practice evidences the absence of a regional collective security mechanism. In addition, as opposed to other regions, most UNSC resolutions are issued under Chapter VI of the UN Charter, which corresponds to the regional pacifistic approach of the maintenance of peace and security.

On the other hand, the internal conflicts in Sri Lanka, Myanmar and Thailand have not seen international involvement. The situation in Myanmar has gained a special media interest, and the political interest of the wider international community, but international involvement in the resolution of the situation has been first declined by ASEAN, of which Myanmar is a member, and subsequently halted at the UNSC by the threat of a Chinese veto.[33] The situation with North Korea keeps both the region and the whole international society alert, due to North Korea's aggressive policy and nuclear weapons. Diplomatic efforts have taken place, not least through the long-term six-party talks, with the participation of North Korea, South Korea, China, Russia, the USA and Japan. The conflict escalation poses a great risk to the region and is, no doubt, of great interest to international community as a whole.

Association of Southeast Asian Nations

General description

ASEAN was established in 1967, and comprises ten States.[34] ASEAN attained a new legal framework and a legal personality in 2008 with the

---

29 'UNMOGIP Facts and Figures', ibid.
30 'UNMOGIP Facts and Figures', ibid.
31 'Current peacekeeping Operations', UN Peacekeeping. Available at <http://www.un.org/en/peacekeeping/operations/current.shtml> (accessed 25 March 2013).
32 'FAQs', UNAMA website. Available at <http://unama.unmissions.org/Default.aspx?tabid=1748> (accessed 25 March 2013).
33 The last attempt to pass a UNSC resolution was made in 2007 by the USA and the UK, the draft being vetoed by China and Russia. Available at <http://www.un.org/apps/news/story.asp?NewsID=21228&Cr=myanmar&Cr1> (accessed 25 March 2013).
34 Indonesia, Malaysia, Philippines, Singapore, Thailand, Brunei Darussalam, Viet Nam, Lao PDR, Myanmar and Cambodia.

new Charter.[35] All preceding ASEAN documents, as stated in Article 52 of the ASEAN Charter, continue to be valid.

ASEAN is mainly a social and economic co-operation forum. Even though peace and stability is listed as one of the main aims and purposes in the ASEAN Declaration[36] and the Charter, the interpretation of peace and security differs greatly from other regions. The fundamental principles of ASEAN for co-operation are enshrined in the Treaty of Amity and Cooperation in Southeast Asia of 1976:[37]

- Mutual respect for the independence, sovereignty, equality, territorial integrity, and national identity of all nations;
- The right of every State to lead its national existence free from external interference, subversion or coercion;
- Non-interference in the internal affairs of one another;
- Settlement of differences or disputes by peaceful manner;
- Renunciation of the threat or use of force; and
- Effective co-operation among themselves.

The same principles derive from the UN Charter and the Declaration on Principles of International Law Concerning Friendly Relations and Cooperation among States in Accordance with the Charter of the UN.[38] Nevertheless, they have not prevented other regions from developing collective security mechanisms (and even the right to regional intervention). ASEAN has stayed true to these principles in their classical interpretation, and has not created a regional collective security mechanism which would imply any coercion or the use of military capabilities as such.

Already from the outset the principles of non-intervention and non-use of force were the basis of the anti-colonialist struggle in Asia.[39] In comparison, the African post-colonial approach was also anti-interventionist, until the international community failed to respond to humanitarian catastrophes in the beginning of the 1990s, such as Somalia and Rwanda. The permissibility of the use of force, however, is inherently higher in Africa than in Asia.

The general approach of ASEAN members is regionalist, i.e. supporting regional autonomy. To avoid out-of-region influence, ASEAN was

---

35 Charter of the Association of Southeast Nations, 20 November 2007, Singapore. Available at <http://www.asean.org/asean/asean-charter/asean-charter> (accessed 25 March 2013).
36 The ASEAN Declaration (Bangkok Declaration), 8 August 1967, Bangkok. Available at <http://www.aseansec.org/1212.htm> (accessed 25 March 2013).
37 Treaty of Amity and Cooperation in Southeast Asia, 24 February 1976, Denpasar, Bali, Indonesia. Available at <http://www.asean.org/news/item/treaty-of-amity-and-cooperation-in-southeast-asia-indonesia-24-february-1976-3> (accessed 25 March 2013).
38 GA 2625(XXV).
39 Acharya, op. cit., n. 15, p. 54.

intentionally created not to be a military pact like the Southeast Asian Treaty Organization (SEATO)[40] or the Central Treaty Organization (CENTO)[41] led by great powers and constituting a form of intervention in the affairs of their members.[42] ASEAN was formed as a rejection of such military pacts, which meant also the unwillingness to participate in multilateral defence co-operation within a regional grouping. A reason for ASEAN not to include military co-operation was also in order not to be perceived as a Western ally in the Cold War,[43] and the principle of non-interference was applied also to protect these States from communist subvergence.[44] The alternative, the ASEAN way, was instead to create co-operation based on consultations and consensus, something said to be unique in the cultural heritage of Southeast Asia.[45]

The legal basis

The institutionalised framework of the ASEAN regional co-operation in the maintenance of peace and security is new, and parts of it are still at the project stage. In 1997, the ASEAN Heads of States and Governments, at their Summit in Kuala Lumpur 'envisioned a concert of Southeast Asian nations, outward looking, living in peace, stability and prosperity, bonded together in partnership of dynamic development and in a community of caring societies'.[46] This was the initiative that led to the first developments in the enhancement of security co-operation within the framework of ASEAN – the ASEAN Vision 2020.

At the ninth ASEAN Summit in 2003, to concretise the ASEAN Vision 2020, the ASEAN Leaders resolved that an ASEAN Community shall be established by 2020.[47] The ASEAN Community would consist of three pillars, namely the ASEAN Political-Security Community (APSC), the ASEAN Economic Community (AEC) and the ASEAN Socio-Cultural Community (ASCC).[48] At the twelfth ASEAN Summit in January 2007, the Leaders

---

40 Established in 1954, dissolved in 1977. Members: Australia, France, New Zealand, Thailand, Pakistan, Philippines, the USA and the UK.
41 Established in 1955, dissolved in 1979. Members: Iran, Pakistan, Turkey, the USA and the UK.
42 Acharya, op. cit., n. 15, p. 54.
43 Ibid, p. 55.
44 Ibid, p. 71.
45 Ibid, p. 55.
46 ASEAN Political-Security Community Blueprint, Jakarta, ASEAN Secretariat, June 2009, p. 1. Available at <http://www.asean.org/archive/5187-18.pdf> (accessed 25 March 2013).
47 'About ASEAN, Overview', ASEAN website. Available at <http://www.asean.org/asean/about-asean/overview> (accessed 25 March 2013).
48 ASEAN Political-Security Community Blueprint.

signed the Cebu Declaration on the Acceleration of the Establishment of an ASEAN Community by 2015.[49] The Blueprint for the Political-Security Community[50] is the newest document that gives an insight into the likely principles relevant in the future for the maintenance of peace and security in ASEAN. In addition, the documents that allow analysing the ASEAN approach to international law are: the ASEAN Declaration[51] and the Treaty of Amity and Cooperation in Southeast Asia[52] and the ASEAN Charter.[53]

Alongside the creation of an ASEAN Community with a political-security pillar, in 2006 an ASEAN defence ministers meeting was established as the highest defence mechanism within ASEAN.[54] The ministers meet annually and exchange views on current defence and security issues. The aim of this forum is to enhance trust-building, openness and transparency. Examples of the work of the ministers' meetings, among others, are the drafting of a Concept paper on Humanitarian Assistance and Disaster Relief, and a concept paper ADMM Plus: Principles for Membership.[55] All issues are on fully peaceful matters.[56] The main focus of the ministers meeting appears to be response to non-traditional threats. There is no mention of use of force, and the use of the military is mentioned only with regard to disaster relief.[57]

As distinct as the general security co-operation in Asia is from other regions, it can be observed that ASEAN has been influenced by the general trend of regional organisations – connecting economic development and security issues. Moreover, the three-pillar model appears to copy that of the EU. The Common Foreign and Security Policy (CFSP) of the EU is reflected in the Political-Security Community of ASEAN. However, the fact that the form is adapted does not imply that the content is adapted in the same way. The blueprint of the Political-Security Community sets out to promote political development in adherence to democracy and human rights and fundamental rights and rule of law,[58] which is a new, more Western-influenced development in the Asian region. On the other hand, the document intends to achieve the results with only very general co-operation activities, such as the creation of targeted academic programmes and networking among schools.[59]

---

49 'About ASEAN, Overview', above, n. 47.
50 ASEAN Political-Security Community Blueprint.
51 The ASEAN Declaration.
52 Treaty of Amity and Cooperation in Southeast Asia.
53 Charter of the Association of Southeast Nations.
54 'ASEAN Defence Ministers Meeting (ADMM)', ASEAN website. Available at <http://www.asean.org/communities/asean-political-security-community/category/asean-defence-ministers-meeting-admm> (accessed 25 March 2013).
55 'ASEAN Defence Ministers Meeting (ADMM)', ibid.
56 'ASEAN Defence Ministers Meeting (ADMM)', ibid.
57 'ASEAN Defence Ministers Meeting (ADMM)', ibid.
58 ASEAN Political-Security Community Blueprint, p. 2.
59 ASEAN Political-Security Community Blueprint, ibid., p. 7 (on promotion of peace and stability in particular).

It must, however, be noted that the creation of a regional human rights mechanism is also named as a future aim.[60] The blueprint repeats the prohibition of the use of force, and limits the actions of the organisation to preventive diplomacy and confidence building, as well as post-conflict peace building. It reads:

> In building a cohesive, peaceful and resilient Political Security Community, ASEAN subscribes to the principle of comprehensive security, which goes beyond the requirements of traditional security but also takes into account non-traditional aspects vital to regional and national resilience, such as the economic, socio-cultural, and environmental dimensions of development. ASEAN is also committed to conflict prevention/confidence building measures, preventive diplomacy, and post-conflict peace building.[61]

The model for co-operation is thus comprehensive security, which means treating security issues with economic and socio-cultural measures, rather than military. In order to deal with traditional threats, the blueprint suggests carrying out technical co-operation with the UN and relevant regional organisations and establishing networks between peacekeeping centres of ASEAN Member States in conducting joint planning and training.[62] More significantly, the emphasis in the blueprint is put on co-operation in combating non-traditional threats.[63] This enhances co-operation in combating transnational crime (e.g. human trafficking, smuggling of people, drug-trafficking, terrorism, illicit trade of arms, cyber crimes, piracy, smuggling, document forgery) in both legislative and practical activities. In sum, ASEAN, more than organisations in other regions, distinguishes between the means to combat traditional and non-traditional threats. The ASEAN Security Community Plan of Action also summarises the general ASEAN approach to regional co-operation, restricting regional action to peaceful settlement of disputes.[64]

The Blueprint is developed in line with the ASEAN Charter that entered into force on 15 December 2008 as the new legal framework of ASEAN. The Charter brings a new era to the ASEAN co-operation and already enhances most of the principles of the ASEAN Vision 2015. The purposes of the organisation laid down in the Charter are, among others, to maintain and enhance peace, security and stability in the region and enhance greater

---

60 ASEAN Political-Security Community Blueprint, ibid., p. 5, A.1.5 and para. 15.
61 ASEAN Political-Security Community Blueprint, ibid., p. 8, para. B. 17.
62 ASEAN Political-Security Community Blueprint, ibid., p. 13, B.2.3.
63 ASEAN Political-Security Community Blueprint, ibid., pp. 14–16.
64 'ASEAN Security Community Plan of Action', ASEAN website. Available at <http://www.asean.org/news/item/asean-security-community-plan-of-action> (accessed 25 March 2013).

political, security, economic and social co-operation. The Charter also provides for creating a single market, promoting democracy and sustainable development. Thus, even though the pillar system is still under development, the co-operation has in fact already, at least on paper, taken shape of that corresponding to the EU. In Article 2(2), all the traditional ASEAN principles are extensively listed, including the non-use of force and non-intervention in internal matters. However, they are followed by adherence to the rule of law, democracy and respect for human rights, which are a new addition to ASEAN principles for co-operation. The Charter provides for establishing a human rights body. Chapter VIII of the Charter is dedicated to dispute-settlement and provides exclusively for the peaceful settlement of disputes through diplomatic talks (dialogue, consultation, negotiation). There are no provisions that would regard military crisis management, peacekeeping or any other kind of use of military assets for peaceful purposes as means of peaceful settlement of disputes. The Charter does not elaborate on Chapter VIII of the UN Charter status of the ASEAN, but rather peculiarly states in Article 45 that ASEAN may seek an appropriate status with the UN system, as well as with other subregional, regional, international organisations and institutions.

Decision-making

Even though ASEAN is a co-operative and not collective security forum, not binding the members to take collective action, a decision-making mechanism is provided for in Chapter VII of the ASEAN Charter. The basic principle for decision-making is consultation and consensus. Even when a consensus cannot be reached, the decision on how to handle the issue further is to be made by the ASEAN summit based on consensus. Article 20 of the Charter also provides that in the case of a serious breach of the Charter or non-compliance, the matter will be referred to the ASEAN summit for decision. Moreover, Article 22 of the Charter provides dialogue, consultation and negotiation as means for peaceful settlement of disputes. Nevertheless, specific dispute settlement mechanisms are to be established by ASEAN. Member States in a dispute may agree to resort to good offices, conciliation or mediation and may request the Chairman of ASEAN or Secretary-General of ASEAN to provide good offices, conciliation or mediation.

The ASEAN summit is named as the highest dispute-settlement authority in Article 26. If disputes are unresolved by the means mentioned above, the dispute is to be referred to the ASEAN summit for decision. The long sequence for the settlement of disputes and control of compliance contains only peaceful, non-coercive means. At no point may force – not only military, but pressure of any kind (political, economic) – be used. Moreover, handling internal conflicts in ASEAN Member States is not within the competence of ASEAN dispute settlement mechanisms.

The practice

While intrastate conflicts in the ASEAN region have been a regular occurrence,[65] the Member States believe that the non-interference policy has prevented the occurrence of military conflicts between any two Member States since 1967 (the establishment of ASEAN).[66] Thus, ASEAN did not interfere in Cambodia in 1975–78,[67] neither did it intervene in the 1986 revolution in the Philippines, nor the Thai conflict in 1992, nor did it object to the admission of the communistic Vietnam in 1995, or the junta-led Burma (Myanmar) in 1997.[68] The principle of non-intervention remained unaltered during the course of the nineties. More recently, ASEAN has refused to intervene and promote a peaceful settlement to the decades-long re-escalated conflict between Cambodia and Thailand regarding the *Preah Vihear* temple,[69] and to take action regarding the political situation in Myanmar.[70]

During the nineties a few bilateral and trilateral military exercises took place,[71] which inspired Malaysia to establish the Malaysian Peacekeeping Training Centre, inaugurated in 2006.[72] This, however, was a unilateral, not a common ASEAN initiative, aimed at training peacekeepers for UN operations.[73]

In 1999 violence broke out after the referendum on the independence of Timor Leste from Indonesia. ASEAN was reluctant to collectively intervene in the Timor Leste crisis, and only some of the ASEAN members participated in the international UN authorised force.[74] The crisis in Timor Leste did lead to institutional developments in the ASEAN structure The ASEAN Troika was established to enable ASEAN to address in a timely manner urgent and important regional political and security issues and situations of common

---

65 For example, Myanmar, Vietnam, Thailand, Indonesia.
66 Acharya, op. cit., n. 15, p. 70, with a reference to Singapore's Foreign Minister.
67 Cambodia was not a member of ASEAN at that time.
68 Acharya, op. cit., n. 15, pp. 72–3.
69 M. Vatikiotis, 'Thailand and Cambodia: Time for ASEAN to Act', *Asia Security Initiative. McArthur Foundation*, 25 January 2010. Available at <http://asiasecurity.macfound.org/blog/entry/353/> (accessed 25 March 2013).
70 J. Aglionby, 'ASEAN gets through with Burmese junta', *The Guardian*, 21 July 2006. Available at <http://www.guardian.co.uk/world/2006/jul/21/burma.johnaglionby> (accessed 26 March 2013).
71 H. McCoubrey and J. Morris, *Regional Peacekeeping in the Post-Cold War Era*, The Hague: Kluwer Law International, 2000, p. 162.
72 Malaysian Peacekeeping Training Centre website. Available at <http://www.mafhq.mil.my/plpm/index.html> (accessed 25 March 2013).
73 Malaysian Peacekeeping Training Centre website, ibid.
74 J. Haacke, 'Regional Security Institutions: ASEAN, ARF, SCO and KEDO', in S. Hoadley and J. Rüland (eds), *Asian Security Reassessed*, Singapore: Institute of South Asian Studies, 2006, p. 132.

concern likely to disturb regional peace and harmony. The mechanism, however, has never come to be used in practice. It was also not used when in 2000 UN Secretary-General Kofi Annan suggested ASEAN to look into the apparent mistreatment of Aug San Suu Kyi in Myanmar.[75] In the continuation of the situation in Myanmar during the twenty-first century, and the civil unrest in Thailand in 2008, ASEAN has maintained the policy of non-interference. In 2006, however, the ASEAN position was not as strict anymore, regarding non-intervention, as in the previous decades. In an interview to *The Guardian* the Foreign Minister of Malaysia, Syed Hamid Albar, said that ASEAN would not intervene in Burma (Myanmar) but would approve of UN action.[76] The attempts of the UNSC to resolve the Myanmar issue, however, failed due to the objections of China and Russia to pass a formal resolution.

In general, regional co-operation in the maintenance of peace and security in the ASEAN framework remains limited and conditioned by the principle of non-intervention, not influenced by the developments of pro-interventionism and 'responsibility to protect' in other regions. In general, ASEAN States rely on the USA for their security, rather than utilising the regional forum.[77] When military operations in Asia are launched, they are limited to peacekeeping and the UN framework, not the regional one, is utilised.

Co-operation with the United Nations

Even though ASEAN does not claim to be a Chapter VIII organisation, it is involved in co-operation with the UN on peace and security, and can be considered as a regional security organisation,[78] especially in today's functional understanding.

It is interesting that ASEAN does not regard itself as a Chapter VIII organisation because its action is allegedly on a lower scale than that of a Chapter VIII organisation, and not because it would exceed the limits of what is appropriate for regional action (as NATO). ASEAN arguably uses less coercion and has less coherence than could be expected of a regional organisation in the understanding of Chapter VIII of the UN Charter. Nevertheless, ASEAN has an Article 52 (Chapter VIII) dispute settlement mechanism, and has been treated by the UN as any other regional organisation summoned to assist the UN in the maintenance of peace and security.

---

75 Haacke, ibid., p. 132.
76 Aglionby, op. cit., n. 70.
77 Haacke, op. cit., n. 74, p. 135.
78 McCoubrey and Morris, op. cit., n. 71, p. 162.

In 2000, the UN Secretary-General called for strengthening the ASEAN-UN co-operation, including that in security matters.[79] Since then ASEAN and the UN have held three Summits.[80] In 2006, ASEAN received an observer status at the UN General Assembly,[81] and in 2007 the two organisations signed a Memorandum of Understanding on co-operation.[82] This memorandum briefly provides also for 'co-operation in the implementation of programmes that are geared towards the maintenance of peace and security'.[83] In his remarks the UN Secretary-General calls for the two organisations to co-operate more closely in preventive diplomacy, peacekeeping and peace building.[84]

On 30 October 2005 in Hanoi, ASEAN and the UN signed a Joint Declaration on Collaboration in Disaster Management, which requires of ASEAN to put into action the ASEAN agreement on Disaster Management and Emergency Response. This agreement entered into force in 2009.[85] Though the documents refer only to natural disasters, the implementation still requires capacity building, which in itself is a challenge to the working methods of the Asian regional co-operation mechanisms. Nevertheless, the co-operation with the UN can be a catalysing factor for the institutionalisation and creation of common ASEAN military capabilities used for peaceful purposes, which have been absent in the past. For now it seems there can still be no talk of any collective ASEAN military activity – neither peacekeeping nor enforcement, neither with, nor without a UN mandate.

Shanghai Cooperation Organisation

General description

The SCO was established on 15 June 2001 in Shanghai with the Declaration on the Creation of the Shanghai Cooperation Organisation. A year later, on 7 June 2002, in Saint-Petersburg, the Charter of the SCO was signed.

---

79 Kofi Annan, *Strengthening ASEAN – UN Partnership*, Remarks at the ASEAN-UN Summit, 12 February 2000, Bangkok. Available at <http://www.asean.org/resources/2012-02-10-08-47-56/leaders-view/item/strengthening-asean-united-nations-partnership-by-mr-kofi-annan> (accessed 25 March 2013).
80 UN Press Release, SG/SM/13212, 29 November 2010.
81 A/RES/61/44.
82 Memorandum of Understanding between the Association of the Southeast Asian Nations (ASEAN) and the UN (UN) on ASEAN-UN Cooperation, 27 September 2007, New York. Available at <http://www.aseansec.org/21918.pdf> (accessed 2 February 2012).
83 Memorandum of Understanding, ibid., Art. 1.
84 SG/SM/13212.
85 ASEAN Agreement on Disaster Management and Emergency Response, Vientiane, 26 July 2005. Available at <http://www.asean.org/news/item/asean-agreement-on-disaster-management-and-emergency-response-vientiane-26-july-2005-2> (accessed 26 March 2013).

The predecessor of the SCO is the Shanghai Five mechanism, founded in 1996. This co-operation framework was initially created for security purposes, especially border security and confidence-building, including mutual reduction of border forces between Russia and China.[86] In the framework of the Shanghai Five, several agreements on border security among the participating States were made.[87] With the establishment of SCO, the co-operation between the participating States was institutionalised, enhanced and extended to include not only security, but also wider social and economic issues. Thus, SCO is one more example in the long row of organisations approaching socio-economic and security co-operation as indivisible for the purposes of regional development. In this case, however, the security issues are the central ones, supplemented by social and economic co-operation.[88]

The SCO could geographically fall both within the Russian sphere of influence and the Asia security region. The Asian region for the placement of this organisation is chosen mainly due to China being both the initiator and the driving force of the organisation.[89] Even though the organisation has only six members – China, Russia, Kazakhstan, Kyrgyzstan, Tajikistan and Uzbekistan – two of its members are great powers and Permanent Members of the UNSC. Moreover, the SCO Member States, having a territory in excess of 30 million square kilometres occupy three-fifths of the Eurasian continent, and having a population of 1.5 billion people make up almost a quarter of the population on Earth.[90] This makes the SCO a 'heavyweight' player both internationally and regionally, even though it is still in the process of development.

A regional organisation with the involvement of China is a new development. There were no regional organisations in Asia before the establishment of the UN, and regional co-operation was weak throughout the Cold War years. Until the 1990s, China was an opponent of multilateralism in general,

---

86 J. Wang. 'China and SCO: Towards a New Type of Interstate Relations', in G. Wu, and H. Landsdowne (eds), *China Turns to Multilateralism. Foreign Policy and Regional Security*, London and New York, NY: Routledge, 2008, p. 104.
87 Such as the Agreement between the People's Republic of China, the Republic of Kazakhstan, the Kyrgyz Republic, the Russian Federation and the Republic of Tajikistan on Strengthening Confidence in the Military Field in the Border Area of 26 April, 1996, and the Agreement between the People's Republic of China, the Republic of Kazakhstan, the Kyrgyz Republic, the Russian Federation and the Republic of Tajikistan on Mutual Reductions of Armed Forces in the Border Area of 24 April, 1997.
88 Wang, op. cit., n. 86, p. 106.
89 T. Kivimäki, 'Security in Southeast Asia', in T. Kivimäki and J. Delman (eds), *War and Security in Asia: Changing Regional Security Structure. How the European Union can support interstate peace*, Copenhagen: Nordic Institute of Asian Studies, 2006, p. 130; Also, Wang, op. cit., n. 86, p. 105.
90 'Brief Introduction to Shanghai Cooperation Organisation', SCO website. Available at <http://www.sectsco.org/EN123/brief.asp> (accessed 26 March 2013).

and used bilateralism in its international relations instead. The reason for that is said to have been China's fear of becoming trapped in institutions not of its own making.[91] The Shanghai Five[92] was an expression of China's new policy for regional co-operation in the maintenance of peace and security, now transformed into the SCO.

The legal basis

The Charter of the SCO[93] lays down the main rules for the co-operation in the organisation. In the Preamble of the Charter adherence to the UN Charter goals and principles is reaffirmed along with commonly acknowledged principles of international law. The principles listed are particularly those related to the maintenance of international peace and security, and the development of good neighbourly and friendly relations and co-operation between the States. They reflect the Five Principles of Peaceful Coexistence promoted by China in its foreign policy.[94] The principles above, which are already rather detailed in the Charter itself, are reconfirmed in even more detail in the 2007 Treaty on Long-Term Good-Neighborliness, Friendship and Cooperation Between the Member States of the SCO,[95] noting the need to jointly combat today's threats to peace and security.

It is evident from Article 1 ('Goals and Tasks') and Article 3 ('Areas of Co-operation'), that the main purpose of co-operation is security. The economic co-operation was, in fact, secondary to China, but was included in the framework of the SCO due to the request of the four smaller Member States.[96] Among the tasks of the SCO in Article 1, protection of human rights, conflict prevention and peaceful settlement of disputes are also listed. With the establishment of the SCO, the focus of the Shanghai Five on traditional security has shifted to non-traditional threats, the 'three evils' – terrorism, separatism and extremism.[97] Yet, the means of combating them remain traditional for the SCO.

All-in-all the provisions on the measures to take in the maintenance of peace and security are very general and brief, mainly restricted to listing of

---

91 Kivimäki, op. cit., n. 89, p. 124.
92 The Shanghai Five consisted of all present SCO Member States except for Uzbekistan.
93 Charter of the Shanghai Cooperation Organisation, 7 June 2002, Saint-Petersburg. Available at <http://www.sectsco.org/EN123/show.asp?id=69> (accessed 26 March 2013).
94 China's Position Paper on the New Security Concept, 31 July 2002, Ministry of Foreign Affairs of the People's Republic of China. Available at <http://www.mfa.gov.cn/eng/wjb/zzjg/gjs/gjzzyhy/2612/2614/t15319.htm> (accessed 25 March 2013).
95 Treaty on Long-Term Good-Neighborliness, Friendship and Cooperation Between the Member States of the Shanghai Cooperation Organisation, Bishkek, 16 August 2007. Available at <http://www.sectsco.org/EN/show.asp?id=71> (accessed 26 March 2013).
96 Wang, op. cit., n. 86, p. 119.
97 Ibid.

the general principles applicable. Only the 15 June 2006 Joint Communiqué of Meeting of the Council of the Heads of the Member States of the SCO[98] calls for 'formulating a mechanism for the Organization to adopt measures in response to developments that threaten regional peace, stability and security', and notes 'that the heads of state believed that the SCO Secretariat should draft the relevant agreement as soon as possible, to ensure that all measures under the mechanism are law-based'. No information on the actual creation of such a document specifying the SCO mechanism for the maintenance of peace and security is made publicly available by the SCO.[99] There are no documents available specifying what is appropriate for regional action by SCO, and what specific co-operation measures may be taken, apart from the anti-terrorism military exercises which have become the annual practice of the organisation.

There are no provisions for peacekeeping or peace enforcement in the SCO Charter. However, the joint military anti-terrorism exercises held by SCO indicate that collective use of force by the SCO is not absolutely unthinkable. The intended targets are not States (thus the intervention would not be against the political integrity and independence of a State), but the 'three evils' – terrorism, separatism and extremism. The procedure of how operations against the 'three evils' would be decided upon and launched is not specified in the SCO legal basis.

Even though the legal regulation of the security and defence measures in SCO is very brief and symbolic, rather than practically implementable, the existence of the organisation in itself is a significant development in the regionalisation of the maintenance of peace and security. Most importantly, a regional organisation in the maintenance of peace and security has come about in Asia, including China. This evidences a trend towards regionalisation that was formerly missing in the maintenance of peace and security in this area of the world.

Decision-making

The structure of the SCO consists of the Council of Heads of States, the Council of Heads of Governments, the Council of Foreign Ministers, meetings of heads of ministries and/or agencies, the Council of National Coordinators, the Regional Counter-Terrorist Structure and the Secretariat.

The Council of the Heads of State is the supreme SCO body. It holds meetings once a year and makes decisions on the most fundamental issues of

---

98 Joint Communiqué of Meeting of the Council of the Heads of the Member States of the Shanghai Cooperation Organisation, 15 June 2006. Available at <http://www.sectsco.org/EN/show.asp?id=95> (accessed 26 March 2013).
99 See the listings of SCO documents by year on the SCO website. Available at <http://www.sectsco.org/EN123/index.asp#> (accessed 25 March 2013).

the organisation. According to Article 16 there is no voting, and decisions are made by consensus. If a Member State does not agree on certain aspects of a decision that does not change a decision in whole, its opinion is placed on the record. There is also the possibility of a State or States opting out, if they do not wish to be involved in a certain project. Thus, in fact, if there are four States opting out, decisions and subsequent action can also be taken by two Member States, thus, in essence – bilaterally. The Charter does not provide specifically for how the regional organisation would decide on the use of force, the possibility of which is supported by the regular common military exercises.

The practice

The little practice of the SCO that there is relates mainly to exercises in combating non-traditional threats and, to a much lesser extent, operations in the field. The SCO Member States have expressed their will to contribute forces to peacekeeping operations, but on an individual basis, not as SCO forces,[100] which is the same as in the case of ASEAN. The SCO is said to have the intention to remain non-military,[101] as opposed to the CSTO.[102] At the same time, the SCO organises military exercises, which does not correspond with the scope of activities of a non-military organisation. If the SCO claims the right to use force against terrorism, extremism and separatism, it can in practice also mean that the SCO would maintain the right to intervene in an internal conflict – civil unrest – on the side of a Member State's government. Thus, SCO action could, in theory, contain intervention with enforcement elements upon invitation within the region. In this way, the SCO differs from ASEAN by the extent to which it applies the principle of non-intervention, and the non-military nature of the SCO is, in fact, contestable.

The SCO does not have a practice of regional operations. The only active SCO project is the SCO-Afghanistan Contact Group which works through consultations to combat drug-trafficking, cross-border crime and weapons smuggling.[103] When violence broke out in Kyrgyzstan in April 2010, the SCO did not react. To that point, the UN Secretary-General urged the SCO to contribute to the security and stability of Kyrgyzstan.[104] Subsequently, also

---

100 P. Guang, 'New Developments in the Shanghai Cooperation Organisation', CACI Forum, Central Asia – Caucasus Institute, Silk Road Studies Program, 22 May 2008. Available at <http://www.silkroadstudies.org/new/inside/forum/CACI_2008_0522.html> (accessed 26 March 2013).
101 Xinhua news agency, 'SCO military co-operation mainly aimed at terrorism', *China Daily*, 23 November 2010. Available at <http://www.chinadaily.com.cn/world/2010-11/23/content_11598151.htm> (accessed 26 March 2013).
102 Guang, above, n. 100.
103 Protocol on Establishment of SCO-Afghanistan contact group between SCO and Islamic Republic of Afghanistan, 4 November 2005. Available at <http://www.sectsco.org/en/show.asp?id=70> (accessed 26 March 2013).
104 UN Press Release, SG/SM/12953, 28 September 2009.

China is said to have shown the will to enhance security co-operation in such situations.[105]

The only application of military capacities by the SCO so far has been the multilateral military exercises. The military exercises evidence that SCO Member States, as opposed to ASEAN, have military capabilities made available for co-operation in the sphere of regional maintenance of peace and security. Regular common military exercises have been carried out throughout the decade of existence of the SCO (in 2003, 2005, 2007, 2009, 2010, 2011). For example, 'Peace Mission 2010' was a 16-day exercise with the participation of 5,000 troops from five Member States. Uzbekistan did not participate. The press release by the SCO on the exercise, however, mentioned riots in Uzbekistan in 2005 as an example of threats to be combated by the SCO.[106] The size of the exercises illustrates how different are the military capabilities of different regions. For the SCO this was merely an annual exercise. In comparison, the AU could hardly gather the same 5,000 troops for the challenging peacekeeping operation in Somalia.

When considering whether a regional right to humanitarian intervention ought to be permitted as a general rule, one needs to apply the scenario to each regional organisation within the context of its composition and capabilities. Whereas African regional capabilities are small, and do not pose a danger outside the region, the SCO combines two great powers and Permanent Members of the UNSC – Russia and China – and the application of a right to unilateral regional humanitarian intervention could have a much greater impact. The limitations of international law on regional humanitarian intervention, however, are not relevant to the way issues are tackled in this mainly Asian organisation. Both China and Russia have historically subjected the surrounding territories to their sovereignty. Russia still has a direct sphere of influence and both Russia and China have incorporated many smaller nations in their territory. Conflicts within these areas of Russia and China – either caused by religious disputes, territorial or self-determination matters – would be regarded as internal matters of each State.

Co-operation with the United Nations

The SCO has been increasingly co-operating with the UN. The SCO has had observer status at the UN General Assembly since 2004.[107] Not only is

---

105 D. Erkomaishvili, 'China's Shanghai Cooperation Organisation Initiative', *Central European Journal of International and Security Studies*, E-contributions, 14 February 2011. Available at <http://www.cejiss.org/econtributions/chinas-shanghai-cooperation-organisation-initiative> (accessed 26 March 2013).
106 Xinhua news agency, 'Peace Mission 2010 concludes, opens a new page for SCO cooperation', *People's Daily Online*, 25 September 2010. Available at <http://english.people.com.cn/90001/90777/90856/7150222.html> (accessed 26 March 2013).
107 A/RES/59/48.

the SCO one of the organisations invited by the UN to the events targeted at enhancing co-operation with regional organisations, that can be interpreted as a recognition of the status under Chapter VIII of the UN Charter. The SCO has also signed a Joint Declaration on Cooperation between the Secretariats of the UN and the SCO in Tashkent in April 2010, which is another means by which the UN can be presumed to tacitly confirm the functional Chapter VIII status of a regional organisation. A Memorandum of Understanding between the SCO and the UN Office on Drugs and Crime was also signed on 15 June 2011.[108] UN-SCO co-operation is, for now, only in the form of talks with the prospects of enhancing practical co-operation in the future.

Summary

Even though ASEAN and the SCO are very different organisations, the basic principle is common for them: strict compliance with the principle of non-intervention. The non-intervention clause enhances even peaceful settlement of disputes by diplomatic means, which cannot be imposed on any State without its request. This approach is rooted in the region's ancient cultural and religious background.

The Asian regional organisations do not have forces made available to the organisations for the maintenance of peace and security. There is no common military force: no regional peacekeeping force, no regional peace enforcement activity with a UN mandate, no regional standby arrangement, and no collective self-defence agreement. All use of force, including the participation of Asian States in peacekeeping operations takes place only on an individual State basis directly under the umbrella of the UN. The only appropriate regional action is regarded to be consultations, diplomatic talks, negotiations – as long as they do not interfere with the matters of a State without its consent. In this context of non-interventionism, regional unilateral humanitarian intervention would also not be accepted. In Asia, the right to unilateral regional humanitarian intervention has, in fact, been seen as an illegitimate imposition of Western interests. On the other hand, the Asian regional organisations fall short of restraining the internal use of force by their Member States. The States in the region are more likely to use force internally, such action not being regarded by them, and the region in general, as a matter of international law.

Notwithstanding the general non-intervention policy, since the end of the 1990s the Asian region has experienced increasing regionalisation in dealing with the matters of peace and security – both in ASEAN and the SCO.

---

108 'UN agency signs accord with Asian countries fighting drugs and crime', *UN News Centre*, 15 June 2011. Available at <http://www.un.org/apps/news/story.asp?NewsID=38726&Cr=unodc&Cr1=> (accessed 26 March 2013).

The global developments have increased both the human rights awareness and the regionalisation of the co-operation in the maintenance of peace and security.

A tendency in Asia exists to separate traditional threats (mainly interstate conflicts and intrastate conflicts in the form of civil wars) from non-traditional treats (terrorism, trans-border crime, etc.).[109] In the case of the latter, regional co-operation is more enhanced, and the use of force is not regarded as generally unacceptable, due to it not being directed against a Member State, but the specific non-State threat instead. This is especially evident from the common military anti-terrorism exercises of the SCO.

Even though Asian States have chosen non-interference as the guarantee for the peace and stability in the region and they do not interfere in either intrastate conflicts or interstate conflicts between two States of the region, this does not mean that conflicts do not exist. An example is the endless and recently escalating threat of North Korea. In addition, there is the decades-long dispute over the Kashmir region between India and Pakistan, and the internal conflicts in, for example, Sri Lanka, Bangladesh, Indonesia and Thailand. The region, as a whole, does not have one united, overarching forum to deal with regional conflicts. The case of UNSC passivity on the matter of Myanmar also gives an example of how a regional power can delimit its regional interests on the universal level, casting doubt onto the advantage of a universal mechanism for the maintenance of peace and security as a more legitimate one, compared to the regional.

The Asian region deals with the maintenance of peace and security in a way that is culturally acceptable. Whereas the African solution to African problems is pro-interventionism, the Asian solution to Asian problems is non-interventionism. In the case of Africa, one may question whether the regional way of dealing with the maintenance of peace and security does not exceed the limits of the prohibition of the use of force. In the case of Asia, the question may, on the contrary, be whether the region does not fall short of its responsibility to protect, even by peaceful means.

---

109 In comparison, terrorism, for example, in the case of Afghanistan was attributed to the State due to its failure to combat it: this is in line with the ICJ judgment in the case Concerning United States Diplomatic and Consular Staff in Tehran of 24 May 1980 (*ICJ Reports* 1980), where Iraq was also found responsible for not ensuring the protection of American diplomats against the rioters.

5 The Americas

Intervention without intervening

General description of the region

Though not the most active region in the matters of peace and security since the end of the Cold War, Latin America remains the cradle of regional maintenance of peace and security. The beginnings of regionalism in the Americas date back to 1826, when the Congress of Panama, summoned by Simón Bolivar took place.[1] In 1889 the framework for an extensive regional co-operation – the First International Conference of American States – was created, later to become the International Union of American Republics, then the Pan American Union, and finally transform into what is today the OAS. The existence of the American regional mechanisms is the reason why regional maintenance of peace and security, as well as the collective right to self-defence were included in the UN Charter in the first place.

The historical autonomy of the Americas developed for two reasons. First, it was due to the fight of the Latin American liberators, the most prominent of which is Simón Bolivar, against the influence of European States, especially Spain.[2] Second, at the same time, the Monroe doctrine was developed in the USA by president Monroe in 1823. The doctrine stipulates:

> [...] a principle in which the rights and interests of the United States are involved, that the American continents, by the free and independent condition which they have assumed and maintain, are henceforth not to be considered as subjects for future colonization by any European powers [...][3]

---

1 H. McCoubrey and J. Morris, *Regional Peacekeeping in the Post-Cold War Era*, The Hague: Kluwer Law International, 2000, p. 93.
2 McCoubrey and Morris, ibid.
3 Monroe Doctrine, 2 December 1823. Available at Yale Law School, Lilian Goldman Law Library, The Avalon Project: Documents in Law, History and Diplomacy. Available at <http://avalon.law.yale.edu/19th_century/monroe.asp> (accessed 25 March 2013).

Or in other words: matters of the Western Hemisphere are to be dealt with without the interference from Europe. Initially, the approach of keeping matters of peace and security regional was of mutual interest to both the Latin American States and the USA. During the next century and a half, however, the Monroe doctrine, applied by the USA, ensured it a nearly undisturbed hegemony in the region of the Americas; also, during the Cold War, marginalising the UN mechanism for the maintenance of peace and security.

In line with the strong American policy that follows the Monroe doctrine, the UN involvement in American, specifically Latin American/Caribbean, conflicts has been limited. In 2010, the UNSC issued three resolutions regarding the presence of UN peacekeeping forces in Haiti, acting under Chapter VII of the UN Charter. UNSC Resolution 1944 (2010) makes a reference to OAS and the Caribbean Community (CARICOM) as 'stakeholders' in the Haiti crisis, and the efforts of OAS in the process of peace-building are recognised. The tasks of the United Nations Stabilization Mission in Haiti (MINUSTAH) peacekeeping force once again depict the realities of the twenty-first century peacekeeping operations. They go beyond merely the 'protection of the civilian population', from a threat perspective characteristic to the Americas: MINUSTAH is mandated 'to assist the Government in tackling the risk of a resurgence in gang violence, organized crime, drug trafficking and trafficking of children'. Thus, the tasks of a UN peacekeeping operation reach into dealing with non-traditional threats.

Altogether the UN has dealt with three conflicts in the Americas since the end of the Cold War: peacekeeping operations in El Salvador (1989–95), Guatemala (1994–97), and most extensively, several subsequent military peacekeeping operations – in Haiti (since 1993[4]). The operation in Haiti is the only remaining Latin American issue dealt with by the UNSC.

Until the end of the Cold War, the appearance of American issues on the agenda of the UNSC was even rarer: the resolutions were limited to a number of six throughout the Cold War period. UNSC Resolution 330 (1973) 'On Peace and Security in South America' is a general resolution calling States to refrain from the use of any coercion in Latin America. UNSC Resolutions 156 (1964) and 203 (1965) deal with the situation in the Dominican Republic. UNSC Resolution 503 (1983) is on the Honduras-Nicaragua conflict, and the Falkland Islands (Malvinas) are dealt with in UNSC Resolutions 502 and 505 (1982). This is not to say that there have not been any other conflicts in the area. During the Cold War period Latin America was suffering from a long row of internal conflicts. The USA, just like in the case of China in Asia, has not been willing to allow the cases from the Western Hemisphere to be dealt with by the UNSC.[5] The OAS was not

---

4 The first resolution was imposing economic sanctions on Haiti S/RES/841(1993).
5 M. Hilaire, *International Law and the United States Military Intervention in the Western Hemisphere*, The Hague: Kluwer Law International, 1997, p. 140.

able to take the internal conflicts of the Member States under its control.⁶ The Americas have seen a wide number of unmandated unilateral interventions by the USA, restrained neither by the regional, nor universal mechanism of the maintenance of peace and security. Thus, the USA has a history of five Cold War interventions in Latin American States: Guatemala (1954), Cuba (1961), the Dominican Republic (1965), Grenada (1983) and Panama (1989). This is only the formal list, that does not contain other *de facto* interventions, as the 'Nicaragua' case evidences.⁷ The USA also used indirect coercion in Latin American civil wars to further its own interests, for example, by supporting rebels and supplying them with arms. In general, the justifications used by the USA in the cases of interventions have been: threats to US national security interests (Guatemala, Cuba and the Dominican Republic), protection of American citizens (the Dominican Republic, Grenada and Panama) and preserving democratic institutions (the Dominican Republic, Grenada, Panama).⁸ In the case of the intervention in Grenada the USA formally used the framework of the OECS and received condemnation by the Council of Ministers of the OAS.⁹

The core reason why the Latin American States are not fond of interventions (pro-democratic and humanitarian) is obvious: traditionally they have had a 'civilized' State intervene to settle their matters for more than a century, just as the Euro-Atlantic organisations intend to export their 'values' (the term used in the legal basis of both the EU and NATO). Such action has the potential of being abused in order to pursue a State's own regional interests. The antipathy of Latin American States towards intervention by such States can be explained by quoting this Theodore Roosevelt's speech from 1904:

> If a nation shows that it knows how to act with reasonable efficiency and decency in social and political matters; if it keeps order and pays its obligations, it need not fear no interference from the United States. Chronic wrongdoing or an impotence which results in a general loosening of the ties of the civilized society, may in America, as elsewhere, ultimately require intervention by some civilized nation, and in the Western Hemisphere the adherence of the United States to the Monroe doctrine may force the United States, however reluctantly, in flagrant cases of such wrong doing or impotence, to the exercise of an international police power ... It is a mere truism to say that every nation, whether in America or anywhere else, which desires to maintain its freedom,

---

6 Hilaire, ibid, p. 140.
7 Hilaire, ibid., p. 139; Case Concerning Military and Paramilitary Activities in and against Nicaragua (Merits), *ICJ Reports* 1986.
8 Hilaire, ibid, p. 127.
9 Hilaire, ibid, p. 76.

its independence, must ultimately realize that the right of such independence cannot be separated from the responsibility of making good use of it.[10]

This quote resonates with the century younger 'responsibility to protect' principle, applicable today. Having had the USA abuse its regional position in the name of a noble goal, the Latin American States are, nevertheless, understandably reluctant to legalise a right to unilateral regional intervention, be it on humanitarian or pro-democratic grounds. Yet, as opposed to Asia where no interference by the regional organisations in the internal matters of a Member State is permissible, in the Americas 'intervention without intervening', i.e. interference by diplomatic means, is practised by the regional organisations.

After the end of the Cold War the USA changed its policy. In the first post-Cold War intervention in the Americas – Haiti – the USA was not willing to take action without a prior UN authorisation. Hilaire explains this change by the loss of US interest to intervene in the absence of a serious threat to national security, and economic interests, as well as the relative post-Cold War easiness of acquiring a UNSC authorisation.[11] Nevertheless, US interventions in Grenada and the Dominican Republic, among others, have been a contributing factor for a re-creation of a separate South American regionalism. In 2008 the Union of South American Nations (UNASUR) was created for the co-operation of South American States and without the participation of the USA.

The new concept of OAS, contained in the Declaration of Security in the Americas of 2008 evidences that today's threats in the Americas are multidimensional,[12] not limited to traditional threats, like civil war or international conflict. Military coups are a specific traditional threat in Latin America, and therefore specific regional provisions have been made against them. The internal conflict in Colombia between the Marxist FARC (Revolutionary Armed Forces of Colombia) as a core insurgent force, and the opposing right-wing paramilitaries, has been plaguing the country since the 1960s.[13] Since the 1980s the internal political conflicts in Colombia have been

---

10 Roosevelt Corollary to the Monroe doctrine, in H. McCoubrey and J. Morris, *Regional Peacekeeping in the Post-Cold War Era*, The Hague: Kluwer Law International, 2000, p. 103, reference 19.
11 Roosevelt Corollary to the Monroe doctrine, ibid, p. 10.
12 Declaration on Security in the Americas, OEA/Ser.K/XXXVIII, Mexico City, 28 October 2003. Available at <http://www.oas.org/en/sms/docs/DECLARATION%20SECURITY%20AMERICAS%20REV%201%20-%2028%20OCT%202003%20CE00339.pdf> (accessed 26 March 2013).
13 'Q&A Colombia's Civil Conflict', *BBC News*, 23 December 2009. Available at <http://news.bbc.co.uk/2/hi/1738963.stm> (accessed 26 March 2013).

interrelated with the drug trade.[14] While North America (USA, Canada) has been dealing with terror threats far away from home in Afghanistan, in the shape of an enforcement operation, Latin America has been faced with a different type of threats. The threat to peace and security through drug-related crime in countries like Colombia and Mexico is of an extent that equals violent intrastate or even interstate conflict. In Mexico, for example, the 'drug war' has taken over 30,000 lives in the period between December 2006 and January 2011,[15] with 15,271 killed in 2010 alone,[16] 1,300 of these being children.[17] The reports of June 2011 bring the number of victims above 40,000.[18] The casualty toll from this asymmetric threat is greater than from any traditional interstate or intrastate military conflict in the region. In comparison, in Argentina's 'dirty war' 1976–83 the estimated number of killed ranges from 9,000 (the official figure) to 30,000,[19] and an estimated 3,197 people were killed during the 17 years of the Pinochet regime in Chile.[20] And again, in the politically and socially unstable Colombia, 26,000 people were killed in homicides in one year – 2001 – making it the most unsafe country in the world to live in.[21] Thus, one can see that the non-traditional post-Cold War threats in the Americas have even more devastating impact, at least as regards the death toll, than the traditional internal (mainly guerrilla warfare) and international conflicts of the Cold War period. The conflict in Colombia is in fact a conflict of mixed nature – it contains both elements of civil war (a rebellious armed group fighting against the government), which is a traditional threat, and organised crime, especially drug trafficking (a source of financing for the guerrillas), which is a non-traditional threat. One can further rhetorically ask how these situations compare to the threshold of a humanitarian intervention in traditional internal conflicts,

---

14 C. Krauss, 'Illicit Crop Cultivation and Drug Trafficking', *International Relations and Security Network*, Zurich, May 2008. Available at <http://www.isn.ethz.ch/isn/Current-Affairs/ISN-Insights/Detail?lng=en&ots627=fce62fe0-528d-4884-9cdf-283c282cf0b2&id=123022&tabid=123967&contextid734=123022&contextid735=123967> (accessed 26 March 2013).
15 'Mexico's Drug War: Number of Killed Passes 30,000', *BBC News*, 16 December 2010. Available at <http://www.bbc.co.uk/news/world-latin-america-12012425> (accessed 26 March 2013).
16 'Crunching Numbers in Mexico's Drug War', *BBC News*, 12 January 2011. Available at <http://www.bbc.co.uk/news/world-latin-america-12194138> (accessed 26 March 2013).
17 'Report: 1300 children killed in Mexico's drug war', *BNO News Wireupdate*, Mexico, 15 July 2011. Available at <http://wireupdate.com/wires/18801/report-1300-children-killed-in-mexicos-drug-war/> (accessed 26 March 2013).
18 'Report: 1300 children killed in Mexico's drug war', ibid.
19 L. DuBois, *The Politics of the Past in an Argentine Working-Class Neighbourhood*, Toronto: University of Toronto Press, 2008, p. 246.
20 'Pinochet's Chile', *The Washington Post Online*, 2000. Available at <http://www.washingtonpost.com/wp-srv/inatl/longterm/pinochet/overview.htm> (accessed 26 March 2013).
21 'Colombia's Mass Exodus', *BBC News*, 5 May 2001. Available at <http://news.bbc.co.uk/2/hi/programmes/from_our_own_correspondent/1314619.stm> (accessed 26 March 2013).

like that of Kosovo or Libya. Intervention in such non-traditional internal conflicts of today is outside the realm of international law, despite their scale and spill-over effects.

There is a row of regional and subregional organisations in the Americas: the Andean Community, the Amazon Cooperation Treaty Organization (ACTO), the Association of Caribbean States (ACS), CARICOM, the Central American Economic System (SICA), the Latin American Integration Association (ALADI), the Latin American Parliament, the OECS, the Southern Common Market (MERCOSUR). The organisations dealing with maintenance of peace and security are the OECS, UNASUR and the OAS itself. The OAS and UNASUR are further analysed in this chapter.

The OAS is the overall and most inclusive regional organisation in the Americas. It is one of the oldest regional organisations, and thus a significant source of practice in the regional maintenance of peace and security. UNASUR, on the other hand, is the newest organisation dealing with regional maintenance of peace and security in the world at the moment of writing. The organisation, established in 2008, illustrates what legal basis is created for a regional organisation of the twenty-first century, reflecting the law and practice accumulated in the region at the time of its establishment. One must, however, keep in mind that what may have developed as a regional rule may not be a universally accepted rule.

Organization of American States

General description

The First International Conference of American States of 1889–90 in which the International Union of American Republics for the prompt collection and distribution of commercial information was created, marks the beginnings of OAS.[22] In 1948, today's OAS was established. At its creation, the OAS had 21 members. Today, the OAS has 35 Member States,[23] including all South-, Central- and North American, and Caribbean States.

The problems of power balance in the Western Hemisphere are as old as the regionalism itself, and still present. After the end of the Cold War, the core problems in the OAS are described to be difficulties in consensus

---

22 'Organization of American States, Our history', OAS official website. Available at <http://www.oas.org/en/about/our_history.asp> (accessed 26 March 2013).
23 Antigua and Barbuda, Argentina, Barbados, Belize, Bolivia, Brazil, Canada, Chile, Costa Rica, Cuba (membership restored on 3 June 2009), Dominica (Commonwealth of), Dominican Republic, Ecuador, El Salvador, Grenada, Guatemala, Guyana, Haiti, Honduras (membership suspended on 5 July 2009), Jamaica, Mexico, Nicaragua, Panama, Paraguay, Peru, Saint Kitts and Nevis, Saint Lucia, Saint Vincent and the Grenadines, Suriname, The Bahamas (Commonwealth of), Trinidad and Tobago, the USA, Uruguay, Venezuela (Bolivarian Republic of).

building, the role of military force, issues of sovereignty, intervention, power disparities and the role of the USA.[24]

The OAS is one of those organisations that hold a strong position on the prohibition of the use of force and non-intervention. Since the end of the Cold War, the OAS has become active in dispute settlement by diplomatic negotiations – a practice that had been lacking throughout the Cold War years – with the USA strongly dominating the organisation. Reverting to military means for peacekeeping, or moreover, peace enforcement, purposes is excluded from the practice of the organisation. The basic documents of the organisation, however, are not simple: the prohibition of the use of force has been overridden in practice, as described below.

The fundamental document of the OAS is the Charter of the OAS of 30 April 1948. Other relevant documents include the American Treaty on Pacific Settlement of Disputes (Pact of Bogotá), also of 30 April 1948,[25] and the Inter-American Treaty on Reciprocal Assistance (Rio Treaty) of 2 September 1947.[26] During the Cold War years some amendments were made to the existing documents: to the Rio Treaty in 1975,[27] and to the Charter of the OAS in 1967 and 1985. More amendments to the Charter were made in 1992 and 1993, both pro-democratic in content.[28] After the end of the Cold War the co-operation in the maintenance of peace and security by the OAS expanded and grew more multifaceted. Thus, in 1995 the Declaration of Santiago on Confidence and Security Building Measures was signed.[29] In 1996, a Treaty establishing the Regional Security System was signed between five Caribbean Islands to establish a close security and defence co-operation, including military co-operation – a type of co-operation not common for the region as a whole. This Regional Security System model rather resembles that of CSTO within the CIS.

In 2003, a new Declaration on Security in the Americas was signed, introducing the concept of multidimensional security – a complex approach to the combination of traditional and non-traditional threats, with a focus on human security.[30] The same year the Santiago Declaration on Democracy and Public Trust was adopted to reaffirm the commitment of American States to

---

24 McCoubrey and Morris, op. cit., n. 1, p. 109.
25 American Treaty on Pacific Settlement of Disputes (Pact of Bogotá), 30 UNTS 55.
26 Inter-American Treaty on Reciprocal Assistance (Rio Treaty), 21 UNTS 77, Art. 1.
27 1975 Protocol of Amendments to the Inter-American Treaty of Reciprocal Assistance (Rio Treaty), 26 July 1975. Available at <http://www.state.gov/p/wha/rls/69869.htm> (accessed 26 March 2013).
28 *Regional Cooperation and Increasing the Peacekeeping Capacity of the U.N.: Role of the OAS*, International Civil mission in Haiti, p. 2. Available at <http://www.un.org/rights/micivih/rapports/arg.htm> (accessed 26 March 2013).
29 Declaration of Santiago on Confidence and Security Building Measures, Santiago, Chile, 10 November 1995. Available at <http://www.state.gov/p/wha/rls/70561.htm.> (accessed 26 March 2013).
30 Declaration on Security in the Americas, above, n. 12.

the promotion of democracy, albeit by peaceful means only.[31] The most relevant provisions of the abovementioned documents are analysed in order to establish the nuanced approach of the OAS on the use of force, and whether the turn of the centuries has introduced a wider support for a right to humanitarian intervention, regional use of force, and more regional autonomy in the maintenance of peace and security in general.

The legal basis

During the establishment of the UN, the regional co-operation system in the Americas was already in place. However, soon after the end of the Second World War the American regional system was significantly elaborated. Thus, the Inter-American Treaty of Reciprocal Assistance (Rio Treaty) signed in 1947, even before the official establishment of the OAS, is still one of its fundamental documents. The core provision of the Rio Treaty is that the contracting parties undertake in their international relations not to resort to the threat or the use of force in any manner inconsistent with the provisions of the UN Charter or the Treaty itself.[32] In case of a conflict between parties, the dispute is to be settled by consultation using peaceful means only.[33] These peaceful means of dispute settlement are regulated in detail in the Pact of Bogotá,[34] the peaceful settlement of disputes being fully voluntary and not subject to pressure from the organisation, similar to ASEAN or the League of Arab States. The post-Cold War developments, however, have amended the role of the OAS in the peaceful settlement of disputes, giving it not only a right, but a duty to intervene by peaceful means.

The other core provision of the Rio Treaty is the collective self-defence clause, in line with Article 51 of the UN Charter.[35] In 1975, the legal aim to amend the voting quorum in the Rio Treaty was set against the political background of lifting the OAS embargo imposed on Cuba, in which the USA was not interested.[36] The Treaty was amended with the 1975 Protocol of Amendment to the Inter-American Treaty of Reciprocal Assistance (Rio Treaty).[37] Thus, the amended treaty text now increased the

---

31 Declaration of Santiago on Democracy and Public Trust: A New Commitment to Good Governance for the Americas, Santiago, Chile of 10 June 2003, AG/DEC. 31 (XXXIII-O/03). Available at <http://www.oas.org/xxxiiga/english/docs/agdoc4224_03rev3.pdf> (accessed 26 March 2013).
32 Rio Treaty, Art. 1.
33 Rio Treaty, Art. 7.
34 Pact of Bogotá.
35 Rio Treaty, Art. 3.
36 'The World. Bringing Down a Ban', *Time*, 28 July 1975. Available at <http://www.time.com/time/magazine/article/0,9171,913333,00.html> (accessed 26 March 2013).
37 Rio Treaty.

required vote to a two-thirds majority vote,[38] replacing an absolute majority vote.[39]

There is a possibility to use force upon the decision of the Organ of Consultation. It can be implied that the pre-condition for such a decision would normally be self-defence, as identified in Article 3 of the Rio Treaty. Article 8 of the Treaty also provides for the possibility to rescind the decision on using force made by the Organ of Consultation, in which case an absolute majority vote is sufficient.

The Protocol amending the Rio Treaty also contains a new Article 12: 'Nothing stipulated in this treaty shall be interpreted as limiting or impairing in any way the principle of non-intervention and the right of all States to choose freely their political, economic and social organization'. This article can be read as a guarantee against US pro-democratic interventions, but in reality it did not prevent the interventions from taking place. After the amendment, interventions in Grenada and Panama took place, along with indirect coercive action, as in Nicaragua.

The Charter of the OAS starts out by declaring that the OAS is a regional agency. It has no powers other than those expressly conferred upon it by the Charter, none of which authorise the organisation to intervene in matters that are within the internal jurisdiction of the Member States.[40] Thus, the OAS is an example of an organisation, the constitutive document of which prohibits adding tasks not expressly delegated to the organisation. The opposite example to that is, most explicitly, NATO, the post-Cold War activities of which are outside the scope of self-defence, provided for in the Washington Treaty. The Charter of the OAS stipulates the right of States to choose, without external influence, their political, economic and social system and the duty to abstain from intervening in the affairs of another State. Article 19 provides that no State has the right to intervene, directly or indirectly, for any reason whatsoever, in the internal or external affairs of any State, including interference through the use of armed force. The repetition on prohibition of the use of force, except for self-defence is found also in Article 22. Article 23, however, makes a reservation: measures adopted for the maintenance of peace and security in accordance with existing treaties do not constitute a violation of the prohibition of use of force. Thus, theoretically, this provision creates a loop-hole for a possibility of regional use of force. Such an example of an exception is, for example, the Caracas Declaration of 1954,[41] which reinterprets the traditional principle of each State being allowed to choose its own system:

---

38 Rio Treaty, Art. 20.
39 Rio Treaty, Art. 16.
40 Charter of the Organization of American States, 119 UNTS 3, Art. 1.
41 Caracas Declaration, 28 March 1954. Available at <http://avalon.law.yale.edu/20th_century/intam10.asp> (accessed 26 March 2013).

> Recognition of the inalienable right of each American state to choose freely its own institutions in the effective exercise of *representative democracy*, as a means of preserving its political sovereignty, achieving its economic independence, and living its own social and cultural life, without intervention on the part of any states or group of states, either directly or indirectly, in its domestic or external affairs, and, particularly, without the intrusion of any form of *totalitarianism*.

In continuation the Declaration resolves that:

> To unite the efforts of all the American States to apply, develop, and perfect the above-mentioned principles so that they will form the basis of firm and solidary action designed to attain within a short time the effective realization of the representative democratic system, the rule of social justice and security, and economic and cultural cooperation essential to the mutual well-being and prosperity of the peoples of the Continent.

Thus, the declaration, in a blurred language, provides for taking regional action in order to restore (establish) representative democracy. In practice the Caracas declaration has provided a loop-hole from the provisions of Articles 19 and 21 of the OAS Charter, in allowing intervention, also by military means, in States that were not perceived as representative democracies – a justification used by the USA in the so-called pro-democratic interventions in Latin America.[42] The interventions by the USA, just as in Guatemala in the same year of 1954, launched as pro-democratic interventions, in order to prevent communist States from forming in the Western Hemisphere, in fact ended up establishing totalitarian military regimes that the declaration, in principle, stated to be against.

The structure of the organisation is complicated, with a number of organs and specialised organisations. Since the end of the Cold War this system has become even more complicated, with different institutions specialising in specific aspects of security, in line with the newly introduced concept of multidimensional security.[43] Some of the new institutions are the Committee on Hemispheric Security (since 1995), the Department of Public Security (since 2006), the Inter-American Committee against terrorism (since 1999). In addition the inactive Inter-American Defense Board (originally established in 1942), an international committee of nationally appointed defence officials, was given new life in 2006, redefining it as an 'entity'[44] under the Charter of the OAS and giving it a new statute.[45] Its task is to develop collaborative

---

42 McCoubrey and Morris, op. cit., n. 1, p. 109.
43 Declaration on Security in the Americas, above, n. 12.
44 Statutes of the Inter-American Defense Board, 15 March 2006, AG/RES. 1 (XXXII-E/06).
45 Statutes of the Inter-American Defense Board, ibid.

approaches on common defence and security issues facing the Americas. The Board is to provide technical advice and services to the OAS, including reporting on confidence and security measures and developing educational programmes on regional security.

In essence, the provisions on the use of force in the OAS remain as they have been since the creation of the organisation, not fully excluding the possibility of the use of force, but strictly limiting it. The abuse of the prohibition of the use of force in the region during the Cold War appears to have led to a great level of elaboration in dealing with threats to peace and security by peaceful means. There is however, an important nuance that characterises the maintenance of peace and security in the Americas in the past two decades: the promotion of democracy by peaceful means has become highlighted. In 1991, the OAS passed Resolution 1080 which calls for OAS action in the cases where representative democracy is threatened.[46] Thus, even though military intervention is prohibited, an obligation of peaceful pro-democratic intervention is imposed on the OAS. Moreover, the post-Cold War pro-democratic peaceful intervention practice led to the signing of the 2001 Inter-American Pro-Democratic Charter.[47] Another relevant document in the promotion of democracy in the region is the above-mentioned Santiago Declaration of 2003, which reaffirms the commitment of American States to democracy. The concept of democracy in the understanding of the OAS documents enhances State responsibility in the protection of human rights.[48] Despite the OAS Member States having the obligation to actively protect human rights regionally, there is clearly no regional right to humanitarian intervention or pro-democratic intervention, using military or any other coercive means. Intervention by peaceful means, which in the case of the Americas excludes military peacekeeping, however, is permissible, and even a duty, since the introduction of the post-Cold War democratisation commitments (as in Resolution 1080). In this way, the OAS differs from ASEAN, where even peaceful intervention is not acceptable, if the State itself has not called for diplomatic efforts from the side of the organisation.

Decision-making

The OAS consists of the following organs: the General Assembly, the Meeting of Consultation of Ministers of Foreign Affairs, the Councils, the Inter-American

---

46 AG/RES.1080 (XXI-O/91).
47 Inter-American Democratic Charter, Lima 11 September 2001, OEA/Ser.G, CP/doc.3508/01; A. F. Cooper and T. Legler, 'A tale of two mesas: the OAS defence of democracy in Peru and Venezuela', *Global Governance*, Vol. 11 (Autumn) 2005, p. 1. Available at <http://findarticles.com/p/articles/mi_7055/is_4_11/ai_n28318060/> (accessed 27 March 2013).
48 See, for example, the Inter-American Democratic Charter, Arts 1 and 3, as well as Chapter II – Democracy and Human Rights.

Juridical Committee, the Inter-American Commission on Human Rights, the General Secretariat, the Specialised Conferences and the specialised organisations, their subsidiary organs, agencies and other entities – as established.[49] An example of such an entity is, for example, the abovementioned Inter-American Defense Board. The General Assembly is the supreme organ of the OAS. It decides on the general action on policy of the organisation and considers any matter relating to friendly relations among the American States[50] with an absolute majority vote, except for where a two-thirds majority vote is specifically provided for in the Charter.[51]

Matters of peace and security have a specific regulation, different from the general provisions of the Charter of the OAS. Article 29 of the Charter contains a special provision for collective security and defence. The provision regards intra-regional conflicts between Member States and a threat from a third State, or any other threat to the peace and security in the Americas. The article provides that in furtherance of continental solidarity and collective self-defence the measures and procedures established in special treaties on the subject shall apply. Such treaties are the Rio Treaty and the Pact of Bogotá. As mentioned above, since 1975 the Rio Treaty provides for a two-thirds majority vote for measures taken by the OAS Organ of Consultation. The Charter provides that it is the Meeting of Consultation of Ministers of Foreign Affairs that serves as the Organ of Consultation in the context of the Rio Treaty, and thus in general considers problems of urgent nature.[52] If the States involved in the conflict have ratified the Rio Treaty, the special rules of the Rio Treaty are applied,[53] if not, the Charter rules are applied. Articles 65 to 68 of the Charter provide the procedure for calling the Meeting of Consultation, without prejudice to the Rio Treaty, in a case of armed attack on the territory of an American State. According to the Charter provisions the Chairman of the Permanent Council calls the Meeting of Consultation after a vote of absolute majority of the Member States, and an Advisory Defence Committee on problems of military co-operation is created for this case, to assist the Organ of Consultation. The Charter does not contain any provisions on the decision-making process by the Meeting of Consultation. Nevertheless, it contains provisions on the functions of the Permanent Council. In addition to serving provisionally as the Organ of Consultation, the Permanent Council has a wide set of functions in the peaceful settlement of disputes, these being of recommendatory nature (Articles 84 to 87).

---

49 Charter of the OAS, Art. 53.
50 Charter of the OAS, Art. 54 a).
51 Charter of the OAS, Art. 59.
52 Charter of the OAS, Art. 61.
53 At the time of writing, 23 OAS Member States have ratified the Rio Treaty. Available at <http://www.oas.org/juridico/english/sigs/b-29.html> (accessed 27 March 2013).

The vote is two-thirds majority, excluding the State parties involved in the dispute (Article 89).

The Rio Treaty, in addition, contains detailed provisions on the decision-making process by the Organ of Consultation. The quorum for making the decision at the Organ of Consultation is the number of votes necessary for making a decision under the Rio Treaty provisions – two-thirds of all State parties (at the time being two-thirds of 23 Member States). Thus, it is not decisive how many of the Member States are present at the meeting. The States involved in the conflict, however, are excluded from the voting process, as in the case of the AU.[54]

It can thus be concluded that that the existing decision-making procedure is very complicated due to a multi-level involvement of different organs and the different treaties that may be invoked depending on the situation. At the same time, the procedures are nuanced and elaborated, and decided by a qualified majority vote, which is transparent and objective in comparison to a consensus decision-making procedure.

The practice

The practice of the OAS can generally be described as one of putting effort into preventing the use of force, rather than using force in the maintenance of peace and security. During the Cold War the preventive practice was impaired due to the inability of the OAS to restrain its strongest member – the USA. McCoubrey and Morris indicate that as opposed to the role of the USA in NATO, it enjoys 'a position of unassailable hegemon' in the OAS. They refer to the relationship between the USA and other OAS States, especially those of Central America and the Caribbean as a relation between a hegemon and subordinates.[55] Such a model of region-State relations is not unique: the same can essentially be witnessed in the CIS/CSTO framework with Russia in the centre, the reason why the present author has defined the region as 'the Russian sphere of influence'.

The Cold War practice of the USA was one of interventionism in the Latin American and Caribbean States, however, the operations were not carried out within the formal framework of the OAS, and at the end of the Cold War, a unilateral US intervention even received condemnation by the OAS. Just like the OAU, the OAS has been accused of inactivity, including the case of the crisis in Panama in 1989. Yet, the USA intervention in Panama was a turning point for OAS inactivity: it was the first time the OAS actually passed a resolution condemning the US unilateral intervention.[56]

---

54 Rio Treaty, Art. 19.
55 McCoubrey and Morris, op. cit., n. 1, p. 93.
56 Ibid, p. 117; OAS CP/Res. 534 (800/89), 22 December 1989.

In the past two decades, US interventionist policy has become more toned down, with the most debated recent US activity being the use of Colombian airbases by the US military.[57] The relaxing of the interventionism policy is most probably due to the disappearance of the communist threat that had been the reason for the so-called pro-democratic US interventions in the States of the region during the Cold War,[58] as well as the loss of strategic US interest in the region.[59]

The policy of the OAS shifted to international defence and promotion of democracy. The next crisis in the region, after Panama, was Haiti in 1991. The OAS took immediate action by condemning the coup and placing demands on Haiti.[60] Since the end of the Cold War, the OAS has dealt with several cases by peaceful means. Cooper and Legler call this phenomenon 'intervention without intervening'. The relevant cases named are Peru,[61] Paraguay, Guatemala, Haiti,[62] Venezuela, Bolivia and Ecuador.[63]

Thus, in 1992 the President in power in Peru, Alberto Fujimori, dissolved the Congress, closed the courts, suspended the constitution and assumed special emergency powers.[64] The OAS intervened in 2000 to prevent Fujimori from securing the illegal third term of power.[65] In Venezuela, Hugo Chavez was ousted by a coup d'état in April 2002. The OAS intervention took place from 2002 to 2004. In this case the OAS helped restore democracy by facilitating dialogue among the country's political elites and the 15 August 2004 presidential recall referendum against Chavez.[66]

In both cases, however, it was not military interventions that took place, but high level diplomatic missions – mesas: Mesa de Negociación y Acuerdos in Venezuela and Mesa de Diálogo in Peru. The mesa in Peru was led by a former foreign minister from the Dominican Republic, Eduardo Latorre, while the Venezuelan mesa was led by the Secretary-General of the OAS himself, Cesar Gaviria.[67] In Peru there were 18 representatives of different actors involved, while in Venezuela there were 12. The actors involved were

---

57 'Regional Conflicts call for urgent meeting of South American Defence Council', *Merco Press. South Atlantic News Agency*, 23 November 2009. Available at <http://en.mercopress.com/2009/11/23/regional-conflicts-call-for-urgent-meeting-of-south-american-defence-counci> (accessed 12 April 2013).
58 A. F. Cooper and T. Legler, *Intervention without intervening? The OAS defense and promotion of democracy in the Americas*, New York, NY: Palgrave Macmillan, 2006, p. 13.
59 Hilaire, op. cit., n. 5, p. 10.
60 McCoubrey and Morris, op. cit., n. 1, pp. 117–18.
61 Elections monitoring in 1992 after an autogolpe (self-imposed coup by the president in power by election fraud).
62 The OAS imposed economic sanctions.
63 Cooper and Legler, op. cit., n. 58, p. 2.
64 Cooper and Legler, op. cit., n. 47, p. 51.
65 Ibid, p. 1.
66 Ibid, p. 1.
67 Cooper and Legler, op. cit., n. 58, p. 2.

government ministers, pro-government and opposition members of the congress and civil society representatives, and in Venezuela, in addition, also state governors.[68] Cooper and Legler conclude that such mesas are not a quick way to fix a problem, and do not guarantee long-term stability, but that they have helped bring the parties of the conflict to a dialogue by OAS remaining a neutral mediator and have prevented the escalation of violence.[69]

The OAS does not have regional military capabilities, such as rapid reaction forces. In principle, any kind of regional military formations under the auspices of the OAS are not and have not been under consideration. The only regional operations envisaged in theory are electoral monitoring missions.[70] The OAS can, in general, contribute to peacekeeping without the use of military force,[71] yet no regional peace enforcement or military peacekeeping operations are permissible.

Co-operation with the United Nations

Co-operation between the OAS and the UN is deep-rooted, as the OAS was in fact the first regional organisation recognised as a Chapter VIII organisation by the UN. The OAS has been an observer at the UN General Assembly since 1996. The formal reciprocal recognition documents of the OAS and the UN have a wider form than the twenty-first century declarations between the UN and regional organisations in the sphere of maintenance of peace and security (e.g. the EU, NATO, the AU, SADC, etc.). The co-operation between the two organisations is formally commended through mutual UN General Assembly resolutions of both organisations. On the side of the UN it is UN General Assembly Resolution 49/5 of 1994 and 51/14 of 1996, both entitled 'Cooperation between the UN and the Organisation of American States'. Both documents praise the efforts of the UN Secretary-General and OAS in co-operation, and refer to the recent examples of co-operation – such as meetings and the operation in Haiti. They also emphasise the UN Charter rules governing the co-operation. On the part of OAS the relevant resolutions are the OAS General Assembly Resolutions 1345 of 1995[72] and 1372 of 1996.[73] OAS General Assembly Resolution 1345 is brief and commends the UN Secretary-General for enhancing co-operation, and refers to the co-operation between the OAS and the UN in Haiti in particular. UN General Assembly Resolution 1372 is a direct response to OAS General Assembly Resolution 49/5, and contains a reference, among others, to the

---

68 Cooper and Legler, op. cit., n. 58, p. 3.
69 Ibid, pp. 8–9.
70 Inter-American Democratic Charter, Art. 24.
71 *Regional Cooperation*, op. cit., n. 28, p. 2.
72 AG/RES. 1345 (XXV-O/95).
73 AG/RES. 1372 (XXVI-O/96).

signing of a Cooperation Agreement between the UN Secretariat and the General Secretariat of the OAS. The signing of the latter has become the standard procedure for formalising UN co-operation with regional organisations in the twenty-first century.

Though formally the co-operation between the two organisations is very elaborated, in practice the only co-operation of the two organisations in the field has been in the two decades-long crisis in Haiti. This co-operation does not involve military assistance on the side of OAS. The OAS has, in fact, reported to the UN that it is willing to participate in UN peacekeeping without the use of military force.[74] An expression of this intent is the OAS/UN International Civilian Mission in Haiti (MICIVIH).[75] In essence, the UN-OAS relations in the maintenance of peace and security can be summed up as undisputed recognition of the distribution of tasks between the two, in accordance with Chapter VIII of the UN Charter, where the OAS deals with the peaceful settlement of disputes locally, leaving the rest of the maintenance of peace and security to the UN.

South American Union of Nations

General description

UNASUR was established in 2008. UNASUR is a continent-wide regional organisation. Its members are all South American States, a total of 12.[76] The declaration of intent to establish the organisation was signed in Cusco, December 2004.[77] UNASUR was officially established by signing the South American Union of Nations Constitutive Treaty on 23 May 2008.[78] The organisation merges two South American organisations for economic co-operation – MERCOSUR and the Andean Community of Nations[79] in an organisation resembling the model of the EU.[80] At the same time, the general post-Cold

---

74 *Regional Cooperation*, op. cit., n. 28.
75 MICIVIH website. Available at <http://www.un.org/rights/micivih/first.htm> (accessed 27 March 2013).
76 Argentina, Bolivia, Brazil, Chile, Colombia, Ecuador, Guyana, Paraguay, Peru, Suriname, Uruguay and Venezuela.
77 Cusco Declaration on the South American Community of Nations, Third South American Presidential Summit, Cusco, 8 December 2004. Available at <http://www.comunidadandina.org/ingles/documentos/documents/cusco8-12-04.htm> (accessed 27 March 2013).
78 South American Union of Nations Constitutive Treaty, Brasilia, Brazil, 23 May 2008. Available at <http://www.comunidadandina.org/ingles/csn/treaty.htm> (accessed 27 March 2013).
79 Cusco Declaration on the South American Community of Nations, op. cit., n. 77.
80 A. Sanchez, 'The South American Defense Council, UNASUR, the Latin American Military and the Region's Political Process', *Council of Hemispheric Affairs*, 1 October 2008. Available at <http://www.coha.org/the-south-american-defense-council-unasur-the-latin-american-military-and-the-region%E2%80%99s-political-process/> (accessed 27 March 2013).

War tendency of regionalisation is maintained – the economic co-operation forum enhances also security co-operation. The organisation has also established its own mechanism of security and defence.

The legal basis

The shape of the new mechanism of UNASUR is sketched in the basic documents of the organisation, while the specific implications are to be decided on and elaborated in documents to follow.[81] The basic legal document of UNASUR is the South American Union of Nations Constitutive Treaty. Even in the twenty-first century the preamble of the treaty refers to the fight for independence of South American leaders, referring to, for example, Bolivar's fight for independence from Spain. Second, co-operation in the political, social and economic fields is in the competence of the organisation. To achieve development, multilateralism, the rule of law in international relations, the sovereign equality of States and a culture of peace need to prevail. The principles at the core of the UNASUR co-operation are listed as: unlimited respect for sovereignty and territorial integrity and inviolability of States, self-determination of the peoples, solidarity, co-operation, peace, democracy, citizen participation and pluralism, universal, interdependent and indivisible human rights, reduction of asymmetries and harmony with nature for a sustainable development. Interestingly, the respect for sovereignty and territorial integrity and inviolability of States is not merely re-quoted from the international legal and political documents setting down these principles: the aforementioned principles are underlined, emphasised and qualified with a single, but significant word 'unlimited'. Thus, the Constitutive Treaty of UNASUR responds to the USA (NATO) and African regionalist pro-interventionist positions with a clearly spelled out articulation of the principle of non-intervention, even more explicitly than in the OAS documents.

The references to compliance with the UN Charter and the Charter of the OAS in the Statute of the UNASUR South American Defence Council[82] subordinate UNASUR to the OAS. Thus, UNASUR is a subregional organisation covering South America in the wider region of the Americas. This means that UNASUR is not a substitute for the co-operation of American

---

81 Extraordinary meeting of the Ministers of Foreign Affairs and Defence of the UNASUR, Resolution of 27 November 2009. Available at http://www.cdsunasur.org/index.php?option=com_content&view=article&id=163:extraordinary-meeting-of-the-ministers-&catid=58:ingles&Itemid=189 (accessed 24 February 2011).
82 Statute of the UNASUR South American Defence Council, 11 December 2008. Available at <http://www.cdsunasur.org/index.php?option=com_content&view=article&id=120:statute-of-the-unasur-south-american-defense-council-&catid=58:ingles&Itemid=189> (accessed 27 March 2013). Article 2 contains such a provision. The Constitutive Treaty, however, holds no reference to the OAS.

States in the OAS, but a supplement – for closer co-operation in order to support the common interests of the South American States.

The provisions on establishing a peace and security mechanism in the framework of UNASUR came a few months after the signing of the Constitutive Treaty. The Statute of the UNASUR South American Defence Council was adopted on 11 December 2008, creating the organ responsible for the maintenance of peace and security in South America.[83] At the time of its creation, it was stressed in the media that the South American Defence Council is not intended to be a military alliance according to the NATO model.[84] In fact, military activity is not included in the UNASUR co-operation at this stage at all – the organisation is to co-operate by peaceful means only. The matters of security vs. defence, however, are two sides of the same coin, and are not distinguished and separated in the legal provisions of UNASUR. The word *defence*, as derived from the content of the Statute, contains the full scope of security measures, including prevention and confidence building.

The leading principles of the Defence Council are repeated from the Constitutive Treaty, among them: unlimited respect for the sovereignty, integrity and territorial inviolability of the States, non-intervention in their internal affairs and self-determination of peoples, promoting peace and the peaceful settlement of disputes and safeguarding the full force of international law in conformity with the principles and standards of the UN Charter, the Charter of the OAS and the UNASUR Constitutive Treaty. In addition, Latin American-specific principles referring to prevention of coups against democratically elected governments carried out by the military in Member States are included.[85]

The objectives of the Defence Council are of co-ordinating nature and exchange of information. For example, promoting the exchange of information and analysis on regional and international status in order to identify risk factors and threats which may affect regional and world peace,[86] contributing to articulating joint positions of the region,[87] promoting and facilitating military training and co-operation between military study centres[88] and sharing experience in UN peacekeeping operations.[89]

The provisions included in the Constitutive Treaty and the Statute of the Defence Council are in a process of elaboration. An example of such provisions is the mechanism for Confidence Building and Security Measures, including specific implementation measures and guarantees, which was established by

---

83 Statute of the UNASUR South American Defence Council.
84 'South American Defence Council meets for the first time', *Latin American Herald Tribune*. N.D. Available at <http://laht.com/article.asp?CategoryId=12394&ArticleId=329400> (accessed 27 March 2013).
85 Statute of the UNASUR South American Defence Council, Art. 3.
86 Statute of the UNASUR South American Defence Council, Art. 5.d).
87 Statute of the UNASUR South American Defence Council, Art. 5.e).
88 Statute of the UNASUR South American Defence Council, Art. 5.h).
89 Statute of the UNASUR South American Defence Council, Art. 5.i).

a resolution of the Ministers of Foreign Affairs and the Ministers of Defence of the UNASUR extraordinary meeting in Quito, Ecuador 15 September 2009.[90]

The resolution contains provisions on the exchange of information on military-related activities, measures in the field of security, guarantees the Member States give one another, verification of compliance and a specific call for co-operation in combating drug problems. The measures in the field of security provide not only for co-operation in border surveillance and arms control. The section requires the States to prevent armed groups from action outside the law, to combat and prevent terroristic activities. A region-specific provision is the requirement for the States to strengthen human rights and democracy and in this regard to resist any attempt of coup d'état.

Section IV of the resolution is dedicated to guarantees. There are four guarantees, three of which repeat and underline the prohibition of use or threat of use of force and any kind of military aggression or threats to the territorial stability, sovereignty and integrity of the UNASUR Member States. While point a) prohibits any use of force among Member States,[91] point c) demands that Member States explicitly include a corresponding provision in their co-operation agreements in the field of defence with third countries. Moreover, point d) requires a Member State that hosts foreign military or even civilians (either from within or outside the region) on its territory to guarantee and ensure that the abovementioned principles will not be broken. In the short practice of UNASUR the main concern has been the use of military bases in Colombia by the US military. Thus, it appears rather clear that like many other UNASUR documents, this resolution has been adopted emphasising the unacceptability of any US interventions within the region. The guarantees also have a character of limiting the possibility of Member States to invite an intervention by another State. Thus, a UN-led, or at least UN-mandated operation appears to be the only legal option for launching military operations in the South American region.

The South American Defence Council Action Plan for 2009–10 serves as an additional tool for interpreting the provisions of the resolution with regard to regional military action: UNASUR military co-operation is possible only to assist in cases of natural disasters. With regard to peacekeeping, Member States only share experience on their lessons learned from the peacekeeping operations they have participated in individually.[92]

---

90 Resolution of the Ministers of Foreign Affairs and the Ministers of Defence of the UNASUR extraordinary meeting in Quito, Ecuador 15 September 2009. Available at <http://www.cdsunasur.org/es/consejo-de-defensa-suramericano/documentos-oficiales/58-ingles/163-extraordinary-meeting-of-the-ministers-> (accessed 27 March 2013).
91 Point b) repeatedly declares South America a nuclear-free zone.
92 UNASUR South American Defense Council, 'Action Plan 2009–2010', January 2009, Santiago, Chile. Available at <http://www.cdsunasur.org/index.php?option=com_content&view=article&id=116:action-plan-2009&catid=58:ingles&Itemid=189> (accessed 27 March 2013).

The final provisions of the resolution list a number of documents that need to be elaborated with regard to the mechanism of maintenance of peace and security in South America, for example, a project for a Protocol of Peace, Security and Cooperation of UNASUR, a project of a Decision for the opening of a debate and negotiation process for an Architecture of Security for UNASUR, and a project for a Code of Conduct on Defence and Security Matters.

The Protocol of Peace, Security and Cooperation of UNASUR contains the principles of the promotion of confidence-building and security measures, including defence expenditures, the rejection of threat or use of force, the respect for territorial integrity and the sovereignty of each one of the Member States of UNASUR, non-interference into the internal affairs, and the settlement of any disputes by peaceful means, among others. This document is intended to become legally binding.[93]

Decision-making

According to its Constitutive Treaty, UNASUR has the following bodies: the Council of Heads of State and Government, the Council of Ministers of Foreign Affairs, the Council of Delegates and the General Secretariat. According to Article 6 of the Constitutive treaty, the Council of Heads of State and Government is the highest decision-making body.

Article 12 provides for the adoption of the legislative measures of UNASUR. All the norms of UNASUR are to be adopted by consensus. The Decisions of the Council of Heads of State and Government, the Resolutions of the Council of Ministers of Foreign Affairs and the Provisions of the Council of Delegates may be adopted with the presence of at least three-quarters of the Member States. The Decisions of the Council of Heads of State and Government, the Resolutions of the Council of Ministers of Foreign Affairs adopted without the presence of all Member States, are to be forwarded by the Secretary-General to the absent States, which are to make their position known. Thus, the participation of all Member States is necessary in decision-making, and the absence of a delegate does not exclude a Member State from the decision-making process. In addition, it can be concluded from Article 21 that resolutions adopted by the bodies of UNASUR are legally binding documents.

The Statute of the South American Defence Council also provides for a special mechanism in dealing with matters of peace and security. The South

---

93 Ambassador Hugo de Zela, Permanent Representative of Peru to the Organization of American States, by CSR Western Hemisphere Team, 'INSS Colleagues for the Americas Seminar "The Rearmament Debate in South America"', Institute for National Strategic Studies, Event Report, 28 April 2010. Available at <http://www.ndu.edu/inss/docUploaded/INSS%20Event%20Report%20-%20April%202010%20Colleagues%20Seminar.pdf> (accessed 27 March 2013).

American Defence Council consists of the Defence Ministers from the Member States. The Defence Council is created as an agency for consultancy, co-operation and co-ordination in defence matters, it is to hold annual meetings and the decisions are to be taken by consensus.[94]

The dispute settlement mechanism in Article 21 of the UNASUR Constitutive Treaty provides a chain of measures that are to be taken, in order to solve a conflict between two Member States. Any dispute that may emerge between States parties regarding the interpretation or implementation of the provisions of this Constitutive Treaty is to be settled through direct negotiations. In the case where a solution is not reached through direct negotiation, the Member States involved have to submit the dispute for the consideration of the Council of Delegates, which is to formulate within 60 days, the appropriate recommendations for the settlement of the dispute. If a solution is not reached by the Council of Delegates, the dispute is to be taken to the Council of Ministers of Foreign Affairs, which has to consider it at its next meeting.

The decision-making rules are very detailed and specified for each organ. For example, the Working Groups on specific issues can hold sessions and make proposals as long as they have a quorum of half plus one of the Member States.[95] The legislative measures emanating from the organs of UNASUR become binding on the Member States once they have been incorporated into each Member State's domestic law, according to its respective internal procedures.

The consensus in the decision-making process is emphasised throughout the Treaty, and is repeated also in Article 13 on the adoption of policies and creation of institutions, organisations and policies, and Article 14 on political dialogue. An equivalent level of regional coherence, where the harmonisation of national legislation is a regional maintenance of peace and security commitment, can be found also in the Euro-Atlantic region and the Russian sphere of influence.

The practice

Even though UNASUR is a new organisation, it already has practice in dealing with regional threats to peace and security. The South American Defence Council was created keeping in mind the Venezuela-Colombia conflict. In November 2009 the Defence Council held an extraordinary meeting to deal with both the Venezuelan-Colombian conflict, and the Peru-Chile conflict. Rafael Correa, the head of UNASUR at the time stated: 'The heart of the fact is that the Colombia/Venezuela differences are because we have seven US military bases in Colombia and that is a matter of concern for the

---

94 de Zela, ibid., Arts 12–13.
95 UNASUR Constitutive Treaty, Art. 12.

whole region'.[96] The origin of the Peru-Chile conflict is the unsettled maritime border, a case on which is pending at the International Court of Justice.[97] Peru has refused the dispute to be handled by UNASUR.[98]

With regard to the USA-Colombia military base agreement, UNASUR issued a Joint Declaration on 28 August 2009.[99] In this declaration the UNASUR states once more emphasise the need to comply in military co-operation with the principles and intentions of the UN Charter and emphasise 'the unconditional respect of sovereignty, integrity and territorial sanctity of the States, the non-intervention in internal affairs and the self-determination of the people are essential for the consolidation of regional integration'. The methods for achieving peace in the region are solely peaceful: 'through the prevention of conflicts, the peaceful solution of controversies and the abstention from reverting to threats or the use of force'. The promotion of dialogue and consensus in topics of defence is to take place through the strengthening of co-operation, confidence and transparency. As in Asia, the emphasis in security is put on combating non-traditional threats – terrorism and transnational organised crime. The document further specifies that in dealing with untraditional threats, just like with the traditional, any applicable mechanisms, including that of the OAS must take into account the unconditional respect for sovereignty, integrity and territorial sanctity and non-intervention in the internal affairs of the States.

The following passage in the declaration is directly addressed towards the USA:

> To reaffirm that the presence of foreign military forces cannot, with its means and resources linked to its own goals, threaten the sovereignty and integrity of any South American nation and as a consequence, the peace and security of the region.

Whereas in the framework of the OAS and the OECS, the USA had a practice of abuse of power through regional interventions, the focus of the security

---

96 Regional Conflicts call for urgent meeting of South American Defence Council', *MercoPress. South Atlantic News Agency*, 23 November 2009. Available at <http://en.mercopress.com/2009/11/23/regional-conflicts-call-for-urgent-meeting-of-south-american-defence-counci> (accessed 12 April 2013).
97 Maritime dispute (*Peru v Chile*). Contentious cases. Case progress available at ICJ website. Available at <http://www.icj-cij.org/docket/index.php?p1=3&p2=3&case=137> (accessed 27 March 2013).
98 'Peru rules out discussing Chile-Bolivia sea outlet talks at Unasur Summit', *Andina*, Peruvian news agency, 29 July 2009. Available at <http://www.andina.com.pe/ingles/Noticia.aspx?id=QN2aQMM54gw=> (accessed 27 March 2013).
99 A joint declaration of the special meeting of the Council of Leaders of UNASUR, San Carlos de Bariloche, Argentina, 28 August 2009. Available at 'Just the Facts' project <http://justf.org/blog/2009/08/31/joint-declaration-unasur-meeting> (accessed 27 March 2013).

and defence mechanism of UNASUR is to prevent the reoccurrence of such practice in the South American continent.

The year 2010 saw an escalation of the conflict between Colombia and Venezuela. The cause for the escalation was that in the OAS Colombia accused Venezuela of being the home of 87 bases of guerrilla groups FARC and ELN. Venezuela, in return, accused Colombia of trying to create the conditions for a US military intervention in the oil-rich socialist country.[100]

The Colombian-Venezuelan crisis was settled through mediation by the Secretary-General of UNASUR, Nestor Kirchner. The president of Venezuela, Hugo Chavez, praised the efforts of UNASUR, stating that by bringing both countries to dialogue UNASUR had prevented a war between them, and that diplomatic relations between the two States have been re-established.[101] The diplomatic ties had been officially broken from 22 July to 7 August 2010, causing a threat of a military escalation of the conflict. UNASUR adjourned for an emergency meeting as soon as 25 July 2010[102] and succeeded in preventing the escalation.

Thus, the practice of UNASUR of the past two years evidences an emphasis of avoiding the use of military force in the continent (by Member States and the USA), emphasising the peaceful settlement of disputes and the principles of non-use of force and non-intervention. The first case of settling a conflict between Member States through mediation has been successful.

Co-operation with the United Nations

As UNASUR is a new organisation, its co-operation with the UN so far is limited. In October 2011, UNASUR received observer status at the UN General Assembly, but has no other practice of co-operation with the UN. Participating in international military operations as an organisation would be against the constitution of UNASUR. UNASUR has not participated in UN civilian peacekeeping either. There is no explicit reference to Chapter VIII of the UN Charter in the Constitutive Treaty and the Statute of the UNASUR South American Defence Council, yet the general context of UNASUR rules is that of a classical Chapter VIII organisation. The UNASUR Constitutive Treaty refers to the UN only in as much as depositing the treaty with the UN.[103] The Statute of the South American Defence Council provides for the

---

100 'UNASUR to meet on Colombia-Venezuela crisis', *Andina news agency*, Lima, 25 July 2010. Available at http://www.andina.com.pe/ingles/Noticia.aspx?Id=AfjbGkjD+M0=> (accessed 27 March 2013).
101 K. Begg, 'Chavez praises UNASUR's mediation of Colombia-Venezuela feud', *Colombia Reports news portal*, 16 August 2010. Available at <http://colombiareports.com/colombia-news/news/11352-chavez-praises-unasurs-mediation-of-colombia-venezuela-feud.html> (accessed 27 March 2013).
102 'UNASUR to meet on Colombia-Venezuela crisis', op. cit., n. 100.
103 Constitutive Treaty, Art. 27.

compliance with the UN Charter, the Charter of the OAS and the UNASUR Charter.[104] In addition the Statute provides a specific form of co-operation: namely, to share experience in UN peacekeeping.[105] Participating in UN peacekeeping operations on an individual State basis – just like in the OAS and ASEAN framework – appears to be the only possibility for military operations in the strictly non-interventionist Statute of the UNASUR South American Defence Council.

Summary

The region of the Americas is, in principle, non-interventionist, yet with a pro-active approach to peaceful settlement of disputes, which has been described as 'intervention without intervening'. The region has been enjoying significant autonomy from the UN since the very beginnings of the latter. It is, in fact the regional co-operation in the Americas that contributed to the inclusion of Chapter VIII in the UN Charter. The regional co-operation in the Americas is thus the model for Chapter VIII provisions. The documents of American regional organisations provide for action to be taken by peaceful means only, excluding military peacekeeping, however, self-defence function is covered. Despite the non-interventionist legal provisions, Latin American States have been subject to US interventions, as well as military coups throughout the years of the Cold War. Therefore, as opposed to Africa, since the end of the Cold War the prohibition of use of force and non-intervention have been re-emphasised by the American regional organisations. While in Africa pro-democratic interventions have a certain level of acceptance, there may be no military pro-democratic intervention in the Americas. The main reason for the difference in attitude is the possibility for a single regional hegemon to abuse its standing in the region. The perception of the concept of pro-democratic intervention is, once more, an example of the region-specific interpretation. What may be acceptable in one region, may not be acceptable in another, yet each region is entitled to pertain its specific view – to a limit set by the general law on the use of force. In the case of the Americas this means that humanitarian intervention and use of force in general are prohibited, but instead the region is pro-active in dealing with conflicts by peaceful means.

The OAS has supplemented the myriad of its legal and political documents on peace and security with new documents, the focus of which is the duty of OAS Member States to promote and protect democracy by peaceful means. UNASUR is a new organisation and has started out by a complete and unlimited application of the principle of non-intervention and prohibition of use of force, stated very explicitly in every single document of the

---

104 Statute of the UNASUR South American Defence Council, Art. 3. e).
105 Statute of the UNASUR South American Defence Council, Art. 4. i).

organisation, and going as far as putting a responsibility on Member States for the prevention of interventions by third States through their territories. This, in principle, appears to imply that even intervention by invitation without a prior UN mandate is not supported.

The American regional documents mainly focus on restraining traditional threats like internal conflicts, especially coups d'état, though need for co-operation in dealing with non-traditional threats is noted. The post-Cold War greatest threats to the peace and security of the region, however, are the non-traditional threats, especially the 'drug wars' with a grave impact on the region. It is interesting, that in the light of the severe drug-wars in Latin American States of the twenty-first century, the emphasis of regional action is still on promoting democracy by peaceful means and on anti-US interventionism measures. The drug-wars are regarded as internal matters of the Member States, where no intervention measures are feasible, even though UNASUR at least notes the need for co-operation in this area.

In both the OAS and UNASUR, the fact whether a Member State is or is not presented at a meeting where the decision is taken, is not decisive: under the Rio Treaty provisions, for example, the majority necessary for making a decision is two-thirds of all Member States, and not two-thirds of the quorum. UNASUR goes as far as creating a procedure where all Member States have to express their position subsequently, even if they have been absent at the meeting, where a legally binding decision has been made. In the OAS, the decisions are made by a qualified majority vote, while in UNASUR they are made by consensus.

In general, the developments in the Americas show a new attempt to implement regional mechanisms for the maintenance of peace and security in a regionally specific way, keeping in mind the experience of the region over the past half century. The new South American mechanism for the maintenance of peace and security of UNASUR is still in the creation stage, but the main point is clear – intervention using military means by this regional organisation, for whatever reason, is out of the question.

6 The Middle East

In the absence of regional unity

General description of the region

The Middle East is a security region of its own, member countries being connected by cultural and religious ties: mainly Arab and mainly Islamic. The region is centred around the Arabian Peninsula, and also covers North Africa, thus overlapping with the African region and the AU. Along with Africa, it is one of the most troubled regions in the world. The core conflict of the region, lasting over half a century, is the Palestinian (Arab)-Israeli conflict, to which there still is no resolution in sight, despite attempts for compromise, such as the 2002 Arab Peace Initiative.[1] In fact, the League of Arab States (Arab League), as such, was created to support Palestinians against Israelis in the conflict, and for this reason Israel contested the Chapter VIII character of the organisation in the first UN debate on the status of the organisation.[2] The region is historically connected to the Islamic collective self-defence concept of *Dar al-Islam* described in Chapter 1, and thus Israel is the manifestation of *Dar al-Harb*, the non-Muslim 'House of War'.[3] This conflict is also said to be the core reason for the impairment of regional co-operation in the Middle East throughout the post-Second World War era. The conflicts of the Middle East, such as the situation in Iraq and the Palestinian-Israeli conflict and Afghanistan (a Muslim, but not Arabic country) taking into consideration their complex and controversial developments, have generally been dealt with by the UNSC, having a constant place reserved in the annual lists of the UNSC resolutions. One of the most recent resolutions,

---

1 The text of the initiative is available at the Embassy of the Hashemite Kingdom of Jordan in Washington DC website. Available at <http://www.jordanembassyus.org/arab_initiative.htm> (accessed 10 April 2013).
2 W. Hummer and M. Schweitzer, 'Chapter VII. Regional Arrangements', in B. Simma (ed.), *The Charter of the UN. A Commentary*, 2nd edn, Oxford: Oxford University Press, 2002, p. 829.
3 H. McCoubrey and J. Morris, *Regional Peacekeeping in the Post-Cold War Era*, The Hague: Kluwer Law International, 2000, p. 192.

UNSC Resolution 1973 (2011), nevertheless, formally named the Arab League as the co-ordinator for the Libya conflict resolution efforts.

There are a few organisations in the Middle East region, of which the most prominent ones dealing with matters of peace and security are the Arab League and the Organization of Islamic Conference (OIC). Most other organisations in the region, such as the Gulf Cooperation Council, the Arab Maghreb Union and the Arab Cooperation Council, deal centrally with economic issues.[4] The activity of the Middle East regional organisations in the regional maintenance of peace and security has been very limited – both during the Cold War, and in the post-Cold War years. A few initiatives, however, have been observed in the last decade.

The information on the organisations in the Middle East region – both the Arab League and the OIC is scarce – since the end of the Cold War both literature, and the documents and materials on current activity are limited.[5] The OIC has not had a vital role in the maintenance of peace and security. It is, however, described very briefly to introduce another example of a regional organisation in the Middle East region other than the Arab League.

League of Arab States

General description

In 1945, when the UN was established, the Arab League was also in creation. Established on 22 March 1945, between the Dumbarton Oaks Conference and the San Francisco Conference, it had no practice that would be of help in drafting Chapter VIII of the UN Charter. At its creation the Arab League had two principal aims: to be anti-colonial and anti-Israel.[6] The organisation has grown from the original seven to 22 Member States.[7]

The record of the Arab League activities in the maintenance of peace and security has been very low during the Cold War years.[8] Of 77 conflicts in

---

4 C. Tripp, 'Regional Organizations in the Arab Middle East', in L. Fawcett and A. Hurrell (eds), *World Politics: Regional Organization and International Order*, Oxford: Oxford University Press, 1995, p. 283.
5 The League of Arab States website. Documents available in Arabic only. Available at <http://www.lasportal.org/wps/portal/las_en/home_page/!ut/p/c5/04_SB8K8xLLM9MSSzPy8xBz9CP0os3gXy8CgMJMgYwOLYFdLA08jF09_X28jIwN_E6B8JG55C3MCuoNT8_TDQXbiNwMkb4ADOBro-3nk56bqF-RGVHjqOioCAKQoUKM!/dl3/d3/L2dBISEvZ0FBIS9nQSEh/> (accessed 8 April 2013).
6 Pact of the League of Arab States, signed in Cairo on 22 March 1945. UN, *Treaty Series*, Vol. 70, p. 237 (Arabic), 248 (English translation).
7 Algeria, Bahrain, Comoros, Djibouti, Egypt, Iraq, Jordan, Kuwait, Lebanon, Libya, Mauritania, Morocco, Oman, Palestine, Qatar, Saudi Arabia, Somalia, Sudan, Syria, Tunisia, United Arab Emirates and Yemen.
8 Specified period 1945–81.

the region, it has successfully intervened in six.⁹ The Arab League has not been active in conflict resolution since the end of the Cold War either, the main reason still being the inability to solve the core conflict since the creation of the organisation, the Israeli-Palestine conflict, and the lenient rules of co-operation, providing no enforcement measures nor imposing strict obligations on its members. For these reasons the organisation has been referred to by some as a dead letter organisation.¹⁰ No enhancement of regional co-operation has taken place after the end of the Cold War, despite the reoccurring crises and operations in the Gulf area throughout the 1990s and the first years of the twenty-first century.¹¹ The last few years, however, appear to be showing a slight sign of re-attempted regionalism.

Despite the little activity the organisation has shown, it still exists. In fact, recent activities regarding an establishment of a mechanism of peace and security have taken place, at least on paper. A new Statute for the newly established Peace and Security Council was signed in 2006, and is formally in force since 2007. The regulation of the regional maintenance of peace and security in the Arab League can be drawn from three documents: the Pact of the League of Arab States of 1945, the Joint Defence and Economic Cooperation Treaty¹² of 1950 and the Statute of the Peace and Security Council of 2006.¹³

The legal basis

The Pact of the Arab League, signed 22 March 1945 is the framework document of the organisation. It provides that the purpose of the organisation is to draw closer the relations between Member States and co-ordinate their political activities with the aim of realising a close collaboration between them, to safeguard their independence and sovereignty, and to consider in a general way the affairs and interests of the Arab countries.¹⁴ Article 2 provides that the co-operation covers economic, cultural and social fields. Individual articles in the Pact are dedicated to both security and defence co-operation. Thus, Article 5 provides for the peaceful settlement of disputes. Recourse to force in the settlement of disputes between two or more Member States is not allowed. The conflicts are to be settled by the Council of the

---

9 R. Tavares, *Regional Security. The Capacity of International Organisations*, Oxford: Routledge, 2009. p. 109.
10 McCoubrey and Morris, op. cit., n. 3, p. 189.
11 M. N. Shaw, *International Law*, 6th edn, Cambridge: Cambridge University Press, 2008, pp. 1032 and 1293.
12 Joint Defence and Economic Cooperation Treaty between the States of the Arab League, *Middle East Journal*, Vol. 6, 2 (Spring) 1952, pp. 238–40.
13 The Statute of the Arab Peace and Security Council, 29 March 2006. Unofficial translation (official version only available in Arabic) available at <http://www.arableagueonline.org/las/picture_gallery/PeaceSecurity2.pdf.> (accessed 8 April 2013).
14 The Statute of the Arab Peace and Security Council, ibid., Art. 2.

Arab League, and the decisions of the Council are binding for the Member States concerned. The involved States are not participating in the decision-making. The Council also mediates in conflicts between a Member State and a third State. There is, however, an interesting condition that significantly limits the competence of the Arab League: the conflict must not involve the independence of a State, its sovereignty or territorial integrity, and the contending States have to apply to the Council to review their case – only then the Council can make a decision obligatory for the parties. Article 6 is a collective self-defence provision in line with Article 51 of the UN Charter. It provides that the State attacked or threatened with attack may request an immediate meeting of the Council which determines the necessary measures to repel this aggression. Its decision is taken unanimously. Yet, if the aggressor is a Member State, its vote is not counted. This article is an example of enhancing security and defence in one regional mechanism: the collective self-defence clause is applicable not only towards an outside aggressor, but also an inside one: self-defence against action taken by a member of the Arab League. Also, the OAS provides for the possible self-defence against another Member State of the same organisation. The African organisations and UNASUR merge self-defence with security measures, also making it applicable against any member. In contrast to the Arab League concept of collective self-defence, the Euro-Atlantic and Russian sphere of influence organisations are alliances that apply the term 'defence' only to outside threats, and the need for a Member State to defend itself against another Member State is, in principle, not an issue. Moreover, the newer mechanisms such as ECOWAS, the AU and UNASUR do not draw a strict line between security measures and collective self-defence.

Article 8 of the Pact represents the old approach to the State system, as stipulated in the 1970 Declaration on Principles of International Law concerning Friendly relations and Co-operation among States in accordance with the UN Charter:

> Every member State of the League shall respect the form of government obtaining in the other States of the League, and shall recognize the form of government obtaining as one of the rights of those States, and shall pledge itself not to take any action tending to change that form.[15]

The States of the region include old monarchies and post-revolution dictatorships, among others. Thus, a pro-democratic intervention would both contradict the basic provision included in the founding document of the Arab League and threaten the fragile political balance among the Member States having different political systems. At the same time, several members of the League are also members of the AU, where humanitarian intervention and pro-democratic intervention is permitted under regional constitutional provisions.

---

15 GA 2625(XXV).

This is only one of many examples that depict how States may face contradicting requirements due to an overlap of functions and territories of the regional organisations.

There is no pre-written scenario of how to choose the forum in case of a situation where regional organisations overlap. The case of Libya (2011) evidences that it is left much to chance: whichever organisation comes up with the feasible measures for action. In the case of Libya it was the Arab League requesting UN intervention, while the AU was still reserved about any enforcement action and offered negotiations instead.[16] If a State or States request their conflict to be settled, they can choose the forum, but if the question concerns coercive, enforcement action, difficulty may arise. In the case of Libya, it was the UN that appointed the Arab League as the co-ordinator of the conflict settlement. Nevertheless, while in reality the Arab League did not show active participation in the conflict resolution, the AU was active in negotiating a peaceful settlement of the dispute parallel to the UN-mandated NATO coalition action. Thus, it can be concluded, that there is nothing that prevents different regional mechanisms from tackling the same issue simultaneously according to the principles of each individual organisation. The Libya case evidences also that regional organisations are not prevented from continuing the procedure for peaceful settlement of disputes while the UNSC is also dealing with the issue, which, nevertheless, could be dubious, as the analysis of the 'Uniting for Peace' procedure reveals. While the procedure for the division of competence is not settled, it is clear that in such situations trans-organisational co-operation is of vital importance. For this reason, it would be useful to conclude agreements between regional mechanisms whose competence overlaps, in order to settle the competence matters in abstract, before the specific conflict arises.

Another important document of the Arab League is the 1950 Joint Defence and Economic Cooperation Treaty. The Treaty elaborates on the provisions regarding common defence. The aim of the co-operation is the realisation of mutual defence and the maintenance of security and peace according to the Pact of the Arab League and the UN Charter, and to consolidate the stability and security and provide means of welfare and development in the countries. The Treaty repeats the commitment to the peaceful settlement of disputes, specifying – both among the Member States, and with other 'powers'. Article 2 is a classical Article 51 provision, which provides for a collective use of force in the case of aggression against a Member State of the League: an act of aggression against one State is regarded as directed against all of them. The organisation would hold consultations upon an invitation of a Member State that would believe that its territorial integrity, independence

---

16 'African Union "ignored" over Libya Crisis', interview with Jean Ping, chairman of the Standing Commission of the AU, *BBC Hardtalk*, 25 March 2011. Available at <http://news.bbc.co.uk/2/hi/programmes/hardtalk/ 9436093.stm> (accessed 11 April 2013).

or security is threatened. Article 3 identifies only war and international emergency as threats. Yet, one has to keep in mind that at the time of the drafting of the Treaty internal threats were not yet a current issue, and the Treaty could also be interpreted as covering them in the light of today's security situation. The involvement of the League in internal conflicts in Lebanon (1976 and 2008) and Libya (2011) is evidence to that.

The Treaty has presumably been invoked only once – in 1976, when establishing the Arab Deterrent Force in Lebanon.[17] In the absence of general Arab unity, however, the organisation was unable to take action in this Middle East crisis, and left the issues to the international community. There have been attempts to reform the Arab League, including the defence provisions, since 1979, though no amendments proposed ever came into force.[18]

The twenty-first century brought about a new wave of reforms in the Arab League. Not only did the Arab Charter of Human Rights mark an era of new regional activism in the Middle East. A new mechanism for the maintenance of peace and security of the Arab League was also established in 2006.[19]

On 29 March 2006, the Council of the Arab League, meeting at Summit level, adopted resolution Res. 331-5-18-29.3.2006, approving the establishment of an Arab Peace and Security Council as a specialised agency within the system of Joint Arab Action.

The Statute is established with reference to Articles 5, 6 and 8 of the Pact of the Arab League – the articles containing provisions on security and defence; Articles 2 and 50 of the UN Charter; and Articles 1, 2 and 3 of the Treaty on Joint Defence and Economic Cooperation among Member States of the League. While the Articles of the Pact and the Treaty are those regarding peace and security, as described above, Article 50 of the UN Charter is not. Article 50 of the UN Charter provides:

> If preventive or enforcement measures against any state are taken by the Security Council, any other state, whether a Member of the UN or not, which finds itself confronted with special economic problems arising from the carrying out of those measures shall have the right to consult the Security Council with regard to a solution of those problems.

There is a possibility that an error may have occurred in the unofficial translation of the Pact, as the original is only signed in Arabic, and that Article 51 would have been meant instead. However, it is not excluded that the provision for economic solutions is intended, as the same request for UN funding is included in the Ezulwini Consensus of the AU.

---

17 McCoubrey and Morris, op. cit., n. 3, p. 198.
18 Hummer and Schweitzer, op. cit., n. 2, p. 831.
19 The Statute of the Arab Peace and Security Council.

The Treaty of Joint Defence and Economic Cooperation also provided for a mechanism for dealing with security and defence issues, consisting of a Permanent Military Commission as an organ with advisory functions and a Joint Defence Council that would take decisions on matters of peace and security. This system has essentially remained on paper. Only around 2,005 new initiatives for a workable mechanism of peace and security in the Arab world came about, including the Statute of the Arab Peace and Security Council.[20]

The new Arab Peace and Security Council mechanism reveals some similarity to the innovative AU security and defence mechanism, several members of which are League members as well. Thus, Article VII of the Statute, alongside a Data Bank and an Early Warning System, provides for a third organ of the Council: a Board of Wise Personalities (in comparison – the AU Panel of the Wise). The board is to consist of prominent Arab personalities enjoying appreciation and respect. The members of the board would be designated by the Chairperson of the Council or the Secretary-General to undertake mediation, conciliation and good offices missions, or to go on investigating missions.

The objectives of the Arab Peace and Security Council are the prevention, management and settlement of inter-Arab conflicts, as well as the analysis of developments affecting Arab national security (Article III). Both the AUPSC and Arab Peace and Security Council have co-ordinating, analytical and implementing functions. However, the Arab Peace and Security Council does not have a decision-making function. It is the Council of the Arab League that takes all decisions based upon the findings of the Peace and Security Council.[21] Article VIII of the Statute, however, provides that the League's Council may charge the Peace and Security Council with an executive function 'to take the necessary action to restore security in tension areas, including dispatching of civil or military observer missions to these areas with specific mandate'. The Peace and Security Council is to be composed of five Member States represented at the level of Foreign Ministers.[22] If a member of the Council is involved in a conflict, a mechanism for substitution with another Council member is provided in the Statute.

Article VI states that in accordance with the Charter of the Arab League and with the principle of sovereignty and territorial integrity of all Member States the Peace and Security Council will, among others, undertake the following duties:

---

20 Tavares, op. cit., n. 9, p. 110.
21 The Statute of the Arab Peace and Security Council. See, for example, Art. III b) and Art. VI, para. 10.
22 The Statute of the Arab Peace and Security Council, Art. IV.

- Propose appropriate measures to be taken collectively in case of aggression, or threat of aggression against an Arab country in accordance with the provisions of Article 6 of the Charter[23] as well as in the case of an Arab country attacking another Arab country or threatening to attack it.
- Strengthen co-operation to confront transnational threats and dangers such as organised crime and terrorism.
- Submit proposals for the establishment of an Arab peace-keeping force whenever necessary.
- In case of aggravation of a conflict the Council, in addition to the measures it proposes to contain it, may request to hold an extraordinary session of the League's Council to take appropriate decisions thereon.

Thus, what can be concluded from the article is that the Arab Peace and Security Council does not make decisions on the Arab League actions in the field of maintenance of peace and security, but makes recommendations to the Council of the Arab League, which then takes the decision. Emergency meetings for collective rapid reaction can be held. The Arab League does have the formal potential for establishing regional peacekeeping, including, or rather – in particular – military peacekeeping. The creation of such a peacekeeping force has, however, proved to be a practical challenge. It can also be concluded that the concept of collective defence enhances both conflicts within the region, and conflicts with a State outside the regional organisation. Thus, the self-defence clause is applicable also when the aggressor is a member of the Arab League. Also, dealing with non-traditional threats has been added to the competence of Arab peace and security mechanism, specifically regarding organised crime and terrorism.

Decision-making

Article 3 of the Pact of the Arab League provides that the League shall have a Council composed of the representatives of the Member States. Each State shall have one vote. The functions of the Council are to realise the purpose of the Arab League, supervise the execution of the agreements concluded between the Member States and determining the means whereby the Arab League will collaborate with the international organisations which may be created in the future to guarantee peace and security and organise economic and social relations.

The collective self-defence clause of Article 6 of the Pact requires unanimity. If the aggressor is a Member State, the unanimity requirement excludes that State. Article 7 of the Pact provides that the decisions of the Council taken by a unanimous vote are binding on all the Member States of the

---

23 The translation of the Statute refers to the Pact of the League of Arab States as the 'Charter'.

League while those that are reached by a majority vote are binding only to those that accept them. In fact, the unanimous decisions can be interpreted as binding on all Member States also by the virtue of each State's own consent. This provision has turned out to be the stumbling block of the Arab League – it is commonly noted as a reason why the Arab League has been reluctant to deal with regional conflicts.[24]

The structure and decision-making process of the Arab League never became as complex and elaborated as, for example, that of its contemporary, the OAS. The Joint Defence and Economic Cooperation Treaty of 1950 and the Statute of the Peace and Security Council, nevertheless contain specific provisions.

The Joint Defence and Economic Cooperation Treaty provides for the creation of a Joint Defence Council under the supervision of the Arab League Council to implement the collective defence provisions.[25] The Joint Defence Council consists of the Foreign Ministers and the Defence Ministers of the Member States or their representatives. Decisions taken by a two-thirds majority are binding on all Member States. Considering the functions delegated to the Joint Defence Council, these would be the decisions regarding the implementation of defence measures. In reality it is the principle that the Arab League Council decisions not taken by unanimity bind only those accepting them that has paralysed the whole Arab League system. Therefore, also, the Joint Defence Council never became effective.[26]

The 2006 Statute of the Arab Peace and Security Council apparently takes the same position in the structure of the Arab League as the Joint Defence Council did – under the supervision of the Council of the Arab League. The function of the Peace and Security Council is merely advisory and executive, as it does not make decisions regarding peace and security, but only makes recommendations, and has an executive function in carrying out the practicalities of the decisions made by the Council of the Arab League. Tavares points to the positive change in the capacity of the Arab League to intervene in disputes concerning sovereignty, independence and territorial integrity of States and acting upon its own initiative.[27] The Statute provides for the possibility of the Peace and Security Council to mediate, negotiate and deal with conflicts with peaceful means upon its own initiative. The Statute, however, does not alter the Pact, the authority of the Arab League Council and the provisions regarding the absence of unanimity. Thus, the problem of the enforceability of the Arab League Council decisions remains valid.

---

24 Tavares, op. cit., n. 9, p. 113; 'Profile: Arab League', *BBC News*, 9 March 2011. Available at <http://news.bbc.co.uk/2/hi/middle_east/country_profiles/1550797.stm> (accessed 11 April 2013).
25 Joint Defence and Economic Cooperation Treaty, Art. 6.
26 'Profile: Arab League', op. cit., n. 24.
27 Tavares, op. cit., n. 9, p. 109.

The unwillingness and inability of the Arab League to intervene into the matters of its members puts it, regional coherence- and commitment-wise, on a level of a co-operative security organisation, like ASEAN, rather than a collective security organisation, as it was intended.

The practice

The Arab League is not an organisation with any considerable practice. In fact, some authors even refer to the Middle East as a region where regional organisations are absent.[28] This is mainly due to the Arab-Israeli conflict. Instead of being a maintainer of peace and security in the region, the Arab League is rather a belligerent in the Palestine-Israel conflict, to use the characterisation by McCoubrey and Morris.[29] While the members of the Arab League have been able to agree on some declarations regarding the Palestinian-Israeli conflict,[30] constant disputes between Member States prevent the League from being able to deal with nearly any other issues, especially due to the specific non-binding decision principle.[31] The 12 March 2011 request to the UNSC to establish a no-fly zone in Libya is a rare example of a joint decision by the Arab League.[32]

The Arab League has taken action with the use of military means in two conflicts over the course of 60 years (while this is not indicative of the absence of military conflicts in the Middle East region). The first time the League established an Inter-Arab Force as a peacekeeping force was in 1961 in the conflict between Iraq and Kuwait. The second time was the peace-keeping operation in Lebanon from 1976 to 1983 carried out by the Arab League:[33] initially by the Arab Security Force, later to be succeeded by the Arab Deterrent Force. In this case, Article 3 of the Joint Defence and Economic Cooperation Treaty was presumably invoked.[34] The provision is: 'The Contracting States shall consult together at the request of any one of them, whenever the territorial integrity, independence or security of any one of them is threatened'. It was the largest and most controversial action carried out by the Arab League. After the collapse of effective government in

---

28 McCoubrey and Morris, op. cit., n. 3, Chapter 8 (p. 187) is entitled 'In the Absence of Regional Organisations' and refers to the Middle East and the League of Arab States in particular.
29 McCoubrey and Morris, op. cit., n. 3, p. 192.
30 For example, 'Arab League backs Palestinian membership bid at UN', *BBC News*, 28 May 2011. Available at <http://www.bbc.co.uk/news/world-middle-east-13586799> (accessed 11 April 2013).
31 'Profile: Arab League', op. cit., n. 24.
32 See the reference to the League of Arab States decision in S/RES/1973 (2011).
33 A. Cassese, *UN Peacekeeping: Legal Essays*, Leiden: Martinus Nijhoff Publishers, 1978, p. 109.
34 McCoubrey and Morris, op. cit., n. 3, p. 198.

Lebanon, the Arab League intervened. The peacekeeping force was essentially Syrian and was accused of lack of impartiality.[35] In addition, the operation was carried out without a UN mandate, and the Syrian forces exceeded their peacekeeping mandate, carrying out enforcement action.[36] The legality of the operation was never discussed by the UNSC,[37] just as it has been characteristic in the post-Cold War African cases. In 1983 a multinational peacekeeping force, comprising of British, French, Italian and US contingents took over in Lebanon. The Syrian forces, however, remained in Lebanon until 2005.[38]

The Arab League took no action in the Gulf conflicts throughout the post-Cold War years.[39] Member States were split in their support to the intervention.[40] During the first Gulf conflict between Iraq and Kuwait in 1990, a coalition of the willing was established to carry out the first ever UN-authorised peace enforcement operation instead.[41] Some individual members of the Arab League, however, have been part of the coalitions both in the Gulf conflicts, and in Libya in 2011.

The Arab League has shown slight improvements to the overall pattern of inactivity during the past few years. For one, those are the legislative initiatives of the organisation described above. In addition, the Arab League was involved in solving the political crisis in Lebanon through mediation in 2008.[42] Though a civil war was avoided, the conclusion of the Doha Agreement of May 2008 on the settlement of the Lebanon conflict did not bring a lasting solution, and in January 2011 the situation in Lebanon was still described as being serious by the Arab League.[43] Moreover, in 2008 the Arab League Council convened for the first time to discuss a conflict – the border dispute between Djibouti and Eritrea and agreed to send a fact-finding mission.[44] Also, as mentioned in the recent case of Libya, the Arab League was the formal framework for inviting a UN intervention in the internal conflict in Libya, by requesting a no-fly zone.

The Arab League was entrusted with the central co-ordination role in the Libyan crisis by UNSC Resolution 1973 (2011). However, in reality the Arab League was left out of the actual resolution of the conflict, even though,

---

35 C. Gray, *International Law and the Use of Force*, 3rd edn, Oxford: Oxford University Press, 2008, p. 399.
36 McCoubrey and Morris, op. cit., n. 3, p. 198.
37 Gray, op. cit., n. 35, p. 391.
38 Ibid, p. 399.
39 Shaw, op. cit., n. 11, p. 1293.
40 'Profile: Arab League', op. cit., n. 24.
41 S/RES/678(1990).
42 Tavares, op. cit., n. 9, p. 113.
43 C. Hilleary, 'Arab League Calls Lebanese Crisis "Serious"', *Voice of America*, 14 January 2011. Available at <http://www.voanews.com/english/news/Arab-League-Calls-Lebanese-Crisis-Serious-113603364.html> (accessed 11 April 2013).
44 Tavares, op. cit., n. 9, p. 114.

as opposed to the AU, it called for enforcement action. The support of the Arab League, though, had already faded after the first coalition bombings.[45] The international enforcement action in Libya did not proceed, as the Arab League and the AU had expected.[46] At the initial stage of the crisis resolution, the Arab League specifically expressed the wish that NATO not get involved in Libya.[47] A coalition operation was initially launched, but taken over by NATO just a few days later. Other than requesting an international enforcement action and later expressing the discontent with the action carried out, the Arab League had no considerable role in resolving the Libyan crisis.

In addition to the establishment of the Peace and Security Council, the Arab League is also working on an initiative of establishing an Arab peacekeeping force 'to regain ownership of the resolution of its conflicts'.[48] Though a very small step, the decision on inviting UN intervention in Libya has also broken the pattern of the Arab League not being able to take common decisions. As long as the conflict with Israel is nearly the only thing that can bring an agreement among Arab States, the other conflicts within the region will remain handled by out-of-region actors, be it the UN, coalitions of the willing or other regional organisations. A wish to avoid outside interference may stimulate regional maintenance of peace and security efforts in the future.

Co-operation with the United Nations

Even though the Arab League was one of the two regional organisations present from the beginnings of the UN, the UN was hesitant to recognise the Chapter VIII status of the organisation. As opposed to the OAS, the claim

---

45 I. Traynor, 'Arab League Chief Admits Second Thoughts about Libya Air Strikes', *The Guardian*, 21 June 2011. Available at <http://www.guardian.co.uk/world/2011/jun/21/arab-league-chief-libya-air-strikes> (accessed 11 April 2013).
46 'African Union demands "immediate" halt to Libya Attacks', *The Times of India*, 20 March 2011. Available at <http://articles.timesofindia.indiatimes.com/2011-03-20/middle-east/29148423_1_african-union-libya-attacks-libyan-authorities> (accessed 11 April 2013). E. Cody, 'Arab League Condemns Broad Western Bombing Campaign in Libya', *The Washington Post*, 20 March 2011. Available at <http://www.washingtonpost.com/world/arab-league-condemns-broad-bombing-campaign-in-libya/2011/03/20/AB1pSg1_story.html> (accessed 11 April 2013). J. Decker, 'Arab League Condemns Bombing in Libya', *Reuters* news agency, 20 March 2011. Available at <http://www.reuters.com/news/video/story?videoId=197411571&videoChannel=5> (accessed 11 April 2013).
47 'Ritzau. Løkke Ønsker større NATO rolle i Libyen', *TV2 News*, 22 March 2011. Available at <http://nyhederne.tv2.dk/article.php/id-38369238:løkke-ønsker-større-natorolle-i-libyen.html> (accessed 11 April 2013).
48 *A Secure Middle East: A Vision from the Arab World*, Introductory Remarks by H. E. Mr. Amr Moussa, Secretary-General of the League of Arab States at the Académie Diplomatique Internationale, Paris, 1 February 2010, p. 7.

of which to be a Chapter VIII organisation was never contested at the UN, there was a fierce debate about the status of the Arab League.[49] It was argued in some UN General Assembly debates that the absence of reference to Chapter VIII in the Pact of the Arab League or the lack of enforcement measures would imply that the Arab League is not a regional arrangement in the meaning of Chapter VIII. Nevertheless, the Arab League was accepted as an observer to the UN General Assembly in 1950 without specifying the status, and further on it has been regarded as a Chapter VIII organisation.[50] Since the debate over the observer status of the Arab League in the UN General Assembly, its status as a Chapter VIII organisation has not been questioned.[51] And there has not been a frequent need for that either – due to the general inactivity of the organisation, which also means that the co-operation with the UN has not been extensive.

The Arab League was created to be an organisation working in compliance with the principles and text of the UN Charter. The only large-scale operation the Arab League has undertaken – in 1976 – was formally launched as a peacekeeping operation without a UN mandate. In addition, the Arab League launched a smaller peacekeeping operation to resolve a conflict between Iraq and Kuwait in 1961. There is no practice of co-operation between the UN and the Arab League with regard to military operations in the field. Over the years the UNSC has been dealing with the Middle East issues without considerable contribution from the Arab League. Myriads of resolutions have been passed by the UN over the decades on the Israeli-Palestinian conflict and the Gulf conflicts. In 1993, the UN General Assembly devoted a resolution to UN co-operation with the Arab League.[52] The only significant point in the resolution is that the Assembly regards the Chapter VIII status of the Arab League as given, based on the claims of the Arab League itself. Otherwise, the document provides for no relevant co-operation or common practice, only a political intent to strengthen the co-operation between the two organisations.

In the twenty-first century, attempts to breathe life into the peace and security mechanisms of the Arab League have come around, but the mention of the League in the UN documents does not show relevant intensification of co-operation between the two organisations. The 2004 UN General Assembly resolution on co-operation with regional organisations[53] mentions the co-operation between the UN and the Arab League, especially with regard to human rights and conflict prevention. The 2006 UN General Assembly resolution on co-operation with regional organisations touches upon formal

---

49 Hummer and Schweitzer, op. cit., n. 2, p. 818.
50 Gray, op. cit., n. 35, p. 384.
51 Hummer and Schweitzer, op. cit., n. 2, p. 828.
52 A/RES/48/21, see also A/RES/47/12.
53 A/59/303 (points 41–43, p. 12).

diplomatic co-operation, including that in the field of security between the two organisations.[54] In December 2010, a draft UN General Assembly resolution on Cooperation between the UN and the League of Arab States (A/65/L.33) was presented by the Arab Group.[55] The UN General Assembly requested the UN Secretary-General and the General Secretariat of the Arab League to intensify their co-operation for the realisation of the purposes and principles embodied in the UN Charter. The two organisations would work to strengthen the capacity of the Arab League.[56] The Resolution project was adopted by the UN General Assembly, welcoming the co-operation of the two organisations.[57] The item was again included in the agenda for the sixty-seventh session of the UN General Assembly, where the UN Secretary-General would have to report on the progress of the actual co-operation.

A case to illustrate the efforts to strengthen the co-operation between the UN and the Arab League is the Libya conflict (2011). In UNSC Resolution 1973 the UN appointed the Arab League as the co-ordinator of the international action taken in Libya, implicitly pointing to the importance of the regional security and defence organisation as a local forum that can grant legitimacy to outside intervention. The AU was, supposedly, not chosen for this purpose due to its support for Gaddafi – who was the author of the initial proposal for an African regional organisation, later established as the AU[58] – was the Chairman of the Assembly of the AU, and had sponsored the organisation financially.[59]

The UNSC resolution not only refers to the decision of the Council of the Arab League of 12 March 2011 requesting an imposition of a no-fly zone on Libyan military aviation and civilian protection in Libya. It also notes the important role of the Arab League in matters relating to international maintenance of peace and security in the region and its status under Chapter VIII of the UN Charter. The Arab League is given the role of the co-ordinator for co-operation with other Member States of the UN, and the implementation of the UN resolution. The States that nationally or through regional organisations and arrangements are to take measures to enforce the no-fly zone, are to report to and co-operate equally with the UN Secretary-General, as well as the Secretary-General of the Arab League.[60] Nevertheless, apart from the formal request for intervention to the UN,[61] and subsequent condemnation,

---

54 A/61/256.
55 GA/11036.
56 GA/11036.
57 A/RES/65/126.
58 B. Kioko, 'The right of intervention under the African Union's Constitutive Act: From non-interference to non-intervention', *International Review of Red Cross*, Vol. 85, 852 (December) 2003, p. 811.
59 'African Union "ignored" over Libya Crisis', op. cit., n. 16.
60 S/RES/1973 (2011).
61 S/RES/1973 (2011).

the Arab League as a whole failed to assume any actual role in the resolution of the conflict in Libya (or any other conflict in the Middle East in 2011, for that matter), despite individual members becoming members of the coalition.

Organization of Islamic Conference

The OIC was established in 1969. It has 57 Member States from a very vast geographical region.[62] The coherent element of the organisation is not geography, but religion – Islam. The organisation is centred around the Middle East, but the map of the organisation is far more extended, consisting of nearly one-third of the UN Member States. In fact, even the regional character of the organisation is questioned, as it spans several regions.[63]

The OIC is a political co-operation organisation that comprises Member States from Africa, Asia, the Russian sphere of influence and the Middle East. The organisation is comparable to OSCE. Just like OSCE, the OIC covers several security regions with different regional mechanisms for the maintenance of peace and security. The OIC is not an overarching organisation to which they are subordinate, but rather a trans-regional organisation that provides a forum for multilateral diplomatic talks. The law and practice of the OIC is only sketched in this chapter to give an additional example of a regional organisation centred around the Middle East, and in addition to the Arab League.

In 2008 the OIC adopted a new Charter.[64] The Charter of the OIC[65] provides that it is an organisation dealing with the maintenance of peace and security. The provisions on the prohibition of the use of force and peaceful settlement of disputes, along with the commitment to the purposes and principles of the UN Charter are included in the OIC Charter. They are followed by a long list of principles relevant in Islam in Article 2. Islamic majority in a State is the main requirement for participation in the organisation.

The Charter contains two articles on the peaceful settlement of disputes. Article 27 provides:

> The Member States, parties to any dispute, the continuance of which may be detrimental to the interests of the Islamic Ummah or may endanger the maintenance of international peace and security, shall, seek a solution by good offices, negotiation, enquiry, mediation, conciliation,

---

62 'About OIC', the Organization of Islamic Conference website. Available at <http://www.oic-oci.org/page_detail.asp?p_id=52> (accessed 11 April 2013).
63 Hummer and Schweitzer, op. cit., n. 2, p. 837.
64 Charter of the Organization of the Islamic Conference, Dakar, 14 May 2008. Available at <http://www.oic-oci.org/is11/english/Charter-en.pdf> (accessed 11 April 2013).
65 Charter of the Organization of the Islamic Conference, Art. 2.

arbitration, judicial settlement or other peaceful means of their own choice. In this context good offices may include consultation with the Executive Committee and the Secretary-General.

Article 28 provides that the OIC may co-operate with other international and regional organisations with the objective of preserving international peace and security, and settling disputes through peaceful means. There is a general absence of specific remedies in the OIC Charter. The decision-making in the organisation is based on consensus, but if that is not possible, on a two-thirds majority. The quorum is two-thirds of the Member States.

The Chapter VIII status of the organisation is not clear. While some authors claim it is not a Chapter VIII organisation,[66] it is also stated that the organisation claims to be one.[67] On the one hand, Hummer and Schweitzer refer to the fact that the OIC has never contacted the UN within the meaning of Chapter VIII of the UN Charter.[68] On the other hand, the OIC has had observer status at the UN General Assembly since 1975.[69] In 2007 and 2009, the UN General Assembly issued resolutions regarding co-operation with the OIC[70] equivalent to those concerning co-operation with the OAS and the Arab League. In the resolutions regarding regional organisations of the 1990s, a reference to the Chapter VIII status was typically made, but the rhetoric of the twenty-first century has changed. Even if the OIC is not a Chapter VIII organisation, the reference by the UN General Assembly is made to the UN co-operation with it as a regional organisation, without specifying any chapters or articles. Essentially, the resolution contains the same co-operation provisions and is made according to the same template as the resolutions regarding co-operation with Chapter VIII organisations in the 1990s. While the 2006 UN General Assembly report on co-operation with regional organisations[71] did not concern security and defence issues, the 2007 and 2009 co-operation resolutions[72] also address co-operation in conflict prevention, peacekeeping and peacebuilding. A draft UN General Assembly resolution on co-operation between the UN and the OIC (document A/65/L.43) was submitted in December 2010. The draft provides that, among other things, the UN General Assembly would affirm that the UN and the OIC shared a common goal of promoting and facilitating the Middle East peace process so that it could reach its objective of establishing a just and comprehensive peace in that region.[73] The project was adopted in UN General Assembly

---

66 Hummer and Schweitzer, op. cit., n. 2, p. 837. Tavares, op. cit., n. 9, p. 11.
67 Tavares, op. cit., n. 9, p. 12.
68 Hummer and Schweitzer, op. cit., n. 2, p. 837.
69 A/RES/3369 (XXX).
70 A/RES/61/49 and A/RES/63/114.
71 A/61/256.
72 A/RES/61/49 and A/RES/63/114.
73 GA/11036.

Resolution A/RES/65/140 where the UN General Assembly welcomed the strengthening between the OIC and the UN. The UN Secretary-General is to report on the actual co-operation at the sixty-seventh session of the UN General Assembly.[74] No practical co-operation between the two organisations has taken place to date in the field of maintenance of peace and security.

No mandate for any kind of military use of force, not even military peacekeeping is specified in the Charter and neither has OIC launched any peacekeeping operations. A general initiative to create an OIC peacekeeping force has, nevertheless, been expressed several times throughout the twenty-first century – for example, in 2007[75] and 2009[76] – but has not been followed up. In 2010 the Secretary-General of the OIC expressed an initiative in the media to establish a department for peace and security within the OIC General Secretariat and an OIC Peace and Security Council.[77] Thus, if there is to be any mechanism for regional maintenance of peace within the framework of the OIC, it is still to be created. In any case, due to the trans-regional composition, the OIC is not likely to bend or challenge the existing rules on the use of force by regional organisations, at least not in the foreseeable future.

Summary

The Middle East shows an irregularity in the general picture of regionalisation in the maintenance of peace and security with its shortage of regional initiatives and practice. Though the Middle East organisations are traditional organisations complying with the UN Charter provisions without controversies about what is appropriate for regional action, they have not been an active part of the post-Cold War UN efforts in utilising regional mechanisms in the maintenance of peace and security. As opposed to other security regions, where the regional mechanisms may be acting too autonomously, in the Middle East the inability to co-operate in the regional mechanisms for the maintenance of peace and security has been the greatest problem in itself. The OIC with a wide trans-regional membership and general competence has consensus as the decision-making principle, and two-thirds vote in the absence of it. The decision-making principle of the Arab League is unanimity.

---

74 A/RES/65/140.
75 'OIC Mulls muslim peacekeeping force', *Daily Times*, Kuala Lumpur, 16 February 2007. Available at <http://www.dailytimes.com.pk/default.asp?page=2007\02\16\story_16-2-2007_pg1_1> (accessed 11 April 2013).
76 K. Zarbaliyeva, 'Organization of Islamic Conference intends to establish a peacekeeping force', *Trend*, Azerbaijan, Baku, 22 April 2009. Available at <http://en.trend.az/news/politics/foreign/1459536.html> (accessed 11 April 2013).
77 M. A. Majin, 'OIC Secy-Gen Calls for establishment of department of peace and security', *Brunei FM*, 27 January 2010. Available at <http://news.brunei.fm/2010/01/27/oic-secy-gen-calls-for-establishment-of-department-of-peace-and-security/> (accessed 11 April 2013).

If unanimity is not reached, the decisions made by majority vote are binding only to the members who have agreed to them.

One of the main reasons for the inactivity of the Middle East regional maintenance of peace and security is the inability to deal with the vast conflicts, like the one with Israel, the wars in Iraq, and others the 2011 internal conflicts resulting from the Arab Spring. Another possible reason for the inactivity of the Middle East regional organisations is fragmentation and organisation overlap. For example, the Arab League overlaps region- and function-wise with the AU. The recent events regarding Libya evidence a theoretical gap for how to solve situations when a conflict falls under the competence of two or more organisations simultaneously, especially if the organisations prioritise different principles and apply conflicting interpretations of what is appropriate for regional action.

In the Middle East, permitted regional action is peaceful settlement of disputes, including military peacekeeping. Regional peacekeeping may take place also without a UN mandate. Humanitarian intervention is not a debated issue. While some States are also members of the AU, where humanitarian intervention is permitted, the Middle East regional organisations are far more reluctant to intervene into the internal matters of Member States. The mandate to intervene by peaceful means only upon an organisation's initiative is new as of 2006.

In the Arab League regional security and defence are integrated, and self-defence measures may also take place against a member of the organisation. The threats that the region faces are both traditional threats of internal and international conflicts, as well as non-traditional threats of terrorism and organised crime.

More than any other region, the Middle East in the post-Cold War era has relied upon the universal mechanism, without using the regional one. It is clear, however, that in case of enforcement action the UN does not intervene as an organisation, but delegates the task to Member States. In reality, this has meant operations by the coalition of the willing with a Euro-Atlantic lead, and operations by NATO. Thus the inability to act collectively within the region has itself contributed to the interventions by out-of-region States and organisations.

7 The Russian sphere of influence

The matryoshka of military peacekeeping

General description of the region

The Russian sphere of influence has historically developed over a vast part of the European and Asian continents as a security region of its own. Since the end of the Second World War and the establishment of the Iron Curtain, a sequence of security and defence organisations has been formed in the region. First of all, in 1955 the Warsaw Pact was signed, establishing a UN Charter Article 51 organisation. After the fall of the Iron Curtain the organisation became redundant and was dissolved in 1991.

The Warsaw Pact (Treaty of Friendship, Co-operation, and Mutual Assistance)[1] was signed by the Eastern Bloc States on 14 May 1955. The Warsaw Pact organisation was essentially established to counter NATO.[2] In practice, Russia (Soviet Union) used the alliance to control its sphere of influence. The most significant abuses of the hegemonic power were the claimed interventions upon invitation[3] in Hungary and Czechoslovakia to crush the anti-Soviet uprisings. In 1956, the Soviet intervention in Hungary was justified by referring to the Warsaw Pact and foreign assistance to insurgents.[4] The intervention was condemned by the UN General Assembly, but the UNSC condemnation was avoided by a Soviet veto.[5] In Czechoslovakia in 1968, where the situation was essentially similar to that in Hungary, the Soviet Union used the justification that the conflict was international subversion where assistance to the government was thus needed.[6] Later, outside the framework of the Warsaw Pact, the same legal basis – intervention by invitation – was used in the Russian intervention in Afghanistan in 1979.

---

1 UNTS, vol. 219, p. 3.
2 M. N. Shaw, *International Law*, 6th edn, Cambridge: Cambridge University Press, 2008, p. 47.
3 C. Gray, *International Law and the Use of Force*, 3rd edn, Oxford: Oxford University Press, 2008, p. 92.
4 I. Brownlie, *International Law and the Use of Force by States*, Oxford: Oxford at the Clarendon Press, 1963 (reprinted 2002), p. 325, also note 6 therein.
5 Gray, op. cit., n. 3, p. 87.
6 Ibid.

The Cold War practice of Russia in its sphere of influence was similar to the US interventionism in Latin America, except, instead of the pretext of pro-democratic aims, questionable invitations were used as the justification for intervention. For this reason, it is not surprising that after the end of the Cold War many of the former Socialist Bloc and Soviet States avoided further alliances with Russia. Russia, which before the Soviet revolution of 1917 had been one of the major European powers, was the hegemon on the East side of the Iron Curtain during the Cold War. What remained in the Russian sphere of influence after the end of the Cold War were 11 of the former Soviet republics, together with which Russia created the new regional organisation – the CIS.

The CIS was established with peace and security as one of its functions. A few years later, in 2002, to improve and enhance the co-operation in the field of maintenance of peace and security and to meet new threats, the CSTO was established within the CIS, but as a separate regional peace and security organisation.

The two existing organisations of the region have a peculiar structure. The CIS and the CSTO are both international organisations with a legal personality and, yet, they have an interlocking relationship, but without clearly separated functions. The CIS and the CSTO are an organisation within an organisation – corresponding to the Russian traditional matryoshka (babushka) doll structure. While the two are legally separate international organisations, they have a common basic document – the Collective Security Treaty of 1992 as the legal basis for the security and defence mechanism in the region. The rest of the basic (founding) documents of each organisation differ. How distinct are the functions of the two organisations is not yet fully clear based on the sources and practice available to date.

The CIS consists of 11 Member States[7] which have committed themselves to co-operation within the field of maintenance of peace and security. The CSTO has further enhanced co-operation in collective security and defence, with an emphasis on military co-operation.[8] The CSTO has seven Member States. While the initial aim of establishing the CIS was to preserve an integrated defence system in the Russian sphere of influence, the aims of the common defence within the CSTO framework were, in addition, extended to combat Islamic terrorism, drug trafficking and ethnic conflict.[9]

---

7 The Member States of the CIS are Armenia, Azerbaijan, Belarus, Kazakhstan, Kyrgyzstan, Moldova, Russia, Tajikistan, Turkmenistan, Ukraine and Uzbekistan. Turkmenistan and Ukraine do not have full member status. Georgia withdrew its membership in 2008, thus there are 11 CIS Member States at the moment.
8 As opposed to general political co-operation.
9 S. Torjesen, 'Russia as a Military Great Power: The Uses of the CIS and the SCO in Central Asia', in E. Wilson Rowe and S. Torjesen (eds), *The Multilateral Dimension in Russian Foreign Policy*, London and New York, NY: Routledge, 2009, p. 184.

There is one thing common for all three organisations of the region (the Warsaw Pact, the CIS, the CSTO), each organisation is centred around a great power – Russia. As opposed to the role of the USA in the OAS, Russia is more open about its hegemonic position, and appears generally to have the acquiescence for such a position from the other States of the region.

Commonwealth of Independent States

General description

The CIS was established in 1991. It consists of 11 Member States that are also all former Soviet republics. The organisation, however, does not have legal continuity with either the USSR or the Warsaw Pact. The reason for creating the CIS was the preservation of the integrated defence system of the Member States of the USSR, after its collapse.[10] The CIS was established with two documents: the Agreement on the Establishment of the Commonwealth of Independent States signed by Belarus, Russia and Ukraine on 8 December 1991 and the Alma-Ata Declaration, signed by 11 CIS Member States on 21 December 1991. The constitutive document of the CIS is the Charter (Statute) of the CIS, signed in Minsk on 22 January 1993.[11] The Collective Security Treaty was signed even before the Charter on 15 May 1992 within the framework of the CIS and with an initial aim to preserve a united security space in the region.

The legal basis

The Charter of the CIS is the constitutive document of the organisation and contains the core provisions on the CIS. In fact, the provisions are some of the most elaborate and specific compared to the constitutive documents of the other regional organisations. The following are listed as the core principles of the CIS: the sovereign equality of States, the right to self-determination, the non-interference in the internal matters of States, territorial integrity, the prohibition of the use of force, the supremacy of international law in international relations, and other principles derived from the UN Charter and the Helsinki Final Act. It is noteworthy that in all its documents the CIS refers equally to compliance with OSCE as with the UN. The purposes of the organisation in Article 2 are listed to be political, economic, social (humanitarian), environmental, and other. Certain areas of co-operation are elaborated on. The maintenance of peace and security is one of these, and the Charter provides also for establishing efficient means in cutting down on armament and armament expenditures, the destruction of nuclear weapons and other

---

10 Torjesen, ibid., p. 181.
11 34 *ILM* 1279 (1995).

WMDs, reaching full and complete disarmament, and protecting external borders. Peaceful settlement of disputes is also included. Interestingly, the Charter does not refer to regional peace and security, but world peace and security as the purpose of the organisation. In concerning itself not only with regional security but also with world security, the CIS is similar to the Euro-Atlantic organisations, NATO and the EU, finding a common framework under the auspices of OCSE with most of those organisations' Member States.

The provisions on collective security and military-political co-operation are very detailed and enhancing the broad sphere of activities. Chapter III (Articles 11 to 15) concern specifically collective security and military-political co-operation. Military peacekeeping (military observers and collective peace-keeping forces) is specified as the primary means by which security is to be maintained in the CIS. The co-ordinated policy of the CIS Member States concerns the field of international security, disarmament and arms control, formation of armed forces and maintenance of security in the CIS. Article 12 is dedicated to collective self-defence:

> Should the threat to sovereignty, security and territorial integrity of one or several Member States or to international peace and security arise, the Member States shall immediately employ the mechanism of mutual consultations to coordinate their positions and to undertake measures to eliminate this threat, including the peace-making actions and the use, in case of necessity, of the Armed Forces as the realization of the right for individual and collective self-protection pursuant to Article 51 of UNO Charter. The decision on the joint use of Armed Forces shall be taken by the Council of Heads of States of the Commonwealth or by the interested Member States of the Commonwealth taking into consideration their national legislations.

Thus, the article reveals that self-defence applies to threats from outside the region. As opposed to the provisions of the Arab League, for example, threats from inside the region appear to be covered not by collective self-defence, but by a range of other security measures provided for in the Charter and other CIS documents, the main one being military peacekeeping. At the same time, self-defence is not limited to a threat to an individual Member State or States – the clause can be invoked also in case a threat to international peace and security arises – not necessarily limited to the CIS region. This can be derived from the wording of Article 12, where a threat to international peace and security is listed after a threat to a Member State or Member States as a condition for invoking collective self-defence. In practice, in compliance with international law, such a provision could mean creating an *ad hoc* coalition with a third State for its defence.[12]

---

12 Brownlie, op. cit., n. 4, pp. 330–31. According to Brownlie there is a customary right to aid third States which have become the object of an unlawful use of force.

A region-specific norm included in the Charter is the duty of the Member States to ensure the stable situation in the external frontiers of the CIS. Such a provision is particular to the organisations with the participation of Russia – the CIS and the SCO.

As to the peaceful settlement of disputes, the emphasis of the CIS is once again region-specific – on the prevention of inter-ethnic and inter-confessional conflicts which are likely to entail the violation of human rights. The Russian sphere of influence is heavily burdened by such conflicts, for example, the conflict between Armenia and Azerbaijan, the Russian internal ethnic conflicts with the separatists in Dagestan and Chechnya, as well as Georgia and the separatists in Abkhazia and Southern Ossetia, Moldova and separatists in Transdnestr. The Member States are to settle their dispute through negotiations as the first step. If that fails, they may (but are not obliged to) submit the dispute to the Council of the Heads of States.[13] At the same time, the Council of the Heads of States may interfere in a conflict that may cause a threat to peace and security at any stage and recommend a proper procedure for settlement,[14] thus the consent of the States in conflict is not required, if the Council of Heads of States decides to qualify the dispute as a threat to peace and security, which is fully at its discretion. The initial action of the Council of Heads of States, nevertheless, may not be coercive, but only recommendatory.

The fact that the document providing specifically for the security and defence co-operation in the CIS came chronologically before the CIS Charter illustrates the CIS emphasis on such co-operation. The Treaty on Collective Security[15] signed in Tashkent on 15 May 1992 gives the core provisions of security and defence co-operation within the framework of the CIS, and has later become the legal basis of the CSTO as well. In the period from 1992 to 1994 the treaty was acceded to by nine members of the CIS.[16] In contrast, upon ratification of the CIS Charter, Moldova made a reservation, that it did not intend to participate in matters of collective security and military and political co-operation of the Charter of the CIS.[17]

The Collective Security Treaty (CST) provides for the prohibition of the use of force and the peaceful settlement of disputes as the guiding principles. It also prohibits the participation of the parties to the Treaty in military alliances[18] or any other groupings or actions that could be directed against any other State party. Article 2 of the CST provides that:

---

13 CIS Charter, Art. 17.
14 CIS Charter, Art. 18.
15 UNTS, vol. 1894, 1-32307.
16 Armenia, Azerbaijan, Belarus, Georgia, Kazakhstan, Kyrgyzstan, Russian Federation, Tajikistan and Uzbekistan.
17 UNTS, vol. 1894, 1-32307.
18 The most obvious example of such would be NATO.

The States Parties shall conduct consultations with each other on all major international security matters that affect their interests and coordinate their positions on these matters. In case of any threat to security, territorial integrity and sovereignty to one or several States Parties, or in case of a threat to international peace and security, the States Parties shall immediately put into action the mechanism of joint consultations in order to coordinate their positions and take measures to eliminate the arisen threat.

A Collective Security Council consisting of the Heads of the States Parties and the Commander-in-Chief of the Allied Armed Forces of the CIS is the decision-making organ.[19] Article 4 provides for collective self-defence under Article 51 of the UN Charter. Article 6 further notes that the Treaty does not affect the right of the States to individual and collective self-defence in conformity with the UN Charter.

The use of the Armed Forces outside the territories of the States Parties is to be made exclusively in the interests of international security in strict conformity with the UN Charter and national legislation of the States Parties to the Treaty. Thus, any military action outside the region is to be taken only with a UNSC mandate.

The Treaty was concluded for a period of five years. It was renewed subsequently, and was revived in 2002, when the CSTO was established.

Being a strongly militarily oriented organisation, the CIS has a number of other documents regulating the maintenance of peace and security, all of which cannot be listed here. Some of the most relevant and region-specific provisions, however, need to be mentioned. These are mainly provisions regarding regional military peacekeeping.

In 1996, the CIS adopted the Concept for Prevention and Settlement of Conflicts in the territory of States members of the Commonwealth of Independent States.[20] The CIS Member States agreed to take steps required to settle conflicts on the territory of Member States in accordance with Chapter VIII of the UN Charter, including peacekeeping operations. Though the traditional means of peaceful settlement of disputes are also used by the CIS (good offices, mediation, negotiation and confidence-building measures), it is interesting that CIS Member States resort to peacekeeping operations, i.e. operations actually containing military capabilities, as a central means for the peaceful settlement of disputes.[21] In comparison, in other regions, such as Asia or the Americas, the understanding of peaceful settlement of disputes would generally translate into diplomatic negotiations, and military peacekeeping would be outside the

---

19 Collective Security Treaty, Art. 3.
20 Concept for Prevention and Settlement of Conflicts in the territory of States members of the Commonwealth of Independent States, A/51/62, 31 January 1996 (CIS Concept).
21 CIS Concept.

permissible scope of measures of peaceful settlement of disputes. Even conflict prevention in the CIS can be a reason for preliminary military deployment. Peacekeepers are permitted to participate in armed combat if a situation arises.[22] The document, however, further states that the collective peacekeeping forces shall not take part in active combat and shall make use, first and foremost, of peaceful means and instruments. They shall refrain from the use of weapons except in cases of armed resistance to their discharge of the mandate to conduct peacekeeping operations. Enforcement measures in the settlement of conflicts (peace enforcement) shall be permitted only if such powers have been mandated by the UNSC in accordance with the UN Charter.

The CIS legal basis also provides for the possibility of action outside the region, as peacekeeping with a UN mandate.[23] Peculiarly, however, the peacekeeping concept described above significantly exceeds the limits of traditional UN peacekeeping, emphasising the permissibility of coercive elements in peacekeeping. The extent of the use of force permissible in CIS peacekeeping, as legalised in CIS documents, equals, and even exceeds that of ECOWAS. Whereas enforcement measures were used in controversial ECOWAS operations in Liberia and Sierra Leone, no other mechanism uses the deployment of foreign military troops as a preventive measure included in the peaceful means of settlement of disputes. With an internal peacekeeping mandate as wide as that of CIS, there is no need to invoke enforcement action, or humanitarian intervention in particular.

The Letter dated 26 January 1996 from the Permanent Representative of the Russian Federation to the UN addressed to the UN Secretary-General,[24] which contains a report on CIS activities in the maintenance of peace and security, contains and lists at least six agreements that evidence the emphasis on military peacekeeping in the CIS mechanism for peaceful settlement of disputes:

(a) The Agreement of 20 March 1992 on Military Observer Groups and Collective Peace-Keeping Forces in the Commonwealth of Independent States;

(b) The Protocol of 15 May 1992 on the status of military observer groups and collective peace-keeping forces in the Commonwealth of Independent States;

(c) The Protocol of 15 May 1992 on the provisional arrangements for the formation and deployment of military observer groups and collective peace-keeping forces in areas of conflict between and within the States members of the Commonwealth of Independent States;

---

22 CIS Concept, Section 2, para. 2.
23 CIS Concept, Section 2, para. 2.
24 CIS Concept, Section 2, para. 2.

(d) The Protocol of 15 May 1992 on the staffing, structure, logistical and financial support of military observer groups and the collective peace-keeping forces in the Commonwealth of Independent States;
(e) The Concept for prevention and settlement of conflicts in the territory of States members of the Commonwealth of Independent States of 19 January 1996; and
(f) The Statute of Collective Peacekeeping Force in the Commonwealth of Independent States of 19 January 1996.

Judging from the documents described above, CIS appears highly military oriented, on a level equivalent only to NATO. And it is, in fact, stated by Russia that the aim, if not through the CIS, then through the CSTO is to match NATO capabilities.[25]

Decision-making

The decision-making on the issues of security, defence and guarding of the external frontiers of Member States of the CIS is in the hands of the Council of the Heads of States. Military activity is co-ordinated by the Councils of Heads of Governments.

Article 12 of the CIS Charter provides that the decision on the joint use of armed forces is taken by the Council of Heads of States or by the interested Member States of CIS. Thus, if some Member States intend to use force, they do not necessarily need to receive the acquiescence of all CIS Member States. In general, issues of security and disarmament in the CIS are to be settled by mutual consultations. Article 5 of the CST provides that co-ordination and joint action is to be taken by the Collective Security Council, which consists of the Council of Heads of States and Commander-in-Chief of the Allied Armed Forces. Deployment and operation of the objects of the collective security system on the territory of the States Parties is to be subject to special agreements.[26]

The Council of Heads of States and the Council of the Heads of Governments take decisions by consensus. However, consensus is conditioned by the abovementioned clause of 'interested Member States' in Article 12 of the CIS Charter. Article 23 of the CIS Charter provides that 'any State may

---

25 Torjesen, op. cit., n. 9, p. 186. 'Post-Soviet security group CSTO to become alternative to NATO – newspaper', *RIA Novosti* News Agency, 17 March 2010. Available at <http://en.rian.ru/russia/20100317/158223926.html> (accessed 12 April 2013). K. J. Møller, 'CSTO. Collective Security Treaty Organisation. En Russisk domineret forsvarsorganisation I udvikling?', DIIS Brief, Dansk Institut for Internationale Studier, Oktober 2007, p. 4. H. Ozdal, 'Putting the CSTO to the test in Kyrgyzstan', International Strategic Research Organisation, 21 October 2010. Available at <http://www.usak.org.tr/EN/makale.asp?id=1747> (accessed 12 April 2013).
26 Collective Security Treaty, Art. 7.

declare its lack of interest in this or that issue which should not be considered as an obstacle for taking a decision'. The abovementioned provisions give Russia a great leeway to act without constraint from the other members of CIS.

The CIS has also other organs for the maintenance of peace and security. Such is the Council of Defence Ministers – an organ of the Council of Heads of States on the issues of military policy and the military construction of the Member States. There is also the Allied Armed Forces Chief Command that rules the Allied Armed Forces as well as groups of military observers and the collective peacekeeping forces.[27] Each of the organs has specific regulation in their respective documents.

The Statute of Collective Peacekeeping Forces in the Commonwealth of Independent States of 19 January 1996[28] further elaborates the special decision-making procedure for launching peacekeeping operations. It provides that the Council of Heads of States takes the political decision on launching a collective peacekeeping operation based on consensus. A precondition is an appeal by one or several Member States involved in a conflict, as well as a request or consent of all conflicting sides. In addition, a peace agreement has to be in place. The document itself is in compliance with UN peacekeeping principles. The concept of 'preventive peacekeepers', however, does not appear to fit in the picture.

The mandate for an operation is ratified by the Council of Heads of States upon a recommendation of the Council of Ministers for Foreign Affairs and the Council of Ministers of Defence. In addition, the UN and the OSCE are to be informed immediately of the decision made. A mandate and financial assistance may be asked from the UN, taking into account the scale of the conflict.

The practice

The CIS belongs to those regional organisations that have considerable post-Cold War practice, including military operations in the field. Since the end of the Cold War the CIS has carried out peacekeeping operations in Moldova, Georgia, Armenia, Azerbaijan and Tajikistan. Apart from the Armenian-Azerbaijani conflict over the territory of Nagorny Karabakh, the abovementioned ones are internal conflicts. In addition, Russia is dealing with an internal conflict in Chechnya. The legitimacy of several CIS operations has been questioned. Russia has been accused of using the disguise of a regional security organisation to further its own political agenda by launching large

---

27 CIS Charter, Art. 23.
28 A/52/61.

scale military interventions in other CIS Member States, disguised as regional peacekeeping operations.[29]

The peacekeeping in the Moldovan Russian separatist region Transdnestr launched in 1992 was the first CIS peacekeeping operation. The operation is still ongoing. The peacekeepers[30] consist of Russian, Ukrainian, as well as Moldovan and Transdnestrian observers.[31] It is not according to the UN principles of peacekeeping that the warring parties are also peacekeepers themselves, because they cannot be neutral. The media refer to Moldova as a 'frozen conflict' and the peacekeeping force has been accused of inefficiency.[32] The Moldovan government has been consistently demanding the withdrawal of the peacekeeping forces,[33] to which the pro-Russian Transdnestrian politicians do not agree,[34] and neither does Russia, despite the appeal of the Moldovan government to the CIS, the OSCE and NATO.[35] Peacekeeping against the will of the hosting State hardly complies with the basic principles of peacekeeping. It can be observed that the reservation of Moldova to the CIS Charter and the non-signing of the CST did not keep Moldova out of Russia's sphere of influence. Russia claims that according to the agreement between the Republic of Moldova and the Russian Federation on the principles of a peaceful settlement of the armed conflict in the Transdnestrian region of the Republic of Moldova, signed in Moscow on 21 July 1992, Russia's peacekeeping forces are to stay there until the complete solution of the conflict.[36] In UN practice, the 1967 UNEF I peacekeeping operation in Egypt sets a precedent for a requirement to withdraw troops, when the State consent ceases.[37] The continuation of an operation after a withdrawal of the host State consent cannot be regarded as non-coercive. Even if combat action is not taking place, the forced presence of foreign troops in another State is

---

29 H. McCoubrey and J. Morris, *Regional Peacekeeping in the Post-Cold War Era*, The Hague: Kluwer Law International, 2000, pp. 85–86.
30 The number of troops and the level of arms have been significantly reduced since the 1999 Istanbul Summit, 'OCSE calls for withdrawal', OSCE website. Available at <http://www.osce.org/moldova/55540> (accessed 18 April 2013).
31 'Russia, Moldova, Transdnestr peacekeepers to hold joint drills', *RIA Novosti*, 24 March 2010. Available at <http://en.rian.ru/world/20100324/158297376.html> (accessed 12 April 2013).
32 'Transdnestr rejects Moldova's accusations of peacekeeping inefficiency', *RIA Novosti*, 8 September 2010. Available at <http://en.rian.ru/world/20100908/160519537.html> (accessed 18 April 2013).
33 'Russia, Moldova, Transdnestr peacekeepers to hold joint drills', op. cit., n. 31.
34 'Transdnestr rejects Moldova's accusations of peacekeeping inefficiency', op. cit., n. 32.
35 'Withdrawal of Peacekeepers from Transdniestria to Lead to Denunciation of Peace Agreements', *Informacionnaja Rossiya*, News Agency, 13 November 2010. Available at <http://inforos.ru/en/?module=news&action=view&id=26690> (accessed 12 April 2013).
36 'Withdrawal of Peacekeepers', ibid.
37 A. Randelzhofer, 'UN Peacekeeping System' ('Host Country Consent'), in R. Bernhardt (ed.), *Encyclopaedia of Public International Law*, Vol. 4, Amsterdam: North-Holland Publishing Company, 1982, p. 261.

against the principles of peacekeeping, yet for an enforcement operation there has been no legitimate authorisation.

In 1992, a civil war broke out in Tajikistan. The CIS failed to act collectively. Instead, Russia and Uzbekistan provided bilateral military assistance to Tajikistan. The operation was transformed into a CIS operation in 1993 with the participation of Russia, Kazakhstan, Kyrgyzstan and Uzbekistan. Nevertheless, the Russian contribution remained predominant, and a common peacekeeping mechanism of CIS never materialised.[38] The operation ceased in 2000.[39] In the extension of the conflict in Tajikistan, internal conflicts caused by the Islamic Movement of Uzbekistan, broke out in Uzbekistan and Kyrgyzstan in 1999 and 2000. The CIS was unable to co-ordinate action and respond to the asymmetric threat with a counter-insurgency operation.[40]

In 1993, in connection with the operation in Tajikistan, Russia accelerated its efforts for the CIS to be recognised as a regional organisation under Chapter VIII of the UN Charter. The steps towards it were the 1994 acquisition of the observer status at the UN General Assembly, and the 1996 Concept for Prevention and Settlement of Conflicts in the territory of States members of the Commonwealth of Independent States, which stipulated the Chapter VIII status of the organisation.

While the legitimacy of the operation in Tajikistan has not generally been questioned, the operation in Georgia raised concerns about the impartiality of the peacekeeping forces, and lead to protests against the presence of the CIS forces.[41] It is noted by McCoubrey and Morris that Russia traded in the UN support for establishing a peacekeeping operation in Georgia in return for a favourable vote on the US-promoted UNSC Resolution 940 on intervention in Haiti.[42] This example once again evidences the significance of power-play in dealing with the international use of force, and that trade-in of interests can equally take place in regional organisations (the SADC case of South Africa and Zimbabwe) as well as in the universal organisation, as in the example given.

Georgia has been subject to an internal conflict since the collapse of the Soviet Union. In 1993, the UNSC resolved on the situation in Georgia and the separatist region of Abkhazia for the first time.[43] In the same year, Russian peacekeeping forces were deployed to Georgia, in the region of Abkhazia.[44] In 1994, the Russian operation was re-hatted as a CIS peacekeeping operation in co-operation with the UN observer mission in Georgia. All the peacekeeping

---

38 Torjesen, op. cit., n. 9, p. 184.
39 R. Tavares, *Regional Security. The Capacity of International Organizations*, Oxford: Routledge, 2009, p. 101.
40 Torjesen, op. cit., n. 9, p. 185; Gray, op. cit., n. 3, p. 407.
41 Gray, op. cit., n. 3, p. 279.
42 McCoubrey and Morris, op. cit., n. 29, p. 119.
43 SC/RES/849 (1993).
44 Tavares, op. cit., n. 39, p. 103.

forces in the CIS peacekeeping operation have been solely Russian.[45] In addition, in 1992, a peacekeeping operation was established by Russia in South Ossetia – also in the territory of Georgia. Tavares points out that, though often mistaken for a CIS operation, the peacekeeping operation in South Ossetia was not only practically, but also formally Russian.[46]

The Georgian conflict with Russia culminated in August 2008, escalating in both regions of operation – South Ossetia and Abkhazia. This time Russia openly took the side of the pro-Russian separatists, violating the territorial integrity of Georgia. The arguments of Russia included the need to act in fulfilment of its peacekeeping tasks, self-defence and the need to protect Russian nationals from 'genocide', with the nuances of its official rhetoric constantly changing.[47] The adding of humanitarian intervention to the list of justifications appears to have been treating the Euro-Atlantic region with its own medicine in the context of Kosovo, rather than supporting the legitimacy of regional humanitarian intervention. At the UNSC, Russia has always declared itself highly opposed to the right to regional humanitarian intervention both before[48] and after[49] Georgia. For example, Putin stated to *Moskocskiye Novosti*:

> [W]hen state sovereignty is too easily violated in the name of this provision [humanitarian intervention], when human rights are protected from abroad and on a selective basis and when the same rights of a population are trampled underfoot in the process of such 'protection,' including the most basic and sacred right—the right to one's life—these actions cannot be considered a noble mission but rather outright demagogy.[50]

In the case of Georgia, Russia acted coercively using the peacekeeping forces already located in the region. After the 'August War' of 2008, Russia unilaterally recognised the independence of South Ossetia and Abkhazia. Georgia withdrew from the CIS on 18 August 2008[51] – just after the reaching of a preliminary peace agreement.

---

45 Tavares, op. cit., n. 39, p. 101.
46 Ibid.
47 G. Hafkin, 'The Russo-Georgian War of 2008: Developing the law of unauthorized humanitarian intervention after Kosovo', *Boston University Law Journal*, Vol. 28, 219, 2010, p. 226.
48 E.g. Kosovo.
49 E.g. Libya and Syria.
50 N. Ottens, 'Putin Rallies Against Soft Power, Humanitarian Intervention', *Atlantic Sentinel*, 3 March 2012. Available at <http://atlanticsentinel.com/2012/03/putin-rallies-against-soft-power-humanitarian-interventions/> (accessed 18 April 2013).
51 *Information on Georgia's withdrawal from the CIS*, Ministry of Foreign Affairs of Georgia. Available at <http://www.mfa.gov.ge/index.php?lang_id=ENG&sec_id=30&info_id=10783> (accessed 12 April 2013).

Co-operation with the United Nations

In the year 1992 most of the Member States of today's CIS were accepted as new members of the UN. Not long after, the conflicts in Georgia[52] and between Armenia and Azerbaijan caught the attention of the UNSC. While the UN only expressed concern with Armenian-Azerbaijani conflict in two resolutions in 1993 – UNSC Resolutions 874 and 884 – leaving the issue up to the CIS, the Georgian conflict received more attention.

With UNSC Resolution 858 (1993) the UN established the UN Military Observer Mission in Georgia (UNOMIG) to observe the ceasefire between the Georgian and Abkhaz forces. In addition a peacekeeping force was called for. Since the establishment of the CIS peacekeeping force, UNOMIG has had the task, among others, of observing that the CIS peacekeeping force operates within the framework of the Agreement.[53] Since 1993, the UN has issued around 30 resolutions on the situation in Georgia. Since 1994[54] these resolutions contain a commendation of UNOMIG co-operation with the CIS peacekeeping force, a lengthy description of the situation, and an extension of the UNOMIG mandate. UNSC Resolution 1839, however differs – being the first resolution issued after the August War, it contains no description of the situation, only an extension of the mandate of the UN mission (not mentioning the name UNOMIG). This is explainable with the highly politically sensitive issue of how to interpret the events of August 2008 in Georgia, namely, the military action taken by Georgia and that of Russia, on which both parties have radically different views. The last resolution on Georgia coincides approximately with the coming into effect of the withdrawal of Georgia from the CIS – 18 August 2009. Along with the ending of the CIS operation (due to Georgia no longer being a member of the regional organisation), the UN mission was also ended. The last UN resolution on Georgia is UNSC Resolution 1866, making a note of the six-point agreement of 12 August 2008 and subsequent implementing measures of 8 September 2008 issued on 13 February 2009, and extending the mandate of the 'UN mission' until 15 June 2009.

In comparison, UN-mandated peacekeeping operations in the former Yugoslavia – Kosovo Force (KFOR) and European Union Force (EUFOR) Althea – are continuing years after the signing of peace agreements. Based on the observation of the reoccurring nature of long-lasting conflicts in different regions of the world, it is not likely that the conflict situation of Georgia with the separatist regions (or the new neighbouring countries – as recognised by Russia) of South Ossetia and Abkhazia is fully resolved. Russian peacekeepers

---

52 SC/RES/849 (1993) and SC/RES/874 (1993).
53 SC/RES/937 (1994), 6 b).
54 SC/RES/937 (1994).

remain in the area, i.e. in the territories of South Ossetia and Abkhazia,[55] yet, without a UNSC authorisation.

This example, along with the examples from the practice of the USA and China, may give room for consideration to how much the Permanent Members of the UNSC can equally control the global agenda of the maintenance of peace and security as well as their respective regional mechanisms. At the same time, it also echoes the African concern with the disinterest of the UNSC in African matters. The selection of issues on the UNSC agenda does not portray the UNSC as a more legitimate forum for deciding on intervening in a conflict than a regional organisation, as it is still the regional interests of the powers that are often either prioritised or held back.

Another example of UN involvement in CIS matters is Tajikistan. In the years 1994 to 1999 the UN deployed a mission of observers in Tajikistan.[56] The resolutions stressed the need and welcomed the co-operation of the UN mission with the collective peacekeeping force of the CIS, Russian border forces and the OSCE.[57]

It appears from the UN-supported, though not mandated, CIS peacekeeping operations that Russia highly regards the UNSC mandate as a provider of extra legitimacy. However, the practice of the CIS shows that though commended, none of the operations within the CIS has been UN-mandated. It is not without reason that Russia has been seeking Chapter VIII status for the CIS. It appears that in the doctrine of the region the classification under Chapter VIII of the UN Charter gives a right to regional peacekeeping without a UN mandate.

The basic documents of the CIS do not state that it is a Chapter VIII organisation. The first time the CIS claimed to be a Chapter VIII organisation was in connection with peacekeeping in Tajikistan.[58] The Chapter VIII status was later included in the abovementioned Concept for Prevention and Settlement of conflicts in the territory of States members of the Commonwealth of Independent States.[59] The CIS has been an observer at the UN General Assembly since 1994.[60] The Chapter VIII status of the organisation has not been contested. The author, however, was not able to establish that the CIS

---

55 'Russia may increase the number of peacekeepers in Abkhazia', *Georgia Times*, 21 June 2011. Available at <http://www.georgiatimes.info/en/news/59293.html.> (accessed 12 April 2013). 'Russian forces in Abkhazia, S Ossetia guarantee peace – Rogozin', *The Voice of Russia*, 31 July 2011. Available at <http://english.ruvr.ru/2011/07/31/53992059.html> (accessed 12 April 2013).
56 Established with SC/RES/968 (1994).
57 Resolutions 968 (1994), 999 (1995), 1030 (1995), 1061 (1996), 1089 (1996), 1099 (1997), 1113 (1997), 1128 (1997), 1138 (1997), 1167 (1998), 1206 (1998), 1240 (1999), 1274 (1999).
58 Gray, op. cit., n. 3, p. 396.
59 35 *ILM* 1996, p. 783.
60 A/RES/48/237.

would have signed a joint declaration with the UN Secretary-General, which in practice means the endorsement of the role of the regional organisation in assisting the UN in the maintenance of international peace and security. Such a declaration on co-operation, however exists between the UN and the CSTO.

Common Security Treaty Organization

General description

The CST signed in 1992 (as analysed above) was transformed into the CSTO framework in 2002. The formal reason for establishing CSTO was the rising threat of Islamic terrorism after 9/11.[61] The CSTO was to become a fully fledged organisation capable of addressing new threats and challenges to the region through a rapid reaction force and a joint military command.[62]

Even though the CSTO was established as a regional organisation with its own legal personality, the CST also provides continuity with the security and defence co-operation within the CIS framework. The CSTO consists of seven members of the CIS: Russia, Kazakhstan, Kyrgyzstan, Tajikistan, Uzbekistan, Armenia and Belarus.[63] The structural interconnection of the two organisations is peculiar, and the division of labour between them is not fully clear, apart from non-traditional threats, which are the realm of the CSTO solely.

Gray describes the CSTO as the functional military core of the CIS, which is in the process of concluding institutional and practical arrangements for peacekeeping.[64] This is not fully descriptive, as the CSTO has not taken CIS peacekeeping and military co-operation out of the game. The CSTO has not carried out any military peacekeeping operations yet, while the CIS has been participating in peacekeeping in Georgia throughout the existence of the CSTO. The UNSC presidential statement on co-operation with regional organisations of 13 January 2010 refers to the CIS (along with the OSCE and the SCO) as a 'close partner' of the CSTO.[65] Thus, it can be concluded that both organisations are regarded as separate entities by the UN, while in practice the CSTO, in the last few years, has been the forum co-operating with the UN in the maintenance of peace and security on the diplomatic level, leaving the CIS framework aside. Meanwhile, the CIS also maintains the matters of peace and security enshrined in its Charter and has been continuing the practice of regional peacekeeping.

---

61 Torjesen, op. cit., n. 9, p. 185.
62 Ibid.
63 The first five are also members of the SCO.
64 Gray, op. cit., n. 3, p. 388.
65 S/PV.6257, p. 11.

The legal basis

The legal basis of the CSTO is the CST signed 15 May 1992, a CIS document preceding even the CIS Charter, but not ratified by all Member States of the CIS.[66] This document analysed above as the core document of the CIS, regulating the matters of security and defence, is also valid for the CSTO. There is, however, another significant legal source of the CSTO. It is the Charter of the Collective Security Treaty Organization of 2002.

The Charter of the Collective Security Treaty Organization[67] is the establishing document of the 'international regional organization of the Treaty on Collective Security'. The Preamble of the treaty declares that the States will be acting in strict accordance with their obligations under the UN Charter and the decisions of the UNSC. The aim of the organisation is to further develop and intensify the military and political co-operation of the Member States to ensure and strengthen national, regional and international security. The Preamble in fact uses the term 'alliance' to describe the co-operation in the sphere of countering transnational challenges and threats to the security of States and peoples, and enhancing effectiveness in the activities within the framework of the organisation.

The treaty stipulates that its provisions, the provisions of international agreements, as well as the decisions adopted for the further development of the treaty by the Council on Collective Security, are to be binding on the Member States of the organisation and on the organisation itself.

The purposes of the organisation are stated to be the strengthening of peace and international and regional security and stability and ensuring collective defence of the independence, territorial integrity and sovereignty of its Member States, giving priority to political measures. The basic principles of international law are cited once again, at the same time, not limiting the organisation's own mandate to regional issues. The concern of the CSTO, just as in the two basic documents analysed regarding the CIS, is international maintenance of peace and security, not only regional. In addition, the document states that the organisation shall promote the formation of a just and democratic world order based on the universally recognised principles of international law. This is a typical twenty-first century provision in basic documents of regional organisations, as seen also in Africa and Asia.

Article 7 of the Statute provides a specified range of joint activities in order to achieve an effective collective security system. These include the establishment of coalition (regional) groupings of forces and corresponding administrative bodies, as well as creating a military infrastructure, training military staff and specialists for the armed forces, and furnishing them with the necessary

---

66 Nine members of CIS had ratified the Treaty at its peak. Georgia, Azerbaijan and Uzbekistan did not extend their participation in 1999.
67 UNTS 2235, I-39775, p. 90.

military technology. In comparison, where the AU has a principal provision on the right to intervention, but is short of capabilities, the CSTO is focusing on establishing military assets capable of carrying out operations.

The Statute differs from the documents of the 1990s by adding combating non-traditional threats to its competence in Article 8. These threats include terrorism and extremism, the illicit traffic in narcotic drugs, psychotropic substances and arms, organised transnational crime, illegal migration and other threats to the security of the Member States. The Statute emphasises that the activities are to be carried out primarily under the auspices of the UN. The CSTO refers to action against non-traditional threats as 'primarily under the auspices of the UN', which then may contain actual use of force against them, as done by NATO in Afghanistan, shortly before the drafting of the CSTO Statute. In addition, CSTO Member States signed an agreement on CSTO peacekeeping activities in Dushanbe on 6 October 2007, stapling the organisation's own mandate for peacekeeping operations.

Decision-making

The CSTO Charter provides that the organisation has the following organs: a Council on Collective Security, a Council of Ministers for Foreign Affairs, a Council of Ministers of Defence, a Committee of Secretaries of the Security Councils[68] and a Secretariat.

The work of the organisation is to be carried out mainly through consultations and negotiations for agreeing upon and co-ordinating policy positions regarding international and regional security problems.[69] The principle for decision-making in all the organs is consensus. The Charter also states that each Member State has one vote. More details on the decision process, however, are left to be specified in other documents. The decisions made by the organs are binding on the Member States and require implementation through national legislation.[70]

The Council on Collective Security is the highest organ of the CSTO. It considers the main questions concerning the activities of the organisation and takes decisions aimed at achieving its objectives and purposes, as well as ensures co-ordination and joint action between Member States. The Council consists of the Heads of the Member States. The Council of Foreign Ministers and the Council of Defence Ministers and the Committee of Secretaries of the Security Councils all act as advisory and executive organs on their respective issues.

The CSTO Charter itself does not provide for exceptions to the consensus clause, as opposed to the CIS Charter. Thus, it appears that the acquiescence

---

68 It is composed of the Secretaries of the national security councils of the Member States.
69 CSTO Charter, Art. 9.
70 CSTO Charter, Art. 12.

of all Member States is necessary in order to make a decision. The decisions made by the Council are, however, not abstract decisions made by an international organisation – they constitute a direct obligation for the Member States to implement the obligation through the national procedure. This way, the CSTO is one of the most committed regional organisations in the field of maintenance of peace and security.

The practice

The practice of the CSTO has to date been preparatory for its intended role as a regional, and even global actor. The CSTO has been involved in diplomatic efforts to receive recognition from the UN in order to be able to carry out peacekeeping operations within the region without a UN mandate, and peacekeeping operations outside the region with a UN mandate. Arms sales at favourable conditions by Russia to other Member States are also a part of the closer co-operation within the framework of the CSTO.[71]

The CSTO has been working actively to create a vast infrastructure for Collective Rapid Response Forces – a rapid reaction force equivalent to the EU Battlegroups, NATO Response Forces and the African Standby Force. The size of the Collective Rapid Response Forces is 20,000[72] to which only the capabilities of NATO Response Force are equal. The Collective Rapid Response Forces consist of elite units of armed forces, law enforcement agencies and emergency ministries. The task for these structures would be to localise military and trans-border conflicts, counter organised crime and conduct rehabilitation after emergencies.

In the meeting of the CSTO in December 2010 the Member States looked back on a year where joint military exercises and operations to prevent drug trafficking, illegal immigration and criminal use of cyberspace were conducted. At the meeting the President of Russia, Dmitry Medvedev, stressed the importance of the Collective Rapid Reaction Force in crisis management. The Member States also approved a declaration on the CSTO peacekeeping force and a declaration of the CSTO Member States, and signed a package of joint documents.[73] The texts of the documents are not publically available, but have been described in the media. They consist of over three dozen decisions taken by the CSTO Council, especially on the formation of a

---

71 K. Parshin, 'CIS: Coming together on paper, still apart in practice', Eurasianet.org, Open Society Institute, 8 July 2007. Available at <http://www.eurasianet.org/departments/insight/articles/eav101007b.shtml> (accessed 12 April 2013).
72 'Opening remarks at meeting of the Collective Security Treaty Organisation', President of Russia website, 10 December 2010. Available at <http://eng.kremlin.ru/transcripts/1458> (accessed 12 April 2013).
73 'Meeting of the Collective Security Treaty Organisation', President of Russia website, 10 December 2010. Available at <http://eng.kremlin.ru/news/1459> (accessed 12 April 2013).

crisis response system. Also the CST was amended, for example, the obligation of collective action (as enshrined in Article 4), would apply not only in cases of external aggression against one of the Member States, but also against any kind of armed attack – including non-traditional threats. Joint response against terrorism and joint recovery operations in the case of natural disasters were also enhanced.[74] In contrast to the extensive structural and formal developments, no peacekeeping operations in the field have taken place during the existence of the CSTO.

In 2007, the Secretary-General of CSTO, Nikolai Bordyuzha, suggested in an interview that the CSTO peacekeeping force could be used in Abkhazia and South Ossetia, through a 'verbal agreement with the UN'.[75] The CSTO framework, however, has not been used – not in Abkhazia and South Ossetia, nor in any other case to date.

In 2010, civil unrest broke out in Kyrgyzstan. The Kyrgyz provisional government turned to Russia individually calling for troops to maintain order. Russia referred the matter further to the CSTO. The official reason for the limited role of the CSTO in the Kyrgyz crisis was that the situation involved an internal political crisis in a member country rather than an act of foreign aggression requiring a collective response. According to Russia and the other Member States, the violence was purely a domestic matter for Kyrgyzstan to resolve.[76] Comparing the case to the previous peacekeeping practice of the CIS (also invoking the CST), the fact that the conflict is internal has not been an obstacle for the organisation not to intervene. In 2012, the Deputy Secretary-General of the CSTO, Valery Semerikov, made a statement that the CSTO considers involvement in a peacekeeping operation in Afghanistan in 2014.[77]

From the organisation's vast diplomatic efforts to receive recognition from the UN, especially in 2010, it appears that the CSTO, as opposed to the CIS, is more outside-region oriented, and is focusing the efforts on establishing rapid reaction units – as a UN Standby Force. How the CSTO will use its military assets within the region, and whether it will actually become utilised for peacekeeping and peace enforcement outside the region by the UN, remains to be seen from its future practice.

---

74 I. Kolchenko, 'CSTO Opens Security Umbrella. Belarus Chairs Collective Security Treaty Organisation in 2011', *Belarus Magazine*, No 2, 2011. Available at <http://www.belarus-magazine.by/en.php?subaction=showfull&id=1249716237&archive=&start_from=&ucat=2&> (accessed 3 August 2011).
75 K. Parshin, 'CIS: Coming together on paper, still apart in practice', op. cit., n. 71.
76 H. Ozdal, 'Putting the CSTO to the test in Kyrgyzstan', op. cit., n. 25.
77 'CSTO Eyes Peacekeeping Operations in Afghanistan after 2014', *The Voice of Russia*, 9 October 2012. Available at <http://english.ruvr.ru/2012_10_09/CSTO-eyes-peacekeeping-operations-in-Afghanistan-after-2014/> (accessed 18 April 2013).

Co-operation with the United Nations

The CSTO has had observer status at the UN General Assembly since 2004.[78] In 2010, a draft UN General Assembly resolution on Cooperation between the UN and the Collective Security Treaty Organization (CSTO) (document A/65/L.6), was introduced by the representative of Belarus, on behalf of the CSTO. A joint declaration of co-operation was signed on 18 March 2010. The Secretary-General of the CSTO referred to the signing of the declaration as giving the CSTO Chapter VIII status,[79] empowering the CSTO with the right to launch regional peacekeeping operations without a UN mandate and launching international military operations outside the region with a UN mandate.[80]

It appears from the UN documents on regional co-operation that the CSTO framework is intended to take over the peacekeeping task of the region from the CIS – both within the region and outside. This can be concluded both from the political statements on the intentions of the CSTO,[81] as well as the fact that the CSTO appears as the organisation representing the Russian sphere of influence at the UN, while the CIS framework is being increasingly left behind.

Summary

The Russian sphere of influence is characterised by the Russian domination and robust regional peacekeeping. The main activities that have taken place within the framework of the CIS have been regional peacekeeping operations, but the extended mandate of the CSTO contains a broad spectrum of tasks, making regional action also outside the region possible as part of UN peacekeeping.

As several CIS Member States have stayed out of closer military co-operation, the main regional efforts for the maintenance of peace and security have transferred to the CSTO. The CSTO is a group of CIS Member States willing to take up closer commitment; it is a military alliance. The CSTO and the CIS have the same basic document – the CST. Security and defence in the region are integrated, and regional self-defence, as opposed to the Middle East, is applicable to outside enemy only. While the mandate of the CIS provides for traditional security and defence co-operation, the CSTO, in addition, also has a mandate for combating non-traditional threats, Islamic terrorism, drug trafficking and ethnic conflicts, and most recently, also natural disasters. It can also be observed that while the CIS has operated only within the region,

---

78 A/RES/59/50.
79 'UN Recognizes Russia-Led Security Bloc', *RTT News, Global Financial Newswire*, 19 March 2010. Available at <http://www.rttnews.com/ArticleView.aspx?Id=1245556> (accessed 12 April 2013).
80 'UN Recognizes Russia-Led Security Bloc', ibid.
81 UN Press Release, GA/11036, 13 December 2010.

the CSTO is also outward oriented with the aim of participating in global peacekeeping.

Permissible regional action beyond political means thus includes military peacekeeping in the region without a UN mandate and theoretically does not exclude military peace enforcement with a UN mandate. The organisations of the Russian sphere of influence recognise the mandatory requirement of a UNSC authorisation for any enforcement operation. Humanitarian intervention without a UN mandate is not accepted. However, use of force internally within a State and peacekeeping within the region, even if very robust, is not regarded as requiring UN authorisation. The CSTO intends not only to take regional action but also to take up peacekeeping outside the region with a UN mandate. The region is among those that both have a broad constitutive mandate for the use of its military assets as well as the actual military capabilities. Both the CIS and the CSTO regard themselves as Chapter VIII organisations.

One of the central concerns for ensuring the legitimacy of regional action in the CIS and the CSTO is the obvious dominance of Russia. While the CIS has 11 Member States and the CSTO has seven, the Russian influence and military capability is overwhelming. The decision-making mechanism of the CIS allows the States that have an interest in the issue to make a decision, based on consensus, without the participation of all CIS Member States, thus strengthening the dominating role of Russia.

The regional practice in peacekeeping shows incompliance of the regional peacekeeping with the accepted UN peacekeeping practices and principles (the limitations to the use of force, invitation, neutrality, impartiality). The CIS and Russian practice is one of several regional examples of the blurring between peacekeeping and enforcement. There are a vast number of cases from different regional organisations that illustrate the incorrectness of the classification of military peacekeeping as a peaceful settlement of disputes. The post-Cold War robust peacekeeping, which in principle contains the Chapter VII clause when authorised by the UN, evidences the presence of enforcement elements. If the UNSC needs to invoke Chapter VII in the authorisation of an operation, it means that the military action is of the level of coercion where UNSC authorisation is mandatory. Thus, any robust military peacekeeping containing enforcement elements, such as that common in the Russian sphere of influence, ought to be authorised by the UN, in line with Article 53 of the UN Charter.

8 The Euro-Atlantic region
Going global

General description of the region

The Euro-Atlantic region encompasses Western Europe, along with the Eastern European States that broke off from the Russian sphere of influence at the end of the Cold War, as well as the North American allies – Canada, and, most significantly the USA. The USA is, unquestionably, the strongest military power and the most influential State of the region.

The security and defence co-operation in the Euro-Atlantic region has been a sensitive issue due to the Second World War, especially concerning the role of Germany in the European security and defence structures after the end of the war. The co-operation process has significantly speeded up only since the end of the Cold War. After the relative calm of the Cold War, the Euro-Atlantic region has experienced outbreaks of violence on its 'doorstep'. The conflicts in the Balkans have been the main concern of the Euro-Atlantic region in the 1990s and beyond. The twenty-first century has brought the Euro-Atlantic security concerns even further outside the region, reaching into the Middle East and Africa.

There are two keywords that distinguish the Euro-Atlantic regions from all the others: 'values' and 'global'. The values of democracy and human rights are embedded in the basic documents of NATO and the EU. The adherence to them is a requirement for membership, and their promotion is a mission of the two organisations. The regional ambition to act globally is a post-9/11 development. It is an ambition that is also echoed in the latest developments of the CSTO. The Euro-Atlantic organisations appear to view global crisis management as their legitimate mission.

The number of organisations dealing with the maintenance of peace and security in the region is not excessive: NATO and the EU. Moreover, the OSCE enhances the Euro-Atlantic region and the Russian sphere of influence. The Western European Union (WEU) never became a significant actor in the maintenance of peace and security, and was formally dissolved in 2011.[1]

---

1 Not operative since 1999, formal dissolution finalised on 30 June 2011. Available at <http://www.weu.int/> (accessed 12 April 2013).

European Union

General description

The history of the European security and defence policy dates back as far as the 1950s. In 1950, the Pleven Plan with the proposal to create a European Defence Community and a European Army was signed, yet never ratified.[2] Just like with the UN armed forces envisaged in Article 43 of the UN Charter, the European countries were not ready to merge their armies into one. In the 1960s, the Fouchet plan proposed a common European foreign and defence policy – no agreement was reached to proceed with the plan.[3] The Davignon proposals in 1970 were the next – more successful, albeit slow – step to set the ground for a common security and defence policy in Europe. The Davignon proposals found expression in the Single European Act of 1986, introducing European Political Cooperation. However, it is not until 1992 that one can talk of an explicit legal basis for a CFSP of the EU. The end of the Cold War and the collapse of Yugoslavia determined the establishment of Pillar II of the EU – CSDP – and it was only in 1999 with the Amsterdam Treaty, that the European Security and Defence Policy (ESDP) specifically took its place in the EU basic documents. The Lisbon Treaty[4] provides a detailed regulation of the common security and defence co-operation (CSDP) within the EU. The main political documents containing provisions on ESDP (now CSDP) are the European Security Strategy, and Headline Goal 2010.

The core security provision of the EU is the so-called 'Petersberg tasks', giving the EU the internal constitutional mandate to participate in the whole spectrum of crisis management operations. Global, not only regional, maintenance of peace and security is a new function for the EU that it has been fulfilling actively in the past decade.

The legal basis

Coming into force in 1993, the Maastricht Treaty was significant by introducing Title V provisions on CFSP to the primary legal regulation of the EU.

---

2 J. W. De Zwaan, 'Foreign policy and defence cooperation in the European Union: legal foundations', in S. Blockmans (ed.), *The European Union and Crisis Management. Policy and Legal Aspects*, The Hague: T.M.C. Asser Instituut, Asser Press, 2008, p. 19.
3 De Zwaan, ibid.
4 [2007] OJ C306/01.

In contrast, the strength of EU and NATO in the maintenance of peace and security has significantly grown since the end of the Cold War, and especially in the twenty-first century. While the EU has mainly had an economic co-operation function until the past decade, NATO is specific by being one of the few organisations dealing exclusively with security and defence.

With this document the European Communities gained the three-pillar framework of the EU, the second pillar of the EU being CFSP. The co-operation in this pillar was to be intergovernmental, as opposed to the supranational, as in the European Communities (Pillar I). The Maastricht Treaty also stated that CFSP 'might in time lead to common defence'.[5]

Another step in European security and defence policy was taken in 1999, when the Petersberg tasks were integrated into the Treaty on European Union through the Amsterdam Treaty. These tasks had originally been set out in the Petersberg Declaration adopted at the Ministerial Council of the WEU in June 1992,[6] and were now included in Article 17, paragraph 2 of the Treaty on European Union. The Petersberg tasks include humanitarian and rescue tasks, peacekeeping tasks, tasks of combat forces in crisis management, including peacemaking.

The EU Constitutional project[7] of 2004 was not ratified by all Member States and never came into force. Nevertheless, the Lisbon Treaty took over much of its unprecedentedly wide regulation of CFSP and ESDP. It came into force in December 2009.[8] The main features of now CSDP are the participation of EU in crisis management operations, facilitating a common defence in the future and creating the framework for enhanced security co-operation between States that have such intentions. The Treaty contains very detailed administrative, decision-making and implementation provisions.

Article 21[9] provides the main principles guiding CFSP and, within it, CSDP: democracy, the rule of law, the universality and indivisibility of human rights and fundamental freedoms, respect for human dignity, the principles of equality and solidarity, and respect for the principles of the UN Charter and international law. In the nuanced political approach of the EU to action without a UN mandate, it is interesting to point to the particular wording of the EU documents regarding the UN. The nuance sought is the distinction between the terms 'compliance with the UN Charter' or 'with the principles of the UN Charter'. The latter implies that the action may possibly not be in compliance with the grammatical text of the Charter, but rather in compliance with the ideas, the values,[10] that the Charter is to represent, such as the protection of human rights.

---

5 Declaration of the Western European Union at Petersberg, Germany, subsequently incorporated into Treaty of European Union, Art. 17.
6 Petersberg Declaration, Western European Union, Western European Union Council of Ministers, Bonn, 19 June 1992. Available at <http://www.weu.int/documents/920619peten.pdf> (accessed 12 April 2011).
7 [2008] OJ C310/01.
8 General Secretariat of the Council of the EU, Information Note, Treaty of Lisbon, December 2009. Available at <http://www.consilium.europa.eu/uedocs/cms_data/docs/pressdata/en/ec/111652.pdf> (accessed 12 April 2013).
9 Treaty on European Union (TEU), consolidated version, [2010] OJ C83/1.
10 P. Allott defines a value as an idea which serves as a ground for choosing between possibilities. P. Allott, *Eunomia. New Order for a New World*, Oxford: Oxford University Press,

The aims of CFSP are defined in eight subparagraphs of Article 22. They include safeguarding EU values (a broad concept only used in the Euro-Atlantic region), fundamental interests, security, independence, supporting human rights and democracy. Other aims are aims of economic and environmental nature, multilateralism, good global governance. With regard to the maintenance of peace and security, the Treaty notes that the purpose of the EU is to preserve peace, prevent conflicts and strengthen international security. Just as in the CIS/CSTO basic legal documents, and as opposed to other regional organisations – the matter of concern is international and not merely regional security. This aim is to be achieved in accordance with purposes and principles of the UN Charter, the principles of the Helsinki Final Act and with the aims of the Paris Charter, including those relating to external borders.

The new Article 42 of the consolidated Treaty contains the core provisions of CSDP. It briefly provides for the full scope of EU tasks in security and defence matters, while details of each point are specified further in the section. Article 42(1) defines ESDP as an integral part of CFSP that shall provide the EU with an operational capacity drawing on civilian and military assets. The paragraph explicitly gives the EU an internal mandate for using the military assets in operations outside the EU for peacekeeping, conflict prevention and the strengthening of international security in accordance with the principles of the UN Charter. Article 43 specifies the types of missions – both civilian and military – that the EU may launch: joint disarmament operations, humanitarian and rescue tasks, military advice and assistance tasks, conflict prevention and peacekeeping tasks, tasks of combat forces in crisis management, including peace-making and post-conflict stabilisation. All these tasks may contribute to the fight against terrorism, including by supporting third countries in combating terrorism in their territories. Thus, even though the EU uses a distinct terminology for peace operations, it is apparent from the list above that both peacekeeping and peace enforcement (e.g. combat forces) are permissible according to the EU's internal mandate.

The EU does not, at the moment, have an established common defence policy. Article 42 provides for the future prospects of CFSP in possible defence co-operation. Section 2 refers to progressive framing of a common Union Defence policy which in time may lead to a common defence when the European Council, acting unanimously, so decides. The future possibility of a common defence has already been included in the Treaty on European Union through the Nice Treaty.[11] The Lisbon Treaty, however, for the first

---

2001, p. 48; See N. D. White, 'The ties that bind: The EU, UN and International Law', *Netherlands Yearbook of International Law*, Vol. 37, 2006.

11 [2002] OJ C325/5.

time, adds an Article 51 collective defence provision to the EU terminology.[12] Provisions in Article 42 sections (2) and (7) point to the priority of the commitment within NATO in common defence matters of the EU Member States which are also members of NATO. Thus, there is a subordination of the EU to NATO in the matters of collective defence.

The Treaty further provides not only that the EU Member States are to make their civilian and military capabilities available for the implementation of the CFSP and that they are obliged to undertake progressive action to improve their military capabilities. It also provides for a possibility of those Member States whose military capabilities fulfil higher criteria and which have made more binding commitments to one another in this area, with a view to the most demanding missions, to establish permanent structured co-operation within the EU framework. This provision resembles the role of the CSTO within the CIS framework, though the EU permanent co-operation is not a separate organisation, does not have a separate legal personality, and is not even in place at the time of writing.

Over the past decade the EU has been concentrating efforts on establishing general as well as rapid reaction capabilities that could be used to assist the UN and for other operations. Thus already at the Cologne European Council in June 1999, the EU leaders agreed that 'the Union must have the capacity for autonomous action, backed by credible military forces, the means to decide to use them, and the readiness to do so, in order to respond to international crises without prejudice to actions by NATO'.[13]

In 2003, the EU agreed on its first strategic document: European Security Strategy, *A Secure Europe in a Better World*.[14] The core idea of this strategic document is that the threats in today's world are far-reaching and interconnected, and in order to provide security within Europe, the EU has to go global in combating threats outside its territory and, more importantly, preventing them. The reason for the EU going global can probably best be described by the following quote from the Strategy:

> Our traditional concept of self-defence – up to and including the Cold War was based on the threat of invasion. With the new threats the first

---

12 Article 42(7) reads: 'If a Member State is the victim of armed aggression on its territory, the other Member States shall have towards it an obligation of aid and assistance by all the means in their power, in accordance with Art. 51 of the UN Charter. This shall not prejudice the specific character of the security and defence policy of certain Member States. Commitments and cooperation in this area shall be consistent with commitments under the North Atlantic Treaty Organisation, which, for those States which are members of it, remains the foundation of their collective defence and the forum for its implementation'.
13 'Military Capabilities', Council of the European Union website. Available at <http://www.consilium.europa.eu/showPage.aspx?id=1349&lang=EN> (accessed 12 April 2013).
14 'A Secure Europe in a Better World', European Security Strategy, adopted by the Council, Brussels, 12 December 2003.

line of defence will often be abroad. The new threats are dynamic ... Conflict prevention and threat prevention cannot start too early.

The Security Strategy defines the EU as 'inevitably a global player' and states its aim: Europe should be ready to share in its responsibility for global security and in building a better world. In that the Security Strategy proclaims full commitment to upholding international law as well as developing it. It is recognised that the fundamental framework for international relations is the UN Charter and that the UN Security Council has the primary responsibility for the maintenance of international peace and security. The EU sets as its priority the strengthening of the UN, equipping it to fulfil its responsibility to act effectively.[15] The intention of the EU is to support the UN in its response to threats to international peace and security.[16]

The key threats to Europe listed in the Strategy are: terrorism, proliferation of weapons of mass destruction, regional conflicts, State failure and organised crime. It is also added in the document that the traditional concept of a threat – large-scale aggression against a Member State is now improbable.

Another major ESDP document is the Headline Goal 2010, which also defines the EU as a global actor, ready to share in the responsibility for global security.[17] The Headline Goal makes it the aim for Member States to be able to respond with rapid and decisive action, in fulfilling the full spectrum of EU crisis management tasks.[18] In addition to the Petersberg tasks included in the Treaty on European Union, both the Security Strategy and the Headline Goal list also joint disarmament operations, the support to third countries in combating terrorism and security sector reform.[19] As in all other relevant EU documents, also in the Headline Goal 2010, the commitment to co-operation with the UN is made, including the readiness to use the new rapid reaction forces (EU Battlegroups) to respond to requests from the UN.

The 2008 Report on Implementing the European Security Strategy, *Providing Security in a Changing World*, further elaborates on the EU role in the international maintenance of peace and security. It states that the UN stands at the apex of the international system, and that everything the EU has done in the field of security has been linked to UN objectives.[20] The attention regarding the maintenance of global peace and security is allocated to the need of the renewal of international order. The EU is concerned with the issues of legitimacy, effectiveness and the decision-making efficiency of

---

15 'A Secure Europe in a Better World', ibid.
16 'A Secure Europe in a Better World', ibid.
17 Headline Goal 2010, approved by General Affairs and External Relations Council on 17 May 2004, endorsed by the European Council of 17 and 18 June 2004, para. 1.
18 Headline Goal 2010, ibid.
19 Headline Goal 2010, ibid, para. 2.
20 Report on Implementing the European Security Strategy, 'Providing Security in a Changing World', Brussels, 11 December 2008, S407/08, p. 11.

the UN, and sets as its goal taking the initiative in the renewal of the multilateral order.[21]

The EU documents do not contain any provisions on regional humanitarian intervention without a UN mandate. The EU is an organisation that pledges compliance with international law, which would, in principle, imply abstaining from enforcement action without a UN mandate. The textual basis in EU documents does not assert the existence of a regional right to humanitarian intervention without a UN mandate. There is, however, other evidence from EU practice for the potential EU consensus on the permissibility of regional humanitarian intervention without a UN mandate in emergency cases.

Decision-making

The Lisbon Treaty is the first primary EU document that provides for clear and detailed procedural guidelines for CFSP and CSDP. Article 24 of the consolidated Treaty provides that 'the rules of CFSP shall be defined and implemented by the European Council and the Council acting unanimously, except where the Treaties provide otherwise'. Regarding CSDP, and, namely, when launching international military operations, unanimity is the applicable principle. The decisions on operational action taken by the EU are taken by the Council. Thus, Article 42(4) requires that decisions relating to the CSDP, including those initiating a mission, are to be adopted by the Council acting unanimously on a proposal from the High Representative of the Union for Foreign Affairs and Security Policy or an initiative from a Member State.

Despite sometimes cumbersome procedures and the strict adherence to the rule of unanimity (which has been the stumbling stone for the Arab League) the EU's peace support operations tend to be launched quickly and efficiently.[22] On the other hand, there is a lack of available civilian and military personnel in the force generation process, a shortage which is attempted to be minimised by enhanced co-operation.[23]

The EU is particular among all the regional organisations in providing detailed and nuanced procedural regulation for decision-making and implementation. For comparison, the core material provisions on CSDP are briefly contained in Articles 42 to 46 (five articles), while the decision-making, implementation and other administrative and co-ordination provisions take up Articles 23 to 41 (19 articles).

---

21 'Providing Security in a Changing World', ibid, pp. 2 and 12.
22 A. Björkdahl and M. Strömvik, 'The decision-making process behind launching an ESDP crisis management operation', DIIS Brief, Copenhagen: Danish Institute for International Studies, 2008, p. 5.
23 Björkdahl and Strömvik, ibid, p. 5.

Until the coming into force of the Lisbon Treaty, the Council decisions on launching EU operations were called 'joint actions', the new provisions entitle them 'decisions'. The Treaty also specifies that the adoption of legislative acts shall be excluded from the CFSP competence of the Council.[24] The abovementioned decisions, however, constitute the EU legal basis for launching international operations.[25]

As distinguishable from other regional organisations in the maintenance of peace and security, in the EU implementation measures are emphasised as corollaries of any decision made: if the Council makes a decision, there has to be clarity on how it will be implemented. Such an example is, among others, Article 28(1), which reads:

> Where the international situation requires operational action by the Union, the Council shall adopt the necessary decisions. They shall lay down their objectives, scope, the means to be made available to the Union, if necessary their duration, and the conditions for their implementation.

Such provisions ensure that decisions are not abstract, but that there is a responsibility to ensure the feasibility of carrying them out in practice. The absence of such a provision has the potential of impairing the work of security and defence organisations. This problem is especially evident in the case of the AU.

The initiatives for CSDP action may come from different directions. The High Representative of the Union for Foreign Affairs and Security Policy has the task of both contributing through his proposals to the development of the common foreign and security policy and ensuring implementation. In addition, any Member State, the High Representative of the Union for Foreign Affairs and Security Policy, or the High Representative with the support of the Commission, may refer any question relating to the common foreign and security policy to the Council and may submit to it initiatives or proposals of the decisions adopted by the European Council and the Council.[26] The European Parliament may also address questions or make recommendations to the Council or the High Representative – though only as an advisory body.

Taking into consideration the 'Kadi' case,[27] the EU is unique with a possible judicial review of the decisions made. The judicial review of CFSP decisions, however, is limited. The Treaty provides that the Court of Justice of the

---

24 TEU, Art. 24(1).
25 Björkdahl and Strömvik, op. cit., n. 22, p. 2.
26 TEU, Art. 27.
27 Joined Cases C-402/05P and C-415/05P *Yassin Abdullah Kadi and Al Barakaat International Foundation v Council of the European Union*, European Court of Justice (Grand Chamber), Judgment of 3 September 2008.

European Union only has jurisdiction to monitor compliance with Article 40 of this Treaty and to review the legality of certain decisions as provided for by the second paragraph of Article 275 of the Treaty on the Functioning of the European Union, i.e. the court has a competence to review that CFSP activities do not affect the exercise of the EU's primary tasks contained in Articles 3 to 6 and restrictive measures against legal and natural persons.

Article 31 provides for the details of the decision-making procedure, such as abstention by declaration, the combination of abstention of one-third of the EU Member States with one-third population, and qualified majority. Article 31(4) specifies that the provisions by qualified majority may not be taken on issues containing military and defence implications. Here unanimity is required. However, the unanimity clause does not prejudice Article 31(1) which allows for abstentions by up to one-third of all Member States having up to one-third of the population of the EU, which does not jeopardise the adoption of the decision. In a case of abstention, as in the case of the Arab League, the decision does not bind the State which abstained, however, even the abstaining States must accept that the decision binds the EU and act in the spirit of mutual solidarity and avoid conflicts with the decision. Thus, it is apparent that there is a rather flexible exit from the potential cases of unanimity-deadlock. The abstention provision in fact puts a question mark on the actual unanimity of the decision-making. Rather, the decision-making procedure can be characterised, in accordance with Article 31, as a two-thirds majority vote, where any Member State has a veto right.

The decision-making process, just as the whole legal basis of the EU, is of unprecedented complexity and efforts to ensure legitimacy of process compared to any other regional organisation. On the one hand, this is good for making legitimate decisions, but on the other hand, the complexity of the process may overshadow the importance of the content and the aim of the decision to be made.

The practice

The EU has been the most active regional organisation in crisis management in the past decade. Even though the EU does not have the capabilities for large-scale operations, it has been very active in smaller-scale operations, including the use of military force. The EU has participated in civilian and military crisis management on three continents: several operations in Europe and Africa, and in addition, a monitoring mission in Aceh, Indonesia in 2005/06. The EU has carried out 27 international operations, nine of which are military.[28] The military operations have taken place in the Balkans and in

---

28 'EU Common Security and Defence Policy (CSDP). Overview of the missions and operations of the European Union. February 2013', European Union website. Available at

African countries where the African regional organisations have not been able to act on their own.

The EU has been co-operating closely with the UN, and the primary reason for establishing EU Battlegroups has been to assist the UN. The Battlegroups, however, have not been used for any operations to date. Instead, however, EU forces have been used in operations Concordia in the Former Yugoslav Republic of Macedonia (FYROM) in 2003, EUFOR Chad/CAR 2008–09, Artemis, DRC 2003, EUFOR DRC 2006, support to African Union Mission in Sudan (AMIS) II Darfur, Sudan 2005–06, Atalanta since 2008, European Union Training Mission (EUTM) Somalia since 2010, and EUTM Mali in 2013.

Operation Concordia in FYROM was the second ESDP operation, and its first military one.[29] Here the EU took over the peacekeeping operation from NATO under the co-operation arrangements between the two organisations.[30] Operation Concordia did not have a UN mandate. It was a peacekeeping operation that was based on the invitation by the FYROM president and was, in principle, endorsed by a general provision in UNSC Resolution 1371 (2001).[31] Nevertheless, Ireland could not participate in the operation, due to its constitutional requirement for a UN mandate for any international military operation.[32] Bearing in mind the case, the legislation of Ireland was subsequently changed.

The EU's next military operation took place far outside the region – in the DRC. In 2003, the EU took over, within the framework of the short-term operation Artemis, the stabilisation operation led by France, which had been authorised by UNSC Resolution 1484 (2003).[33] The actual authorisation of UNSC Resolution 1484 was made for an Interim Emergency Multinational Force to be created by the UN Member States, and was mandated under Chapter VII of the UN Charter, authorising the force 'to use all necessary means'. The operation, being based on a host State invitation and having enforcement elements, thus, was a combination of peacekeeping and peace enforcement.[34] The mandate for the EU operation was renewed through UNSC Resolutions 1493 (2003) and 1505 (2003).

<http://www.consilium.europa.eu/showpage.aspx?id=268&lang=EN> (accessed 12 April 2013).
29 F. Naert, 'ESDP in Practice: Increasingly Varied and Ambitious EU Security and Defence Operations', in M. Trybus and N. White (eds), *European Security Law*, Oxford: Oxford University Press, 2007, p. 68.
30 Naert, ibid, pp. 68–69.
31 Naert, ibid, p. 70.
32 Naert, ibid, p. 69.
33 Naert, ibid, p. 72.
34 Naert, ibid, p. 74.

In 2006, a new short-term military operation was launched to monitor the elections in the DRC, named EUFOR DR Congo.[35] The mandate for this operation was UN Resolution 1671 (2006). The EU force was authorised to assist the UN force – MONUC – in election monitoring. The resolution made a reference to peacekeeping, and at the same time, the UNSC acted under Chapter VII of the UN Charter, using such phrases as 'to use all appropriate steps' and 'to take all necessary measures', in order to carry out the mandate. Thus, the EU operations launched in Africa have continued the pattern established by ECOWAS – the operations blur the concepts of peacekeeping and peace enforcement by being authorised to use force beyond self-defence, while having a formal host State consent.

The operations EUFOR Althea in Bosnia-Herzegovina (since 2004), Operation Atalanta, the European Union Naval Force (EUNAVFOR) counter-piracy operation in the Gulf of Aden and Somali Basin, and EUTM Somalia (since 2010) are still ongoing.

EUFOR Althea in Bosnia-Herzegovina is the largest and longest EU military operation. In 2004 the EU took over from NATO, which had already been present in the area for a decade, the task of ensuring peace, security and adherence to the Dayton Agreement. The legal basis for the operation is the Dayton Agreement itself and UNSC Resolution 1575 (2004). Here the UNSC has once again acted under Chapter VII of the UN Charter. Even though the task of Althea is to ensure the observance of the peace agreement, the mandate of the forces is rather wide:

> The parties shall continue to be held equally responsible for compliance [...] and shall be equally subject to such enforcement action by EUFOR and the NATO presence as may be necessary to ensure implementation [...] and the protection of EUFOR and the NATO presence and to take all necessary measures to ensure compliance.[36]

It can be observed that the EU in its joint actions (called 'decisions' since December 2009) for launching the respective operations[37] does not qualify the operations as peacekeeping or peace enforcement operations, but refer to them as 'military operations' and 'crisis management operations'. The UN resolutions, though issued under Chapter VII, contain both peacekeeping and enforcement authorisation elements, making the EU practice yet another example of the reluctance of strict division between peacekeeping operations

---

35 'EUFOR DR Congo', EU website. Available at <http://www.consilium.europa.eu/showPage.aspx?id=1091&lang=EN> (accessed 12 April 2013).
36 S/RES 1575 (2004).
37 2003/423/CFSP of 5 June 2003 (Artemis), Council Joint Action 2004/570/CFSP of 12 July 2004 (Althea), 2006/319/CFSP of 27 April 2006 (EUFOR DR Congo), Council Joint Action 2008/851/CFSP of 10 November 2008 (Atalanta), and others.

and peace enforcement in the post-Cold War maintenance of peace and security.

A peculiar example of an EU military operation is EUNAVFOR's counter-piracy operation in the Gulf of Aden and the Somali Basin – operation Atalanta. This operation illustrates the combating of non-traditional threats by international military means (also evident in the CSTO and the SCO), rather than diplomatic co-operation between States on what is regarded as an internal matter of each State (as observed in the examples of ASEAN and UNASUR). The EUNAVFOR mandate is based on UNSC Resolutions 1814 and 1816 (2008)[38] and its own Council Joint Action 2008/851/CFSP of 10 November 2008, and subsequent documents. The joint action lays down the mission for the operation. First, the protection of vessels of the World Food Programme delivering humanitarian aid to displaced persons in Somalia, in accordance with the mandate laid down in UNSC Resolution 1814 (2008). Second, the protection of vulnerable vessels cruising off the Somali coast, and the deterrence, prevention and repression of acts of piracy and armed robbery off the Somali coast, in accordance with the mandate laid down in UNSC Resolution 1816 (2008).[39] For this purpose the military units are authorised to take action in the form of providing protection to vessels chartered by the World Food Programme and on a case-by-case basis also to merchant vessels, keep watch in the Somali territorial waters and, if necessary, take measures, including the use of force, to deter, prevent and intervene in order to bring to an end acts of piracy and armed robbery, as well as arrest, detain and transfer persons who have committed, or are suspected of having committed acts of piracy and armed robbery. The mandate also provides for the co-ordination with the equivalent NATO operation (Combined Task Force 150 in the framework of Operation Enduring Freedom).[40] This way the military has been given an international policing function alongside an enforcement task.

In general, the practice of the EU in military operations is in compliance with international law – host State consent and/or UNSC authorisation has been received for all military operations, and in most cases, even both. The practice of States (and regional organisations), however, is not limited to what they do, it includes also what they say.[41] Here there is more to add on the practice of the EU. There is relevant practice of the EU and its Member States that evidences a potential unilateral regional humanitarian intervention without a UN mandate.

Many EU Member States are also members of NATO, which launched the intervention in Kosovo, and the position of which on the issue of a UN

---

38 The mandate was extended with Resolutions 1838 (2008), 1846 (2008), and 1897 (2009).
39 Council Joint Action 2008/851/CFSP of 10 November 2008.
40 Council Joint Action 2008/851/CFSP of 10 November 2008.
41 M. Akehurst, 'Custom as a Source of International Law', *The British Year Book of International Law*, Vol. 47, 1974–75, p. 53.

mandate is controversial in general. All NATO member countries, of which 19 are also EU Member States, agreed on the intervention in Kosovo in 1999, though not arguing that it was legal. There are, however, statements and documents which evidence the potential for repeated practice, analysed below, in the section on NATO.

Sweden, though a neutral EU member, is one of those countries whose official political position has been stated to be that in extreme cases intervention should be considered even without a UNSC resolution. It may be that in exceptional cases the UNSC does not authorise action, although the contemplated measure is clearly in conformity with the UN Charter. In such cases States should be able to consider an intervention even without UNSC authorisation in exceptional circumstances to save people from genocide and other serious violence.[42] In this context, at the 2005 UN summit the Swedish Prime Minister, Göran Persson, also stressed the need for the Security Council to better live up to its responsibilities, namely, that greater emphasis must be put on early prevention of conflict and early action.[43]

The only situation in which an operation can, theoretically, be launched without an explicit UNSC mandate is a peacekeeping operation based on acceptance or invitation from the government(s) in the area of operation.[44] If the operation contains enforcement elements, it requires an authorisation from the UNSC. Björkdal and Strömvik note the 'grey zone' of humanitarian intervention when the EU could potentially carry out enforcement action without a UN mandate. They, however, do not consider as realistic the scenario of the EU launching such an operation without a UN mandate.[45] There is other literature suggesting the possibility for unauthorised EU military action. Thus, Lindström writes that the need for a UN mandate although politically desirable, may not be feasible in certain situations requiring rapid response.[46] He raises the question whether, in such cases, an invitation by the host country and a request by the UN Secretary-General would suffice for the deployment of an EU Battlegroup as has been the case for certain ESDP actions,[47] and whether in an urgent situation resembling crimes against humanity materialises, a request by the UN Secretary-General would be enough. He continues by noting that while several EU Member States point to a need for a UN or OSCE mandate prior to engaging in a significant

---

42 D. Amneus, 'Swedish State Practice 2004–5: the Responsibility to protect', *Nordic Journal of International Law*, Vol. 75, 2006, p. 313.
43 Amneus, ibid. pp. 313–14.
44 A. Björkdahl and M. Strömvik, EU Crisis Management Operations. ESDP Bodies and Decision-making procedures, DIIS Report 2008:8, Copenhagen: Danish Institute for International Studies, 2008, p. 22.
45 Björkdahl and Strömvik, ibid.
46 G. Lindström, *Enter the EU Battlegroups. Chaillot Paper N 97*, Paris: Institute for Security Studies, 2007, p. 52.
47 Lindström does not specify which cases this refers to.

military operation, others highlight the drawbacks such as time delays and the implicit subjugation of EU foreign policy to non-European countries represented in the UNSC.[48] The dislike for being subject to the discretion of the Permanent Members of the UNSC also reflects in the example of Irish State practice.[49] Legally, the UN Secretary-General has no power to authorise a regional enforcement operation, which a humanitarian intervention would be. It would rather be the UN General Assembly under the 'Uniting for Peace' procedure, and not the UN Secretary-General unilaterally, who could act in an exceptional case. Moreover, Tsagourias argues that a coercive EU operation without a UNSC cannot be ruled out because the UNSC is not a linchpin for legitimacy and efficiency and that the EU could launch coercive peacekeeping operations by virtue of them not being inconsistent with UN principles and purposes.[50]

The 'Kadi' case[51] is a case where a UNSC resolution restricting the rights of individuals under Chapter VII of the UN Charter was contested. The decision of the court has raised a legal pluralist debate on international law and EU law as two distinct legal systems.[52] Whilst the debate specifically concerns the supranational EC law in the first pillar of the EU, it concerns CFSP as well, and gives relevant evidence of the EU approach towards international law, the UN Charter and human rights.

The facts of the case are that the UNSC, under Resolutions 1267 (1999) and 1333 (2000), among others, blacklisted individuals – suspected members of Al Qaeda and the Taliban. The resolutions were passed under Chapter VII of the UN Charter. They were then implemented in the EU through an EC regulation. The Court of First Instance concluded in the 'Yusuf' case that:

> The Community may not infringe the obligations imposed on its Member States by the Charter of the UN or impede their performance and, second, that in the exercise of its powers it is bound, by the very Treaty by which it was established, to adopt all the measures necessary to enable its Member States to fulfil those obligations.[53]

---

48 Lindström, op. cit., n. 46, p. 52.
49 Parliamentary debates, Senead Éireann (upper house) (Official report – Unrevised), Vol. 184, No. 7, Wednesday, 28 June 2006, pp. 502–42.
50 N. Tsagourias, 'EU Peacekeeping Operations: Legal and Theoretical issues', in M. Trybus and N. White (eds), *European Security Law*, Oxford: Oxford University Press, 2007, pp. 129–30.
51 Joined Cases C-402/05P and C-415/05P, above, n. 27.
52 See, for example, M. Scheinin, 'Is the ECJ Ruling in "Kadi" Incompatible with International Law?', *Yearbook of European Law*, Vol. 28, 2010. P. J. Cardwell, D. French and N. White, 'Case and Comment. Frozen in time? The ECJ finally rules on the *Kadi* Appeal', *The Cambridge Law Journal*, Vol. 68, 1 (March) 2009, pp. 1–45. G. de Búrca, 'The European Court of Justice and the International Legal Order After *Kadi*', *Harvard International Law Journal*, Vol. 51, 1, 2010.
53 Case T-306/01 *Ahmed Ali Yusuf and Al Barakaat International Foundation v Council of the European Union and Commission of the European Communities* [2005] ECR II–3533, para. 254.

The European Court of Justice (ECJ) wisely separated the UNSC resolution from its implementing measures in the EU. Thus, the court contested the EU regulations by which the relevant UNSC resolutions were implemented, and not directly the UNSC resolution itself. Nevertheless, annulling the regulation as incompatible with the fundamental rights of the European Community (EC), namely, the right to fair trial and the right to property, the court did *de facto* set aside the UNSC resolutions.

De Búrca notes that the ECJ treats the UN Charter in the 'Kadi' case as a simple international treaty in a separate legal system, without any superiority,[54] even though the provisions regarded action undertaken by the UNSC under Chapter VII of the UN Charter. Even though the court states that it is not judging the decision of the UNSC, but only the measures by which it was implemented in the EU, the practical effect of the decision was overruling a decision made by the UNSC. The decision gave ground for the perception that the EU may prioritise its fundamental values over Article 103 obligations. The rights involved in the case are not even the human rights which may be deemed to be *jus cogens*, yet, in essence, the ECJ decided in favour of human rights rather than obligations under Articles 24(2) and 103 of the UN Charter.[55] Protection of human rights, though having been neglected in practice due to lack of consensus, is also a principle contained in the UN Charter. Thus, though not having used this argumentation, but *de facto* prioritising fundamental EU rights over international obligations, the 'Kadi' decision gives an indirect example of how the commitment to UN purposes and principles included in many EU documents may mean direct discrepancy from the UN Charter text. In such cases potential unilateral regional action by the EU with the purpose of human rights protection, its extreme expression being humanitarian intervention, may not be excluded either.

Another evidence to the potential for EU unilateral action are the changes to the legislation of the traditionally neutral EU countries in order to be able to participate in EU Battlegroups even in the absence of a UNSC authorisation. While most of the EU Member States have not had a constitutional restraint for participating in international military operations, even without a UN mandate, a few countries, such as Ireland and Finland, have had such restraints. By the entry into force of the EU Battlegroups concept in 2007, all the EU Member States had their national legislation in place, in order to be able to participate in EU military operations, even if the operation is not authorised by the UNSC.

Ireland has been the last EU Member State resisting participation in military operations and even any operations that use military assets, without an explicit UN mandate. The reason for this is the formal status of Ireland as

---

54 de Búrca, op. cit., n. 52, pp. 23 and 30.
55 Cardwell *et al.*, op. cit., n. 52. This is one of the central arguments analysed in the article.

a neutral State. As noted, in 2003 Ireland was the only EU country that did not participate in the EU operation Concordia in FYROM, specifically due to constitutional restraints, even though Concordia was a peacekeeping operation.[56]

The main safeguard for ensuring the constitutionality of Irish military action is the so-called 'triple lock'. This means that the mandate for the operation has to be approved by resolutions from three institutions: the UNSC, the government of the Republic of Ireland and the lower house of Parliament, the Dáil Éireann. Until June 2006, the official statements of Ireland emphasised the commitments to the triple lock, however, the situation changed with the Irish participation in the Nordic Battlegroup (active in the first half of 2008). While maintaining the general constitutional commitment to the triple lock system and the Irish neutrality, a Defence (Amendment) Bill 2006 of 12 July 2006[57] was passed to allow more flexibility for participation of the Irish troops in military operations without a UNSC authorisation. The parliamentary debates in the upper house of Parliament, the Senead Éireann, contain the explanation by the Irish Minister of Defence, Willie O'Dea, for circumstances in which Irish troops should be deployable, also without a UN mandate, and the additional arguments of the members of Parliament in support of such provisions. The most relevant points of the parliamentary debate are the following:

- The mode of work of the UNSC – with 'petty squabbles' and abuse of the veto power is criticised.[58] This criticism corresponds to the general debate on the legitimacy of the UNSC, which has been wide-spread since the optimism about the newly gained ability of the UNSC to work efficiently after the end of the Cold War faded. Most significantly, in the Irish parliament debate UNSC action is being distinguished from UN purposes and principles, where the purposes and principles are assumed to have higher inherent legitimacy.[59]
- The possibility for providing troops for a humanitarian mission in the absence of a UN resolution is necessary. While not a requirement in other countries, providing troops for humanitarian missions was not possible in Ireland before the amendment. The UNSC does not have a practice of issuing a resolution on authorising a humanitarian assistance operation, yet the Irish troops could not be committed even for civilian purposes without such a mandate.[60] Thus even civilian humanitarian

---

56 Naert, op. cit., n. 29, p. 69.
57 Defence (Amendment Act) 2006, No. 20 of 2006, 12 July 2006. Available at <http://www.irishstatutebook.ie/2006/en/act/pub/0020/print.html> (accessed 18 April 2013).
58 Parliamentary debates, op. cit., n. 49, pp. 502–42.
59 Parliamentary debates, op. cit., n. 49, p. 520.
60 Parliamentary debates, op. cit., n. 49, p. 528.

aid operations after a natural disaster, or similar, and not only cases of humanitarian intervention were out of the scope of the national mandate for the deployment of Irish troops. The way around the provision until the amendment was that troops volunteered and were seconded to non-governmental organisations (NGOs) as part of an NGO operation.[61] (It is peculiar that the seconding of the State military troops to a non-governmental organisation has been a more legally feasible option than the deployment of troops for humanitarian assistance purposes without a UN mandate.)

The amendment is not limited only to civilian operations. The Minister clarifies that the amendment proposes to eliminate any requirement for a UNSC mandate, including for a peace enforcement mission, once the Dáil Éireann is satisfied that it accords with the purposes and principles of the UN.[62]

After a vast debate, the Defence (Amendment) Act 2006 was passed. The amendment (Section I) significantly contains the definition of an International UN Force – 'an international force or body established, mandated, authorised, endorsed, supported, approved or otherwise sanctioned by a resolution of the Security Council or the General Assembly of the UN'. This amendment widely extends the concept of a UN force, not only stating the authority of both the UNSC and the UN General Assembly, but also giving a very wide interpretation of what is to be seen as acceptance by the UN of action taken. 'Endorsed', 'supported' and 'otherwise sanctioned' loosely extends the range of interpretations of a UN-authorised force, in contrast to 'established', as the only term used before the amendment.

In such manner, Ireland manages to make the core provision on the requirement for a UN mandate flexible, without formally changing the constitutional requirement of the triple lock, which includes a UN mandate. In fact, the UN authorisation requirement now encompasses also *ex post facto* endorsement.

Finland is another case where the national legislation was altered to allow for the participation of the neutral State in EU operations. Traditionally, Finland, being a neutral country, had strict requirements for a UN mandate.[63] The 1984 Act on Peace Support Operations, No 514/1984, as amended on 31 December 2000, contained a specified prohibition to participate in coercive action.[64] Section 1 of the 1984 (2000) Act limited Finnish participation

---

61 Parliamentary debates, op. cit., n. 49, p. 528.
62 Parliamentary debates, op. cit., n. 49, pp. 528–29.
63 A. J. K. Bailes, G. Herolf and B. Sundelius (eds), *The Nordic Countries and the European Security and Defence Policy*, Stockholm International Peace Research Institute, Oxford: Oxford University Press, 2006, p. 71.
64 The 1984 Act on Peace Support Operations, No. 514/1984, as amended on 31 December 2000. Available at <http://www.finlex.fi/en/laki/kaannokset/1984/en19840514/> (accessed 12 April 2013).

in military crisis management and peace support operations implying only peacekeeping activities. A further requirement was a UN or OSCE mandate with a specified aim – preserving international peace and security or protecting the execution of humanitarian aid and the civilian population. The Act specifically excluded participation in coercive military measures governed by Articles 42 and 51 of the UN Charter. Section 2 of the Act further limited the peacekeeping that the Finnish forces may be involved in, by requiring additional co-ordination consultation of the government with the Parliament, if the peacekeeping activity exceeded 'traditional peacekeeping'.

The year 2006, the time of creation of the EU Battlegroups, brought about radical changes to the Finnish legislation on its participation in military operations. The 2006 Act on Military Crisis management[65] now gave a different context for the participation of Finnish military forces in international operations:

> Finland may participate in international military crisis management authorized by the UN Security Council, or exceptionally in other international military crisis management, with the purpose of maintaining or restoring international peace and security or supporting humanitarian assistance operations or protecting the civilian population, taking into account the purposes and principles of the Charter of the UN (Finnish Treaty Series 1/1956) and other rules of international law (military crisis management).

Thus, the new law does not limit the applicability of the crisis management provisions only to peacekeeping. 'Crisis management' is the EU terminology. In line with the Petersberg tasks enhanced in the Treaty on European Union, this includes the full range of crisis management operations, also enforcement. Most significantly, the Act directly states that in exceptional cases Finland may participate in crisis management without a UN mandate, while taking into consideration the purposes and principles of the UN Charter. Thus, the previously unconditional requirement for the UN mandate has been made flexible, and the purposes and principles of the UN Charter have been counter-positioned to the actual authorisation by the UNSC, just like in the case of Ireland. The amendments to the Finnish legislation are thus depictive of an implicit EU consensus of the regional permissibility of an unauthorised regional humanitarian intervention, which the organisation has though not expressed directly in its legal acts.

The cases of Ireland and Finland depict the reaction of the most militarily restrained – neutral – States in the EU to the establishment of the

---

65 The Act on Military Crisis Management, 11 April 2006, Statute Book of Finland, 211/2006. Available at <http://www.finlex.fi/en/laki/kaannokset/2006/en20060211.pdf> (accessed 12 April 2013).

ESDP mechanism. The other EU Member States have also joined the EU Battlegroups arrangement – a commitment which includes the possibility of out-of-area action – also without a UN mandate. It must be noted that individual States, according to the principles for the establishment of the EU Battlegroups and the individual battlegroup arrangements, maintain the right to opt-out from participation in a specific operation at their own discretion.[66]

The examples of Ireland and Finland must not be viewed narrowly as expressions of national law but rather as an expression of national implementation of the regional consensus on the rules of regional use of force in the EU framework. This EU consensus thus implies the commitment to the UN purposes and principles, but waives an unconditional compliance with the decisions, or rather, abstentions from action, by the UNSC, the Permanent Members of which, are, in fact, two of the EU's own Member States.

The small examples above, put together, produce a mass of evidence that humanitarian intervention without a UN mandate has a serious potential of being a politically acceptable option in the EU. Yet, if there were a true consensus on the legality of such action, it would not have to be sought for in materials containing indirect evidence, but would be included in the main EU documents, as it is in the AU and ECOWAS.

Co-operation with the United Nations

Despite the abovementioned controversies, the EU is the organisation that has one of the strongest co-operation relations with the UN. This is reflected, among other things, in the EU operations launched in support of the UN, upon UN request and mandated by the UN.

The EU was also the first organisation to sign a co-operation declaration with the UN in 2003, which can be interpreted as the twenty-first century practical recognition of Chapter VIII status. In addition, the EU (initially, the EC) has had observer status at the UN General Assembly since 1974,[67] having its rights extended with a right of reply and right of oral amendment in May 2011.[68] Despite the close co-operation with the UN, as the Treaty on European Union does not contain a reference to Chapter VIII, the status of the organisation has been debated, in particular due to the fact that its scope

---

66 The Nordic Battlegroup Memorandum of Understanding, Section 4 (2). Text available at the Government Offices of Sweden website at <http://www.regeringen.se/content/1/c6/04/49/80/60960599.pdf> (accessed 12 April 2013). EU BG 2010, Section 3.2, Text available at the Cabinet of Ministers of the Republic of Latvia website at <http://www.mk.gov.lv/doc/2005/AIMss_170306.doc> (accessed 12 April 2013).
67 A/RES/3208 (XXIX).
68 A/RES/65/276.

of action is exclusively outside the region, and not within its own region.[69] Nevertheless, there is no reason to regard the EU as less of a Chapter VIII organisation than any other organisation analysed above. In its practice the UN refers to the EU as a Chapter VIII organisation.[70] Also, the EU itself declares that it is 'working intensely with the Secretary-General and with the Security Council to support the maintenance of international peace and security, in line with Chapter VIII of the UN Charter'.[71] The direct statement that the EU is a Chapter VIII organisation is not necessary, because the EU acts as one, in fact, more than any other regional organisation.

The commitments of the EU to assist the UN in the efforts to maintain global peace and security can be found in a wide range of EU political documents, as already mentioned: in the Treaty on European Union, the European Security Strategy, the Headline Goal 2010, and reinforced in a row of other documents. The commitments have not been only unilateral. In 2003, the EU and the UN signed the Joint Declaration,[72] which was followed-up in 2007 by a Joint Statement on UN-EU co-operation in Crisis Management.[73] In addition, the EU has issued the EU-UN Cooperation in Military Crisis-Management Elements of Implementation of the EU-UN Joint Declaration.[74] The Joint Declaration states that in order to deepen the co-operation and provide it with reliable and sustainable mechanisms, the UN Secretary-General and the Presidency of the Council of the EU, among others, have agreed to be united by the premise that the primary responsibility for the maintenance of international peace and security rests with the UN Security Council, in accordance with the UN Charter. Within this framework, the EU reasserts its commitment to contribute to the objectives of the UN in crisis management.[75]

---

69 C. Gray, *International Law and the Use of Force*, 3rd edn, Oxford: Oxford University Press, 2008, p. 386.
70 One of many examples: remarks at a forum on 'The UN and the European Union: Joining Forces for the Challenges of the 21st Century', UN Secretary-General Ban Ki-moon, Vienna (Austria), 25 April 2008, *UN News Centre*. Available at <http://www.un.org/apps/news/infocus/sgspeeches/search_full.asp?statID=226> (accessed 12 April 2013).
71 S/PV. 6257, p. 11.
72 Joint Declaration on UN-EU Co-operation in Crisis Management, New York, 24 September 2003. Available at <http://www.consilium.europa.eu/uedocs/cmsUpload/st12730.en03.pdf> (accessed 12 April 2013).
73 Joint Statement on the EU-UN Cooperation in Crisis Management. Council of the European Union Brussels, 7 June 2007, p. 4. Available at <http://www.consilium.europa.eu/uedocs/cmsUpload/EU-UNstatmntoncrsmngmnt.pdf.4> (accessed 12 April 2013).
74 EU-UN Cooperation in Military Crisis-Management Elements of Implementation of the EU-UN Joint Declaration, adopted by the European Council 17–18 June 2004. Available at <http://consilium.europa.eu/uedocs/cmsUpload/EU-UN%20co-operation%20in%20Military%20Crisis%20Management%20Operations.pdf> (accessed 12 April 2013).
75 Joint Declaration on UN-EU Co-operation in Crisis Management.

Despite the political debates and claims for potential action without a UNSC mandate if an emergency situation arises, the EU has been an exemplary regional organisation as regards compliance with the UN Charter provisions and principles. It has received praise from the UN on several occasions and the action by the EU in operations in the field has not caused legality and legitimacy debates. In fact, the experience with the already launched operations shows, that when the regions are short of resources – especially the African region – they prefer to address the EU for assistance, rather than NATO, thus evidencing the higher legitimacy of the former. Such cases are, for example, East Timor and Darfur.

North Atlantic Treaty Organization

General description

NATO[76] was established in 1949 as a collective self-defence alliance, in compliance with Article 51 of the UN Charter. Today, NATO has 28 member countries.[77]

NATO is particular among all the major regional organisations, being an organisation, the competence of which is exclusively the maintenance of peace and security. The only other major regional organisation with solely security and defence functions is the relatively newly created CSTO. The fact that NATO and CSTO are the only such considerable examples, allows parallels to be drawn with the Cold War situation, where the Warsaw Pact had the place of the CSTO today. The two organisations are not adversaries. Yet, a kind of competition persists: CSTO has expressed its determination to become a competitor to NATO in being an agent for the UN in global peacekeeping.[78] Until now, however, NATO has unquestionably been, and still is, the most militarily capable organisation in the world. On several occasions the UN has turned to NATO for assistance with enforcement action.

---

76 The initial NATO members were Belgium, Canada, Denmark, France, Iceland, Italy, Luxembourg, Norway, the Netherlands, Portugal, the UK and the USA.
77 Today, NATO members are Albania, Belgium, Bulgaria, Canada, Croatia, Czech Republic, Denmark, Estonia, France, Germany, Greece, Hungary, Iceland, Italy, Latvia, Lithuania, Luxembourg, the Netherlands, Norway, Poland, Portugal, Romania, Slovakia, Slovenia, Spain, Turkey, the UK and the USA.
78 For example, S. Torjesen, 'Russia as a Military Great Power: The Uses of the CIS and the SCO in Central Asia', in E. Wilson Rowe and S. Torjesen (eds), *The Multilateral Dimension in Russian Foreign Policy*, London and New York, NY: Routledge, 2009, p. 186; 'Post-Soviet security group CSTO to become alternative to NATO – newspaper', *RIA Novosti*, 17 March 2010. Available at <http://en.rian.ru/russia/20100317/158223926.html. (accessed 14 April 2013).

NATO was specifically established with regard to Article 51 of the UN Charter, as opposed to being a Chapter VIII organisation.[79] The information found in the literature suggests that the reason NATO declared itself not to be a Chapter VIII organisation was specifically not to be subject to UNSC decisions, and thus, the direct influence of the USSR.[80] One of the official purposes of creating NATO was the intention to fill the gap left by the UNSC, until it would function effectively.[81] The Vanderberg resolution adopted by the US Senate on 11 June 1948 regarding the objectives of international co-operation shortly before the establishment of NATO contains the aim of progressive 'development of regional and other collective arrangements for individual and collective self-defence in accordance with the purposes, principles and provisions of the Charter', and notes the great input of the drafters of the North Atlantic Treaty to stay within the confines of the UN Charter. By explicitly placing itself under Article 51 of the UN Charter, instead of Chapter VIII, NATO brought about the distinction of the two categories of regional organisations: Chapter VIII and Article 51. Action under Article 51 in self-defence would be legal under the UN Charter without an authorisation from the UNSC, with or without an institutionalised regional framework. NATO was, nevertheless, proclaimed to be, by some authors, inconsistent with the prohibition of the use of force, and thus, by no means a Chapter VIII organisation.[82] For example, Pernice wrote:

> Unions of States concerned with the maintenance of peace and security are therefore, according to the 'philosophy' of the UN Charter, inadmissible not only when they contradict the Purposes and Principles of the UN, but also, and to a greater extent, when they fail to subordinate themselves to the UN as 'regional organizations' within the meaning of Chapter VIII.[83]

Classifying NATO as an 'outlaw organisation' is not a widely supported view, though a similar view has been expressed regarding the Arab League in the debates on its status.[84] Today's NATO, however, is hardly what it was in 1949 with the limited self-defence function.

---

79 J. Delbrück, 'Collective Security' (Regional Systems of Collective Security), in R. Bernhardt, *Encyclopedia of Public International Law*, Vol. 3, Amsterdam: North-Holland Publishing Company, 1982, p. 113.
80 Delbrück, ibid.
81 M. Zwanenburg, 'NATO, its Member States, and the Security Council', in N. Blokker and N. Schrijver (eds), *The Security Council and the Use of Force. Theory and Reality – A Need for Change?*, Leiden and Boston, MA: Martinus Nijhoff Publishers, 2005, p. 192.
82 M. Hummer and W. Schweitzer, 'Chapter VII. Regional Arrangements', in B. Simma (ed.), *The Charter of the United Nations. A Commentary*, 2nd edn, Vol. 1, Oxford: Oxford University Press, 2002, p. 819.
83 Hummer and Schweitzer, ibid, p. 820, reference 84 – Pernice, R.
84 The debate is described by Hummer and Schweitzer, ibid, p. 829.

The organisation is said to be the first military alliance being a security community of values — democracy, individual liberty and the rule of law.[85] The national adherence and implementation of these values is, in fact, along with practical commitment requirements, the main precondition for membership in NATO. The organisation has been in constant transformation since the end of the Cold War, when NATO's functions changed dramatically. In the so-called 'transformation' process NATO has become rather a pro-active security organisation than a collective self-defence organisation.

The legal basis

The North Atlantic Treaty or Washington Treaty is the founding document of NATO. The text of the Treaty has remained unaltered, even though significant changes in the functioning of NATO have come about since the end of the Cold War.[86] The internal mandate of the organisation has been altered by the three Strategic Concepts instead. The Strategic Concepts are defined as authoritative statements of the objectives of the organisation and provide the highest level of guidance on the political and military means to be used in achieving them; they are the overarching NATO doctrine.[87] Since the end of the Cold War the North Atlantic Council (NAC) at the summit level has approved three Strategic Concepts: in 1991, 1999 and 2010. The Concepts give the best understanding of what is regarded by the organisation as the current threats, the law, its mandate, and what is considered to be appropriate for regional action. The provisions of the strategic documents have added new concepts to the work of NATO, such as crisis management, action outside the region, fight against terrorism, pre-emptive self-defence and others, reaching far outside the classical scope of tasks of a self-defence alliance.

The North Atlantic Treaty was signed in Washington on 4 April 1949. It is a relatively brief document establishing a defence alliance. It is one of the oldest documents including a reference to the principles of democracy and rule of law in its preamble. Even though NATO does not regard itself as a Chapter VIII organisation,[88] and is regarded not to be one by a number of

---

85 A. Greciu, *Securing Civilization? The EU, NATO, and the OSCE in the Post-9/11 World*, Oxford: Oxford University Press, 2008, p. 80, see also reference 1 therein.
86 The only official amendment to the Treaty text is the definition of the territories to which Art. 5 applies. It was revised with the Protocol to the North Atlantic Treaty on the accession of Greece and Turkey, signed on 22 October 1951.
87 *NATO Handbook*, Chapter II, The Transformation of the Alliance: The Strategic Concept of the Alliance. Available at <http://www.nato.int/docu/handbook/2001/hb0203.htm> (accessed 28 August 2011). R. Tavares, *Regional Security. The Capacity of International Organizations*, Oxford: Routledge, 2009, p. 145.
88 B. Simma, 'NATO, the UN and the Use of Force: Legal Aspects', *The European Journal of International Law*, Vol. 10, 1999, p. 10; Zwanenburg, op. cit., n. 81, p. 194.

scholars due to its doctrine on autonomy of action,[89] the provisions of the Washington Treaty regarding compliance with international law do not stand out from other basic documents of the regional organisations dealing with the maintenance of peace and security. The Washington Treaty, in fact, starts out by reaffirming the faith in the purposes and principles of the UN Charter. Article 1 of the Treaty provides for the compliance with the relevant principles enhanced in the UN Charter. Article 1 stipulates the requirement to settle any international dispute by peaceful means, as set forth in the UN Charter, and to refrain from threat of use of force in any manner inconsistent with the purposes of the UN.

Thus, whatever incompliance and non-subordination with the UN Charter has become attributed to NATO over the years of its existence, it is not due to an inherently wrongful legal basis, but the political interests of the Member States constituting the organisation. Even if the intention at the time of the creation of NATO was to avoid the interference of the UNSC, the text of the Washington Treaty does not contain provisions in contradiction with international law. Article 51 of the UN Charter – collective self-defence – provides for the right of States to exercise the right without a prior UN mandate.

The North Atlantic Treaty provides also for internal requirements for the Member States: eliminating conflict between the economic policies[90] and strengthening the individual military defence capacity of the Member States.[91] Article 4 provides that the State parties will consult together when the territorial integrity, political independence or security of any one of them is threatened. Thus, the provisions of the Treaty are not in stark contrast with those of any other organisation analysed above.

The core provision of the Washington Treaty is Article 5, the first paragraph of which reads:

> The Parties agree that an armed attack against one or more of them in Europe or North America shall be considered an attack against them all and consequently they agree that, if such an armed attack occurs, each of them, in exercise of the right of individual or collective self-defence recognised by Article 51 of the Charter of the UN, will assist the Party or Parties so attacked by taking forthwith, individually and in concert with the other Parties, such action as it deems necessary, including the

---

89 D. A. Leurdijk, 'UN Reform and NATO Transformation: the Missing link', in O. M. Ribbelink (ed.), *Beyond the UN Charter. Peace, Security and the Role of Justice*, The Hague: Hague Academic Press, 2008, p. 142; Simma, op. cit., n. 88; D. S. Yost, 'NATO and International Organizations', Forum Paper, Rome: NATO Defence College, 2007, pp. 32–35, and others.
90 Washington Treaty, Art. 2.
91 Washington Treaty, Art. 3.

use of armed force, to restore and maintain the security of the North Atlantic area.

Thus, the treaty provides for self-defence in line with Article 51 of the UN Charter, though implying that the right is customary (and 'recognized by Article 51'). How exactly each party contributes to the collective self-defence is, however, up to it individually. The article also further provides for reporting the action taken to the UNSC immediately, also in line with Article 51 of the UN Charter.

To date, Article 5 of the Washington Treaty has been invoked only once – 50 years after the signing of the Treaty. It was done by the USA after the 9/11 attacks.[92] The invocation of the clause was general; it was not as a specific military operation. The first NATO operation following the invocation of Article 5 was launched in Afghanistan as a UN-mandated NATO peace enforcement operation, and not self-defence.[93] The initial unilateral US intervention in Afghanistan had been defined as self-defence. However, it was individual self-defence, not collective – in the NATO framework. It must be noted that Article 6(1) of the Washington Treaty specifies what is an armed attack, limiting it substantially to the territory of the Member States.

When the Cold War ended, the need for the continuation of the Alliance was cast into doubt, and therefore it started the still continuing process of transformation.[94] Even though Article 12 of the Treaty required a review after 10 years, having regard for the factors affecting peace and security in the North Atlantic area, including the 'development of universal as well as regional arrangements under the Charter of the UN for the maintenance of international peace and security', this was never done.[95] Instead, NATO established the practice of changing its own rules through political documents: declarations[96] and strategic concepts. The strategic concepts are the most significant and highest level NATO documents, adopted by the NATO decision-making organ, the NAC, at its summits.[97] The strategic concepts reveal the current agreement of Member States about the functions and priorities of the organisation.

---

92 E. Buckley, 'Invoking Article 5', *NATO Review*, Summer 2006.
93 SC/Res/1386 and the subsequent ones regarding ISAF. In 2003, NATO took over the lead of the force under Chapter VII provisions: see UNSC Resolution 1510 (2003).
94 Zwanenburg, op. cit., n. 81, p. 198.
95 It appears from the Washington Treaty that at the creation of NATO it was not clear what could be the regional arrangements provided for in Chapter VIII.
96 NATO Summit Declarations include Oslo Declaration of 1992, Prague Summit Declaration of 2002, Istanbul Summit Declaration of 2004, Riga Summit Declaration of 2006, Bucharest Declaration of 2008, Strasbourg-Kehl Summit Declaration and Lisbon Declaration of 2010 and others. Prague Summit Declaration, for example, is significant with the fact that it included an anti-terrorism concept, and that the Member States agreed on establishing NATO response forces.
97 Zwanenburg, op. cit., n. 81, p. 198.

The 1991 Strategic Concept[98] is the first in a row of, so far, three strategic concepts, amending the basic provisions of NATO in the post-Cold War era. This document is ground-breaking: it creates a whole new context for NATO. This Strategic Concept reaffirms that NATO is a defence alliance. However, it emphasises that the threats to NATO member countries are 'less likely to result from calculated digression against the territory of the Allies, but rather from the adverse consequences of instabilities that may arise from the serious economic, social and political difficulties, including ethnic rivalries and territorial disputes, which are faced by many countries in Central and Eastern Europe'.[99] These conflicts are recognised as potential risks that could lead to armed conflicts. They could then have spill-over effects in NATO countries, thus having a direct impact on the security of the Alliance. Such a case were the conflicts in the Balkans throughout the nineties, culminating in the 1999 NATO intervention in Kosovo. Moreover, the Strategic Concept provides for a broad list of new threats that the Alliance has to respond to in addition to those included in Articles 5 and 6 of the Washington Treaty. The new potential threats include also proliferation of WMD, disruption of the flow of vital resources and actions of terrorism and sabotage. Already in this document the global context is mentioned.

The 1991 Strategic Concept reiterates that NATO's essential purpose is to safeguard the freedom and security of all its members by political and military means in accordance with the principles of the UN Charter. The work of the Alliance is based on common values of democracy, human rights and the rule of law, with the purpose of the establishment of a just and lasting peaceful order in Europe. This Alliance objective remains unchanged. There are, nevertheless, other things that have changed. One of the most relevant, besides expansion and widening the understanding of threat, is the broadening of NATO tasks – a new internal mandate is given to NATO – participation in crisis management and conflict prevention. Moreover, security measures in the European (OSCE) context, confidence-building activities, dialogue, co-operation, enhancement of transparency and improvement of communication, as well as other security activities are envisaged. With the wide range of security tasks added to the NATO internal mandate, NATO cannot be regarded as a pure Article 51 collective defence organisation in the post-Cold War era. The security activities carried out by the 'transformed' NATO are not covered by the self-defence clause.

Most of the new provisions included in the 1991 Strategic Concept are picked up and elaborated on in the next two strategic concepts. The 1999

---

98 The Alliance's New Strategic Concept, agreed by the Heads of State and Government participating in the Meeting of the North Atlantic Council, 7–8 November 1991. Available at <http://www.nato.int/cps/en/natolive/official_texts_23847.htm> (accessed 18 April 2013).
99 The Alliance's New Strategic Concept, ibid, para. 7.

Strategic Concept[100] is an update of the post-Cold War status and in a great part repeats (almost wholescale) the 1991 concept. In many ways the 1999 concept continues the 1991 one by elaborating on the topics included. In this strategic concept the old and new tasks of NATO are defined and categorised explicitly. These are: security, consultation, deterrence and defence, crisis management and partnership.

The definition of 'security' contains also commitment to peaceful resolution of disputes, in which no country would be able to intimidate or coerce any other through the threat or use of force. Security, consultations and defence and deterrence are named as the fundamental tasks of the Alliance in order to achieve its essential purpose. Thus, the organisation has, in fact, the peaceful settlement of disputes function characteristic to Chapter VIII organisations. Crisis management and partnership are additional tasks to enhance security and stability in the Euro-Atlantic area. Crisis management refers also to rapid response capabilities, which have found practical expression in the NRF[101] – NATO's rotating stand-by brigade-size rapid reaction units.[102] Crisis management is a matter with significant legal implications, as it implies NATO's action outside the region.

The list of threats to the Alliance is, once again repeated and elaborated, listing both military and non-military threats, and focusing on non-traditional threats. The main distinguishing feature in the 1999 security concept from the 1991 one can be summed up to be the broad approach to security, which encompasses complementary political and military means, and emphasising co-operation with other States that share the Alliance's objectives.[103]

The strategic concepts do not express a revolution in the perception by NATO of the international law enshrined in the UN Charter in clear language. On the other hand, the widening of the threats NATO is to respond to and the broadening of NATO's tasks subjects the Alliance to rules that have not been relevant before. The new rules include those on enforcement action outside the region, bringing along controversy. The question of action without a UN mandate does not appear directly in the strategic concepts. Yet, it is pointed out that the Strategic Concept of 1999 was drafted ambiguously,[104]

---

100 The Alliance's Strategic Concept, 24 April 1999, Washington D.C. Available at <http://www.nato.int/cps/en/natolive/official_texts_27433.htm> (accessed 15 April 2013).
101 The establishment of the NRF was first announced at the Prague Summit in 2002 and approved by the Ministers of Defence in June 2003 in Brussels.
102 For more information, see 'NATO Response Force. At the Centre of Transformation', NATO website. Available at <http://www.nato.int/cps/en/natolive/topics_49755.htm> (accessed 15 April 2013). Stand-by rapid reaction forces have been created also by CSTO, the EU and the AU, the latter two being smaller in size.
103 'The Strategic Concept of the Alliance', NATO Handbook. Available at <http://www.nato.int/docu/handbook/2001/hb0203.htm> (accessed 27 August 2011).
104 Zwanenburg, op. cit., n. 81, p. 201 notes that the ambiguity is intentional to allow for broad interpretation.

which is officially interpreted by, for example, the USA, in the way that it does not impair NATO's ability to act in the absence of a UN mandate.[105] The Strategic Concept makes the requirement for a UN mandate a constitutional – national law issue,[106] thus leaving it up to the member countries to decide nationally whether they are willing to act without a UN mandate. Zwanenburg notes that the USA understood this paragraph as nothing in the Strategic Concept modified the position taken by the USA regarding NATO's ability to act in the absence of a UNSC mandate.[107]

NATO military doctrine, Allied Joint Publication 3.4.1 on peace support operations, however, evidences in clear language, that even though normally an OSCE or UN mandate is required, in exceptional circumstances, the NAC may decide on unilateral action.[108] Such approach is echoed also in the EU context, and is actually enshrined in the basic documents of the AU. At the same time, it is noted that other NATO Member States, such as France, Belgium and Canada, have on occasions expressed and emphasised a need for a UNSC mandate as a prerequisite for launching an operation.[109]

The 2010 Strategic Concept is entitled 'Active Engagement, Modern Threats'. Though based on the argument that the world has changed since 1999, the 2010 concept still copies the previous strategic concepts in part, but is more detailed and daring. The distinguishing features of the 2010 Strategic Concept are: the addition of an even wider range of new threats, altering the order of priority of the functions of the organisation and being very explicit about NATO's military capabilities. The preamble of the 2010 Strategic Concept once again describes NATO as a unique community of values, committed to the principles of individual liberty, democracy, human rights and the rule of law. The document states that, while the world is changing, NATO's essential mission will remain the same: to ensure that the Alliance remains an unparalleled community of freedom, peace, security and shared values.[110]

The Strategic Concept, in line with the previous strategic concepts declares a firm commitment to the purposes and principles to the UN Charter and the

---

105 Zwanenburg, op. cit., n. 81, p. 201.
106 Ibid, p. 202.
107 Statement of Ambassador Marc Grossman, Assistant Secretary of State for European Affairs before the Senate Armed Services Committee, 28 October 1999: see Zwanenburg, op. cit., n. 81, p. 202, reference 49.
108 Peace Support Operations, in NATO, Allied Joint Publications 3.4.1: NATO Doctrine for Peace Support Operations (2001), para. 0102.
109 Zwanenburg, op. cit., n. 81, p. 208; H. McCoubrey and J. Morris, *Regional Peacekeeping in the Post-Cold War Era*, The Hague: Kluwer Law International, 2000, p. 51.
110 Strategic Concept for the Defence and Security of The Members of the North Atlantic Treaty Organisation 'Active Engagement, Modern Defence', adopted by Heads of State and Government in Lisbon, 19 November 2010. Available at <http://www.nato.int/lisbon2010/strategic-concept-2010-eng.pdf> (accessed 15 April 2013).

Washington Treaty, which affirms the primary responsibility of the UNSC for the maintenance of international peace and security.[111]

The list of potential threats is updated and includes the acquisition of advanced military capabilities by third States (including ballistic missiles), proliferation of nuclear weapons and other WMD, terrorism, spill-over effects of instability beyond the regional borders (containing potential for extremism, terrorism, and trans-national illegal activities such as trafficking in arms, narcotics and people). A new threat, not mentioned before, is cyber-attacks. Also transport, energy and environmental security concerns are listed, alongside with the development of technology (laser weapons, electronic warfare and impeded access to space). The scope of threats is extended to an unprecedented level, while excluding the probability of a conventional armed attack. Most of the threats listed have the character of requiring action outside the region, yet not necessarily the use of military force.

NATO's intent to 'go global' was carefully included as a new task in the form of crisis management in the 1999 Security Strategy. The 2010 Strategy prioritises it as one of three core tasks of NATO, which contribute to safeguarding NATO interests and are said to be always carried out in compliance of international law: collective defence, crisis management and co-operative security. Collective defence is the classical provision of Article 5 of the Washington Treaty. However, the provision of the Strategic Concept also states that NATO will deter and defend against any threat of aggression, and against emerging security challenges where they threaten the fundamental security of individual Allies or the Alliance as a whole. This statement, namely the deterrence aspect, can be interpreted as allowing even pre-emptive self-defence. Crisis management definition resembles the wording found in the EU documents: 'to address the full spectrum of crises – before, during and after conflicts'. Crisis management, though global,[112] is not defined as altruistic, but rather, carried out in cases where the crises outside the region threaten the security of the Alliance.

Co-operative security is emphasised in the new concept. Such co-operation is established through partnerships beyond NATO borders with third countries in various co-operation programmes, for example, the general networks of Partnership for Peace programme and Mediterranean Dialogue and individual co-operation frameworks of NATO-Ukraine Commission or NATO-Russia Council.

It must be noted that the 2010 Strategic Concept supplements the statement of previous strategic concepts, that the Alliance does not consider any

---

111 Strategic Concept, ibid, Preamble.
112 The shift from being a regional actor to becoming a global actor was first declared in May 2002 foreign ministers meeting in Reykjavik. The Member States declared the commitment to confront the threats to its members' security, no matter what their origin. In the aftermath of the Declaration, the first NATO-led peace-support operation outside the Euro-Atlantic area was launched, taking over the US-led operation in Afghanistan (Leurdijk, op. cit., n. 89, p. 125).

country to be its adversary with a new one: 'However, no one should doubt NATO's resolve if the security of any of its members were to be threatened'.

According to NATO's own new strategic concept it will always act in accordance with international law. In the common understanding of international law this would mean no enforcement action without a UNSC mandate. This appears not to be the guaranteed interpretation by NATO. It is clear from both practice of NATO and the quote above, regarding the response to threats, that NATO is not shy about using force. The conclusion of the 2010 Strategic Concept reads:

> We, the political leaders of NATO, are determined to continue renewal of our Alliance so that it is fit for purpose in addressing the 21st Century security challenges. We are firmly committed to preserve its effectiveness as the globe's most successful political-military Alliance. Our Alliance thrives as a source of hope because it is based on common values of individual liberty, democracy, human rights and the rule of law, and because our common essential and enduring purpose is to safeguard the freedom and security of its members. These values and objectives are universal and perpetual, and we are determined to defend them through unity, solidarity, strength and resolve.

In the context of unilateral interventions, Allain Pellet criticises the USA for sacrificing the UN collective security system and commonly accepted international law, as well as the legitimacy as perceived by the rest of the world, to define unilaterally their own legitimate interests, usually presented under the veneer of values.[113] The same criticism can be addressed to NATO as a whole. Even if the values that NATO stands for are universal, NATO's pro-interventionist approach to spreading them may not be.

Decision-making

Article 9 of the Washington Treaty provides that the parties establish a Council, in which each of them is represented. The Council is to be organised so that it is able to meet promptly at any time. The Council is to set up subsidiary bodies as necessary, including the specified defence committee as an advisory body recommending measures for the implementation of Article 3 and 5 provisions. The NAC has established several specialised committees: the Policy Coordination Committee, the Political Committee, the Military Committee and Defence Planning Committee. There is also an advisory body, the NATO Parliamentary Assembly.

---

113 A. Pellet, 'Legitimacy of Legislative and Executive Actions of International Institutions', in R. Wolfrum and V. Röben (eds), *Legitimacy in International Law*, Berlin, Heidelberg and New York, NY: Springer, 2008, p. 75.

The Washington Treaty does not specify further provisions on decision-making. Over the years NATO has developed a practice for decision-making in its two structures: political (civilian) and military, supplementing the rules included in the Treaty. Consensus, which is the decision-making principle in the NAC, has developed in practice, but is not stipulated in the Treaty.

In the NAC, Member States do not vote on an issue. A document is accepted, unless a Member State explicitly objects to it.[114] Consensus is used, for example, for approving NATO Strategic Concepts, the NATO budget, deployment of forces for peace operations and invocation of Article 5.[115] In the everyday work of NATO, 'silence procedure' is used, where Member States are informed about the issue before the meeting and can send statements on their objections to the secretary-general before the meeting, if they oppose. If there is 'silence', the item is accepted. Thus, in practice, there is no voting, but only a general possibility of objection – potentially with a veto power – by any single one of the member countries.[116] The consensus decision-making procedure has been deemed to be too lengthy and inefficient for the expanded NATO, improvement suggestions on the expert level have been submitted.[117] With the weekly meetings of NAC on the permanent representative level, NAC is the most alert decision-making body of all the organisations in the maintenance of peace and security. NAC meets at different levels: the permanent representative level, the level of Foreign Ministers, Defence Ministers, and Heads of Government. Nevertheless, NAC has the same authority and power of decision-making on all the levels, and the decisions have the same status and validity at all levels.[118] Such documents as Summit Declarations and Strategic Concepts are, naturally, accepted at Summit levels.

The decision-making procedure in NATO is no exact science, as, for example, the intervention in Libya evidences. While on 19 March 2011 a coalition operation was launched, and a NATO operation was strongly opposed by Germany and other countries, such as Poland and Turkey,[119] already on

---

114 Tavares, op. cit., n. 87, p. 147.
115 P. Gallis, 'NATO's Decision-Making procedure', CRS Report for Congress, Congressional Research Centre, The Library of Congress, 5 May 2003, p. 2.
116 Tavares, op. cit., n. 87, p. 147.
117 E. Buckley and K. Volker, 'NATO Reform and Decision Making. Atlantic Council Strategic Advisors Group', Issue Brief, February 2010. Available at <http://www.acus.org/files/publication_pdfs/403/NATOReform_SAGIssueBrief.pdf> (accessed 18 April 2013).
118 *NATO Handbook*, Chapter 7 'Policy and Decision-Making. The North Atlantic Council'. Available at <http://www.nato.int/docu/handbook/2001/hb070101.htm> (accessed 30 August 2011).
119 M. Knigge, 'Berlin's stance on Libya has isolated Germany in NATO', interview with Nicholas Burns, *Deutsche Welle* news portal, 13 April 2011. Available at <http://www.dw-world.de/dw/article/0,,14985036,00.html> (accessed 18 April 2013). 'Who's in Charge? Germans pull forces out of NATO as Libyan Coalition falls apart', *Daily Mail*.

25 March 2011 the operation was re-hatted as a NATO operation. Just as in the SADC, ECOWAS, the CIS and CSTO, the decision-making procedure is rather a negotiation process among the more influential members of the organisation, than a vote-count of all its members. In essence, however, the result of the procedure does not differ from that of the political decision-making procedure in the UNSC where the powerful States negotiate their interests, having the potential ace of veto power up their sleeve.

The practice

NATO may not hold the record of the greatest number of operations launched by a regional organisation but it is notable for having launched the largest-scale and some of the most challenging, and also controversial, operations in the post-Cold War era.

The first NATO operations were carried out in the Balkans. In 1992, NATO's ships and aircraft were deployed to monitor the UN arms embargo against all the republics of former Yugoslavia. In November 1992, NATO, alongside the WEU, began peace enforcement operations in the same area.[120] NATO operations in the Balkans were carried out with a UN mandate. Even though these operations were peace enforcement operations and peacekeeping operations with enforcement elements (as authorised by the UN) and, in addition, large scale, they did not create a general legal concern. NATO operations in the Balkans include the Operation Deliberate Force (1992–95), IFOR (1995–96), Stabilisation Force (SFOR) (1996–2004) in Bosnia, and Taskforce Harvest (2001), Operation Amber Fox (2001–02) and Operation Allied Harmony (2002–03) in FYROM.[121]

The first UNSC mandate for a NATO operation was UNSC Resolution 770 (August 1992), not directly, but implicitly addressing the organisation by calling upon States acting nationally and through regional arrangements or agencies to take all measures necessary to facilitate, in co-ordination with the UN, the delivery by relevant UN humanitarian organisations and others of humanitarian assistance to Sarajevo and other parts of Bosnia.[122] It was followed by UNSC Resolution 816 (1993), calling States to ensure a no-fly zone. The actual addressee of this resolution was NATO, which, in turn, set up the Operation Deny Flight. The following resolution, UNSC Resolution 836 (1993), provided for the protection of safe havens. This was

---

Daily Online, 23 March 2011. Available at <http://www.dailymail.co.uk/news/article-1368693/Libya-war-Germans-pull-forces-NATO-Libyan-coalition-falls-apart.html> (accessed 18 April 2013).

120 SC/Res/713 (1991) – the initial resolution introducing the embargo, and the resolutions following it; SC/RES/770 (1991), SC/Res/787 (1992), SC/Res/795 (1992), and others.
121 Tavares, op. cit., n. 87, p. 148.
122 S/Res/770.

the first resolution containing the phrase 'all necessary means', which refers to enforcement action in UNSC practice. After the Dayton Peace Agreement was signed in 1995, IFOR became the first NATO peacekeeping operation.[123]

As opposed to the operations listed above, operations in Afghanistan and Kosovo, however, are some of the most controversial in the history of regional maintenance of peace and security. In fact, Kosovo appears to have spurred a debate on the legality and legitimacy of the use of force of unprecedented vastness.[124] The 1999 NATO intervention in Kosovo was expressly launched as a humanitarian intervention and without a UN mandate. Some NATO countries, led by the USA and the UK, also used an implied authorisation argument as additional legal justification for the intervention in Kosovo.[125] While the UNSC had resolved on the situation in Kosovo in UNSC Resolutions 1160 (1998), 1199 (1998) and 1203 (1998), none of the resolutions authorised the use of force. It was the indirect wording of UNSC Resolution 1199 (1998) that was invoked implicitly: 'Should the concrete measures demanded in this resolution and resolution 1160 (1998) not be taken, to consider further action and additional measures to maintain or restore peace and stability in the region'.[126] In addition France, the Netherlands and Slovenia argued that the UNSC had actually resolved under Chapter VII, affirmed the existence of a threat to international peace and security, and imposed enforcement (non-military) measures, thus, NATO had been entitled to act.[127] The implied authorisation argument is far-reaching, as the UNSC clearly had not invoked the 'all means necessary' clause. Though surrounded by great public and legal debate, the bombings of Serbia were not officially condemned by neither the UNSC, nor the UN General Assembly, even though the opposition and support in both UN organs were split.[128] The UNSC did not condemn the operation due to the same reason it had not authorised it in the first place – the use of veto by the Permanent Members of the UNSC. Instead, the UN took over the control of the operation in Kosovo, subsequently authorising it by UNSC Resolution 1244. This was deemed by some scholars to account for a retroactive authorisation (authorisation

---

123 S/Res/1031; 'NATO's relations with the UN', NATO website. Available at <http://www.nato.int/cps/en/natolive/topics_50321.htm> (accessed 18 April 2013).
124 The authors who have dedicated significant articles to the topic include Bruno Simma (*EJIL* Vol. 10, 1999), Alain Pellet, Vera Gowland-Debbas and Ruth Wedgwood (*EJIL* Vol. 11, 2, 2000), and Frederik Harhoff (*Nordic Journal of International Law*, Vol. 70, 1–2, 2001), among many others. Comprehensive reports have also been prepared by groups of researchers, such as the Independent International Commission on Kosovo Report and the report on legal and political aspects of humanitarian intervention by the Danish Institute of International Affairs.
125 Gray, op. cit., n. 69, p. 352.
126 S/Res/1198.
127 Gray, op. cit., n. 69, p. 352.
128 UN Press Release, GA 9599, 21 September 1999.

ex post facto).[129] Viewing the sequence of events in a context, the argument about the retroactivity of the authorisation is not to be accepted uncritically. Retroactivity does not derive from the text of UNSC Resolution 1244. The UNSC authorisation amounted to getting the situation under the control of the UNSC in circumstances that did not give other choices. The launching of an operation in Kosovo with a UN mandate was not possible due to a veto from Russia and China. The condemnation of the operation would not have been feasible due to the veto power of the three Euro-Atlantic Permanent Members of the UNSC. The immediate cessation of the operation would not have been possible due to the necessity for damage-control and the veto of the Euro-Atlantic members of the UNSC. The best option that was available to the UN at the time was to gain control of the operation, issuing UNSC Resolution 1244. Therefore the subsequent authorisation by the UNSC ought not to count as *ex post facto* authorisation, but rather as assuming UN control over a previously illegal situation.

In the aftermath of the Kosovo intervention Serbia filed the 'Legality of Use of Force' cases against NATO Member States at the ICJ. The ICJ, however, did not review the matter, basing it on the lack of jurisdiction.[130] Later, the academic debate moved on to the nuances of legality and legitimacy of humanitarian intervention in principle. One of the central conclusions that appeared to have gained acceptance was, as for example, in this quote by Simma, that 'only a thin red line separated NATO's action in Kosovo from international legality'.[131] Another significant conclusion was the 'emergency exit'[132] concept (humanitarian intervention as an exceptional solution), gaining support in the policy of the Euro-Atlantic region and its Member States, and included as a clearly spelled-out legal right to humanitarian intervention in the African regional documents.

Nevertheless, following the intervention, there also appeared to dominate the fear that if the Kosovo case were to be accepted as a precedent for establishing law, the right to humanitarian intervention could be abused. Twelve years after the launching of the unilateral regional operation in Kosovo

---

129 Pellet, for example, views authorisation *ex post facto* automatically retroactive. A. Pellet, 'Brief Remarks on the Unilateral Use of Force', *European Journal of International Law*, Vol. 11, 2, 2000, p. 389; I. Österdahl, 'Preach what you practice. The Security Council and the Legalisation *ex post facto* of the Unilateral Use of Force', *Nordic Journal of International Law*, Vol. 74, 2005, pp. 252–55.
130 'Legality of Use of Force' (*Yugoslavia v United States of America*) (*Serbia and Montenegro v Belgium*) (*Serbia and Montenegro v Canada*) (*Serbia and Montenegro v France*) (*Serbia and Monténégro v Germany*) (*Serbia and Montenegro v Italy*) (*Serbia and Montenegro v Netherlands*) (*Serbia and Montenegro v Portugal*) (*Yugoslavia v Spain*) (*Serbia and Montenegro v United Kingdom*).
131 Simma, op. cit., n. 88, p. 22.
132 J. E. Rytter, 'Humanitarian Intervention without the Security Council: From San Francisco to Kosovo – and Beyond', *Nordic Journal of International Law*, Vol. 70, 2001, pp. 148–51.

diverse reactions have been witnessed, though depicting a general fear of repetition of such action. The practice of the use of force by NATO has decreased the organisation's legitimacy in the eyes of other regions of the world, the position being stated by Asian States, and re-emphasised in the unconditional prohibition of all use of force by UNASUR. The only region that has openly taken over the Kosovo relay is Africa, namely, the AU and ECOWAS. The positions of NATO and the EU on the issue are unequivocal. The possibility to launch international operations without a UN mandate is not stipulated in the basic documents of the organisations, but has widely appeared in other documents, national positions and legislation of Member States, and other sources since the Kosovo intervention, including those described above regarding the EU.

There is one more NATO operation that needs to be mentioned, as it affects the legitimacy of NATO action – the International Security Assistance Force (ISAF) in Afghanistan. It is the first NATO operation out of the North-Atlantic area. It is also the longest and most challenging of NATO operations. Though against NATO's own constitutional provisions of the Washington Treaty, the operation was permitted by the Strategic Concept of 1999, allowing out-of-area operations (i.e. 'going global'). ISAF also had a UNSC mandate. The operation that was formally launched in August 2003 has continued longer and with greater setbacks and losses, than expected. With little visible progress, high levels of local corruption and continuous fighting, the NATO forces have been competing with the Taliban for the support of the local population for a decade. On the one hand, in the aftermath of 9/11, the operation received the most important assurance of legality – a UNSC mandate. The UN did not express objections against the global ambitions of a regional organisation in this case. The legitimacy matter, on the other hand, cannot be limited to the fulfilment of formal criteria. The fact that NATO intends to act globally is not warmly accepted by other regions which regard themselves as the potential interveneable regions. In addition, the local support in the theatre of operations is very split. Critics characterise the out-of-region pro-interventionist activities of the Euro-Atlantic region, especially humanitarian intervention, a cover for US interventionism and as a new form of colonialism.[133] This perception, along with, for example, the wish to avoid NATO involvement in other regions (e.g. as expressed by the Arab League before the enforcement of the no-fly zone in Libya[134]),

---

133 K. Watanabe, 'The Debate on Humanitarian Intervention', in K. Watanabe (ed.), *Humanitarian Intervention. The Evolving Asian Debate*, Tokyo: Japan Centre for International Exchange, 2003, pp. 12–20.
134 For example, 'Arab League backs a no-fly zone in Libya', *CNN World*, 12 March 2011. Available at <http://articles.cnn.com/2011-03-12/world/libya.civil.war_1_arab-league-libyan-people-opposition-forces?_s=PM:WORLD> (accessed 18 April 2013). The article

evidence a lower external legitimacy of NATO's out-of region action than the internally perceived one.

Alongside the examples of the EU Member States, the example of the decision of the Supreme Court of Denmark should be noted to illustrate the potential for a NATO consensus for regional action without a UN mandate.

On 17 March 2010, the Supreme Court of Denmark ruled on the legality of the Danish participation in the Iraq war. The question of the requirement for a UN mandate was brought up in connection with the legality of the Danish participation in the Iraq war. On 21 March 2003, the Danish Parliament gave its consent according to Section 19, paragraph 2 of the Constitution, to place a Danish military force at the disposal of a multinational operation under American leadership. A group of citizens, represented by the 'Constitution Committee on the Iraq War' sued the Prime Minister. They alleged that the decision of the Parliament on the Danish participation in the war violated Section 19, paragraph 2, of the Constitution, since the war against Iraq was illegal according to international law.

The court dismissed the claim on the ground that the appellant had no right of action with regard to the lawsuit. However, the Court did make clear its standing on the constitutionality of participation in military action without a UN mandate.[135] The Supreme Court emphasises the dualistic position of Denmark, drawing a strict line between national law and international law. The court notes that there is no unclarity in the understanding of Section 19, paragraph 2 of the Constitution and no incompliance with the textual interpretation or rules of procedure has taken place. The Court states that if the appellant's point of view were to be taken, the Constitution, from its very inception in 1953 ought to have left it up to the UNSC – with the veto rights of its Permanent Members – to decide whether Denmark, outside the situations recognised by international law, may use military force.[136]

The decision is significant in verifying the absence of national constraint to use force without a UN mandate, be it the context of an *ad hoc* coalition or a regional organisation framework, like NATO.

---

quotes the foreign minister of Oman, Youssef bin Alawi bin Abdullah, 'Be assured the Arab countries will not accept the intervention of the NATO coalition'.

135 UfR 2010.1547H. The details of the Court's opinion have been omitted in the release on the Court's decision in English.

136 The precise wording of the judgment in Danish, summarised in the description above: 'Hertil bemærker Højesteret, at der ikke foreligger nogen særlig uklarhed om forståelsen af grundlovens § 19, stk. 2, i overensstemmelse med ordlyden som en procedureregel, der regulerer forholdet mellem regering og folketing. En forståelse som hævdet af appellanterne ville indebære, at Danmark i 1953 skulle have overladt det til FN's Sikkerhedsråd – med vetoret for de permanente medlemmer – at afgøre, om Danmark uden for folkeretligt anerkendte situationer ville kunne anvende militære magtmidler. En sådan forståelse ville også stride mod den grundlæggende ordning i dansk ret af forholdet mellem national ret og international ret, hvorefter folkeretten ikke har grundlovskraft'.

A regional consensus for the use of force by a regional organisation is built up of the national positions of its Member States and has international implications. The intention not to be bound unconditionally by UNSC authorisation in the Euro-Atlantic region is underlined, among others, by the changes of legislation in the EU (not NATO) Member States Ireland and Finland, by the USA claiming that the decision to use force without a UN mandate is a national constitutional matter, and by the Danish judgment above. Thus, if the Member States of a regional organisation do not have a constitutional provision prohibiting the use of force without a UN mandate and do not regard themselves restricted by general international law on the prohibition of the use of force, the regional organisation may decide to act accordingly. Such a consensus was reached by NATO in the case of Kosovo, and is not excluded in the future.

In addition to the large-scale military operations, NATO has been engaged in many other activities concerning the maintenance of peace and security. The NRF has been created and so far used for civilian purposes, the most significant involvement being to assist after hurricane Katrina in 2005[137] and the earthquake in Pakistan, also in 2005.[138] NATO has also assisted other regional organisations. In Darfur, NATO gave training and technical assistance to the AU Mission in Sudan. In Somalia, NATO supported the AU Mission by providing airlift to the African States willing to deploy to Somalia under AMISOM.[139] NATO has also participated in a training mission in Iraq based on UNSC Resolution 1546 and at the request of the Iraqi Interim Government.[140] At the same time, there is a reserve on the side of the involved regional organisations and States to involve NATO directly in their regional conflicts.

The practice of NATO clearly evidences the strongest and most active outward-oriented military action of all organisations dealing with the maintenance of peace and security. Despite the claims of NATO itself for the high standards and the legitimacy of action carried out by the organisation, its coercive military nature holds a danger of breach of international law and abuse of power.

---

137 'Support to US in the response to hurricane Katrina', September 2005, Allied Command Operations, Supreme Headquarters Allied Powers Europe. NATO website. Available at <http://www.nato.int/shape/news/2005/10/051025a.htm> (accessed 18 April 2013).
138 'NATO Response Force Arrives in Pakistan', Allied Command Operations, Supreme Headquarters Allied Powers Europe, 25 October 2005. NATO website. Available at <http://www.nato.int/shape/news/2005/10/051025a.htm> (accessed 18 April 2013).
139 Tavares, op. cit., n. 87, p. 147.
140 'NATO's relations with the UN', NATO website. Available at <http://www.nato.int/cps/en/natolive/topics_50321.htm> (accessed 18 April 2013).

Co-operation with the United Nations

NATO is the only regional organisation analysed in this book not having an observer status with the UN General Assembly. The Alliance strongly claims itself not to be a UN Charter Chapter VIII organisation, basing it on the Cold-War defensive alliance argument (UN Charter Art. 51),[141] while the UN approach towards NATO in recent practice resembles its practice towards Chapter VIII organisations.[142]

It cannot be denied that with the end of the Cold War NATO stepped out of its Article 51 role and entered the sphere of the maintenance of peace and security, which is the realm of the UNSC, namely, peace operations, and in particular, peace enforcement. While the UN has utilised several other regional organisations for peacekeeping, NATO is the organisation that has been mainly carrying out peace enforcement tasks, generally with but – in relation to Kosovo – also without a UN mandate.

Apart from the other US-led operations and coalitions of the willing,[143] NATO has been the one framework the international community, in the shape of the UNSC, has utilised to enforce collective action. Such cases of UN-mandated NATO operations are the abovementioned operations in the Balkans (FYROM and Bosnia and Herzegovina) and Afghanistan. In addition, the UN has mandated a NATO training mission in Iraq.[144]

The two organisations have co-operated in smaller-scale field activities, as well as established more formal co-operation. NATO and the UN have worked together in areas like Darfur, Somalia, Pakistan and Afghanistan.[145] On a formal level, NATO and the UN have co-operated through staff-level meetings, high-level visits, and consultations between specialised bodies on issues of crisis management, civil-military co-operation, combating human trafficking, mine action, the fight against terrorism, and others.

In September 2008, NATO and the UN signed a joint declaration on the co-operation of the secretariats. Such a development is peculiar, because it is the same type of co-operation declarations that the UN signs with almost all regional security organisations, and which can be interpreted as a confirmation of the Chapter VIII status of the regional organisation it is signed with.

---

141 See Simma, op. cit., n. 88, and Zwanenburg, op. cit., n. 81.
142 See, for example, Security Council meeting S/PV.6257 and the Joint Declaration between the secretariats, in 'Secret UN-NATO Cooperation Declaration', The Transnational Foundation for Peace and Future Research. Available at <http://www.oldsite.transnational.org/Resources_Treasures/2008/TFFBoard_UN-NATO.html> (accessed 21 April 2013).
143 For example, operations in Iraq in 1991 and 2003, Operation Enduring Freedom in Afghanistan.
144 'NATO's relations with the UN', NATO website. Available at <http://www.nato.int/cps/en/natolive/topics_50321.htm> (accessed 18 April 2013).
145 'NATO's relations with the UN', ibid.

The 2010 NATO Strategic Concept makes the following reference to the declaration:

> We are committed to strong and productive cooperation between NATO and the UN. We welcome the strengthened practical cooperation following the Joint Declaration on UN/NATO Secretariat Cooperation of September 2008. We aim to deepen this practical cooperation and further develop our political dialogue on issues of common interest, including through enhanced liaison, more regular political consultation, and enhanced practical cooperation in managing crises where both organisations are engaged.[146]

The declaration states that the co-operation is guided by the UN Charter, internationally recognised humanitarian principles and guidelines, and consultation with national authorities. Yet, at no place in the declaration NATO states that it subordinates itself to the primacy of the UNSC, but rather, that both organisations work together for the maintenance of international peace and security. Interestingly, the wording 'We also reaffirm our willingness to provide, within our respective mandates and capabilities, assistance to regional and sub-regional organizations, as requested and as appropriate' in the declaration may also be interpreted as distinguishing NATO as a category separate from regional and subregional operations.

It appears that NATO intends to be an equal partner to the UN, independent of it, but respectful of the fact that the UN is in the centre of a network of regional organisations that are subordinate to it. For such a position of NATO there is no explicit legal status under international law. The law does not provide for an alternative mechanism of the international maintenance of peace and security other than the UN one. Even though the position of NATO with regard to the role of the UN in the maintenance of peace and security is controversial under international law, the UN co-operates with NATO, avoiding potential confrontations, and instead utilising the capabilities of NATO to the best of its ability.

Summary

The EU and NATO are relevant not only in the regional maintenance of peace and security but also in the global context. The significance of these organisations in comparison to other regional organisations is catalysed by the strong regional identity: the Euro-Atlantic region is one of the most

---

146 Lisbon Summit Declaration, issued by the Heads of State and Government participating in the meeting of the North Atlantic Council in Lisbon, Press release (2010) 155, 20 November 2010. Available at <http://www.nato.int/cps/en/natolive/official_texts_68828.htm?mode=pressrelease> (accessed 15 April 2013).

coherent regions in the world. The regional co-operation is based on common values of democracy and the protection of human rights. The Euro-Atlantic region is a very distinct region from the rest of the world with its wide post-Cold War practice and the ambitions for going global, i.e. acting outside the region, even with its military capabilities. While CSTO has expressed an intention to assist in UN peacekeeping globally, in addition to its core task of intra-regional maintenance of peace and security, most other organisations have no ambition to step outside their respective regions. In the case of the Euro-Atlantic region, the threats are seen as coming from outside the region, not inside. While traditional threats are not excluded, main emphasis is on non-traditional ones. The threats listed are of a very wide range – starting from terrorism and spill-over effects of an internal conflict outside the region, to cyber-attacks.

The decision-making mechanisms differ in the Euro-Atlantic organisations. In the EU it is a very (perhaps too) detailed and regulated process and a unanimity vote with a possible abstention. In NATO it is an intransparent consensus procedure.

Peaceful conflict prevention (outside the region) is very highly emphasised, and both military peacekeeping and peace enforcement are permissible. The region has extensive practice in peacekeeping and peace enforcement with a UN mandate outside the region, as well as in peacekeeping without a UNSC mandate. There is, however, ambiguity about potential enforcement action by the Euro-Atlantic organisations outside the region without a UN mandate, as was the case of Kosovo.

Though not stated in the basic regional documents, different national legal acts, judgments and political statements evidence that there is support in the Euro-Atlantic region for the possibility of launching a humanitarian intervention without a UN mandate. The right to unilateral regional action, just like in the case of the African region, would be applicable only in exceptional, extreme cases. On the other hand, there is a reservation against speaking it out directly and including such a clause in legal documents. Thus, a legal right is not established, but a corresponding political acceptance is evident.

There is also controversy about the legal status of the Euro-Atlantic regional organisations. First, it has been questioned whether a Chapter VIII organisation may act outside the region. Second, NATO claims to be an Article 51, not Chapter VIII, organisation. The functions of the Euro-Atlantic region are blurred: while the EU deals with security issues, also in NATO the defence function has become secondary in its twenty-first century practice as a pro-active global maintainer of security. Nevertheless, all organisations, not least formally recognised Chapter VIII organisations have the duty to respect the primary responsibility of the UNSC in the maintenance of peace and security, at least by virtue of Article 24 of the UN Charter.

It is essentially the combination of the global ambition and the permissibility of enforcement action, generally with a UN mandate, but possibly also as unilateral regional humanitarian intervention, that makes the maintenance of peace and security of the Euro-Atlantic region challenging in an international law context. Some of the most challenging issues are whether or not the Euro-Atlantic organisations – the EU and NATO – are organisations that have more legitimacy to use force due to the democratic values enshrined in them. It can also be questioned whether the claim to act globally is legitimised by the fact that threats to the Euro-Atlantic region come from outside the region while other regions are troubled by threats from within, or are these organisations simply acting as agents of the international community, assisting the UN in the global maintenance of peace and security? Perhaps the central concern of legalising the right to humanitarian intervention as a Euro-Atlantic regional norm is not the potential breach of a *jus cogens* norm, but rather that the norm may be accepted by other regions as well, and thus increase the general extent of regional use of force without a UN mandate.

9 Comparison of the regions

The house of mirrors

The approaches of six security regions of the world (Africa, Asia, the Americas, the Middle East, the Russian sphere of influence and the Euro-Atlantic region) towards relevant provisions of Chapter VIII of the UN Charter have been established through their legal documents and practical activity. The central issues analysed include the perception of a regional right to humanitarian intervention, the permissible scope of regional use of force, the general limits for regional action in the maintenance of peace and security, if short of use of force. The analysis of the individual regions reveals widely differing approaches towards the core legal issues of maintenance of peace and security, which creates a great challenge of establishing what can be regarded as appropriate for regional action. So to speak, each mirror provides a different reflection, making the global network of the maintenance of peace and security a veritable house of mirrors at a fair.

Factors influencing different regional approaches

Despite the UN collective maintenance of peace and security system being formally in place for over 65 years, it is still difficult to find a common denominator regarding the permissibility of the use of force and to define a uniform understanding of what is appropriate for regional action in the regions. Even though the same international law has theoretically applied to all Member States of the UN, non-legal factors strongly influence the understanding and application of the concepts of use of force and maintenance of peace and security. The differences in regional approaches have varied reasons. Some regions are influenced by recent events, while the approach of others is formed during the Cold War, and even their pre-Charter history.

The history of individual regions shows an angle illustrating why in the UN system, which has vitally contributed to maintaining peace and security globally, it has not been possible to establish a homogenous approach to regional use of force and a uniform network of regional organisations in the maintenance of peace and security under the UN umbrella. The historical factors analysed are not exclusive, but only illustrative of the wide range of social, economic, cultural, political and historical factors having an impact on the application of the rules of international law on the use of force by regional organisations.

From ancient times to early Middle Ages one can note the examples of ancient Greek leagues, China and Islamic collective security – *Dar al-Islam* – being religion-based. While religion is generally not the formal determinant co-operation element in today's secular world, it still plays an important role in the formation of regions. The Middle East regional organisations – the Arab League and the OIC – are the only ones that have religion as the formal participation criterion, reflecting the continuation of *Dar al-Islam* in the contemporary world. Nevertheless, while medieval Islam provided for a strong Islamic collective security and defence system, it has not been truly implemented over the course of centuries. The level of unity in the Middle East has been too low to sustain an efficient system of maintenance of security. The Middle Eastern security and defence mechanisms have shown such a low level of efficiency and ability to co-operate, that some authors refer to the Middle Eastern/Islamic regional maintenance of peace and security as absent. Collective security in the Middle East for a group of States having religious and ethnic ties does not appear to work. Nevertheless, the structure of regional co-operation is still maintained, in line with the Islamic tradition.

In Asia, religion plays an important role in the principles applied to regional maintenance of peace and security: peaceful coexistence, non-intervention and non-interference connect with the Eastern religions like Confucianism and Buddhism. Regarding China specifically, its ancient perception of the world order as Chino-centric globalism influenced by Confucianism is still valid to an extent. The Chinese approach is still dominantly globalist and non-interventionist, not accepting the right to regional use of force, and often opposing the Western initiatives for interventions at the UNSC. At the same time Chino-centrism finds its expression in the seclusion of Asian matters from outside influence, and regarding issues of self-determination in the sphere of interest of China (e.g. Tibet) as its internal matter. China, being a Permanent Member of the UNSC has been using its position to keep the majority of the Asian conflicts off the agenda of the UNSC. One of the most explicit cases is Myanmar, on which, in decades of an internal conflict, the UNSC has not resolved once. The Confucian thought is also strongly evident in the non-interfering approach and co-operative security (as opposed to the more committing collective security) in the work of ASEAN.

In Europe, the Christian religious thought is also evident, especially since the revival of the doctrine of humanitarian intervention. It is still the ideas of St Thomas Aquinas and the just war clause that influence the European approach towards responsibility to protect and intervention in the case of necessity. The prioritisation of an individual and its human rights are inherent in the 'love thy neighbour' and 'good Samaritan' Christian philosophy. The present-day Euro-Atlantic action outside the region and promotion of European values of human rights and democracy, often by military means, resemble the medieval crusades and Christian missions. The dark side of the just cause related to Christian religion is the convenience of misusing altruistic aims for specific political interests. The Euro-Atlantic approach of 'going global' has therefore, unsurprisingly, caused concern about masked colonialism in other regions.

The shadow of the Euro-Atlantic colonialism of the sixteenth to twentieth centuries is still present in the twenty-first century maintenance of peace and security. The Euro-Atlantic region is the only region where the two central regional organisations for the maintenance of peace and security have the internal mandate to 'go global'.

Russia, which is the uncontested hegemon of the CIS and CSTO region, is also one of the traditional (eighteenth to twentieth centuries) European powers that have ruled major parts of the world. Russia was politically split off from the rest of the European region by the Cold War, which at the same time merged Europe and North America into one security region. Russia still retains its direct sphere of influence, which, in comparison, the other former imperialist States have lost. Moreover, Russia maintains a political and military surplus as a potential global maintainer of peace and security.

It is only in the past decade that China has opened up for regionalism, initiating the SCO (the Shanghai Five). Also ASEAN has been intensifying its work and institutionalising, while maintaining a non-interference principle as its fundament. In Asia, the Euro-Atlantic humanitarian intervention doctrine has, nevertheless, been rejected, claiming that it is a new form of colonialism.

On a similar note as in Asia, regional activism in the Americas has intensified to prevent interference from outside the region. Just as the predecessor of the OAS was established to counter European colonialism, UNASUR was established in 2008 to significantly limit the influence of the USA on the matters of peace and security in South America. Thus, it can be said that the South American security mechanism is not only aimed at ensuring regional peace and security, but also at ensuring non-interference and non-intervention from the side of the Euro-Atlantic region with its global ambitions.

It is only the region of Africa that, after discarding of the inefficient anti-colonialism-focused maintenance of peace and security mechanism within the framework of the OAU, at the turn of the century opted for an 'all means necessary' solution. While the OAU constituting document concentrated on anti-colonialism, the AU constitutive document was the first to provide a legalised right to regional intervention: both humanitarian and pro-democratic intervention. Africa is the region of the world most plagued by military conflicts, and the inability to guarantee peace through the use of the universal mechanism has eventually brought about a pro-interventionist regional solution.

The generally continuously Eurocentric character of the global maintenance of peace and security is evidenced by the overwhelming majority of military and civilian operations carried out by Euro-Atlantic organisations globally. The ambition of NATO and the EU to act globally highlights the continuously Eurocentric power politics, in line with the historical role of Europe as the dominant region of the world, even if the regional action is (still) taken for a just cause.

The Westphalian power-balance system in the present-day maintenance of peace and security is difficult to disregard. Even though in the post-UN Charter era international law strictly limits elements of power politics, such as the use of force in general, and has eliminated the right to go to war as a means of settlement of disputes, the power-balance element is still of great importance in the modern maintenance of peace and security. The UN primary organ responsible for the maintenance of international peace and security, the UNSC, was in fact, established on a power-balance basis. The drafting of the UN Charter as a compromise among the victors of the Second World War ensured the continuation of the system of power balance – an essentially Western one, with the addition of China. The rest of the world would have to comply with the consensus of these five powers. The main guarantee included in the UN Charter for maintaining the system of balance of power was the inclusion of a veto right for the Permanent Members of the UNSC. The veto right has also conserved the European influence on the maintenance of peace and security at the post-Second World War level, allowing Eurocentrism to linger.

The balance of power can also be witnessed as an important element in the regional practice of maintenance of peace and security. The examples of Russia and USA trading off interventions in Georgia and Haiti in the UNSC, as well as South Africa and Zimbabwe trading off interventions in Lesotho and the DRC, evidence how the balance of power can override the reliance on international law provisions for the use of force both on the regional, as well as the universal level. As much as the role of international law has been strengthened since the creation of the UN, its application still, very much, rests on the principle of power-balance.

The recent history examples of Cold War interventionism in the Americas and in the Russian sphere of influence can be compared. Both regions experienced a strong hegemon intervening in the States of the region throughout the Cold War years. The first example is the case of Latin America where the Cold War interventionism has led to two types of developments: intra-OAS and extra-OAS. The intra-OAS development can be summarised as the introduction of measures for the promotion of democracy carried out by peaceful, diplomatic means only, abolishing the use of military force regionally. The use of military capabilities is unacceptable for Latin American States due to the wave of military dictatorships supported by the USA in the fight against communism during the Cold War. Thus, even peacekeeping in the OAS framework is to be only civilian, and not military. The second – extra-OAS – development is the creation of UNASUR – a South American regional organisation dealing with the maintenance of peace and security in a pacifistic way, and excluding the USA from having a role in the regional co-operation forum.

A different example of the development of post-Cold War regional security is the case of the Russian sphere of influence. The States of the former Socialist bloc that were also members of the Warsaw Pact moved away from the Russian sphere of influence. Countries like Hungary, the Czech Republic and Slovakia (formerly Czechoslovakia) that were subject to interventions by the Soviet Union are now members of the EU and NATO instead. Nevertheless, the former USSR, though dissolved, still generally remains the sphere of influence of Russia. Of all the former Soviet Republics, only four (the Baltic States with a more recent addition of Georgia) out of 15 are not members of the CIS. Russia is essentially still exercising influence in the countries around it, often through military peacekeeping operations. The Member States of the region appear to lack the leverage to counter Russia's unilateral policy in the regional forums. Yet, the countries subject to the Russian policy have acquiesced to this model for the regional maintenance of peace and security. As opposed to the developments in the Americas, in the Russian sphere of influence military capabilities have been constantly strengthened since the end of the Cold War. Moreover, in the future CSTO military capabilities are to be utilised for peacekeeping globally under the UN umbrella. Thus the Cold War practice of unilateral interventions in the region of Americas by the USA has highly strengthened the respect for the unconditional prohibition of the use of force, non-intervention in internal matters and dispute settlement by peaceful means only (military peacekeeping not among those). On the contrary, the strengthening of regional military capabilities is still ongoing in the Russian sphere of influence, where the Russian freedom of action regionally is taken for a fact. Despite the theoretical adherence to all the same UN Charter rules and principles guiding regional use of force and a similar history of interventions by the regional power, the post-Cold War paths of the Americas and the Russian sphere of influence in the maintenance of peace and security differ considerably.

There are also other region-specific elements in the maintenance of peace and security that evidence the presence of regional tradition. They do not crucially influence the regional approach towards what is appropriate for regional action, including the use of force, nevertheless, they evidence the strong impact of individual cultural roots. Such are, for example, the Panels of the Wise. The African regional organisation basic documents (the AU and ECOWAS; also the Arab League, which contains African Member States), provide for an advisory body in the form of the Panel of the Wise that can, among other tasks, be used for mediation and good offices. Such a body would provide popular legitimacy to the efforts of the organisation in tribal societies where the word of the elders is respected. Such panels, however, have been recently implanted into formal organisations, the experiences of their workability need to be gathered.

Also the 'civilised nations' self-perception of the Euro-Atlantic region resembles the ancient Greek and medieval Christian security region model present previously in the region. The Euro-Atlantic region is based on democratic values and this, according to some, gives the Euro-Atlantic region a greater legitimacy to intervene in other regions in the same vein as during the just wars of the Middle Ages. In this sense, the Euro-Atlantic security and defence is still in the essence the civilised 'us' against 'them', even if the purposes for intervention may be altruistic, based on the values of human rights and democracy.

The history of the maintenance of peace and security does not start with the creation of the UN Charter, and not even with the League of Nations. The history of different regions contains events and developments not only over decades, but sometimes even over hundreds and thousands of years, directly impacting the post-Cold War regional maintenance of peace and security. It can be concluded that political-historical factors have a major impact on the interpretation and implementation of the UN Charter rules on maintenance of peace and security in individual regions. Religious ties, power-balance, European dominance, the memory of colonialism and regional cultures in general are still strongly influential elements which provide diverging regional perspectives. The Euro-Atlantic organisations continue a proactive policy for the maintenance of peace and security, while regions like Asia and Americas wish to avoid all use of force. In the case of Asia it is based on the ancient teachings of the Oriental religions, while in the Americas it is due to the abuse of regional power in the past century. The historical regional backgrounds are not beneficial for establishing an idealistic uniform global maintenance of peace and security system with an even network of regional organisations. Yet, it is the reality that has to be taken into consideration. With the extra-legal pre-conditions influencing the mind-set of different security regions, it is difficult to implement democratic rules on regional maintenance of peace and security, providing 'one law, one justice for all'. Subsequently, it is also difficult to achieve a uniform understanding globally of what is appropriate for regional action. This conclusion supports the mode of co-operation with regional organisations that the UN has chosen: to flexibly accommodate the regional peculiarities for the maintenance of peace and security.

Appropriate for regional action

The comparative analysis of the practice of the six security regions makes answering the question of what is the content of 'appropriate for regional action', as cited in Article 52 of the UN Charter, a nearly impossible task. The level of coercion provided for in the constitutive documents and practice of the regional organisations is strikingly diverging. The extent of the permissibility of the use of force ranges from absolute exclusion of any kind of interference in the internal matters of regional members to a full constitutional mandate for regional peace enforcement by military means.

The most non-interventionist region is Asia, where regionalisation in the maintenance of peace and security has accelerated only in the past decade, and where regional maintenance of peace and security is only co-operative, as opposed to a more binding collective security. Co-operative security means having a regional forum only for consultation and negotiations. Any political, economic, and, by all means, military interference in a Member State by the regional organisation is unacceptable. The internal affairs of Member States are respected, and no interference is made, not even in large-scale internal conflicts and civil wars. Though this approach may be fully in compliance with the prohibition of the use of force, it may also be questioned, whether such a mechanism would be able to contribute to the 'responsibility to protect' principle also deriving from the human rights commitments enshrined in the UN Charter itself.

The next level of commitment towards regional maintenance of peace and security can be observed in the Arab League, which is organised as a Western mechanism for regional maintenance of peace and security, but does not have provisions that could bind its members. The fact that the decisions of the organisation are optional in most cases has rendered the organisation unable to achieve commitment from its Member States. The practice of the Arab League, however, does not depict the theoretical level of permissibility of regional action. The Arab League is, in fact, also a collective defence organisation, and regional use of military assets for peacekeeping is permitted.

The following level of commitment is found in the Americas. The Americas are to be a 'zone of peace', which is to be achieved by peaceful means only. The decisions of the regional organisations, however, are binding for the Member States. Interestingly, as opposed to ASEAN, the prohibition of the use of force in the Americas does not preclude the OAS mechanisms for collective self-defence, and intervention by peaceful means is widely practised.

The scope of what is permissible for regional action is furthermore wider in the Euro-Atlantic organisations and the Russian sphere of influence organisations, especially CSTO, made to a great extent according to the NATO model. All of these organisations have an ambition to act globally and permit out-of-area operations. While CSTO constitutionally permits enforcement action within the region with a UN mandate, only peacekeeping with a UN mandate can be contemplated outside the region. The Euro-Atlantic regional organisations, on the other hand, act primarily outside the region, both in peacekeeping and peace enforcement operations.

The highest level of regional commitment however, is found in Africa. Here, not only does the regional organisation take binding decisions for all Member States, but it actually has a constitutional right to intervene militarily in a Member State.

The use of military capacities under the umbrella of the regional organisation is allowed in four out of six regions. The regions of Asia and the Americas have provisions on contributing peacekeeping forces to the UN on an individual basis, but a regional peacekeeping force is intentionally excluded from the multilateral co-operation framework. In the Middle East organisations peacekeeping is theoretically permissible and contemplated, yet non-existent at the time of writing. The other three regions: the Euro-Atlantic, the Russian Sphere of Influence and Africa all have forces available for the regional organisation, and to be used for UN-led or mandated peacekeeping, if called for. In addition, in line with the calls of the Brahimi Report of 2000 and several subsequent documents, the EU, NATO, CSTO and the AU have also established rapid reaction forces. Also, enforcement action is theoretically allowed in all of these organisations. It is, however, only the AU that has, in its basic legal document, explicit provision for potential enforcement action without a UN mandate. The position of the EU, and, moreover, NATO, regarding enforcement outside the region without a UN mandate controversial, but is not formally stated in the official documents of the organisations.

The regions with provisions prohibiting the use of military force and the establishment of regional military capabilities rely on the efficiency of preventive measures. Nevertheless, the regional organisations cannot intervene in the individual States' discretion of establishing national military capabilities. Neither can they interfere in other non-Member States' and regions' establishment of regional capabilities. Thus, while preventive measures may help maintain peace, if a conflict to which military response is required occurs, these regional organisations may lack the ability to respond rapidly. Of course, the UN system would have to come into play in such situations, but the force contributions and the duration of time that is required for gathering them by the UN is one of the core problems of the efficiency of the UN system. In the twenty-first century world, it is the reliance and proper utilisation of Chapter VIII organisations that may save the authoritative position of the UN collective system of maintenance of peace and security.

If a region does not have its own capabilities, the UN is most likely to request assistance from one of the most capable regional organisations – perhaps not only Euro-Atlantic, but also from the Russian sphere of influence. If the region does not have its own capabilities and is intervened into by another regional organisation, even with a UN authorisation, there is a risk of *ultra vires* action – exceeding the limits of the UN authorisation. Thus, it is, in fact, in the interests of all security regions to establish regional mechanisms for the maintenance of peace and security, if not with a military capacity to deal with conflicts in the area, then at least with a diplomatic capacity to take charge of the situation.

A Chapter VIII organisation

The UN Charter regulates regional co-operation very briefly, only regarding the maintenance of peace and security. During the Cold War years the UN took a narrow approach towards Chapter VIII organisations, granting the status to very few organisations. Following the end of the Cold War, the UN has taken a broad functional approach towards regional organisations. With and without reference to Chapter VIII of the UN Charter, the UN co-operates equally with all the regional organisations analysed, despite the differences. The co-operation contains formal agreements and meetings, as well as co-operation in the field with a part of the regional organisations. It appears from the practice of the UN that setting the limits of what is appropriate for regional action is left up to the discretion of the regional organisations themselves. The UN is willing to sign co-operation agreements with the widest scope of regional actors, in order to promote their activity in ensuring the maintenance of peace and security by the means that are culturally acceptable within the individual region. This does not mean that all the action taken by regional organisations is automatically legal under international law. Rather, it means that the UN is not willing to intervene where a regional solution to regional problems would be more efficient and culturally suitable, even if some controversy with regard to legality may arise.

From the practice of the UN in its co-operation with the regional organisations analysed, one cannot distinguish co-operation with Chapter VIII organisations as differing from that with non-Chapter VIII organisations. It has been argued by NATO that it is not a regional organisation in the understanding of Chapter VIII, and therefore not subordinate to the UNSC and subject to limitations set for the Chapter VIII organisations. Even if NATO is an Article 51 organisation with regard to collective self-defence, when it carries out action in a wider security context, the Chapter VIII rules apply. NATO is also treated by the UN the same way as any other regional organisation regarded as a Chapter VIII organisation. The subordination to the UN, in case of regional enforcement action, including humanitarian intervention, remains a valid concern of the UNSC, even if the organisation is defined as an Article 51 organisation. According to international law, the ambition of a regional organisation to provide for the maintenance of peace and security globally while not fully recognising the primary responsibility of the UNSC under Article 53 is unjustified. It is the constitutional character of the UN Charter provisions that determines the requirement of compliance from all UN Member States. If a regional organisation avoids the Chapter VIII classification which imposes compliance with Article 53, it is still subject to the provisions of Articles 24, 39 and 103 of the UN Charter by virtue of individual Member State obligations.

Security and defence

NATO and the Warsaw Pact Organisation were examples of organisations created under Article 51 of the UN Charter, and not as Chapter VIII organisations, thus having an alternative status under the UN Charter, as opposed to Chapter VIII organisations. Today, security and defence have become overlapping and integrated functions of the same organisations dealing with the maintenance of peace and security. The concept of self-defence, however, is perceived differently in different regions – in some regions, namely the Euro-Atlantic region and the Russian Sphere of Influence, threats that trigger collective self-defence can come only from the outside. These regions are 'alliances', stapling the unity of the region according to the 'one for all, and all for one' principle. Even though the EU may potentially have collective self-defence capabilities under the Lisbon Treaty provisions in the future, it does not have them at the moment. Nevertheless, the EU security strategy, which is fully outward-facing, depicts the reliance on its allies and the mutual trust, creating a regional coherence that counter-positions the region to the rest of the world. The same trust principle is also in the core of NATO: an alliance is the term that characterises mutual trust. In addition, CSTO is also defined in its Statute as an alliance.

In contrast, the legal acts of the OAS (Article 7 of the Rio Treaty) and the Arab League (Article 6, paragraph 2 of the Arab League Charter) provide for the possibility to call for collective action against an internal aggressor, i.e. a Member State of the organisation, under the general collective self-defence provisions. The absence of mutual trust within the region may be a hindering factor for strengthening co-operation in the maintenance of peace and security through, for example, sharing information or organising common projects. In Africa, defence co-operation is also enhanced in the wider regional security co-operation, and collective action against a faulted Member State is permissible.

The Asian regional organisations are the only ones that exclude defence co-operation from their regional maintenance of peace and security. ASEAN is said to omit a defence function specifically to avoid outside influence on regional matters. In addition there are no organisations remaining that deal only with collective self-defence. Most of the organisations analysed in this book enhance defence in their maintenance of peace and security mechanisms. A simple explanation for this fact is that response to asymmetric and non-traditional threats that are the most common ones today is not covered by the concept of self-defence. Self-defence refers to an imminent armed attack by another State, which, in fact, is the least likely threat of today, as concluded also in the NATO Strategic Concept of 2010. The merging of collective security and collective self-defence elements in today's regional organisation practice deem the scholarly separation of Chapter VIII organisations as opposed to Article 51 organisations inapplicable in practice. Thus, it can be concluded that the division of organisations into distinct security organisations and distinct defence organisations is obsolete, and that all are subject to Chapter VIII provisions. The general limitations of Chapter VIII on what is appropriate for regional action apply to all of them, without prejudice to the inherent right to individual and collective self-defence.

The threats in various regions differ and thus the types of means of response to the threats and the level of necessity to use of force differ as well. While terrorism has become a global threat, regions face specific threats that attention is paid to. For example, in the Americas it is the military coups frequent in the past and the currently raging drug wars that cause the greatest threats to peace and security. South Americans have chosen preventive limitations on the use of force in the region to avoid future military coups. Drug dealing has been left for internal resolution by Member States, and thus untreated regionally, has become a threat greater and deadlier than the Cold War period coups.

In Africa civil wars and spill-over effects, such as flows of refugees, are the more likely threats to peace and security, along with general poverty and social problems. As to the military threats, Africa has opted for a pro-interventionist action on its own. The implementation of the policy, however, is hindered by the shortage of financial means and practical capabilities.

In the Russian sphere of influence extremism and separatism are a central concern. On this issue Russia finds common ground with China in the SCO. Traditional military means are used to combat these threats.

It is however, only the Euro-Atlantic region that treats the regional threats in principle as coming from outside, and not inside the region. Hence comes the Euro-Atlantic ambition to act outside the region as the principal *modus operandi*. Thus, the action outside the region is, in fact, a means of maintaining the Euro-Atlantic regional, and not international peace and security, which is the realm of the UN according to international law.

Regions have a varying approach to combating threats. All the regions today have to focus on both traditional and non-traditional threats. The regions differ in combating untraditional threats by traditional or non-traditional means. The Euro-Atlantic region and the Russian Sphere of Influence, including the SCO, base their security on traditional military means in combating even non-traditional threats, such as terrorism and extremism. As in the case of Afghanistan, NATO has become a vivid example of how terrorism, and even drug-dealing, is combated through traditional security co-operation. Also in Africa and the Middle East, the security concept is traditional. ASEAN is different from the SCO, even though they both represent Asia. ASEAN and the American regional organisations UNASUR and the OAS are based on the concept of avoidance of all military force, thus, security co-operation contains a different co-operative approach to dealing with the abovementioned threats. ASEAN and UNASUR emphasise co-operation of the appropriate civilian institutions without coercion and interference into internal matters of any State. Looking from a practical perspective, the regions that do have a military capability, as a rule, have chosen to include traditional means (military force) for combating regional threats in their constitutive documents. The regions that do not have the means to build up a military capability, mainly limit themselves to the peaceful settlement of disputes, and finding non-traditional solutions to non-traditional threats like terrorism or trans-border crime. Africa, however, does not correspond to this pattern, by containing provisions on military response to regional crises, even though the capabilities are low.

It can be concluded that the scope of action regional organisations take to respond to threats is an issue of a regionally determined balance of three factors:

(a) The threats that are relevant to the region. As described above, the regions face some common threats and some specifically regional threats. The response to threats may depend on whether the treats are intra- or extra-regional. The specific threats may need to be addressed by economic and social measures, diplomatic means, or may only be combated by military means. Thus the types of threats a region faces influence the type of action taken by a regional organisation.
(b) The military capabilities of each regional organisation. The organisations that do not have the funding and infrastructure for the military use of force are more likely to approach threats from a non-traditional perspective, which excludes the use of military force. The regions that have military capabilities put less restraint on using them.
(c) The culturally acceptable way of dealing with matters of peace and security. This may limit regional action to peaceful settlement of disputes or allow the full scope means, including the use of military force.

Humanitarian intervention

Support for unilateral regional humanitarian intervention

The analysis of the security regions shows that the right to unilateral regional humanitarian intervention continues to be a controversial legal topic. Post-Cold War developments with regard to the right to regional humanitarian intervention can be found in two out of six security regions: the Euro-Atlantic region and the African region, even though Russia used the terminology of humanitarian intervention regarding the 'August War' in Georgia, if half-heartedly.

Even though the African regional interventions of the mid-nineties were conducted without UNSC authorisation (Liberia – 1990, Sierra Leone – 1997), the formalisation of a legal right to regional humanitarian and even pro-democratic interventions in Africa followed only after the NATO intervention in Kosovo in March 1999 (ECOWAS – December 1999, the AU – 2001).

In Africa the right to regional humanitarian intervention has been adopted as a legal norm, as it is stapled in the basic regional documents, such as the Constitutive Act of the AU, the Protocol relating to the establishment of Peace and Security Council of the African Union and the ECOWAS Protocol relating to the Mechanism for Conflict Prevention, Management, Resolution, Peacekeeping and Security. Though there is significant legal-theoretical doubt about whether or not a regional right to intervention can coexist with the *jus cogens* norm on the prohibition of the use of force, in practice no authoritative institution, such as the UN (any organ) or another international organisation, or State, known to the author, has contested the existence of such a regional right in Africa.

Even though Kosovo was directly classified as a humanitarian intervention, the regional organisations – the EU and NATO – have been cautious about clearly establishing a right to humanitarian intervention as a principle. Most importantly the cautiousness may be due to the theatre of action of both organisations, which is mostly outside the Euro-Atlantic area and, thus, directly within the realm of the UN. At the same time, evidence exists, indirectly proving that the Euro-Atlantic region does not exclude the repetition of the Kosovo precedent, if a case may arise. Some of the evidence includes the changes to the legislation of the Member States of the Euro-Atlantic region, allowing for more flexibility for participation in military operations without a UN mandate, especially, EU operations. Other examples are statements made by the politicians of the Euro-Atlantic regional organisations and their Member States, along with the absence of constitutional restraints on action without a UN mandate in Member States.

The reasons for the different regional approaches towards the right to regional humanitarian intervention in Africa and the Euro-Atlantic region are both political, and capability-determined. Africa is a region that is struggling with numerous regional conflicts, practice evidencing that at least ten serious regional conflicts ongoing simultaneously is a common occurrence. The UN has been constantly struggling with gathering Member State force contributions for operations in Africa. The failures of major military powers, such as the USA in Somalia in 1993 and France in Rwanda in 1994 have not increased the out-of-region enthusiasm in involving themselves in the African conflicts. In a situation where African conflicts are too many and international interest too insignificant, it is in the interest of the international community that the African region is capable of resolving its own conflicts. The existing African capabilities, in addition, are not only too small to threaten other regions, but even too small to cope with intra-regional conflicts. The author believes that because of the need for African conflict resolution and the low African military capability the international community has not objected to a regional right to intervention in the African region, even though it may contradict the *jus cogens* principle of the prohibition of use of force. Thus, there exists an African regional right to humanitarian (and perhaps even pro-democratic) intervention. As the practice of the past decade shows, the formalisation of the right has not brought about an increase of regional interventions. Not even in cases where the situation may have been qualified as appropriate, as, for example, the humanitarian catastrophe in Darfur.

The Euro-Atlantic approach is a different matter. The post-Kosovo developments in the establishment (or non-establishment) of a right to regional humanitarian intervention, to the author's mind, evidence a fear of establishing a precedent that may be taken up by other regions. The potential acceptance of a right to regional humanitarian intervention is based on the Euro-Atlantic belief in their inherent justness due to the underlying values of human rights and democracy in the Western society, authorising them to be the fighters for a just cause outside the region. As Martti Koskenniemi has ironically noted: 'Speaking the language of human rights becomes a coverted carte blanche, an unsurpassed marker of legitimacy'.[1]

Needless to say, other regions, most significantly Asia and South America, are not positively inclined towards the Euro-Atlantic superior legitimacy self-perception. Even though the World Summit Outcome of 2005 declared democracy to be a universal value,[2] and recognised the 'responsibility to protect' principle, it did not create the right of individual democratic Member States to intervene coercively in non-democratic States without a UN mandate, not even for humanitarian purposes.

The role of the UN Security Council

The UN Charter provides both for the prohibition of the use of force and for the protection of the human rights. Though ignored for decades, the human rights provisions have been highlighted in the post-Cold War period, as evidenced by the establishment of the 'responsibility to protect' principle. The protection of human rights *per se* does not amount to an authorisation of unmandated use of force. The prohibition of the use of force is still the underlying principle of the UN Charter. While the use of force for humanitarian purposes may be the necessary evil, it has a great potential of furthering the suffering of the people it is intended to protect. For this reason, it is important to stress that the existence of the responsibility to protect does not waive the UN Charter provisions on the prohibition of the use of force. The UN Charter provides for a procedure on how to deal with threats to peace and security which include also humanitarian catastrophes. The procedural provisions provided therein, with the primary responsibility of the UNSC, are to be respected. If the UNSC is accused of not reacting, the cause may not automatically be presumed to be a dysfunctional UNSC. It is very probable that if the UNSC does not agree on action, it is because the majority of the international community, in fact, does not agree on the need for it, and not only because of the veto of one or two members of the UNSC. The view of the majority of the international community may not always be considered by those wanting to intervene upon their own judgement, and a UNSC abstention from action is easily misused as justification for action.

The UN itself has in general been quiet about the developments on the right to regional humanitarian intervention. The African regional operations have not received legal analysis by UN organs, and the *ex post facto*

---

1 M. Koskenniemi and P. Leino, 'Fragmentation of International Law? Postmodern Anxieties', *Leiden Journal of International Law*, Vol. 15, 2002, p. 570.
2 In contrast, the 1970 Declaration of Principles of International Law concerning Friendly relations and Co-operation among States in accordance with the Charter of the UN (GA 2625(XXV)), which provided that every State has an inalienable right to choose its political, economic, social and cultural systems, without interference in any form by another State. I.e. democracy was not stated as the correct form of governance.

authorisations for African regional interventions (such as the widely studied cases of Liberia (1990) and Sierra Leone (1997), along with the less highlighted cases of Côte d'Ivoire (2002) and the DRC (2003)) have been granted on a political basis, without an analysis of the legality of the regional action undertaken. The tumult concerning the Kosovo case ended in the same way it had started – with no joint formal statement made due to the use or threat of use of veto by the Permanent Members of the UNSC.

The UNSC in its post-Cold War (and also earlier) practice does not express itself on theoretical matters of regional right to humanitarian intervention, and hardly even on practical cases of regional intervention (humanitarian, or other). It appears that the matters are left up to those capable and willing to intervene, rather than stirring up the issue politically, such as the cases of African interventions in Liberia, Sierra Leone, Lesotho, and even Russian coercive practice of peacekeeping operations evidence. A greater concern for the international community is, in fact, the inability to intervene when necessary.

Counter-reaction in other regions

The other security regions have been more or less explicit in contesting a regional right to humanitarian intervention, both inside their own region, and as an inter-regional right. None of the regions, however, according to the materials gathered by the author, has explicitly contested the African internal right to regional intervention.

In Asia, both the internal regional right to humanitarian intervention, and the Euro-Atlantic interventionism have been strongly rejected. The Euro-Atlantic claim of spreading the values of democracy and human rights is generally regarded as imperialism in Asia. The aims of the Euro-Atlantic organisations may be just, but the question on the interests of the intervening States is also present in any intervention. Humanitarian interventions without UN authorisation by an organisation from another region would be most highly contestable in regions that deny such a right locally. It is, according to Asian States, members of ASEAN, exactly non-interventionism that has prevented them from potential escalation of interstate conflicts and regional power interventions. Coercive outside interference is feared to have long-term negative effects, even if it were to be carried out with a noble short-term aim, such as the protection of human rights.

South America is the most explicit practical regional example for the denial of a right to regional intervention. All military force is prohibited in regional relations, to avoid military interventions for any purposes. Moreover, a new mechanism for the maintenance of peace and security has been established by South American States without the presence of the USA, which has a wide record of Cold War interventions within the region. Not only is a rule emphasising the prohibition of any kind of use of force included in the basic documents of UNASUR, but also the most likely potential abuser of the prohibition is excluded from membership *ab initio*. The OAS continues to be the central organisation in the maintenance of peace and security in the Americas, but also within the OAS context in the post-Cold War era peacekeeping operations have been limited to civilian operations, without the use of military forces.

It is hard to say whether the re-activation of the Middle East regional organisations is connected to the UN calls for regional contributions to universal maintenance of peace and security or the activity of the members of the Euro-Atlantic region (coalitions, organisations) in the Middle East. It can be noted that the creation of a workable regional mechanism of its own in the Middle East region could have the potential of limiting outside intervention in the region, including that by the Euro-Atlantic regional organisations. Nevertheless, the Middle East region has not directly expressed its position on regional humanitarian intervention. It appears from the reaction to the 2011 row of riots that the discrepancies between the groups of States (e.g. members of the AU, vs. the other Member States) in the Arab League, do not allow for a common position, in line with the unfortunate tradition of the Middle East maintenance of peace and security. The absence of a common position has been often named as the reason for the failures of the Middle East regional mechanism of maintenance of peace and security.

The Russian Sphere of Influence provides, once again, a different approach to humanitarian intervention. Russia, which openly dominates the region, has clearly expressed in the UNSC that it is against a regional right to humanitarian intervention. Such a right is not supported by regional legal documents either. The exception has been claiming a 'humanitarian intervention' in Georgia during the August War in 2008, among many other justifications, but returning to a very strict denial of the right subsequently. Nevertheless, Russia has a broad record of interventions in the region which, though classified as peacekeeping operations by Russia and the CIS, are characterised by extensive use of force and the absence of a verifiable invitation and lack of neutrality. Thus, even though in the Russian Sphere of Influence a right to humanitarian intervention, as part of a general right to enforcement action without UNSC authorisation, does not exist, the actual effects through very robust peacekeeping may be regarded as equivalent. The examples of Russian peacekeeping operations within the region strongly support the High-Level Panel on Threats, Challenge and Change recommendation for setting the same UN authorisation requirements for regional peacekeeping, as for regional peace enforcement. There is, however, no doubt that the right to out-of-region humanitarian intervention without a UN mandate gains no support in the Russian Sphere of Influence.

Possible justifications of intervention

The argumentation in support of a regional right to humanitarian intervention is that crimes against humanity and severe atrocities cannot be tolerated, even if the UNSC is not in a position to make a decision on taking action.

In such situations the regional organisations can provide more efficiency in reacting to humanitarian catastrophes. The opposing argument is that the risk of abuse of a regional right to humanitarian intervention is too high.

The analysis of the African region reveals that the argument used by the region in support of regional right to intervention is the history of absence of a proper reaction by the international community to African regional conflicts, which requires the African region to take matters into its own hands. In this case intervention is only an African regional matter that does not interfere with the maintenance of peace and security in other regions.

In the Euro-Atlantic region, however, the theatre of action is global. The justification for a potential humanitarian intervention in the Euro-Atlantic region is a combination of necessity, just cause, altruism and spreading of values of democracy and human rights, even outside the region. Such evidence, as the changes to the legislation of the EU Member States, the NATO member argumentation used in the case of Kosovo and even the ECJ judgment in the 'Kadi' case, all analysed above, witness that the Euro-Atlantic region does not bow to the unconditional superior legitimacy of the UNSC decisions, but conditions them with national or regional considerations. In the Euro-Atlantic region, the UNSC is not perceived as an infallible mechanism for the maintenance of peace and security. The recent Euro-Atlantic regional developments, questioning the exclusive authority of the UNSC to authorise enforcement action, resemble a revolt against the existing structure of the UNSC with the veto rights of the Permanent Members, even though three out of five Permanent Members of the UNSC are, in fact, Euro-Atlantic. Even though other regions are also interested in reforming the UNSC, the legitimacy of the Euro-Atlantic regional patronising position over the global maintenance of peace and security, marginalising the UN, cannot be expected to be recognised in other regions of the world.

Qualifying factors for the legitimacy of action

Even though the regional right to humanitarian intervention is controversial in general, action within the region holds less danger for the international order than humanitarian intervention by a regional organisation outside its own region. Intra-regional interventions are likely to affect the whole international community less than trans-regional action. Most importantly, while intra-regional action even without a UNSC mandate may be in line with the spirit of Chapter VIII of the UN Charter, action outside the region is rather taking over the global UN functions than staying within the realm of what is appropriate for regional action. In the case of intervention from outside the region, the issue of legitimacy may further be determined by the consideration of whether there is a local regional organisation for the maintenance of peace and security, to which the State in conflict is a member. Outside interference might (but not unquestionably) have a higher legitimacy if a local regional mechanism is not present. If a local mechanism is present but the regionally available remedies are not sufficient, an out-of-region actor ought to receive the consent of the local regional mechanism.

The distinction of action within or outside the region is not the only criterion for evaluating the legitimacy of a regional intervention. Some of other factors may be the following:

(a) A proper decision-making process (whether it is democratic and transparent).
(b) A UN review possibility (unauthorised action by regional organisations that do not contain a UNSC Permanent Member may be regarded as more legitimate because it can be reviewed).
(c) Action is taken within the region among States that have signed for the specific provision, and not from outside the region, unless an agreement between the involved regional organisations is concluded.

First, regarding point (a), a proper, transparent and democratic decision-making process is vital. It can be noted that all the regional organisations have come up with different bids for what the best decision-making procedure may be. The larger organisations are likely to have a majority vote, while in the organisations with fewer Member States, consensus is more common. The balance is often to be found between democracy and efficiency. Thus the EU with its requirement for unanimity of all CSDP participants is perhaps the most democratic mechanism, but has also made it very difficult to agree on action. An example is that of the EU Battlegroups mechanism, which has never been used in practice. The new provisions of the Lisbon Treaty, however, make the unanimity procedure more flexible, with an actual effect equivalent to a majority vote, though maintaining a veto right for every Member State.

Peculiarly, a significant difference between unanimity and consensus can be observed. Whereas unanimity requires a clearly expressed position of each single member, consensus is a negotiation, rather than vote, by requiring an agreement 'in principle'. Thus, the consensus procedure actually provides for an agreement of the dominating States (or a strong position of a single dominating State), to which smaller States do not explicitly oppose. Such a mechanism can be found in NATO, the CIS, CSTO, the SCO, the SADC and UNASUR. Consensus is the decision-making procedure that gives more leverage to the regional powers in regional decision-making. In other organisations majority vote is applied. Such organisations are the OAS, the OIC, the AU and ECOWAS. The Arab League uses both unanimity and majority principles, but with decisions, in effect, only applying to those who have agreed to them. In a unanimity procedure the always present possibility of a veto impairs efficiency. In a consensus procedure, the decision is politically weighed. It is difficult to establish the actual support of all members, as the votes are not counted, but issues negotiated, until there is no opposition preventing the taking of the decision. In a majority procedure the States that do not agree with a decision may be unwilling to comply with a regional decision made (e.g. imposition of sanctions), or in the long term may be willing to denounce membership of the organisation. The qualified majority vote may hold a better balance between democratic vote by all States and ensuring an efficient possibility to take action, yet some States may have to comply with a decision not in their full interest. Concerning regional humanitarian intervention the transparency of the decision-making process is crucial, in order to ensure that the action has the right purpose, and is not used as a cover for the national interests of a single Member State or a smaller group of States.

The review possibility of regional decisions, noted in point (b), should be a basic rule of law requirement. There is a significant difference between regional organisations that have a Permanent Member of the UNSC as their member and those that do not. Regional organisations that have a permanent UNSC member are not likely to have their decision reviewed by any superior authority. The practice of the UNSC explicitly shows that the matters concerning the sphere of influence of a Permanent Member of the UNSC are either vetoed by the member in question or never brought up for debate at all, due to the expected veto by this same Permanent Member. Organisations containing a Permanent Member of the UNSC are the EU, NATO, the SCO, the OAS, CSTO and the CIS. The organisations that do not have a permanent UNSC member are all the African organisations: the AU, ECOWAS, the SADC; Latin-American UNASUR; the Asian ASEAN and the Middle East organisations: the Arab League and the OIC. The legality and legitimacy of the regional interventions carried out by organisations that do not include a Permanent Member of the UNSC is more likely to be practically reviewable by the UNSC. The practice, however, evidences that the UNSC tends not to interfere with the action that has been taken by this category of regional organisations, most likely for the reason that they do not interfere with the interests of the Permanent Members of the UNSC and do not impact the global balance of power. The condemnation of regional interventions by the UNSC is very rare in general, and it is non-existent in the case Permanent Members are involved. Optimally, the UNSC member involved in a matter concerning regional use of force (humanitarian intervention, or any other justification), as a rule, ought to abstain on an issue regarding it. This is not the case in reality. The feasibility of such a provision is not very high, as the Permanent Members of the UNSC are not likely to give up their privileges included in the UN Charter. A review possibility of actions of UNSC Permanent Members has proved to be an irresolvable issue in the practice of the UN, evidenced by both individual cases and the stalemate in UN reform.

The right to regional humanitarian intervention legalised in the African regional documents gives an example of a contractual right to unilateral regional intervention referred to in point (c). The legitimacy of such a contract may be debated from the perspective of a breach of *jus cogens*. However, the fact that Member States in principle agree mutually that they may collectively exercise the right to humanitarian intervention in order to protect people, though possibly against the government that has signed for it, is logically a more legitimate ground for intervention than an out-of-region humanitarian intervention without UNSC authorisation. Possibly even more legitimate than a robust intra-regional peacekeeping operation for which the humanitarian atrocities threshold does not need to be met. The regional States, as evidenced by UN acquiescence, may agree on how to deal with internal regional matters among themselves. There ought not to be action by organisations of one region in another region, without an authorisation. Primarily, the UN ought to authorise such interventions. In cases of failed States there is no one to invite international assistance, thus an intervention may be the only solution to a humanitarian crisis. An invitation issued by the regional organisation in the area, preferably approved by the UNSC, would amount to more legitimacy than a humanitarian intervention without any consent or approval. Thus, the local regional organisation could act as a representative of a failed State within the region. In order to avoid the abuse of power by a regional hegemon, such invitations ought to be reviewed and approved by the UNSC in an urgency procedure or, if not feasible, by the UN General Assembly.

In conclusion, it must be noted that the right to humanitarian intervention does not constitute the only, or the most common post-Cold War risk of the *de facto* action outside the scope of what is appropriate for regional organisations. In fact, the lion's share of unauthorised post-Cold War regional use of force, as evidenced by the practice of the CIS and ECOWAS, has been legally defined as peacekeeping, i.e. means of peaceful settlement of disputes that does not require an authorisation by the UNSC. The right to regional humanitarian intervention within the confines of a region is not likely to create the ultimate danger of regional use of force. The need of proof that crimes against humanity have taken place creates a higher threshold for intervention than, for example, a peacekeeping operation to resolve an internal conflict, or a pro-democratic intervention. An unauthorised intervention by a regional organisation into another region, even on humanitarian grounds, nevertheless, remains most contestable.

Summary

It can be concluded that, generally, regional organisations dealing with the maintenance of peace and security have discretion in stipulating themselves what they regard as appropriate for regional action. The regional mechanisms for the maintenance of peace and security provide the full spectrum between two poles: the unconditional adherence to the principle of the prohibition of the use of force, and the contradicting pursuit of the principle of the responsibility to protect at the cost of the prohibition of the use of force. Today, the understanding of what is appropriate for regional action, depends on the region. It can be limited to the peaceful settlement of disputes upon the request of the parties, or include the use of military capabilities in regional peacekeeping and UN authorised enforcement action within and outside the region. Peacekeeping action may be internally permitted to take place outside the region without a UN authorisation. Defence against external threats within and outside the region is also included in the scope of regional action. In exceptional cases of humanitarian catastrophes, even an intra-regional use of military force without a UN authorisation may be appropriate for regional action. The scope of the action taken by regional organisations depends on three factors: the threats the region is facing, the military capabilities the regional organisations have, and the cultural peculiarities of the region.

The need for a defence function of regional organisations in its traditional shape has become unlikely due to the different nature of threats in the twenty-first century. Defence functions are thus, in practice, melted into the broader regional security co-operation of most regions. The only clearly set limitation for regional action is enforcement action outside the region without a UN mandate, which also encompasses humanitarian intervention. The danger of humanitarian intervention by one region into another without an invitation derives from the contradicting perceptions of the legitimacy of the intervention in the region intervening, the region intervened into and other regions globally.

It is clear that the UN needs all the regional assistance available to support it in the global maintenance of peace and security. Therefore, the UN approach to what is appropriate for regional action is very flexible, and enhances the individual culture, mentality and capabilities of each region. At the same time, in the practice of the UN all organisations are treated as Chapter VIII organisations, which are to respect the primary responsibility of the UNSC in the maintenance of peace and security and the prohibition of unauthorised enforcement action.

10 Suggestions

Where there's a (political) will, there's a (legal) way

Regional organisations differ by their size, composition, global impact, internal democracy and decision-making procedure, internal constitutional limitations, actual military capabilities, political ambitions and other significant factors that influence the legitimacy of their action. For this reason, it is a near-impossible task of making one single set of rules for ensuring the compliance of regional organisations with the international law essentially enshrined in the UN Charter. Even the interpretation of the UN Charter rules itself is vastly diverging in different regional organisations. Thus, the use of force that is claimed legal by one region may be regarded as directly illegal or at least controversial by another region. International law is not an exact science, international relations even less, and politics of the use of force – least of all, due to the high sensitivity of State interests involved.

This chapter contains two categories of suggestions for ensuring better adherence to the rule of law, transparency and procedural legitimacy in the greatly politics-determined sphere of regional use of force. First, there are the measures that can be taken by UN organs to improve the subordination and co-operation of regional organisations. Second, there are suggestions for regional efforts in ensuring greater procedural legitimacy of their own action.

Measures taken by the United Nations

A core difficulty of ensuring regional organisation compliance with international law and full subordination to the UN lies in the fact that the constraint and review of regional actions is impaired in the UNSC itself. The greatest difficulty is posed by the fact that most militarily capable organisations contain a Permanent Member of the UNSC. These organisations are: NATO, the EU, the CIS, CSTO, the SCO and the OAS. Ensuring the compliance of these organisations with international law is the greater challenge.

UNSC practice during its whole existence proves the impossibility to take collective action against a Permanent Member of the UNSC. The Permanent Membership of the UNSC has been the 'carrot method' for gaining the co-operation in the global maintenance of peace and security of the powers against which the 'stick method', such as sanctions or the collective use of force, would not work. UNSC reform where the Permanent Members would not be able to veto the review of their actions would limit their impunity. Such a reform could work as a preventive measure against unilateral regional use of force with the participation of the Permanent Members of the UNSC. The change, however, is clearly not in the interests of the Permanent Members of the UNSC. UNSC reform was pending long before the UN Secretary-General's report, *In Larger Freedom*, without result. Article 108 of the UN Charter provides:

> Amendments to the present Charter shall come into force for all Members of the UN when they have been adopted by a vote of two thirds of the members of the General Assembly and ratified in accordance with their respective constitutional processes by two thirds of the Members of the UN, including all the Permanent Members of the Security Council.

As all the Permanent Members of the UNSC would have to give up their dominant role in the international maintenance of peace and security, it is not likely that such a reform could possibly take place in the foreseeable future. The author therefore suggests other, smaller-scale procedural, rather than significantly political, means for ensuring more transparency and UN control over regional use of force.

When the UNSC endorses regional operations, it tends to abstain from making a formal statement on the legality of a regional operation, or even debating it. The absence of the UNSC legal debate may depict the lack of consensus on the issue of legality or may simply reflect the intention to avoid a subsequent political tumult. The abstention of the UNSC from making statements on certain aspects of legality of regional operations prevents the establishment of a clearer understanding of concepts crucial for determining the limits of regional use of force. Thus, the same gaps and difference in interpretations can be found highlighted in legal literature for decades without a contribution to their clarification from the side of the UN. The international community would, nevertheless, benefit from clarification of controversial issues of the use of force from the UN itself, not only based on the majority views of scholars. For this reason, the UN Secretary-General could take up the task of providing the legal analysis of specific regional operations, and also contribute to the doctrine of regional maintenance of peace and security through the clarification of some of its central concepts.

Whenever an operation is launched, one is to search in political statements of different authorities for the facts and formal argumentation on the legality of an operation. In the case of Kosovo, for example, there was a long row of nuanced individual NATO member country political statements of what they consider to be the justification for the intervention. There is no one single source that compiles the legally significant facts on any single regional military operation. If a complex analysis were prepared by an authoritative organ on each regional operation launched, it would serve as an example-setting and uniformity-establishing tool, contributing to the elaboration of the rules for launching regional military operations.

As the UNSC is a political organ, it would not be proper to require it to make a legal statement on a regional operation. Nevertheless, a post-Cold War practice of the UN Secretary-General has developed for recommending solutions to security problems, promoting the development of law and its clarification. Such are both the UN Secretary-General's own reports, starting with the *Agenda for Peace*, and reports prepared for the UN Secretary-General, such as the High-Level Panel on Threats, Challenges and Change report, *A More Secure World: Our Shared Responsibility*.

Similarly, it is submitted, the international community would benefit from an analysis presented by the Secretary-General to the UN General Assembly and UNSC on the objective legal facts of every regional operation. As the chief administrative officer of the UN, the UN Secretary-General would be the appropriate authority to submit a neutral account of the legality of regional operations. In line with Article 100 of the UN Charter the UN Secretary-General has the discretion to bring to the attention of the UNSC any matter which in his opinion may threaten the maintenance of international peace and security. The means by which it is to be done are not specified. Boutros Boutros-Ghali thus used this discretion to start a line of several UN Secretary-General reports and expert reports prepared for the UN Secretary-General to make recommendations for the improvement of the universal mechanism of the maintenance of peace and security, with a special attention devoted to regional organisations. The report containing the legal analysis of operations could be either prepared in the context with each single operation or submitted to the UN General Assembly as part of the annual report on the work of the Organisation, as provided in Article 98 of the UN Charter.

The UN Secretary-General report could be technically prepared in co-operation between DPKO, which has the field expertise of peacekeeping operations, and the Office of the Legal Adviser, which has the general legal expertise. The reason why the report should be submitted as a UN Secretary-General report is to attribute to it a high authoritative status, relevant when evaluating the legality of subsequent regional operations. A UN directory of legal analyses of regional operations established through these reports would prevent illegal action from being established as a precedent, at least to a greater extent than the present UNSC response. As the UNSC works mainly in the interests of the great powers, and strict compliance with international law is in the interest of the small States, such formal reports to the UNSC and UN General Assembly, along with the feedback of the UN General Assembly on these reports could help strengthen the rule of law in regional action. It is essential that legal evaluation of the operations is made at the level of the principal organ of the UN, to give it the necessary importance and credibility, and not merely the status of a working-level analytical paper. Even if the organs of the UN fail to condemn an illegal operation due to political reasons, an objective legal analysis prepared under the authority of a principal UN organ holds weight. It is not sanctions that make States comply with international law. It is primarily their standing and reputation that motivates States and organisations to justify their actions in legal terms, even the actions that are apparently in breach of international law. It is also a fear of States setting a precedent to others by their own wrongdoings. Thus, an objective report with an authoritative status would serve as a preventive tool for launching military operations in contradiction to international law.

There is a post-Cold War practice of the UN Secretary-General issuing reports on important developments in the maintenance of peace and security doctrine. These reports serve as the basis for the debate in the UNSC and UN General Assembly on how the practice ought to develop in the future. The same document form could be used to specify the scope and limitations of what is appropriate for regional action in abstract. In UNSC meetings, regional organisation representatives have noted the lack of clear division of labour as a significant problem in co-operation practice. Chapter VIII of the UN Charter itself is full of unclarified terms, such as the very fundamental questions of what are regional arrangements and agencies, what is appropriate for regional action and what enforcement action encompasses.

It is clear from the individualised approach of the UNSC that the UN is favourable towards using different rules of the game for different organisations. The use of force is a political matter, not decided by the UNSC by uniform legal considerations. Even though the significant differences between regional mechanisms of maintenance of peace and security do not allow for very detailed specifications, there are some concepts which can and should be uniformly qualified. An issue identified in the preceding chapters as the likely means for by-passing the obligations of regional organisations under international law is, for example, the abuse of the concept of peacekeeping for *de facto* enforcement action.

In the post-Cold War practice regional organisations have dealt with threats to peace and security using the whole spectrum of means. At one end, diplomatic means have been used to resolve conflict situations, at the other end, humanitarian intervention has also found partial recognition. In the wide range of means used by regional organisations, military peacekeeping has become the middle way. Military peacekeeping has been accepted as falling within the domain of regional autonomy as a means of peaceful settlement of disputes and thus, not requiring a UNSC authorisation. In the Russian Sphere of Influence, military peacekeeping is the maximum constitutionally permissible use of military force without a UN mandate. In Africa also, peace enforcement without a UN mandate is permissible. Nevertheless, both the Russian Sphere of Influence and Africa are examples of the temptation and danger of qualifying all regional use of military force as peacekeeping.

Coercive robust peacekeeping ought to also to be regarded as enforcement action, and not peaceful settlement of disputes. Peacekeeping was originally intended as means of maintaining peace in an area of conflict with the consent of the conflicting parties, and permitting the use of force only in self-defence. In its development peacekeeping has grown ever more complicated and ever more robust. In fact, most UN peacekeeping itself is mandated under Chapter VII of the UN Charter, entailing enforcement measures. Not only does the dubious character of invitations (often verbal or given by questionable authority) indicate enforcement in, for example, the CIS, ECOWAS and the SADC so-called peacekeeping operations, even the mere extent of the use of force, involving the peacekeeping forces in direct combat action against one or more combating parties deems such peacekeeping not peaceful, let alone keeping any peace. The modern-day robust peacekeeping, leaving aside the legitimate concerns of invitation, cannot be classified as a peaceful means of settlement of disputes. The UN Secretary-General in his report, *In Larger Freedom*, did not pick up the recommendation by the High Level Panel on Threats, Challenge and Change that regional peacekeeping ought to be subject to the same requirements for a UNSC authorisation as enforcement action. The study of the regional organisations above evidences a coercive effect of operations formally justified as peacekeeping. For this reason the UN Secretary-General ought to bring the issue to the attention of the UNSC. Where the UNSC decides the majority of matters on a case-by-case basis, the UN Secretary-General is in the position to shape the UN doctrine on the regional use of force. The UN needs to set stricter limits for regional military peacekeeping to retain control over regional use of force, instead of having to authorise regional operations *ex post facto* despite their dubious legality.

Another issue that needs clarification from the side of the UN is the legal status of regional organisations. While three Permanent Members of the UNSC are NATO members the controversial legal status of this organisation calls for a clarification. As concluded by the author of this book, there is no alternative status in the UN Charter that would allow a regional organisation not to subordinate itself to the UN, whenever not in its political interest. The solutions for a definition of a regional organisation or arrangement have been sought far and wide, and yet there is no single accepted definition. From an academic point of view it may be of interest to clarify the nuances of the criteria the organisations ought to meet in order to qualify as Chapter VIII organisations. From a practical point of view, what matters is that the collective system of maintenance of peace and security works. To achieve this, it is necessary that the whole clockwork of the international maintenance of peace and security, including each single wheel (regional organisation), functions. The whole network of regional organisations has to work in concert to maintain peace and security globally. For this reason all organisations dealing with the maintenance of peace and security, despite their internal differences, need to be classified as Chapter VIII organisations subordinated to the UN, solely by virtue of their functions. The establishment of a Regional Council as an advisory body to the UNSC may work as a motivating factor for regional organisations to comply with and declare themselves as Chapter VIII organisations.

It is suggested that a Regional Council consisting of Chapter VIII organisations is established as an advisory body to the UNSC. The advisory Regional Council would be involved in discussing action (including potential military action) in any international crisis. The Regional Council would be established in line with Article 29 of the UN Charter, which provides that the UNSC may establish such subsidiary organs as it deems necessary for the performance of its functions.

Through the establishment of a Regional Council the regional organisations would gain the opportunity to be heard in a formal, permanent co-operation framework, as international actors with an administrative, political, and, in the case of a part of the organisations, even military capacity. The UN would gain a better potential for receiving more rapidly organised region-based contributions for peace operation from more closely involved security partners.

If regional organisations are invited to advise the UNSC on the resolution of a crisis, it may have the potential of promoting regional contributions to UN peacekeeping – a problem that is still awaiting a solution. The Regional Council could serve also as a diplomatic forum for balancing the interests of different regions of the world: the militarily capable ones and the pacifistic ones. The ability to be heard in the decision-making procedure of the UNSC would stimulate the initiative of regional organisations to contribute to solutions. The decisions of the Regional Council would not be binding on the UNSC but would provide an additional input to the practical resolution of international conflicts.

The advisory Regional Council would give the opportunity to the regional organisation in whose area a crisis has occurred to give its opinion to the UNSC, and to discuss potential force contributions. This procedure could shorten the time span between the UNSC decision and the completion of the force-generation process, which follows the making of the decision, by provisionally initiating both procedures simultaneously. Region-generated contributions could replace the generation of forces from voluntary State contributions. The regional organisations may also be delegated the task to gather voluntary force contributions on behalf of their region. Thus the overwhelming UN task of force-generation would be split up. In organisations where there is a collective peacekeeping force, a contribution of such a force or individual member contribution could be made, depending on the regional position towards the crisis in question. In regions where a collective regional peacekeeping capacity does not exist, the regional organisations would be in charge of gathering individual member contributions on behalf of the UN. Such a force-generation model is suggested because the twenty-first century security geography of the globalised world is primarily regional, and not individual-State determined. The Regional Council could also be used as the forum for expressing regional calls for assistance, including, if necessary, for military assistance.

The question of how to compose the Regional Council could pose a practical difficulty. As noted, half of the regional organisations contain Permanent

Members of the UNSC, and thus there is a concern that their representation in the Regional Council would overlap.

The UN practice for the composition of its organs and agencies according to a regional representation system could also be used in the Regional Council. The respective regional division used in UN practice is: Africa, Asia-Pacific, Central and Eastern Europe, Latin America and the Caribbean, and Western Europe and others.

A challenging factor is the overlapping of the security regions. Organisations that have Member States in different regions are therefore to be counted as representing both regions. The composition of the Council is to be left up to the UNSC to establish, but the approximate composition is suggested as follows, for the reasons of geographical equality, actual influence and the capacity of regional organisations for the maintenance of peace and security:

- Africa: the AU and the Arab League (overlapping with Asia), the OIS (overlapping with Asia);
- Asia-Pacific: the Arab League (overlapping with Africa), ASEAN and the SCO (overlapping with Central and Eastern Europe);
- Central and Eastern Europe: a significant part of States in this region are in the Euro-Atlantic security structures, the core of which falls under the category of Western Europe, therefore the organisations represented here would be CSTO and the SCO (overlapping with Asia), OSCE (overlapping with Western Europe);
- Latin America and the Caribbean: UNASUR and the OAS;
- Western Europe and others: OSCE (overlapping with Central and Eastern Europe), NATO and the EU.

It is difficult to draw strict lines between the regions and achieve a precisely arithmetic division of power between the regions: that would not correspond to the political reality. Nevertheless, the provided model attempts the closest feasible equality. As noted, the Regional Council is to serve as a consultative, not a decision-making organ. If a vote is to be made on, for example, a recommendation to the UNSC, each one of the 11 organisations is to have a single vote, even if it covers more than one region.

From a positive perspective, a Regional Council would provide an opportunity for the regional organisations in the maintenance of peace and security to express their position at the UNSC in a formalised framework, and not only on an *ad hoc* basis, upon an invitation by the UNSC. Second, the regional positions of pacifistic and interventionist regions could be balanced before advising the UNSC on the measures to be taken. Third, it would be a forum for regional organisations to express their requests for international assistance. Fourth, a direct involvement of regional organisations in the work of the UNSC could motivate their Member States to contribute forces to UN-led and UN authorised (requested) operations. Fifth, the direct availability of regional positions on a conflict in question could provide the UNSC with a position of the international community from an additional – regional – angle, helping prevent a stalemate in the decision-making process.

Noting the negative aspects of the Regional Council, if there is a regional power dominating an individual organisation, the regional organisation voice in the Regional Council would dub the voice of the regional power. In addition, it may be difficult to draw a line between which organisations are to be included in the Regional Council and which are not. In order to become part of the Regional Council, the organisations ought to have a Chapter VIII status (equal to subordination to the UNSC in practice). Nevertheless, the representation has to be regionally even, and cannot be quantitatively unlimited, as then the Regional Council would lose practical efficiency. For comparison, representation too wide to be efficient, in combination with a lack of enforcement capability, is the reason why no particular suggestions here are made regarding the UN General Assembly.

If the UN wishes to use specific organisations as its agents for global maintenance of peace and security, such as NATO, the EU, or perhaps CSTO, special agreements with such organisations could contribute to the uniformity, transparency and predictability of their co-operation. A specified agreement on the scope of rights and obligations of the regional organisations in carrying out military operations for the international maintenance of peace and security would serve the purpose of having a standing commitment of the most capable organisations to assist the UN on clear terms and would grant these organisations the legitimacy to act globally, if the UN would intend so.

It is a fact that NATO carries out the most complicated and most effort-requiring military operations in the world. However, when acting out-of-area, NATO ought to pledge its compliance with the UN Charter obligations, the decisions of the UNSC and efforts in the interest of the entire international community. If a regional organisation is to act outside its region as a global maintainer of peace and security on a regular basis (as NATO and the EU are), their status ought to be specified and legalised by the UN through an agreement, thus granting the regional forces the status of universal agents of the UN in the maintenance of peace and security. This way a slight turn towards the implementation of Article 43 of the UN Charter could be achieved, making forces available to the UN on a formal basis. The problem with this suggestion is that NATO is not willing to subordinate itself fully to the UN and would not be willing to be obliged to launch any operation upon the request of the UN, if not in its own strategic interests.

Following the path of suggestions made regarding the establishment of the Regional Council, signing such agreements with a wide range of regional organisations could contribute to a faster and more predictable force generation process. If the UN had equivalent agreements with a wide range of regional organisations, the regional contribution system could replace a State-based force contribution system, with force generation possibly negotiated in the Regional Council. The agent status granted to the organisations could be reviewed by the UNSC, for example, biannually, or once every five years, to ensure control over the regional agents. The question to the UNSC ought to be posed in the form of whether to renew the contract periodically, and not whether to cancel it in case of breach. The reason for this nuance is to minimise the impunity of the regional organisations in case of ultra vires action, dependent on a veto from a Permanent Member of the UNSC which is also a member of the regional organisation in question.

Measures taken at the regional level

Some regional organisations analysed have a shortage of capabilities, while others have an overwhelming military potential. For this reason the possibilities of establishing a uniform network of mechanisms for the regional maintenance of peace and security are hard to find. Some regions may be the ones intervening, while others may be the potential regions to be intervened into. Combining popular legitimacy in a region that needs a solution to a conflict by military means, and efficiency of action by an out-of-region actor can be a challenge. Even though States and organisations always attempt to justify their actions on legal grounds, there are some measures that can be taken to increase the transparency and legitimacy of regional action if established as the general practice.

Not all regions are equally active in collectively maintaining peace and security, and that not all UN Member States belong to a regional security organisation. The problem of regional inactivity is that if there is no functional regional mechanism for the maintenance of peace and security, the intervention is most likely to be carried out by forces from another region. The regions of Americas, the Middle East and even Asia have recently intensified their regional activity, possibly to avoid outside interference.

It would be optimal if all States of the world belonged to a security region. The regions, on their part, should have the discretion of how to deal with the maintenance of peace security in a culturally acceptable way. As noted above, the organisations analysed range from organisations with a non-interventionist co-operative security model to collective security alliances with strict enforceable commitments and strong common military capabilities, depending on the individual character of the region.

If all regions were to have a working mechanism for the maintenance of peace and security, it could become a default principle that the regional organisation not only deals with regional matters by peaceful means, but also is the primary negotiating partner with the UN concerning a regional conflict that calls for military peacekeeping or even peace enforcement action. Only if the region does not have a military capability itself, yet expresses its consent to the use of military force, can forces from other regions be called in. The request for assistance by the region could either be placed with the UN, or with another regional organisation directly, yet subject to approval by the

UN. In the request or invitation process for the assistance from another organisation the Regional Council framework could be invoked to increase transparency of the potential use of force.

It may be necessary to verify that a regional mechanism is in place and is actively dealing with the peace and security issues of the region, even if its action is limited to peaceful means of dispute settlement. The verification could be done by means of all regional organisations in the maintenance of peace and security submitting annual reports on their activity to the UNSC: information on the meetings held, diplomatic activity, issues discussed, possibly operations launched or participated in. In this way, outside interference in the region could be avoided. Additional efforts could be called in by the UN if no regional resolution were to be found, after having exhausted the means for the peaceful settlement of disputes. The first priority ought to be given to the local regional use of force, calling in out-of-region forces only in the absence or shortage of local capabilities. In the case of outside interference, a regional consent would be preferable, as this would give the use of force more local and international legitimacy than invoking outside interference before all reasonable regional means have been exhausted. In particular, the prioritisation of each region's own mechanism would help rebuke the neo-colonialism accusations that have been expressed, for example, in Asia, regarding the Euro-Atlantic out-of-region interventions. Each region maintains also the right to call for international assistance immediately, if it is clear that regional means are not sufficient.

Intervention by invitation of a State is a ground for launching military action that has often been contested both in practice and theory. States where civil war is raging uncontrollably become failed States, where there is no true authority that holds power. The situation can then be manipulated by more powerful States forcing their interventions masked with alleged invitations. These side-effects of the right to intervention by invitation pose as much a threat to global peace and security as the legalisation of a right to unauthorised humanitarian intervention.

While the suggestion to substitute State invitation with a regional invitation is less likely to help in intra-region interventions where a single power dominates the organisation, in other cases regional invitation replacing State invitation, especially in the case of failed States, could increase the trustworthiness and legitimacy of the invitation.

A right to a regional invitation for intra-regional conflicts is actually included (though not classified as such) in the Constitutive Act of the AU, as the right to intervention based on the decision of the organisation. While in a failed State there is no one to either invite an intervention, nor protect the affected neighbouring States from threatening spill-over effects, these other affected States in the region have a legitimate interest to call for intervention among the members of a regional organisation. The same way a region also has a legitimate right to call for help from outside the region: from another regional organisation, or the UN. The fact that other regional

States are burdened by a conflict in a neighbouring State is thus a direct reason why these States ought to have a legitimate right to call for military assistance. However, as suggested above, an invitation, which gives a legal ground for a peacekeeping operation ought to be approved by the UN as well. If a need for a regional call for intervention has arisen, it means that the situation is so severe that it cannot be resolved by peaceful means only. Thus, if the operation is to be qualified as a peacekeeping operation because it is launched based on a host region request, and because it is to protect the civilians from the warring parties, it is still almost certain to contain enforcement measures. For this reason, an invitation issued directly to another State or region is to be submitted to the UNSC for approval. Regarding intra-regional interventions, the same approval is necessary. In Africa, where a right to humanitarian intervention is legalised, if it is invoked an account of the facts and action taken is to be submitted for endorsement to the UNSC without delay. The right to humanitarian intervention specifically regarding Africa has been acquiesced to by the UN, and does not create a general regional right to humanitarian intervention without a UN mandate. Even in Africa, a UN *ex post facto* endorsement for the rapidly taken humanitarian action is necessary.

The regional decision regarding intervention by invitation would be subject to the internal constitutional rules of the regional organisation on the decision-making procedure for such matters. Even though the effects of different procedures of decision-making were criticised in the conclusions, the process for internal decision-making is a matter of internal discretion of each regional organisation.

A relevant concern in the maintenance of peace and security is the lack of a defined division of labour between organisations: both in the global-regional interaction and in cases of overlap of regional organisations. Such an overlap problem is evident, for example, concerning the division of labour between the AU and the Arab League. There are also other overlaps. Trans-regional overlaps are, for example, the Euro-Atlantic NATO overlap with the American OAS, the Asian SCO overlap with the Russian Sphere of Influence organisations. Intra-regional overlaps of organisations without a clear separation of functions and containing the same Member States are, for example, NATO and the EU in the Euro-Atlantic region, the OAS and UNASUR in the Americas and CSTO and the CIS in the Russian Sphere of Influence. Such overlaps of organisations pose a technical challenge of who is to take charge intra-regionally. Moreover, if the competence of organisations overlaps trans-regionally, this may even create a controversy on what principles of international law are valid, due to the diverging approaches in different regions. Such contradictions can be, for example, the radically different constitutional provisions regarding democracy and pro-democratic interventions in the AU and the Arab League (e.g. Libya is a member of both organisations), a rather theoretical and practically irrelevant issue of radically different approaches to the prohibition of the use of force in the OAS and NATO (concerning USA and Canada), and the permissibility of non-UN autonomous regional peacekeeping in the States members of both CSTO and the SCO.

There are no pre-written rules on how to deal with the choice of a forum in case of a regional organisation overlap. If it concerns non-coercive means the task is simple – the State or States in need of a resolution of a dispute, conflict or crisis can refer their request to the organisation of their choice. The issue is far more complicated if it concerns intervention, i.e. interference by any means (both peaceful and coercive) in the conflict without the consent of the State (States) concerned. One organisation may not interfere at all, another may deal with the crisis by peaceful means only, while another one would use military capacities in robust peacekeeping without delay, or even peace enforcement. How to determine which organisation is to take charge of the situation if their territory of competence overlaps?

The UN has the primary role in the maintenance of peace and security and has the right to determine a threat to peace and security and decide on the measures to be taken. The UN may thus also call upon a specific organisation of its choice to carry out the task. On a regional level there is nothing that prevents different organisations from tackling the same issue simultaneously according to the principles of each individual organisation. Regional organisations are not prevented from continuing peaceful settlement of disputes while the UNSC also is dealing with the issue, and may have delegated peace enforcement or peacekeeping to another organisation or a group of States. Other organisations are not legally prohibited from pursuing a resolution of the crisis by peaceful means, if their internal constitutional provisions do not explicitly prevent them from interfering. Parallel peacekeeping and peace enforcement operations of different organisations in the same area is a common post-Cold War practice. The efficiency of such practice, however, is a debatable topic.

Trans-organisational co-operation and co-ordination is of vital importance for settling organisation competence overlaps. The conclusion of agreements between overlapping regional mechanisms, settling the division of competence in abstract, before the specific conflict arises, could be useful, but not a prerequisite for co-operation. If organisations with a majority of differing Member States overlap, the issue may be discussed in an agreement-based framework or an *ad hoc* co-ordination meeting. If the Member States greatly overlap, it can be the vote of the Member States of both (all) organisations that determines which framework is primarily selected for dealing with the case.

There are, however, principles that ought to be observed. In line with international law, the measures for peaceful settlement of disputes need to be exhausted before force is used. Thus, if one regional organisation has started diplomatic talks, another regional organisation ought not to intervene militarily (even with robust peacekeeping) without consulting and agreeing with the organisation that has already started efforts for the peaceful settlement of the dispute. In addition, a UNSC authorisation is to be received, informing it not only of the intent to intervene, but also of the peaceful efforts taking place. The advisory Regional Council suggested above could be exactly the framework necessary for resolving the issues of overlapping competence areas of different regional organisations, facilitating and speeding-up the exchange of information.

Alternatively, using the example of the AU consensual agreement of Member States on being subject to regional intervention, a similar, yet somewhat less controversial arrangement can be made. The States that are members of more than one security organisation may add declarations to the treaties of the organisations they are members of, in which forum they would primarily prefer to deal with a potential crisis (or specify the conditions for choosing one forum or another) up to the threshold of enforcement action, which is the competence of the UNSC. The UN is also to be informed of such declarations. Such declarations may sound like forum-shopping, nevertheless, they would place the primary regional responsibility on a specified regional forum, helping to avoid chaos. The declaration would be relevant evidence of consent in cases where it is not possible to legitimately express the will of the State, as in a failed State situation or a case of humanitarian atrocities by the government. The organisations would be required to respect the request, if the UNSC would not interfere and decide differently.

The problem of maintenance of peace and security is not necessarily that all organisations compete in wishing to contribute to crisis resolution. The problem may also (and perhaps more likely) be that no organisation wishes to intervene. Dealing with this scenario is, in fact, the greatest challenge of international maintenance of peace and security. The abovementioned unilateral declarations would, at the same time – morally, though not in a legally binding way – point to which regional organisation has the responsibility to address the situation.

It is also suggested that regional organisations conclude co-operation agreements among themselves. For security organisations with overlapping competence it would be useful not only to hold meetings on relevant topics in common and to organise joint training, but also to stipulate the basic principles of how to tackle the cases when their competence over a zone of conflict overlaps: who is to take a primary role in organising a process for the peaceful settlement of disputes, how is potential military response to be organised and how to deal with inviting outside assistance.

Trans-regional co-operation ought to concentrate on common assistance in training and exchange of experience. In addition, these agreements could contain the clause that the regions may mutually call for assistance in case of a military conflict. In this way, the regional organisations that do not have military capacity themselves could specify which other regional organisation they would preferably involve in the military resolution of their conflicts. In addition, States (and regions) do not intervene without a political interest. Having a security co-operation agreement that provides for mutual interest could increase trans-regional will to contribute forces to operations in the region of co-operation.

The possibility of the execution of any of the suggestions is, of course, conditional upon State will. The law on the use of force does not exist in a separate universe from political interests, and has not been able to eliminate *realpolitik*. No law can give a guarantee against the abuse of power by the more powerful States or what have been called the 'rogue States'. Setting the rules, nevertheless, is in the interest of the majority of States. If there is no uniform practice and the general rules are not clear, it is harder to distinguish a breach from a creative interpretation of how to fill a legal gap. Creating general guidelines and setting general rules makes discrepancies more obvious and reduces the temptation to those who may consider breaching the uniform practice. The 'small steps' for constraining illegal and illegitimate regional use of force suggested above are more likely to be accepted by States than ground-breaking political suggestions. The role of political power in the matters of the use of force, including regional, can neither be ignored, nor eliminated. Yet, by specifying and clarifying certain procedural rules, the abuse of material norms in the regional use of force can be limited.

Bibliography

Abass, A., *Regional Organizations and the Development of Collective Security: Beyond Chapter VIII of the UN Charter*, Oxford and Portland, OR: Hart Publishing, 2004.
Acharya, A., 'Conclusion: Asian norms and practices in UN peace operations', *International Peacekeeping*, Vol. 12, 1 (Spring) 2005.
Acharya, A., *Constructing a Security Community in Southeast Asia. ASEAN and the problem of regional order*, 2nd edn, New York, NY: Routledge, 2009.
Akehurst, M., 'Custom as a Source of International Law', *The British Year Book of International Law*, Vol. 47, 1974–75.
Akehurst, M., 'Enforcement Action by Regional Agencies, with Special Reference to the Organization of American States', *British Year Book of International Law*, Vol. 42, 1967.
Allott, P., *Eunomia. New Order for a New World*, Oxford: Oxford University Press, 2001.
Amneus, D., 'Swedish State Practice 2004–5: the Responsibility to protect', *Nordic Journal of International Law*, Vol. 75, 2006.
Arend, A. C. and Beck, R. J., *International Law and the Use of Force*, London and New York, NY: Routledge, 1993 (republished 2003).
Bailes, A. J. K., Herolf, G. and Sundelius, B. (eds), *The Nordic Countries and the European Security and Defence Policy*, Stockholm International Peace Research Institute, Oxford: Oxford University Press, 2006.
Bailey, S. D. and Daws, S., *The Procedure of the UN Security Council*, 3rd edn, Oxford: Clarendon Press, 1998.
Bellamy, J. A., *Responsibility to Protect. The Global Effort to End Mass Atrocities*, Cambridge: Polity Press, 2009.
Bernhardt, R. (ed.), *Encyclopedia of Public International Law*, Vols 3 and 4, Amsterdam: North-Holland Publishing Company, 1982.
Blockmans, S. (ed.), *The European Union and Crisis Management. Policy and Legal Aspects*, The Hague: T.M.C. Asser Instituut, Asser Press, 2008.
Blokker, N., and Schrijver, N. (eds), *The Security Council and the Use of Force. Theory and Reality – A Need for Change?*, Leiden and Boston, MA: Martinus Nijhoff Publishers, 2005.
Brownlie, I., *International Law and the Use of Force by States*, Oxford: Oxford at the Clarendon Press, 1963 (reprinted 2002).
Brownlie, I., *Principles of International Law*, 6th edn, Oxford and New York, NY: Oxford University Press, 2003.
de Búrca, G., 'The European Court of Justice and the International Legal Order After Kadi', *Harvard International Law Journal*, Vol. 51, 1, 2010.

Cardwell, P. J., French, D. and White, N., 'Case and Comment. Frozen in time? The ECJ finally rules on the *Kadi* Appeal', *The Cambridge Law Journal,* Vol. 68, 1 (March) 2009.

Cassese, A., *United Nations Peacekeeping: Legal Essays*, Leiden: Martinus Nijhoff Publishers, 1978.

Chesterman, S., *Just War or Just Peace? Humanitarian Intervention and International Law*, Oxford: Oxford University Press, 2001.

Coleman, K. P., *International Organizations and Peace Enforcement. The Politics of International Legitimacy*, Cambridge: Cambridge University Press, 2007.

Cooper, A. F. and Legler, T., 'A tale of two mesas: the OAS defence of democracy in Peru and Venezuela', *Global Governance*, Vol. 11 (Autumn) 2005.

Cooper, A. F. and Legler, T., *Intervention without intervening? The OAS defense and promotion of democracy in the Americas*, New York, NY: Palgrave Macmillan, 2006.

Danish Institute of International Affairs, *Humanitarian Intervention. Legal and Political Aspects*, Copenhagen: DUPI, 1999.

Deen-Racsmány, Z., 'A Redistribution of Authority Between the UN and Regional Organizations in the Field of the Maintenance of Peace and Security?', *Leiden Journal of International Law*, Vol. 13, 2000.

Department of Peacekeeping Operations, Department of Field Support, *United Nations Peacekeeping Operations. Principles and Guidelines*, New York, NY: United Nations, 2008.

Dienstein, Y., *War, Aggression and Self-Defence*, 3rd edn, Cambridge: Cambridge University Press, 2001.

Dixon, M. and McCorquodale, R., *Cases and Materials on International Law*, 4th edn, Oxford: Oxford University Press, 1991.

Doswald-Beck, L., 'The Legal Validity of Military Intervention by Invitation of the Government', *British Year Book of International Law*, Vol. 56, 1985.

DuBois, L., *The Politics of the Past in an Argentine Working-Class Neighbourhood*, Toronto: University of Toronto Press, 2008.

Erkomaishvili, D., 'China's Shanghai Cooperation Organisation Initiative', *Central European Journal of International and Security Studies*, E-contributions, 14 February 2011. Available at <http://www.cejiss.org/econtributions/chinas-shanghai-cooperation-organisation-initiative> (accessed 22 April 2013).

Espersen, O., Harhoff, F. and Spiermann, O., *Folkeret*, København: Christian Ejlers' Forlag, 2003.

Fawcett, L., 'Exploring regional domains: a comparative history of regionalism', *International Affairs*, Vol. 80, 3, 2004.

Fawcett, L. and Hurrell, A. (eds), *World Politics: Regional Organization and International Order*, Oxford: Oxford University Press, 1995.

Franck, T., 'Legitimacy in the International System', *The American Journal of International Law*, Vol. 82, 1988.

Gowland-Debbas, V., 'The Limits of Unilateral Enforcement of Community Objectives in the Framework of UN Peace Maintenance', *European Journal of International Law*, Vol. 11, 2, 2000.

Gray, C., *International Law and the Use of Force*, 3rd edn, Oxford: Oxford University Press, 2008.

Greciu, A., *Securing Civilization? The EU, NATO, and the OSCE in the Post-9/11 World*, Oxford: Oxford University Press, 2008.

Hafkin, G., 'The Russo-Georgian War of 2008: Developing the law of unauthorized humanitarian intervention after Kosovo', *Boston University Law Journal*, Vol. 28, 219, 2010.

Harhoff, F., 'Unauthorized Humanitarian Interventions – Armed Violence in the Name of Humanity?', *Nordic Journal of International Law*, Vol. 70, 1–2, 2001.

Hehir, A., *Humanitarian intervention after Kosovo. Iraq, Darfur and the Record of Global Civil Society*, New York, NY: Palgrave Macmillan, 2008.

Hilaire, M., *International Law and the United States Military Intervention in the Western Hemisphere*, The Hague: Kluwer Law International, 1997.

Hoadley, S. and Rüland, J. (eds), *Asian Security Reassessed*, Singapore: Institute of South Asian Studies, 2006.

Holzgrefe, J. L. and Keohane, R. O. (eds), *Humanitarian Intervention. Ethical, Legal and Political Dilemmas*, Cambridge: Cambridge University Press, 2003.

Hough, M., 'Collective security and its variants: A conceptual analysis with specific reference to SADC and ECOWAS', *Strategic Review for Southern Africa*, Vol. 20, 2 (November) 1998.

Independent International Commission on Kosovo, *Kosovo Report. Conflict. International Response. Lessons Learned*, Oxford: Oxford University Press, 2000.

International Commission on Intervention and State Sovereignty, *Responsibility to Protect*, Report of the International Commission on Intervention and State Sovereignty, Ottawa: International Development Research Centre, 2001.

Kioko, B., 'The right of intervention under the African Union's Constitutive Act: From non-interference to non-intervention', *International Review of Red Cross*, Vol. 85, 852 (December) 2003.

Kivimäki, T. and Delman, J. (eds), *War and Security in Asia: Changing Regional Security Structure. How the European Union can support inter-state peace*, Copenhagen: Nordic Institute of Asian Studies, 2006.

Köhler, H., 'The United Nations Organization and Global Power Politics: The Antagonism between Power and Law and the Future of the World Order', *Chinese Journal of International Law*, Vol. 5, 2, 2006.

Koskenniemi, M. and Leino, P., 'Fragmentation of International Law? Postmodern Anxieties', *Leiden Journal of International Law*, Vol. 15, 2002.

Kuwali, D., 'Protect Responsibly: The African Union's Implementation of Article 4(H) Intervention', *Yearbook of International Humanitarian Law*, Vol. 11, 2008.

Levitt, J., 'Pro-Democratic intervention in Africa', *Wisconsin International Law Journal*, Vol. 24, 3, 2006.

Lindström, G., *Enter the EU Battlegroups. Chaillot Paper N 97*, Paris: Institute for Security Studies, 2007.

Malan, M. (ed.), *Boundaries of Peace Support Operations: The African Dimension*, Pretoria: Institute for Security Studies, 2000.

Malan, M., 'Peacekeeping in the New Millennium: Towards Fourth Generation Peace Operations?', *African Security Review*, Vol. 7, 3, 1998.

Månsson, K., 'Reviving the "Spirit of San Francisco": the Lost Proposals on Human Rights, Justice and International Law to the UN Charter', *Nordic Journal of International Law*, Vol. 76, 2007.

McCoubrey, H. and Morris, J., *Regional Peacekeeping in the Post-Cold War Era*, The Hague: Kluwer Law International, 2000.

Mersiades, M., 'Peacekeeping and legitimacy: lessons from Cambodia and Somalia', *International Peacekeeping*, Vol. 12, 22 (June) 2005.

Murphy, S. D., *Humanitarian Intervention. The United Nations in an Evolving World Order*, Vol. 21, Procedural Aspects of International Law Series, Philadelphia, PA: University of Pennsylvania Press, 1996.

Neff, S. C., *War and the Law of Nations. A General History*, Cambridge: Cambridge University Press, 2005.

Orakhelashvili, A., 'Legal Stability and Claims of Change: The International Court's Treatment of *Jus ad Bellum* and *Jus in Bello*', *Nordic Journal of International Law*, Vol. 75, 2006.

Orwell, G., *Animal Farm. A Fairy Story*, Harmondsworth: Penguin Books in Association with Martin Secker and Warburg, 1945 (reprinted 1977).

Österdahl, I., 'Preach what you practice. The Security Council and the Legalisation *ex post facto* of the Unilateral Use of Force', *Nordic Journal of International Law*, Vol. 74, 2005.

Ozdal, H., 'Putting the CSTO to the test in Kyrgyzstan', International Strategic Research Organisation, 21 October 2010. Available at <http://www.usak.org.tr/EN/makale.asp?id=1747> (accessed 21 April 2013).

Pellet, A., 'Brief Remarks on the Unilateral Use of Force', *European Journal of International Law*, Vol. 11, 2, 2000.

Ribbelink, O. M. (ed.), *Beyond the UN Charter. Peace, Security and the Role of Justice*, The Hague: Hague Academic Press, 2008.

Rytter, J. E., 'Humanitarian Intervention without the Security Council: From San Francisco to Kosovo – and Beyond', *Nordic Journal of International Law*, Vol. 70, 2001.

Sanchez, A., 'The South American Defense Council, UNASUR, the Latin American Military and the Region's Political Process', *Council of Hemispheric Affairs*, 1 October 2008. Available at <http://www.coha.org/the-south-american-defense-council-unasur-the-latin-american-military-and-the-region%E2%80%99s-political-process/> (accessed 21 April 2013).

Sarooshi, D., *The United Nations and the Development of Collective Security. The Delegation by the UN Security Council of its Chapter VII Powers*, Oxford: Clarendon Press, 1999.

Scheinin, M., 'Is the ECJ Ruling in *Kadi* Incompatible with International Law?', *Yearbook of European Law*, Vol. 28, 2010.

Schreuer, C., 'Regionalism v. Universalism', *European Journal of International Law*, Vol. 6, 1, 1995, p. 478.

Severino, R. C., *The ASEAN Regional Forum*, Singapore: Institute of Southeast Asian Studies, 2009.

Shaw, M. N., *International Law*, 6th edn, Cambridge: Cambridge University Press, 2008.

Simma, B., 'NATO, the UN and the Use of Force: Legal Aspects', *The European Journal of International Law*, Vol. 10, 1999.

Simma, B. (ed.), *The Charter of the United Nations. A Commentary*, 2nd edn, Vols 1 and 2, Oxford: Oxford University Press, 2002.

Svensson, E., *The African Mission in Burundi. Lessons Learned from the African Union's First Peace Operation*, Stockholm: Swedish Defence Research Agency, 2008.

Tavares, R., *Regional Security. The Capacity of International Organizations*, Oxford: Routledge, 2009.

Thürer, D., 'The "failed state" and international law', *International Review of Red Cross*, No. 836, 1999.

Tomuschat, C., 'Uniting for Peace General Assembly Resolution 377 (V) New York 3 November 1950', UN Audiovisual Library of International Law, Codification Division, Office of Legal Affairs, 2008. Available at <http://untreaty.un.org/cod/avl/ha/ufp/ufp.html> (accessed 21 April 2013).

Trybus, M. and White, N. (eds), *European Security Law*, Oxford: Oxford University Press, 2007.

United Nations, *The Blue Helmets. A review of United Nations Peace-keeping*, 3rd edn, New York, NY: United Nations Department of Public Information, 1996.

Watanabe, K. (ed.), *Humanitarian Intervention. The Evolving Asian Debate*, Tokyo: Japan Centre for International Exchange, 2003.

Watters, R. F. and McGee, T. G. (eds), *New Geographies on the Pacific Rim: Asia Pacific*, Vancouver: University of British Columbia Press, 1997.

Wedgwood, R., 'Unilateral Action in the UN System', *European Journal of International Law*, Vol. 11, 2, 2000.

White, N. D., 'The ties that bind: The EU, UN and International Law', *Netherlands Yearbook of International Law*, Vol. 37, 2006.

Wilson, G., 'Regional Arrangements as Agents of the UN Security Council: Some African and European Organisations Contrasted', *Liverpool Law Review*, Vol. 29, 2, 2008.

Wilson Rowe, E. and Torjesen, S. (eds), *The Multilateral Dimension in Russian Foreign Policy*, London and New York, NY: Routledge, 2009.

Wolfrum, R. and Röben, V. (eds), *Legitimacy in International Law*, Berlin, Heidelberg and New York, NY: Springer, 2008.

Wu, G. and Landsdowne, H. (eds), *China Turns to Multilateralism. Foreign Policy and Regional Security*, London and New York, NY: Routledge, 2008.

Yost, D. S., *NATO and International Organizations*, Forum Paper Series, Rome: NATO Defence College, 2007.

Zwanenburg, M., 'Regional Organizations and the Maintenance of International Peace and Security: Three Recent Regional African Peace Operations', *Journal of Conflict and Security Law*, Vol. 11, 3, 2006.

Index

Abass, Ademola 68
Abkhazia 148, 154–7, 162
Aceh, Indonesia 173
Afghanistan: CSTO 162; drugs 216; invitations/requests for intervention 144; legality/legitimacy of interventions 199; NATO 85, 160, 189, 197, 199, 216; Russian sphere of influence 144, 162; SCO 97–8; terrorism 216; UN 84–5, 95, 126, 160, 178–9, 199; United States 38, 105, 189, 202
Africa 49–79: authorisation/mandate for intervention 52–9, 61, 64, 67–71, 77–9, 130, 213, 217–20; colonisation 4, 49, 208; contributions 218; description of region 49–53; Euro-Atlantic region 4, 51–2, 165, 173–5, 186; Eurocentricism 4; fragmentation 51; humanitarian intervention 78–9, 204, 217–20, 222, 224–5; inaction 157; internal conflicts and civil wars 78–9, 216; *jus cogens* 224; legality/legitimacy of interventions 79, 136; list of conflict situations 50; military capabilities 230; non-intervention doctrine 53; non-traditional threats 52–3, 516; out-of-region operations 218; *pacta sunt servanda* 78–9; piracy 51, 175–6; pro-intervention/non-indifference doctrine 52–3, 78–9, 208, 216–17; Regional Council, proposal for advisory 233; responsibility to protect principle 79; traditional threats 216; UN 41, 49–53, 78–9, 157, 219–20; unilateral action 53, 56, 59–60, 64, 70–2, 74, 76, 78, 217–18 *see also* African Union (AU); ECOWAS (Economic Community of West African States); individual countries; SADC (Southern African Development Community)
African Union (AU) 51–3, 66–78: AL 129–32, 237; Assembly 71, 73; authorisation/mandate for intervention 67–71, 77–8, 213; Chapter VIII status 76, 78; collective security and self-defence 69, 129–31; colonialism 43, 66, 208; consent 75, 239; Constitutive Act 52, 62, 66–71, 73, 75–6, 217; decision-making 72–4, 212, 223; description 66; ECOWAS 52, 54, 56, 58–60, 66–7, 71, 72–4; EU 73–4, 174; humanitarian intervention 68–73, 76, 129, 143, 183, 217; hybrid operations 34–5; invitations/requests for intervention 67–8, 236; *jus cogens* 71–2, 217; legality/legitimacy of interventions 66–74; majority voting 223; Mechanism on Conflict Prevention, Management and Resolution 58–9; Middle East 126, 143; military capabilities 213; NATO 199, 201; non-intervention, principle of 67–8, 72; number of members 11; OAS 66, 73, 76; overlapping ROs 237; *pacta sunt servanda* 72; Panel of the Wise 74, 210; Peace and Security Council (AUPSC) 51, 67, 73–6, 217; peacekeeping operations 11, 69–70, 72, 77; practices 53, 66–7, 74–6; pro-democratic intervention 70–1, 129; pro-intervention/non-indifference

doctrine 67–8, 72; rapid reaction forces 47, 76, 213; regionalisation 53; resources 68–9, 74, 76, 98; responsibility to protect principle 67, 72; SADC 52, 62, 65; unilateral interventions 70–2, 74, 76, 217; UN 43, 45–6, 59–60, 62, 65, 67–9, 71–7, 224

Agenda for Peace 6, 7, 12, 39–41, 46–7, 60, 229

Al Qaeda 178–9

Americas 101–25: authorisation/mandate for intervention 9, 109, 119, 125; Cold War 101–5, 124, 209–10; colonialism 101, 211; cooperation 101, 104, 108, 124–5; CSTO 107; description 101–6; Euro-Atlantic region, influence of 101–4, 208; humanitarian intervention 104–6, 124, 220–1, 219; internal conflicts and civil wars 102–3, 105; intervention without intervening 104, 124; military capabilities 212; non-interventionism 124; non-traditional threats 104–5, 125, 215–16; peacekeeping operations (UN) 102, 212; pro-interventionism 104, 124, 209; Regional Council, proposal for advisory 233; responsibility to protect principle 104; traditional threats 104; unilateral interventions 103–4, 108, 219, 224; United States 9, 101–4, 124, 145, 209–10 *see also* Organization of American States (OAS); Union of South American Nations (UNASUR)

amphictyonic (neighbour) leagues of ancient Greece 2–3, 5, 207

ancient Greece 2–3, 5, 207, 210–11

ancient world 2–3, 5, 207, 210–11

Andean Community of Nations 114–15

Angola 64

Annan, Kofi 40, 92

apartheid 61

appropriate for regional action, meaning of 23, 25–6, 211–13, 230

Aquinas, Thomas 207

Arab League (AL) 6, 127–40, 173: AU 129–32, 237; authorisation/mandate for intervention 132, 136, 138; Chapter VIII status 10, 126, 137–9; Charter of AL 132–3; collective security and self-defence 129–35, 143, 147, 212, 215; cooperation 128, 135, 137–40, 141; Council of the Arab League 133–6; decision-making 129, 133–5, 142–3, 173, 212, 223; description 127–8; enforcement measures 128, 130, 136, 138; humanitarian intervention 129, 221; inaction 127–30, 134–40, 143, 212; invitations/requests for intervention 130–1, 139–40; legality/legitimacy of operations 128–33, 136; majority voting 223; mediation, conciliation and good offices 129, 132, 136, 210; NATO 130, 186, 199; non-traditional threats 133, 143; number of members 11, 127; overlapping ROs 129–30, 143; Pact of AL 128–9, 131, 133, 138; Peace and Security Council 128–9, 132–4, 137, 210; peacekeeping operations 10, 132, 135–8, 212; practices 135–7; pro-democratic intervention 129–30; rapid reaction forces 133; religion 207; UN 7, 127–31, 135–40, 141; unanimity 133–4, 142–3, 171, 223; Uniting for Peace procedure 130

Argentina 105

Armenia 148, 152, 156

arms 37, 82, 84, 89, 103, 119, 146–7, 151, 160–1, 196 *see also* disarmament; nuclear weapons

Article 51 (collective self-defence): Africa 69, 129–31; Article 51 organisations 16, 144, 185–6, 190, 202, 204, 214–15; authorisation/ mandate for intervention 9, 23; CIS 147, 149; EU 169; NATO 16, 185–6, 188–90, 202, 204, 214–15; OAS 108; Warsaw Pact 16, 144 *see also* collective security and self-defence

ASEAN (Association of Southeast Asian Nations) 81–93: Amity and Cooperation Treaty 86, 88; ASEAN 10+3 82; ASEAN Community, establishment of 87–90; 'ASEAN' way 82; authorisation/mandate for intervention 91, 93; Blueprint for the Political-Security Community 88,

89–90; Cebu Declaration 88; Chapter VIII status 92; Charter of ASEAN 86, 88–90; collective security and self-defence 86, 215; composition 85; cooperation 81, 83–4, 86, 88–9, 92–3, 135; decision-making 90; Declaration on Friendly Relations and Cooperation 86, 88; description 85–72; Heads of State and Governments 87; human rights 88–90; humanitarian intervention 88, 208; internal conflicts and civil wars 90–1; legality/legitimacy of interventions 87–90; legal personality 85–6; mediation 90; military capabilities 91; non-interventionism 81–2, 86–7, 90–2, 99, 208; non-traditional threats 88–9; number of members 11, 85; out-of-region operations 221; peacekeeping operations 90, 92; practices 91–2; pro-intervention/non-indifference doctrine 92; responsibility to protect principle 81, 92; summits 84, 87–8, 90–1, 93;traditional threats 216; TROIKA 91–2; UN 84, 86, 89, 90, 92–3; unilateral interventions 86–7; Vision 2015 89; Vision 2020 87

Asia 80–100: Amity and Cooperation on SE Asia Treaty 81; authorisation/mandate for intervention 9, 22, 26, 29, 35, 219; bilateral agreements 82–3; collective security and self-defence 83–5, 215; cooperation 80, 82–5, 99–100, 207, 212; description 80–5; human rights 82, 100, 212; humanitarian intervention 81, 99, 219–20; internal conflicts and civil wars 85, 99–100, 212; military capabilities 212; NATO 199; non-interventionism 80–1, 100, 207, 212, 220–1; non-traditional threats 83, 88–9, 100, 122; out-of-region operations 86–7, 236; pro-interventionism 82, 100; responsibility to protect principle 81–2, 100, 212; traditional threats 89; UN 81, 84–5, 99; unilateral action 99, 219 *see also* ASEAN (Association of Southeast Asian Nations); individual countries; Shanghai Cooperation Organization (SCO)

Asia-Pacific Economic Cooperation (APEC) 82
Association of Southeast Asian Nations *see* ASEAN (Association of Southeast Asian Nations)
Atlantic region *see* Euro-Atlantic region
AU *see* African Union (AU)
Aung San Suu Kyi 92
authorisation/mandate of Security Council for intervention 9–10, 18, 23: Africa 52–9, 61, 64, 67–71, 77–9, 130, 213, 217–20; Americas 9, 109, 119, 125; Asia 81, 84, 91, 93, 99; contributions 233–4; criteria for legitimacy of decisions 43; enforcement measures (Chapter VII) 16, 23, 26, 35–8, 150, 222, 231; Euro-Atlantic region 130, 167, 171, 174–85, 188–205, 213, 217–19, 222; humanitarian intervention 18–22, 48, 177–83, 204–5, 217, 219–22, 225–6, 236–7; implied authorisation 197; legality/legitimacy of interventions 27, 40–1; Middle East 130, 132, 136, 138, 143; out-of-region operations 27, 221, 223, 226; peacekeeping operations 28–9; pro-intervention/non-indifference doctrine 52–3; Regional Council, proposal for 238–9; retrospective authorisation 38, 48, 54–6, 197–8, 220, 237; Russian sphere of influence 149–50, 154–7, 161–4, 212–13, 221, 230; UN 9, 22–3, 26, 29, 35, 42–5, 52, 119, 125, 219, 223–4, 229–31; United States 104; Uniting for Peace procedure 31
autonomous activities of ROs *see* unilateral interventions
Azerbaijan 37, 148, 152, 156

balance of power 3–5, 21, 106–7, 209, 224
Balkan Pact 6
Balkan Union 6
Balkans conflict 165, 173–4, 190, 196–7
Ban Ki-moon 84
Bangladesh 100
Battlegroups (EU) 170, 174, 177, 179–80, 182–3

Belarus 146
Belgium 33–4
bilateral agreements 82–3
Björkdahl, A 177
Bolivar, Simón 4, 101, 117
Bordyuzha, Nikolai 162
Bosnia Herzegovina 175
Boutros-Ghali, Boutros 39, 229
Brahimi Report 41–2, 47–8, 213
Brownlie, Ian 30–1
Buddhism 207
Burundi 74–5

Camara, Moussa Dadis 58
Cambodia 33, 91
Canada 165
capacity-building 77, 93
Capstone doctrine 28
Caribbean 10, 102 *see also* individual countries
CARICOM 102
ceasefires, supporting 32, 34
Central African Economic and Monetary Community (CEMAC) 51
Central African Republic (CAR) 34–5, 50, 67, 74
Central and Eastern Europe 190, 233 *see also* particular countries; Russian sphere of influence
Central Treaty Organization (CENTO) 87
Chad 34–5, 50–1, 74–5, 174
Chapter VII *see* enforcement measures (Chapter VII)
Chapter VIII status: AL 10, 126, 137–9; appropriate for regional action, meaning of 23, 25–6, 211–13; ASEAN 92; AU 76, 78; CIS 154, 157–8, 164; collective security and self-defence 214–15; cooperation 213–14; criteria 12; CSTO 164; doctrinal developments post-Cold War 38–40, 45–6; ECOWAS 55, 59, 78; EU 183–4, 204; humanitarian intervention 226; NATO 10, 16, 186, 187–8, 191, 204, 214 ; OAS 16, 115–16, 137–8; OAU 10, 76, 78; OIC 141; regional arrangements and agencies 23–5; Regional Council, proposal for advisory 231–5; regional organisations, use of term 24–5; report regional action, duty to 22; SADC 61, 65, 78; SCO 99; UN, subordination to 231; UNASUR 123; Warsaw Pact 10, 16
Charter of UN: Africa 55, 58, 59, 61–2, 69, 71, 76, 78–9; *Agenda for Peace* 12; AL 129–31, 138–9; Americas 9, 108–9, 115, 124; ASEAN 86, 90, 92; Atlantic Charter of 1941 17; authorisation/mandate for intervention 9, 22–3, 26, 29, 35, 219; balance of power 4, 209; 'Chapter Six and a Half' 28; collective security and self-defence 22–3, 16, 215; common interest, actions in the 17–18; drafting 7–8; enemy States, use of force against 16–17, 23; EU 167–8, 170, 175, 178–9, 182–5, 204; human rights 18, 179; humanitarian intervention, right to 17–19, 22, 81; internal conflicts and civil wars 22; international law 14–18; interpretation 15–16, 211, 227; Middle East 129–31, 138–9, 142; modern regionalism, beginning of 7–9; NATO 185–6, 188–90, 192–3, 203, 204, 234; OIC 140; out-of-region operations 26, 234; peacekeeping operations 14, 27–30, 35–6; Permanent Members of UNSC 4, 21–2; Preamble 18; primacy of UN 22–3, 231; responsibility to protect concept 22, 44–5, 219; Russian sphere of influence 8, 146, 149, 154, 157, 159–60, 164, 210; SCO 95; Security Council (UN), responsibilities of 20–3; treaty, as 179; UNASUR 117–18, 122, 124; Uniting for Peace procedure 17, 21, 31 *see also* Article 51 (collective self-defence); Chapter VIII status; enforcement measures (Chapter VII)
Chavez, Hugo 114, 123
Chechnya 148, 152
Chile 105, 121–2
China: ancient China 2–3, 207; balance of power 209; bilateralism 95; Charter of UN, drafting of 8; Chino-centricism 207;common security concept 80–1; Confucianism 2, 207;

humanitarian intervention 81; non-interventionism 81; Permanent Members of UNSC 157; Russia, reduction of border forces with 94; SCO 94–5, 97–8
Christianity 2–4, 207–8, 210–11
Churchill, Winston 8
CIS *see* Commonwealth of Independent States (CIS)
citizens, protection of own 57, 102–3
civil wars *see* internal conflicts and civil wars
civilian operations 32–3, 168–9, 173, 180–1, 201
civilised, club of the 5
coalitions of the willing 35, 37–8, 40, 81, 137, 143, 202
Cold War and development of regionalism 9–10
collective security and self-defence 7, 9, 32–6: Africa 50, 58, 61–2, 69, 129–31; Americas 108–9, 112, 124, 129, 212, 215; Asia 83–6, 215; Chapter VIII status 214–15; Charter of UN 16, 22–3; customary international law 189; *Dar al-Islam* 2, 3, 126, 207; definition of self-defence 215; enforcement measures (Chapter VII) 16; Euro-Atlantic region 129, 166, 169, 185–90, 193, 204, 214–15; Middle East 126, 129–35, 143, 147, 207, 212, 215; peacekeeping operations (UN) 33–4, 36; pre-emptive self-defence 187, 193; Russian sphere of influence 129, 145–53, 214–15 *see also* Article 51 (collective self-defence)
Collective Security Treaty Organization (CSTO) 146, 158–63, 208; Americas 107; authorisation/mandate for intervention 164, 213; Chapter VIII status 164; Charter of CSTO 159–61; Charter of UN 159–60; CIS 145, 148, 158–61, 163, 237; collective security and self-defence 145, 215; Collective Security Treaty 145, 163, 158, 159; consensus 160, 223; cooperation 145, 158–9, 161, 163, 169; Council on Collective Security 159, 160–2; decision-making 160–1, 196; description 158; establishment 158; humanitarian intervention 164; joint military exercises and operations 158, 161–2; legal personality 145, 158; legality/legitimacy of interventions 159–60; military capabilities 145, 158, 160, 163–4, 210, 212; NATO 151, 185; non-traditional threats 145, 160–4, 216; number of members 145, 158, 164; organs 160; out-of-region operations 212; overlapping ROs 145, 158–61, 163, 237–8; peacekeeping operations 158, 160–3, 210; practices 160–2; rapid reaction forces 47, 158, 161–2, 213; SCO 97, 238; UN 158–64, 210, 224; universalism 159, 163–4; Warsaw Pact 185
colonialism/imperialism: Americas 101, 211; anti-colonialism 209; Asia 86, 220; decolonisation 43, 49, 66; Eurocentricism 4; impartiality 33–4; out-of-region operations 199–200, 208, 236
Colombia 104–5, 114, 121–2, 123
common interest, actions in the 17–18
Commonwealth of Independent States (CIS) 145–58, 208, 210: Agreement on establishment of CIS 146; Allied Armed Forces 149, 152; Alma-Ata Declaration 146; authorisation/mandate for intervention 149–50, 155–7, 164; Chapter VIII status 154, 157–8, 164; Charter of CIS 146–8, 151–3, 160–1; collective security and self-defence 146–52; Collective Peacekeeping Forces, Statute of 152; Collective Security Council 149, 151; Collective Security Treaty 145, 146, 148–9, 153, 163; Concept for Prevention and Settlement of Conflicts 149, 154; consensus 151–2, 164, 223; consent to intervention 153–4; contributions 153–4; cooperation 146, 156–8, 163, 169; Council of Defence Ministers 152; Council of the Head of States 148, 151–2;

Council of the Heads of Governments 151–2; CSTO 145, 148, 158–61, 163, 237–8; decision-making 149, 151–2, 164, 196; description 146; enforcement measures 37, 150, 164; humanitarian intervention 150, 155, 221, 225; internal conflicts and civil wars 152–4; invitations/requests for intervention 231; legality/legitimacy of interventions 145–54; military capabilities148–51; NATO 151, 153; number of member states 145, 146, 164; OSCE 146–7, 152, 153, 157; overlapping ROs 145, 158–61, 163, 237–8 ; peacekeeping operations 11, 147, 149–55, 157, 163–4; practices 152–5; SCO 148; separatism 148, 153–7; structure 145; trade-offs 154; UN 146, 149, 152, 153–4, 156–8, 164, 224; withdrawal of troops when consent ceases 153–4
Comoros 74–5
Concert of Europe 3–4, 5
conciliation *see* mediation, conciliation and good offices
Conference on Security and Cooperation in Europe (CSCE) 10
confidence building 32, 89, 94, 107, 111, 118–20, 122, 149, 190
Confucianism 2, 207
Congress of Panama 4
consent to intervention: AU 75, 239; Chapter VIII status 26; CIS 153–4; declarations 239; doctrinal developments post-Cold War 40; humanitarian intervention 223; international law 19–20; out-of-region operations 223; overlapping ROs 238–9; peacekeeping operations (UN) 29, 33, 34; pressure to consent 19; regional consent 236; Uniting for Peace procedure 31; withdrawal of troops when consent ceases 153–4
Conté, Lansana 58
contributions: ad hoc contributions 27; Africa 218; authorisation/mandate for intervention 233–4; Brahimi Report 41; CIS 153–4; impartiality 33; Middle East 221; neighbouring states 34; peacekeeping operations (UN) 27, 28, 33–4, 37–8, 84–5; Permanent Members of UNSC 29, 34; Regional Council, proposal for advisory 232–4; Secretary-General (UN), reports of 43
Cooper, AF 114–15
cooperation: Asia 80–6, 88, 92–100, 207, 212; Chapter VIII status 213–14; CIS 146, 156–8, 163, 169; CSTO 145, 158–9, 161, 163, 169; ECOWAS 53–4, 59–60; Euro-Atlantic region 167–71, 183–6, 193, 202–4; formal agreements and meetings 214; Middle East 141–2, 207; OAS 107–8, 110, 112, 115–16; SADC 61; UNASUR 114–21, 123–5, 209 *see also* cooperation with UN; economic cooperation/development
cooperation with UN: Africa 41–2, 45–6, 59–60, 65–6, 75, 76–7; AL 137–40, 141; Americas 101, 104, 108, 115–16, 123–5, 141; Asia 84–5, 89, 92–3, 98–9; CSTO 158, 163; doctrinal developments post-Cold War 41–2, 45–6; Euro-Atlantic region 41–2; 45–6, 170–1, 184, 183–5; OIC 141–2; Permanent Members of UNSC 227–8; resolutions (SC) 45–6
Correa, Rafael 121–2
Côte d'Ivoire 57–8, 67, 71, 75, 220
coups 104, 125, 215–16
crimes against humanity 221, 225
crisis management: EU 166–7, 170, 173, 175, 181–2, 184; NATO 187, 190–1, 193
Croatia 36, 84
crusades 208
CSTO *see* Collective Security Treaty Organization (CSTO)
Cuba 10, 103
culture 80, 87, 99–100, 110, 126, 217, 226
customary international law 18, 19–21, 71, 189 *see also jus cogens*
cyber-attacks 193, 204
Czechoslovakia 10, 144–5, 210

Dagestan, Russia 148
Dar al-Harb (House of War) 3, 126

Dar al-Islam collective security of medieval Islam 2, 3, 126, 207
Darfur, Sudan: AU 24–5, 34–5, 75–6, 201; contributions 218; EU 174, 185; NATO 201
Dayton Agreement 175, 197
De Búrca, G 179
Deen-Racsmány, Z 56
decision-making: AL 129, 133–5, 142–3, 173, 212, 223; ASEAN 90; AU 72–4, 212, 223; CIS 149, 151–2, 164, 196; criteria for legitimacy of decisions 42–4; CSTO 160–1, 196; ECOWAS 59, 72–3, 196, 223; EU 73–4, 167, 170–3, 204; invitations/requests for intervention 237; NATO 194–6, 204; OAS 111–13, 134, 223; OIC 141, 142, 223; SADC 62–3, 196; SCO 96–7; UN model 73; UNASUR 120–1 *see also* majority decision-making; unanimity
Declarations of Security in the Americas 104–5
default principle 235
definition of ROs 231
democracy: Asia 83, 88, 90; consensus 223; Euro-Atlantic region 165, 167–8, 187–8, 190, 192, 204, 207–8, 210–11, 218–19, 222; humanitarian intervention 220, 222–3; OAS 108, 110–11, 114, 124; responsibility to protect principle 219; UNASUR 119
Democratic Republic of Congo (DRC) 63, 64–5, 74, 174–5, 209, 220
Denmark 200–1
Department of Peacekeeping Operations (DPKO) (UN) 28, 229
Dienstein, Yoram 71
diplomacy: AL 139; Americas 103, 107, 114–15, 123; Asia 85, 89, 93, 99; authorisation/mandate of SC 213; CSTO 158, 161–3; OIC 140; post-Cold War 230; prevention 39–40; Regional Council, proposal for advisory 232 *see also* negotiations
disarmament 32, 34, 40, 147, 151, 168, 170
disasters 88, 93, 119, 162–3, 181, 201
Djibouti 51, 136

division of labour between regions 129–30, 143, 233, 237–9
doctrinal developments post-Cold War 14, 38–49
Dominican Republic 10, 18, 102–4
drugs 105, 125, 145, 160, 163, 216
Dumbarton Oaks 18, 21–2, 127
Dushanbe, Tajikistan 160

early regionalism 2–5, 207, 209–11
early warning capabilities 44, 68, 132
East Pakistan 18
East Timor 185
Economic Community of Central African States (ECCAS) 51
Economic Community of West African States *see* ECOWAS (Economic Community of West African States)
ECOWAS (Economic Community of West African States) 51–60; AU 52, 54, 56, 58–60, 66–7, 71–4; authorisation/mandate for intervention 54–9, 64, 78; Chapter VIII status 55, 59, 78; collective security and self-defence 58, 129; consensus 59, 62; cooperation 53–4, 59–60; decision-making 59, 72–3, 196, 223; description 53–4; enforcement measures 37, 54–6, 58, 64; humanitarian intervention 18, 58, 183, 225; impartiality 55; internal conflicts and civil wars 57–8; invitations/requests for intervention 64, 231; legality/legitimacy of interventions 55–6, 58–9; maintenance of peace and security 53; majority voting 223; Mechanism on Conflict Prevention 52, 54, 58–9; mediation 57–9; Mutual Assistance in Defence Protocol 54; number of members 11; OAU, references to 52, 54; peacekeeping operations 11, 22, 55–7, 63–4, 175; practices 53, 54–8; pro-democratic interventions 57–8, 71; pro-interventionist doctrine 54, 56, 64; Treaty 52, 53–4, 59; UN 55–60, 64–5, 224; unilateral interventions 59
Egypt 30, 153
El Salvador 102

Index   253

elections 41–2, 57–8, 53, 65–6, 71, 78, 115
enemy states, action against 16–17, 23
enforcement measures: Africa 37, 50, 54–6, 58, 64, 75, 78; AL 128, 130, 136, 138; Americas 105; CIS 37, 150, 164; coercive measures 230–1; EU 171, 174–9; NATO 191, 197, 204–5, 213; out-of-region operations 27 *see also* enforcement measures (Chapter VII)
enforcement measures (Chapter VII): authorisation/mandate for intervention 16, 23, 26, 35–8, 150, 222, 231; Chapter VIII status 26; CIS 164; criteria for legitimacy of decisions 43; CSTO 212; distinction from peacekeeping 36–7; economic enforcement 28; ECOWAS 57, 64; enemy States, measures against 16; Euro-Atlantic region 177–9, 197, 204–5; human rights 178; ICJ 26, 34–5; international law 14–15; invitations/requests for intervention 231; peaceful settlement of disputes 230–1; peacekeeping operations 26, 28, 34, 35–7, 102; political enforcement 28; practices 17; resolutions (UN) 84; responsibility to protect principle 44; traditional threats 35–6
erga omnes obligations 72, 79, 82
Eritrea 61, 136
ethnic conflict 44, 145, 148, 163, 190, 207
EU *see* European Union (EU)
Euro-Atlantic region 165–205: Americas 101–4, 208; ancient Greece 2–3, 5, 207, 210–11; authorisation/mandate for intervention 130, 167, 171, 174–85, 188–205, 213, 218–19, 222; Christian times, medieval Europe in 2, 3, 210–11; collective security and self-defence 129, 214–15; cooperation 41–2, 203–4; democracy 165, 204, 207–8, 210–11, 222; description 165–6;human rights 165, 204, 207–8, 211, 222; humanitarian intervention 204–5, 220–2; just war 3, 207–8; Middle East 143, 165; military capabilities 204, 213; non-traditional threats 165, 168, 170, 187, 190, 193, 202, 204, 216; out-of-area enforcement 26–7, 212, 216; primacy of UN 42; UN 41–2, 204–5; values 81, 99, 165, 204, 207–8, 210–11 *see also* European Union (EU); NATO (North Atlantic Treaty Organization)
Eurocentricism 4–6, 208–9
European Union (EU) 66, 166–85, 203–5: Africa 51–2, 173–5, 185; Amsterdam Treaty 167; authorisation/mandate for intervention 167, 171, 174–85, 204–5, 213, 218; Battlegroups 170, 174, 177, 179–80, 182–3, 222; Chapter VIII status 183–4, 204; civilian operations 168–9, 173, 180–1; Commission 172; common defence policy 168–9; common foreign and security policy 166–8, 171–3, 178–9; common security and defence policy 166–8, 171–2, 223; consensus 182–3; cooperation 167–71, 183–5, 203–4; Council 171–2; Court of Justice 172–3, 178–9; crisis management 166–7, 170, 173, 175, 181–2, 184; Davignon proposals 166; decision-making 73–4, 167, 170–3, 204; decisions (joint actions) 172, 175–6; democracy 165, 167–8, 204, 218–19; description 166; enforcement measures 171, 174–9, 204–5, 213; European Council 171–2; European Parliament 172; European Political Cooperation 166; European Security and Defence Policy 166–8, 170, 174, 182–3; European Security Strategy 166, 169–70, 184; Fouchet Plan 166; Headline Goal 2010 166, 170, 184; High Representative of the EU for Foreign Affairs and Security Policy 171–2; human rights 165, 167–8, 178–9, 204, 218–19; humanitarian intervention 167, 171, 176–83, 204–5, 217–18, 222–3; hybrid operations 34; international law 167, 170–1, 176, 178; invitations/requests for intervention 174, 177; joint actions 172, 175–6; *Kadi* case 172–3, 178–9, 222; legality/

legitimacy of interventions 166–71, 173, 179–85, 204–5; Lisbon Treaty 166–9, 171–3, 215, 223; Maastricht Treaty 166–8, 170, 182–4; military capabilities 168–9, 171, 173–4, 177–82, 184, 204; NATO 169, 174–7, 185, 203–4, 237; neutral countries 179–83, 201; Nice Treaty 168; non-traditional threats 168, 170, 176, 204; number of members 11; OSCE 177–8, 182; out-of-region operations 27, 183; peacekeeping operations 11, 167–8, 171–2, 174–82; Petersberg tasks 166–7, 170, 182; Pleven Plan 166; practices 173–83; rapid reaction forces 169–70, 174, 177, 179–80, 182–3, 213, 223; rescue operations 167–8; Single European Act 166; UN 167–8, 170–1, 174–85, 201, 204, 224; unanimity 171–3, 204, 223; unilateral action 169, 178–83, 217–19; values 165, 167–8, 178–9, 204, 218–19
experience, exchange of 239
experts 34, 39, 43, 45, 60, 195, 229
extremism 95–7, 160, 193, 216
Eyadéma, Faure 58
Eyadéma, Gnassingbé 58
Ezulwini Consensus 68–9, 131

factors influencing regional approaches 206–11
failed states 20, 54, 225, 236, 239
Falklands/Malvinas 102
Finland 179, 181–3, 201
first generation operations 33–4, 35
Five Principles of Peaceful Co-existence 80, 95, 207
former Yugoslavia 156 *see also* Balkans; individual countries
forum shopping 239
fourth generation operations 35
France 18, 33–4, 57, 218
Fukimori, Alberto 114

Gaddafi, Muammar 139
Gavira, Cesar 114
General Assembly (UN): AL 138–9; ASEAN 93; AU 68–9; CIS 154, 157–8; CSTO 163; ECOWAS 60; emergency sessions 29–30; EU 181, 183; OAS 111–12, 115; OIC 141–2; peaceful settlement of disputes 26; peacekeeping operations 29–30, 35–6; Permanent Members of UNSC 29; SADC 65; SCO 98–9; Security Council (UN) 21, 29–31; subsidiary organs, right to establish 28; UNASUR 123; Uniting for Peace procedure 17, 21, 29–31
genocide: AU 67, 69–70; Cambodia 33; CIS 155; ECOWAS 57–8; inaction 33, 53, 67, 78, 86, 177, 218; pro-democratic interventions 57–8; Rwanda 33, 53, 67, 78, 86, 218; World Summit Outcome 44
Georgia 22, 37, 148, 152, 154–8, 209, 217, 221
globalism 165–6, 170, 203–5, 208–9, 212, 215
good offices *see* mediation, conciliation and good offices
Gray, C 28, 56, 158
Greece, amphictyonic (neighbour) leagues of ancient 2–3, 5, 207
Grenada 103–4, 109
Guatemala 102–3
Guinea 58, 67
Guinea-Bissau 58, 67, 74

Haiti 102, 104, 114–16, 154, 209
Hammarskjöld, Dag 28
Hartslief, Robbie 65
Hehir, Aidan 12
High-Level Panel on Threats, Challenges and Change (UN) 42–4, 221, 229
Hilaire, M 104
historical development of regionalism 1–13, 207
Honduras 102
human rights: AL 131, 212; Asia 82, 88–90, 95, 100; Euro-Atlantic region 165, 167–8, 178–9, 187, 190, 192, 204, 207–8, 211, 218–19, 222; humanitarian intervention 220, 222; OAS 111; UN 15, 18, 178–9, 219; UNASUR 119
humanitarian intervention 217–26: Africa 18, 55, 68–73, 76, 78–9, 129,

143, 183, 204, 219–20, 222, 224–5; Americas 104–6, 108, 124, 220–1; Asia 82, 88, 98, 100, 208, 220; authorisation/mandate for intervention 18–19, 48, 204, 217, 219–22, 225–6, 236–7; Chapter VIII status 226; Christianity 207; colonialism/imperialism 199, 208, 220; decision-making 223–4; democracy 220, 222–3; Euro-Atlantic region 167–8, 178–9, 197–9, 204–5, 214, 217–19, 220–3; human rights 220, 222; invitations/requests for intervention 237; legality/legitimacy of interventions 222–4; Middle East 129, 143, 221; military capabilities 225–6; neutral states 180–3; out-of-region operations 27, 225; pro-intervention/non-indifference doctrine 76; responsibility to protect principle 72; Russian sphere of influence 150, 155, 164, 220, 221, 225; UN 17–19, 22, 41, 78–9, 219–20, 221–6; values 81, 99 *see also* unilateral humanitarian intervention

Hummer, W 24, 25–6, 141
Hungary 10, 144, 210
hybrid operations 34–5

ILC Draft Articles on State Responsibility 20
impartiality 33–4, 55, 136, 153–4
imperialism *see* colonialism/imperialism
inaction: AL 127–30, 134–40, 143, 212; AU 67, 75; genocide 33, 53, 67, 78, 86, 177, 218; Middle East 212–13; OAS 113; ROs, where there are no 235; UN 42, 67, 75
in-between measures 28
India 18, 29, 81
Indonesia 100, 173
individual self-defence 16, 149, 186, 188–9, 215
innovation 27–8
internal conflicts and civil wars: Africa 57–8, 71–2, 76, 78–9, 216; AL 143, 212; Americas 102–3, 105, 112; Asia 85, 90–1, 99–100; CIS 152–4; customary international law 19–20; drugs 105; national liberation movements 17; UN 22, 33, 102–3
international community, concept of 50
International Court of Justice (ICJ) 13, 22, 30, 198
international humanitarian law 2, 12
international law 14–27; balance of power 209; EU 167, 170–1, 176, 178; international humanitarian law 2, 12; invitation, intervention by 19–20; NATO 188, 191, 193–4, 200–1, 203; overlapping ROs 237–8; sources of international law, respect for 15; UN 14–18, 227, 229–30; universalism 14–27
International Union of American Republics (IUAR) 6, 11, 101, 106
invitations/requests for intervention: AL 130–1, 139–40; Americas 125, 145; AU 67–8, 236; authorisation/mandate for intervention 237; decision-making 237; dubious governments, from 19–20, 63–4, 231; ECOWAS 64, 231; EU 174, 177; humanitarian intervention 236–7; internal conflicts and civil wars 19–20, 236; international law 19–20; out-of-region operations 27; peacekeeping, exceeding 19; *pro forma* invitations 19; purpose of invitation 20; Russian sphere of influence 144–5, 231; SADC 63–4, 231; spillovers 236; UN 235–6
Iraq: AL 136; humanitarian intervention 18; invasion 22, 81, 136, 200–1; Kuwait 135–6, 138; NATO 200–1; Security Council (UN) 126; September 11, 2001 terrorist attacks 81
Ireland 174, 178–83, 201
Islam: *Dar al-Harb* (House of War) 3, 126; *Dar al-Islam* collective security of medieval Islam 2, 3, 126, 207; jihad 3; militancy 154; OIC 127, 140–2; terrorism 145, 158
Israel/Palestinian conflict 30, 126–8, 135, 137, 138, 143
Ivory Coast 57–8, 67, 71, 75, 220

Japan 81–2
judicial affairs 34
judicial review 21, 172–3

jus cogens 15, 71–2, 79, 179, 217, 205, 218
just war 3, 207–8

Kabila, Laurent 64
Kadi case 172–3, 178–9, 222
Kampuchea 18
Kazakhstan 154
Kellogg-Briand Pact of 1928 4
Kirchner, Nestor 123
Korean War 29, 37
Koskenniemi, Martii 218–19
Kosovo, NATO intervention in 12–13, 81, 197–9: authorisation/mandate for intervention 21–2, 197, 204, 217; democracy 218–19; EU 172–3, 178–9, 204; humanitarian intervention 18–19, 106, 155, 197–9, 217–19, 222; legality/legitimacy of interventions 197–9; NATO 31, 34, 37–8, 190, 197–9; responsibility to protect principle 18–19; UN 41–2, 156, 176–7, 197–8; unilateral interventions 217–19;
Kuwait 10, 37–8, 135–6
Kuwali, Dan 72
Kyrgyzstan 97–8, 154, 162

Latorre, Eduardo 114
League of Arab States *see* Arab League
League of Nations 1, 5–6, 9–10, 21
Lebanon 10, 131, 135–6
legal status of regional organisations 231
legality/legitimacy of interventions: Africa 55–6, 58–74, 79, 136; ASEAN 87–90; authorisation/mandate for intervention 27, 40–1; CIS 145–54; civilians, protection of own 57; consensus 223, 228; criteria for legitimacy of decisions 42–4, 222–4; CSTO 159–60; Euro-Atlantic region 166–71, 173, 179–85, 187–94, 197–200, 204–5, 211; humanitarian intervention 217, 222–4; international law 14; invitations/requests for intervention 19–20; OAS 108–11; out-of-region operations 26–7, 235; SCO 95–6; Secretary-General (UN), reports of 228–30; statements of legality 228–30; UNASUR 117–20; Uniting for Peace procedure 30;

universalism 14
Legler, T 114–165
Lesotho 63–4, 65, 67, 209
Levitt, Jeremy 56, 57, 70–1, 73
Liberia: AU 51, 84; authorisation/mandate of UN 54–6; ECOWAS 18, 22, 37, 51, 54–9, 64, 150; humanitarian intervention 55, 220; inaction 67; peacekeeping operations (UN) 55–6; pro-democratic intervention 58; resolutions (UN) 50–1
Libya: AL 127, 130–1, 135–40, 143; AU 75, 130, 137, 139; humanitarian intervention 106; invitations/requests for intervention 130, 139–40; NATO 137, 195–6, 200; no-fly zone 135, 136, 139; resolutions (SC) 136–7, 139
Locarno Treaty 6

Macedonia (FYR) 174, 180
majority decision-making: AL 134, 143, 223; AU 73–4, 223; ECOWAS 59, 223; EU 173; legality/legitimacy of intervention 223–4; OAS 109, 112–13, 125, 223; OIC 140–1, 223
Malan, Mark 38
Malaysian Peacekeeping Training Centre 91
Mali 174
Malvinas/Falklands 102
mandate for intervention *see* authorisation/mandate of Security Council for intervention
Mauritania 75
McCoubrey, H 113, 135, 154
mediation, conciliation and good offices: AL 129, 132, 136, 210; ASEAN 90; ECOWAS 57–9; peaceful settlement of disputes (Chapter VI) 28; UNASUR 123
Medvedev, Dmitry 161
Memoranda of Understanding 20
MERCOSUR 114–15
Mexico 105
Middle Ages 2, 3, 210–11
Middle East 126–43: Arab Cooperation Council 127; Arab Maghreb Union 127; AU 126, 143; authorisation/

mandate for intervention 130, 132, 136, 138, 143; contributions 221; cooperation 142, 207; *Dar al-Harb* (House of War) 126; *Dar al-Islam* 126, 207; description of region 126–7; Euro-Atlantic operations 143, 165; humanitarian intervention 143, 221; inaction 212–13; Islam 126, 207; non-interventionism 143; out-of-region operations 137, 143; peacekeeping operations 29, 143, 212–13; traditional threats 216; UN 29, 126–7, 142–3; unilateral interventions 142 *see also* League of Arab States; Organization of Islamic Conference (OIC)
military capabilities: Africa 160, 213, 230; AL 212; Americas 10, 115, 209, 212; appropriate for regional action, meaning of 212–13; Asia 97–8, 212; Euro-Atlantic region 168–9, 171, 173–4, 177–82, 184, 195, 204, 213; humanitarian intervention 225–6; non-traditional threats 217; OIC 142; resources 217; Russian sphere of influence 145, 148–51, 158, 160, 163–4, 210, 212, 230; traditional threats 216 *see also* rapid reaction forces (RRFs)
modern regionalism, beginnings of 5–9
Moldova 148, 152, 153
Monroe Doctrine 4, 5, 101–2
Morris, H 113, 135, 154
municipal services 34
Myanmar 85, 91–2, 100

Nagorny Karabakh 152
Namibia 64
Napoleonic Wars 3
national liberation movements 17
NATO (North Atlantic Treaty Organization) 185–205: Afghanistan 85, 160, 189, 197, 199; Africa 52, 199, 201; AL 137, 186, 199; Article 51 16, 185–6, 188–90, 202, 204, 214–15; authorisation/mandate for intervention 130, 188–205, 213, 217; Chapter VIII status 10, 16, 186, 187–8, 191, 204, 214; CIS 151, 153; collective security and self-defence 166, 169, 185–90, 214–15; consensus 195, 200–1, 204, 223; cooperation 186, 193, 202–4; crisis management 187, 190–1, 193; CSTO 151, 185; decision-making 194–6, 204; democracy 187–8, 190, 192, 165, 204; description 185–6;enforcement measures 191, 197, 204–5, 213; EU 169, 174–7, 185, 203–4, 237; Eurocentrism 208–9; globalism 165, 193, 203–5, 208–9, 212; human rights 165, 187, 190, 192, 204; humanitarian intervention 197–9, 204–5, 214, 217–19, 221–2; international law 188, 191, 193–4, 200–1, 203, 214; legality/legitimacy of interventions 187–94, 197–200, 204–5; military capabilities 195, 204; non-traditional threats 187, 190–3, 202, 204 ; North Atlantic Council 187, 194–5; number of members 11, 185; OAS 237–8; OSCE 192; out-of-region operations 27, 199–200, 234; overlapping ROs 237–8; peacekeeping operations 11, 37–8, 192, 195–6; practices 196–201; pro-intervention/non-indifference doctrine 199; rapid response force (NRF) 47, 191, 201, 213; Regional Council, proposal for advisory 234; security and defence organisation, as 185–7, 190, 193, 204; Security Strategy 193; spillover effects 190, 193, 204; Strategic Concepts 187, 189–95, 199, 203, 215; Summit Declarations 195; transformation process 187, 189–90; UN 21–2, 185–6, 188–90, 191–5, 199, 200–5, 214, 224, 231, 234; unilateral operations 12, 188, 194, 217–19; United States 113, 189, 192, 197, 199, 201; values 165, 187–8, 190, 192, 194, 204; Vanderberg resolution 186; veto 195–6, 198; Warsaw Pact 144; Washington (North Atlantic) Treaty 186–90, 192–5, 199 *see also* Kosovo, NATO intervention in
natural disasters 88, 93, 119, 162–3, 181, 201
neighbouring states 34
neutral countries 179–83, 201

Nicaragua 102–3, 109
Nigeria 55–6
no-fly zones 135, 136, 139, 196–7
non-indifference doctrine *see* pro-intervention/non-indifference doctrine
non-interventionism: Africa 62, 86; Americas 107, 117, 122, 124–5, 208; Asia 80–2, 96, 90–2, 99, 100, 207–8, 220–1, 211–12; communist subversion 87; cooperation with UN 67–8, 72; Five Principles of Peaceful Co-existence 80, 207; Middle East 143; UNASUR 117, 122, 124–5, 208
non-traditional threats: Africa 52–3, 216; Americas 104–5, 119, 122, 125, 215–16; Asia 83, 88–9, 95–7, 100, 122, 216; drugs 105, 125, 145, 160, 163, 216; Euro-Atlantic region 165, 168, 170, 176, 187, 190–3, 202, 204, 216; international community, concept of 50; military capabilities 217; natural disasters 88, 93, 119, 162–3, 181, 201; organised crime 160–1, 122; Russian sphere of influence 95–7, 145, 148, 153–7, 160–4, 216; State, concept of 50; traditional intervention, moves from 32–3, 35–6, 50 *see also* terrorism
North Atlantic Treaty Organization *see* NATO (North Atlantic Treaty Organization)
North Korea 84–5, 100
Northeast Asia Cooperation Dialogue (NEACD) 82
nuclear weapons 84–5, 146–7, 193

OAS *see* Organization of American States (OAS)
observer operations 29, 32–3, 37–8, 55, 64, 132, 150–7
O'Dea, Willie 180–1
Office of the Special Adviser on Africa (UN) 60
OIC *see* Organization of Islamic Conference (OIC)
organised crime 122, 133, 143, 160–1, 170
Organization for Security and Cooperation in Europe (OSCE): Cold War 10; EU 177–8, 182; NATO 192; number of members 11; Russian sphere of influence 146–7, 152, 153, 157, 165
Organization of African Unity (OAU) 10, 52, 54, 66, 73, 76, 208
Organization of American States (OAS) 102–16: authorisation/mandate for intervention 109; Caracas Declaration 109–10; Chapter VIII status 10, 16, 115–16, 137–8; Charter 107–13; Cold War 106–7, 111, 113, 209; collective security and self-defence 108–9, 112, 129, 212, 215; cooperation 107–8, 110, 112, 115–16, 141; Council of Ministers 103; creation 106; decision-making 111–13, 134, 223; Declaration of Santiago 107; Declaration of Security in Americas 104; democracy 108, 110–11, 114, 124; description of region 106–8; humanitarian intervention 108, 111, 220–1; inaction 113; Inter-American Defense Board 110–12; Inter-American Pro-Democratic Charter 111; internal conflicts and civil wars 102–3, 112; intervention without intervening 114; legality/legitimacy of interventions 108–11; majority voting 223; military capabilities 10, 115, 209; NATO 237–8; non-interventionism 107; number of members 11, 106; Organ of Consultation 109, 112–13; organs, list of 111–12; overlapping ROs 237–8; Pact of Bogotá (American Treaty on Pacific Settlement of Disputes) 107–8, 112; peacekeeping operations 107, 115, 221; practices 106, 114–15; pro-democratic interventions 110–11, 114, 124, 209; quorum 108–9, 125; rapid reaction forces 115; Regional Security System, Treaty establishing the 107; Rio Treaty (Inter-American Treaty on Reciprocal Assistance) 107–9, 112–13, 125; Santiago Declaration on Democracy and Public Trust 107–8, 111; Secretariat, cooperation agreement between UN Secretariat and 116; structure 110–11; terrorism 110; traditional threats 122, 216; UN 102,

108–12, 115–16, 141; UNASUR 237; United States 10, 103, 109, 113–14, 122–3, 209, 224; voting 108–9, 113
Organization of Eastern Caribbean States (OECS) 10, 122–3
Organization of Islamic Conference (OIC) 127, 140–2: Chapter VIII status 141; Charter of OIC 140–2; decision-making 141, 142, 223; geographical range 140; majority voting 223; military operations 142; number of members 140; quorum 141; religion 207; UN 140–2
Oriental Pact 6
OSCE *see* Organization for Security and Cooperation in Europe (OSCE)
out-of-region operations: Africa 218; authorisation/mandate for intervention 27, 221, 223, 226; Asia 86–7, 236; Charter of UN 26, 234; colonialism 199–200, 208, 236 ; consent to intervention 223; Euro-Atlantic region 26–7, 183, 199–200, 212, 216, 234; humanitarian intervention 27, 225; invitations to intervene 27; legality/legitimacy of interventions 26–7, 235; Middle East 137, 143; Russian sphere of influence 212, 221
overlapping ROs 129–30, 143, 145, 158–61, 233, 237–9

pacta sunt servanda 72, 78–9
Pakistan 18, 29, 100
Palestinian-Israeli conflict 30, 126–8, 135, 137, 138, 143
Pan American Union 101
Panama 103, 109, 113
peace agreements, supporting 32, 34
Peace of Westphalia 4
peacekeeping operations: Africa 11, 63, 69–70, 72, 77–8, 175; ASEAN 90, 92; CIS 147, 149–55, 163–4; consent of State 19–20, 153–4; enforcement measures (Chapter VII) 26, 28, 34, 35–7, 102; EU 11, 167–8, 171–2, 174–82; international law 19–20; invitations/requests for intervention 177, 237; Kosovo 41–2, 156; legality/legitimacy of interventions 19; Middle East 10, 132, 135–8, 143; NATO 11, 192, 195–6; OAS 107, 115, 221; SCO 96; UNASUR 119; unilateral interventions 26, 35, 47, 53 *see also* UN peacekeeping operations
Pellet, Allain 194
Permanent Members of UNSC: AU 224; authorisation/mandate for intervention 223–4; balance of power 21, 209, 225; 'carrot and stick' method 227–8; Charter of UN 4, 21–2; CIS 157, 225; Cold War 9; contributions 29, 34; cooperation 227–8; CSTO 224; doctrinal developments post-Cold War 47; ECOWAS 56, 224; EU 178, 224; Eurocentricism 209; humanitarian intervention 220, 222–4; modern regionalism, beginnings of 7–8; NATO 224, 231; OAS 224; post-Cold War 11, 47; preventive measures 228; reform 228; Regional Council, proposal for advisory 233, 235; SADC 224; SCO 94, 98, 224; United States 157; Uniting for Peace procedure 29; veto 209, 222, 224, 228
Pernice, R 186
Persson, Göran 177
Peru 114–15, 121–2
Philippines 91
Pinochet, Augusto 105
piracy 51, 176
post-Cold War doctrinal developments 14, 38–48
power blocs 8
practices: AL 135–7; AU 53, 66–7, 74–6; Charter of UN, exceptions to 17; CIS 152–5; CSTO 160–2; ECOWAS 53, 54–8; EU 173–83; NATO 196–201; OAS 106, 114–15; peacekeeping operations (UN) 27–38; SADC 53, 63–5; SCO 97–8; UNASUR 121–3
primacy of UN: AU 60, 68; authorisation/mandate for intervention 52; Charter of UN 22–3, 231; Euro-Atlantic region 42, 186, 188, 234; hierarchical relationship with ROs 23; League of Nations 5–6, 9; prioritisation of region's own

mechanism 236; Secretary-General (UN), reports of 46, 48; Security Council (UN) 9, 203, 214, 234
pro-democratic intervention: Africa 57–8, 70–1, 78, 129; AL 129–30; Americas 104, 110–11, 114, 124, 145, 209; Russian sphere of influence 209
pro-intervention/non-indifference doctrine: Africa 53–4, 56, 62, 64, 68, 72, 76, 78, 208, 216; Asia 82, 92, 97, 100; authorisation/mandate for intervention 52–3; humanitarian intervention 76; NATO 199
see also pro-democratic intervention
provisional measures 28
Putin, Vladimir 155

rapid reaction forces (RRFs): AL 133; AU 47, 76, 213; authorisation/mandate of SC 213; Civilian Police Capabilities (UN) 47; criteria for legitimacy of decisions 43; CSTO 47, 158, 161–2, 213; doctrinal developments post-Cold War 42, 43, 46–8; EU 47, 169–70, 174, 177, 179–80, 182–3, 213, 223; NATO 47, 191, 201, 213; OAS 115; responsibility to protect principle 44; SADC 65; Secretary-General (UN), reports of 46–7; Stand-by Forces High Readiness Brigade (SHIRBRIG) 47; UN Standby Arrangement System (UNSAS) 45, 47
Regional Council, proposal for 231–6, 238–9
regional level, mechanisms taken at 235–40
regional organisations, use of term 24–5
religion 2, 126, 207–8, 210–11 *see also* Islam
report action, duty to 22–3, 58
reports of Secretary-General *see* Secretary-General (UN), reports of
requests for intervention *see* invitations/requests for intervention
rescue operations 17, 167–8
resources: Africa 57, 68–9, 74, 76, 78, 98, 171, 216–17, 235
responsibility to protect principle: Africa 67, 72, 79; Americas 104; Asia 81–2, 100, 212; Charter of UN 22, 219; democracy 219; human rights 18; humanitarian intervention 72; International Commission on Intervention and State Sovereignty 48; World Summit Outcome 44
rogue states 17, 240
Rome 2–3
Roosevelt, FD 8
Roosevelt, Theodore 103
RRFs *see* rapid reaction forces (RRFs)
rule of law 83, 88, 90, 117, 167, 187–8, 190, 192, 224
Russian sphere of influence 144–64: authorisation/mandate for intervention 149–50, 154–7, 161–4, 212–13, 221, 230; balance of power 209; China, mutual reduction of border forces with 94; collective security and self-defence 129, 214–15; description of region 144–6; humanitarian intervention 217, 220, 221; invitations/requests for intervention 144–5; military capabilities 230; NATO 186; non-traditional threats 148, 153–7, 216; OSCE 204; out-of-region operations 221; pro-intervention/non-indifference doctrine 209; SCO 94, 98; separatism 148, 153–7, 216; trade-offs 209; traditional threats 216; UN 8, 210; unilateral interventions 210, 217, 230, 238; Warsaw Pact 144–5, 146, 210 *see also* Collective Security Treaty Organization (CSTO); Commonwealth of Independent States (CIS)
Rwanda: AU 67, 75; enforcement measures (Chapter VII) 37; genocide 33, 53, 67, 78, 86, 218; humanitarian intervention 218; impartiality 33–4; inaction 33, 53, 67, 78, 86, 218

SADC (Southern African Development Community) 51–3, 60–6: AU 52, 62, 65; authorisation/mandate for intervention 61–2; Chapter VIII status 61, 65, 78; composition 60; consultations and consensus 62–3, 223; decision-making 62–3, 196; description 60–1; elections 63, 65–6;

impartiality 63; invitations/requests for intervention 63–4, 231; legality/legitimacy of operations 61–5; non-interventionist principle 62; Organ on Politics, Defence and Security Cooperation 52, 62–3; practices 53, 63–5; pro-intervention/non-indifference doctrine 62; Protocol on Politics, Security and Defence Cooperation 61–2; rapid response forces 65; Southern African Development Coordination Conference (SADCC) 60; Summit 62, 65; Treaty 52, 60–2; UN 52, 61–6, 224; unilateral interventions 49, 64

San Francisco conference 21–2, 27, 127

Schweitzer, M 24, 25–6, 141

SCO *see* Shanghai Cooperation Organization (SCO)

second generation operations 34, 35

Secretary-General (UN), reports of: AU 43, 68–9, 77; authorisation/mandate for intervention 42–5, 229–31; CIS 158; doctrinal developments post-Cold War 38–46; EU 177–8, 184; High-Level Panel on Threats, Challenges and Change 42–4, 229; *In Larger Freedom* 43, 45, 228, 231; international law 229–30; modern regionalism, beginning of 7–9; Office of Legal Adviser 229; OIC 142; primacy of UN 46, 48; rapid reaction forces 46–7; responsibility to protect principle 44; Retreat with Heads of Regional and other Organisations 46; Security Council 40–4

security *see* collective security and self-defence

Security Council (UN): abstentions 224; Afghanistan 84, 126; Africa 55–6, 61–9, 71–6, 157, 219–20; Americas 102; appropriate for regional action, meaning of 26, 230; Asia 84; balance of power 21; Charter of UN 20–3; common interest, actions in the 18; composition 8; consensus 228; doctrinal developments post-Cold War 40–5; EU 170, 201; General Assembly (UN) 21, 29–31; humanitarian intervention 219–26; inaction 42; individualised approach 230; internal conflicts and civil wars 102–3; international law 214, 227; Middle East 126–7, 130, 135–8 ; NATO 21–2, 186, 188–9, 192, 194–5, 200–3, 214; number of members 11; out-of-region intervention 225; overlapping ROs 238–9; peacekeeping operations (UN) 27–31, 35–8; primacy of UN 9, 203, 214, 234; reform 42; Regional Council, proposal for advisory 231–5; Russian sphere of influence 144, 149, 150, 154–7, 164; Secretary-General (UN), reports of 40–4; statements of legality 228–30; Uniting for Peace procedure 29–31; veto 85, 144 *see also* authorisation/mandate of Security Council for intervention; Permanent Members of UNSC

self-defence *see* Article 51 (collective self-defence); collective security and self-defence; individual self-defence

self-determination 20, 98, 117–18, 146, 207

Semerikov, Valery 162

separatism 95–7, 148, 153–7, 216

September 11, 2001 terrorist attacks 1, 81, 165

Shanghai Cooperation Organization (SCO) 66, 82–4, 93–9: Charter of SCO 93, 95–7; China 94–5, 97–8; consensus 97, 223; cooperation 84, 94–9; Councils 96–7; decision-making 96–7; description 93–5; Five Principles of Peaceful Coexistence 95; Foreign Ministers, Council of 96; Heads of State, Council of 96–7; human rights 95; humanitarian intervention 98; legality/legitimacy of operations 95–6; list and number of members 94; Long-Term Good-Neighbourliness, Friendship and Cooperation, Treaty on 95; military capabilities 97–8; National Coordinators, Council of 96; non-interventionism 99; non-traditional threats 95–7, 100, 216 ; overlapping ROs 237; Peace Mission 2010 98; practices 97–8; pro-intervention/non-indifference

262 *Index*

doctrine 97; Regional Counter-Terrorist Structure 96; Russian sphere of influence 94, 97–8, 148, 237–8; Secretariat 96, 99; Shanghai Five Mechanism 94–5, 208; traditional threats 216; UN 84, 94–5, 98–9, 224
Sierra Leone 18, 37, 54, 56–8, 67, 75, 150, 220
Small Entente 6
small steps approach 240
smaller states 8, 83, 223
social progress, promotion of 15
Somalia: AU 75, 98, 201; contributions 75, 218; EU law 174, 176; inaction 67, 75; NATO 176, 201; pro-intervention/non-indifference doctrine 53; resources 98; UN 50, 75, 176
South Africa 63–4, 209
South American Defence Council 117–24
South Korea 81
South Ossetia 148, 155, 156–7, 162
South Sudan 75
Southeast Asian Treaty Organization (SEATO) 87
Southern African Development Community *see* SADC (Southern African Development Community)
Spain 101
spillovers 190, 193, 204, 216, 236
Sri Lanka 85, 100
standby forces *see* rapid reaction forces (RRFs)
Status of Forces/Mission Agreements 19
Strömvik, M 177
subordination to UN *see* primacy of UN
Sudan 53, 67, 75, 174 *see also* Darfur
Suez crisis 29, 30
Sweden 177
Syed Hamid Albar, Tan Sri 92
Syria 136

Tajikistan 37, 152, 154, 157, 160
Taliban 178–9, 199
Tanzania 18
Tavares, R 155
territorial integrity of States 15–16, 80, 86, 117, 120, 129–35, 146–9, 155, 159, 188

terrorism: AL 132–3, 143; Americas 105, 110, 119, 122; Asia 83, 89, 95–7, 100, 122; CSTO 145, 158, 160, 162–3, 216; Euro-Atlantic region 165, 168, 170, 187, 190, 193, 202, 204, 216; global threat, as 215; Islamic terrorism 145, 158; September 11, 2001 terrorist attacks 1, 81, 165
Thailand 85, 91–2, 100
third generation operations 34–5
Timor Leste 34, 84–5, 91–2, 94
Togo 58, 75
trade-offs 154, 209
traditional threats: Afghanistan 216; Africa 216; Americas 104, 122, 216; Asia 89, 216; enforcement measures (Chapter VII) 35–6; Euro-Atlantic region 182, 216; international community, concept of 50; Middle East 216; military capabilities 216; non-traditional threats 32–3; Russian sphere of influence 216; State, concept of 50
training 41–2, 89, 91, 118, 159, 174, 201–2, 239
Transdnestr 148, 153
treaty law 15, 71–2
truces, supervision of 29
Tsagourias, N 178

Uganda 18, 53, 67
Ukraine 146
UN peacekeeping operations 9–10, 14, 27–38: ad hoc contributions 27; Americas 102, 212; ceasefires, supporting 32, 34; Chapter VIII 14, 27, 32, 35–6; Charter of UN 14, 27–30, 35–6; CIS 154–5, 157; civilian operations 32–3; contributions from member states 27, 29, 33–4, 37–8, 84–5; CSTO 158, 160–3, 210; Department of Peacekeeping Operations (DPKO) 28, 229; ECOWAS 22, 55–7; enforcement measures (Chapter VII) 28, 34, 35–7; first generation operations 33–4, 35; fourth generation operations 35; General Assembly (UN) 28–30, 35–6; generally agreed principles 29; hybrid operations 34–5; impartiality 33–4;

in-between measures 28; innovation 27–8; internal conflicts and civil wars 33; invitations/requests for intervention 235–6; Middle East 212–13; multi-dimensional processes 34; municipal services 34; NATO 37–8; number of operations 32–3, 38; observer operations 29, 32; out-of-region operations 27; outsourcing 37–8; peace agreements, supporting 32, 34; Permanent Members of UNSC 29; practices of UN 27–38; SADC 64–5; second generation operations 34, 35; Security Council (UN) 27–31, 35–8; third generation operations 34–5; Uniting for Peace procedure 29–31; universalism 14, 27–38

unanimity: AL 133–4, 142–3, 171, 223; consensus 223–4; EU 171–3, 204, 223; humanitarian intervention 223–4

UNASUR *see* Union of South American Nations (UNASUR)

uniform network of mechanisms 235

unilateral humanitarian intervention: Africa 217–18, 224–5; Americas 103–4, 219; Asia 99, 219; authorisation/mandate for intervention 177–83, 217; Euro-Atlantic region 176, 177–83, 204, 217–19; UN 217–19

unilateral interventions: Africa 53, 56, 59–60, 64, 70–2, 74, 76, 78, 217–18; Americas 103–4, 108–9, 113–14, 219, 224; ASEAN 86–7; Brahimi Report 47–8; EU 169, 178–83, 217–19; illegal enforcement 26; international law 19; Middle East 142; NATO 12, 188, 194, 217–19; peacekeeping operations 26, 35, 47, 53; Russian sphere of influence 210, 217, 230, 238 *see also* unilateral humanitarian intervention

Union of South American Nations (UNASUR) 106, 116–24: Action Plan (South American Defence Council) 119; Architecture of Security 120; authorisation/mandate for intervention 119, 125; border surveillance 119; Chapter VIII status 123; Charter of OAS 117, 124; Code of Conduct on Defense and Security Matters 120; consensus 120–2, 125, 223; Constitutive Treaty 116–21, 123; cooperation 114–21, 123–5, 209;Council of Delegates 121; Council of Ministers of Foreign Affairs 120–1; decision-making 120–1; description 116–17; human rights 119; humanitarian intervention 220–1; invitations/requests for intervention 125; legality/legitimacy of interventions 117–20; mediation 123; non-interventionism 117, 122, 124–5, 208; non-traditional threats 119, 122; OAS 237; overlapping ROs 237; practices 121–3; quorum 121, 125; traditional threats 122, 216; UN 117–19, 122–4; United States 104, 119, 122–3, 209

United Kingdom 8, 197

United Nations (UN) *see* Charter of UN; cooperation with UN; General Assembly (UN); primacy of UN; Security Council (UN); Secretary-General (UN), reports of; UN peacekeeping operations

United Kingdom 8, 18

United States: abuse of power 122–3; Afghanistan 38, 105, 189, 202; Americas 101–4, 145, 209–10; ASEAN 92; Cold War 102–4, 113–14; Colombian Airbases, use of 114, 122; Euro-Atlantic region 113, 165, 176–8, 183–5, 189, 192, 197, 199, 201; humanitarian intervention 199; internal conflicts and civil wars 103; Iraq, invasion of 18, 38, 202; military dictatorships, support for 209; modern regionalism, beginnings of 8; Monroe Doctrine 4, 5, 101–2; NATO 113, 189, 192, 197, 199, 201; OAS 10, 103, 109, 113–14, 122–3, 209; OECS 122–3; Permanent Members of UNSC 157; pro-democratic interventions 114, 145, 209; Russia, trade-off with 209; September 11, 2001 terrorist attacks 1, 81, 189; UN 8–9, UNASUR 104, 119, 122–3, 209; unilateral interventions 103–4, 109, 113–14

Uniting for Peace procedure 17, 21, 29–31, 130
universal perspective 1, 3, 5–48, 143, 159, 168
Uzbekistan 98

values: Asia 91; EU 165, 167–8, 178–9, 204, 218–19; Euro-Atlantic region 81, 99, 165, 204, 207–8, 210–11; NATO 165, 187–8, 190, 192, 194, 204 *see also* democracy; human rights; rule of law
Venezuela 114–15, 121–2, 123
verification procedure 236
vetoes 73, 85, 144, 195–6, 198, 224, 228
Vietnam 19, 33

war, law of 2, 12
war, right to go to 4
Warsaw Pact 10, 16, 144–6, 185, 210, 214
weapons 37, 82, 84, 89, 103, 119, 146–7, 151, 160–1, 196 *see also* nuclear weapons
Westphalian sovereignty 3, 4, 209
Western European Union (WEU) 165, 167, 196
wise, panels of the 74, 132, 210
World Food Programme (WFP) 176
World Summit Outcome 44–5, 49, 76, 219

Zimbabwe 64, 209
Zwanenburg, M 192